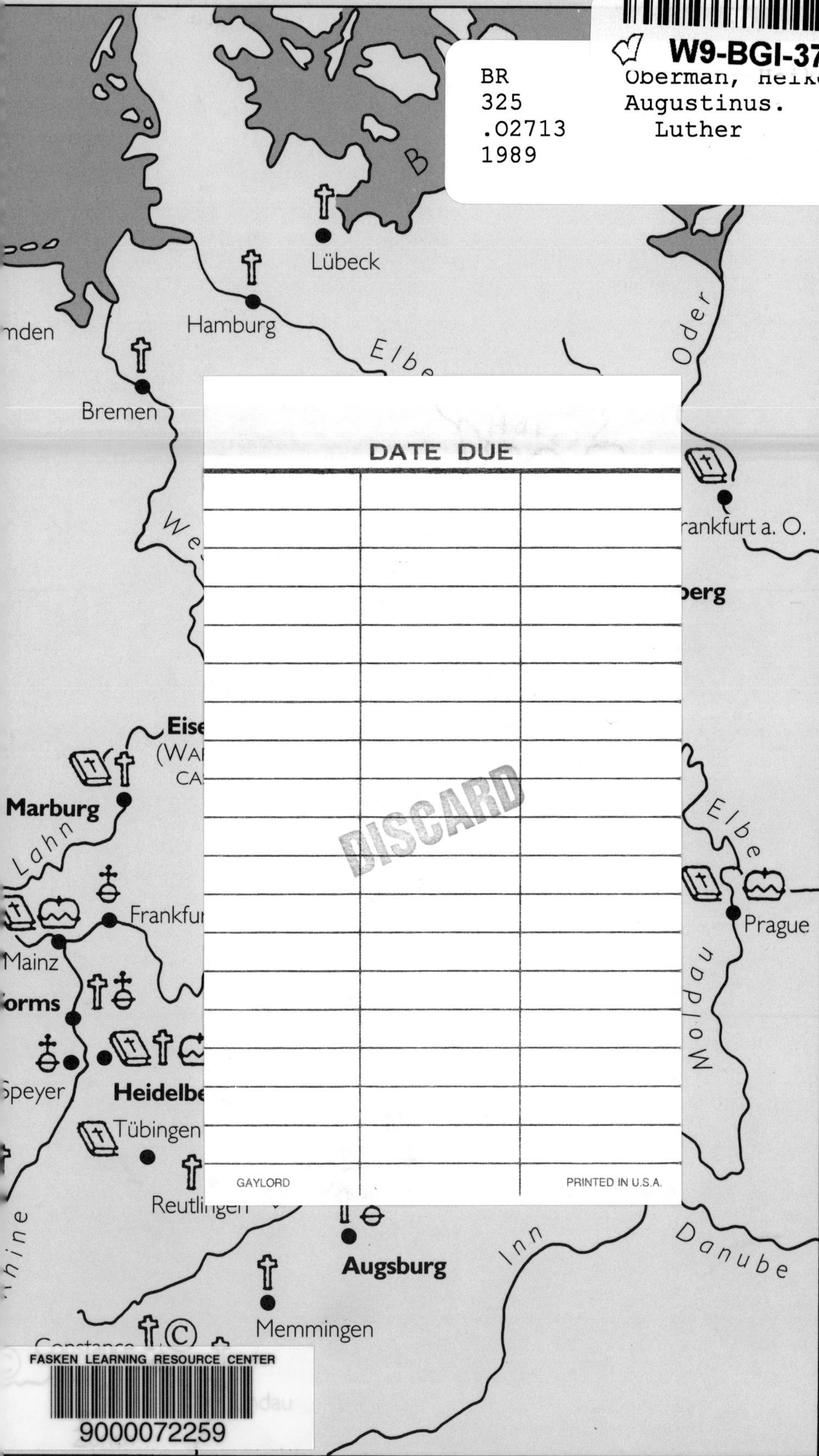

Lübeck
Hamburg
Elbe
Oder
Bremen
Marburg
Lahn
Mainz
Tübingen
Elbe
Prague
Moldau
Augsburg
Memmingen
Inn
Danube

Luther

AETHERNA IPSE SVAE·MENTIS SIMVLACHRA LVTHERVS
EXPRIMIT·AT VVLTVS CERA LVCAE OCCIDVOS
·M·D·X·X·

HEIKO A. OBERMAN

Luther

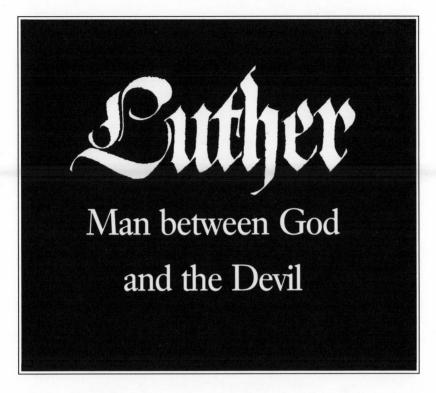

Man between God and the Devil

Translated by Eileen Walliser-Schwarzbart

YALE UNIVERSITY PRESS

New Haven & London

Designed by Richard Hendel
and set in Erhardt type
by G&S Typesetters, Inc., Austin, Texas.
Printed in the United States of America by
Vail-Ballou Press, Binghamton, New York.

Library of Congress Cataloging-in-Publication Data
Oberman, Heiko Augustinus.
[Luther. English]
Luther : man between God and the Devil/Heiko A. Oberman ;
translated by Eileen Walliser-Schwarzbart.
p. cm.
Translation of: Luther.
Bibliography: p.
Includes index.
ISBN 0–300–03794–5 (alk. paper)
1. Luther, Martin, 1483–1546. 2. Reformation—Germany. 3. Reformation—Germany—Biography. 4. Germany—Church history—16th century. I. Title.
BR325.O2713 1989
284.1'092—dc20
[B] 89–5747
CIP

The paper in this book meets the guidelines for permanence and durability of the Committee on Production Guidelines for Book Longevity of the Council on Library Resources.

10 9 8 7 6 5 4 3 2 1

Dedicated to the memory of

Yale's Titus Street Professor

ROLAND H. BAINTON

1895–1984

who combined the gifts of profound penetration and powerful presentation to make Martin Luther come alive for generations of students of the Reformation, on both sides of the Atlantic.

"Simon, the aged, held the baby Jesus, one would assume, for less than a quarter of an hour. Yet he could say that he had seen a light for revelation. Life is so full of brief encounters . . ."

Roland H. Bainton, Christmas letter, 1978

CONTENTS

ILLUSTRATIONS

PREFACE TO THE ENGLISH EDITION

Amidst the conflicting claims about what makes a good historian, one area of common ground is uncontested: the primary task is to become bilingual, gaining control of the languages of the past *and* of the present—not merely languages frozen in dictionaries, but also those gleaned from the historical record and perceived in contemporary experience. Both kinds are hard to master, yet for very different reasons; distance and proximity provide for equally formidable "sound barriers."

The translation enterprise is as hazardous as it is necessary; nuances are easily lost, especially when once vitally important existential expressions are rendered as antiquated parts of an obsolete "belief-system." In the case of Martin Luther this problem is all the more acute, as his interpreters, intent on mining his riches, have been given to present him as "relevant" and hence "modern." Thus they have been inclined to bypass or remove medieval "remnants"—first among these, the Devil Himself.

This book has been written with the double assumption that, first, the Reformer can only be understood as a late medieval man for whom Satan is as real as God and mammon; and, second, that the relevancy so sought after is not found by purging the record and hence submitting to post-Enlightenment standards of modernity, but rather by challenging our condescending sense of having outgrown the dark myths of the past.

What has been said about the risky venture of the historian applies also to this translation from German into English. Over the course of more than two years, I reworked large sections of the original translation, but would not have dared to let this version see the light of day if my truly bilingual cultural mentors in the New World, Kathy and Tom Brady, had not been prepared to normalize names and expressions. I must extend my gratitude as well to Elsie Vezey and Robert Bast for preparing respectively the name and subject indices, and to Cynthia Wells of Yale University Press, who with great diligence saw this work through to its completion. With these heartfelt thanks, of course, I do not transfer the responsibility for the final form in which this book is laid in the hands of the reader. Fortunately, since Luther's voice has proved powerful enough to be heard five hundred years later, crossing the waters should not be too much of an obstacle for this *Luther.*

April 1, 1989 University of Arizona

PREFACE TO THE FIRST EDITION

Discovering Luther the man demands more than scholarship can ever expect to offer. We must be prepared to leave behind our own view of life and the world: to cross centuries of confessional and intellectual conflict in order to become his contemporary. When the Church was still equated with Heaven, and the Emperor represented the might of the world, a monk named Luther rose up against these powers of Heaven and Earth: he stood alone with only God and his omnipresent adversary, the Devil.

Surprisingly, the discoveries and experiences of a life marked by battle raging within and without make him a contemporary of our time, which has learned to sublimate the Devil and marginalize God.

It is not the "Catholic," "Protestant," or even "modern" Luther we are looking for. We will encounter them as well, but our objective is Martin Luther between God and the Devil. Precisely this "narrow" perspective will, in fact, open to us the total vista of the Reformation and the part it played in Luther's time and life; how unexpected it was when it became reality; how imperiled it remained after Luther's death. We will be turning our attention to his personality and its complexities, discovering where he came from and where he was going, where he got in his own way and where he robbed himself of the fruits of his labors.

Getting to know Martin Luther requires more than just following him to the various scenes of the Reformation and more than just compiling theological highlights, though all this is part of our pursuit. The crucial point is to grasp the man in his totality—with head *and* heart, in *and* out of tune with the temper of his time.

Although our presentation comes with all the claims of scholarship, it is by no means academic, because it has to be true to a man who believed his cause far too important to limit it to the confines of the university. He knew not only how to draw boundaries but how to bridge them, thus leaving a lasting mark on contemporaries of all estates.

The notes at the end of the book are not intended solely as factual documentation; they are there to give the reader an opportunity to get a sense of the excitement of the author-at-work. The bibliography will have done its job if the reader is enticed to turn to Luther's own works.

A particular word of thanks must be spoken here. The Institute for Advanced Studies of the Hebrew University in Jerusalem generously provided me with the space and time to write this book. But they offered me even more than hospitality. Israel highlights the alien, alienating, sometimes horrifying Reformer to his heirs: it is the ideal place to prevent one's respect for Luther from lapsing into that kind of blind love which he himself would have rejected as fanaticism.

Jerusalem, in the summer of 1982

one

The Longed-for Reformation

PROLOGUE

Controversy Beyond the Grave

"The Charioteer of Israel has fallen"

"Reverend father, will you die steadfast in Christ and the doctrines you have preached?" "Yes," replied the clear voice for the last time. On February 18, 1546, even as he lay dying in Eisleben, far from home, Martin Luther was not to be spared a final public test, not to be granted privacy even in this last, most personal hour. His longtime confidant Justus Jonas, now pastor in Halle, having hurriedly summoned witnesses to the bedside, shook the dying man by the arm to rouse his spirit for the final exertion. Luther had always prayed for a "peaceful hour": resisting Satan—the ultimate, bitterest enemy—through that trust in the Lord over life and death which is God's gift of liberation from the tyranny of sin. It transforms agony into no more than a brief blow.

But now there was far more at stake than his own fate, than being able to leave the world in peace, and trust in God. For in the late Middle Ages, ever since the first struggle for survival during the persecutions of ancient Rome, going to one's death with fearless fortitude was the outward sign of a true child of God, of the confessors and martyrs. The deathbed in the Eisleben inn had become a stage; and straining their ears to catch Luther's last words were enemies as well as friends.

As early as 1529, Johannes Cochlaeus, Luther's first "biographer," had denounced Luther in Latin and German as the seven-headed dragon, the Devil's spawn. Slanderous reports that he had died a God-forsaken death, miserable and despairing, had circulated time and again. But now the end his friends had dreaded and his enemies had longed for was becoming reality. Who now would lay claim to Luther and fetch him, God or the Devil?

While simple believers imagined the Devil literally seizing his prey, the enlightened academic world was convinced that a descent into Hell could be diagnosed medically—as apoplexy and sudden cardiac arrest. Abruptly and without warning, the Devil would snip the thread of a life that had fallen to him, leaving the Church unable to render its last assistance. Thus, in their

The seven-headed Luther as "agitator": doctor, Martinus, Lutherus, preacher, fanatic, visitant, and Barrabas. Frontispiece (woodcut) from Johannes Cochlaeus, Lutherus septiceps *(Leipzig, 1529).*

Damned and dragged into the jaws of Hell by Satan's demons. Drawing from Der Antichrist *(Constance, 1476).*

first reports, Luther's friends, especially Melanchthon, stressed that the cause of death had not been sudden, surprising apoplexy but a gradual flagging of strength: Luther had taken leave of the world and commended his spirit into God's hands.

For friend and foe alike his death meant far more than the end of a life.

Shortly after Doctor Martinus died at about 3:00 A.M. on February 18, Justus Jonas carefully recorded Luther's last twenty-four hours, addressing his report not to Luther's widow, as one might expect, but to his sovereign, Elector John Frederick, with a copy for his university colleagues in Wittenberg. Had Luther—born on November 10, 1483, as a simple miner's son—died young, history would have passed over his parents' grief unmoved. But now his death was an affair of state. The day after his birth—the feast of St. Martin—he had been baptized and received into the life of the Church as a simple matter of course, but now there was open dispute over whether, having been excommunicated by the pope, he had departed from this world a son of the Church.

IN THE last days before his death Luther had been the cheerful man his friends knew and loved. He had successfully completed a difficult mission: a trip from Wittenberg to Eisleben to mediate in a protracted quarrel between the two counts of Mansfeld, the brothers Gebhard and Albert. Hours had been spent sitting between the parties, listening to the clever reasoning of administrative lawyers—a breed he had despised ever since his early days as a law student in Erfurt. After two tough weeks of negotiation, the parties had narrowed their differences and a reconciliation had finally—though only temporarily—been achieved. So there was reason to be cheerful. Luther had suspected that he would die in Eisleben, the place of his birth. But this did not worry him, although he was quite sure he had little time left: "When I get home to Wittenberg again, I will lie down in my coffin and give the worms a fat doctor to feast on." By highlighting the skeleton within the human body, late medieval art had urgently reminded everyone that health, beauty, and wealth were only a few breaths away from the Dance of Death. The "fat doctor" was well aware of this, not as a moralistic horror story, but as a reality of life poised on the brink of eternity.

On the eve of his death, as so often before, there was jocular theologizing at the table in Wittenberg: will we see our loved ones again in Heaven, Doctor? he was asked. It is very likely, he replied, that we shall be so renewed by the Spirit that, like Adam, who woke up and recognized the newly created Eve as his wife, we shall know one another. Nor will body and spirit be separated in the darkness of Hell. Luther told the story of a man so badly plagued by hunger that he sold his soul to the Devil so that he could for once eat his fill. When he had feasted to his heart's delight, the Devil came to collect his debt. Satan was curtly reminded that he had to wait until the debtor died, since the man had, after all, sold only his soul. The Devil had his answer

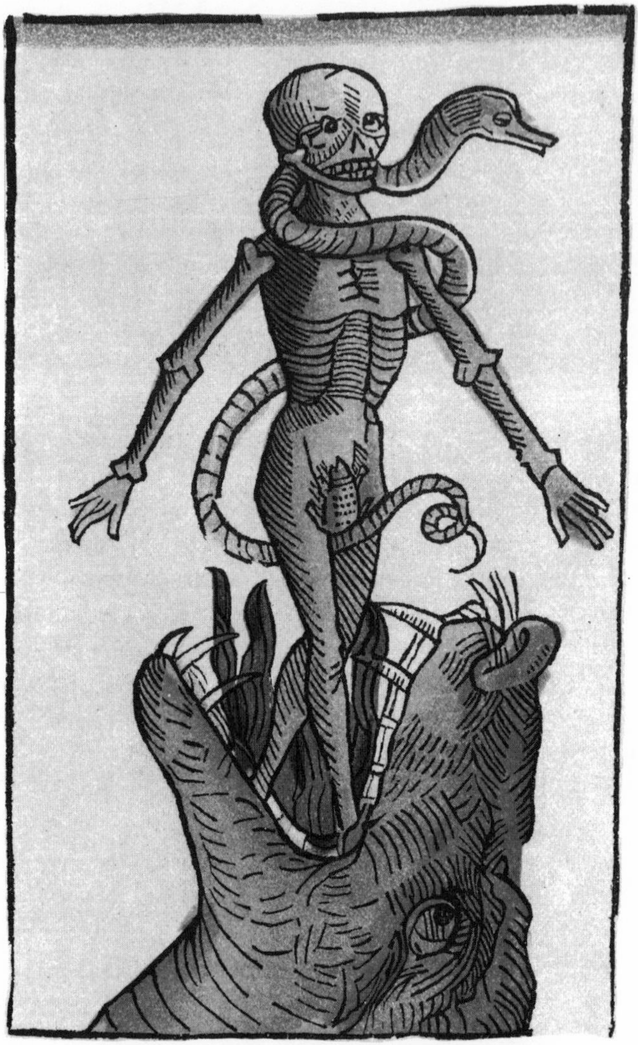

Whether master or servant, rich or poor, all the living are alike: a framework of bones, threatened by Hell, Death, and the Devil. Woodcut from Ulm.

ready: If you buy a horse, don't you also get the reins? Yes, the man had to admit. Well, said the Devil, the soul is the horse and the body the reins. And he grabbed the man—body and soul.

Luther's premonitions of death came true one day later. He was never to return alive to Wittenberg, the site of his greatest achievements. On the morning of February 18, an artist was called in to execute a painting of the

Portrait of the dead Luther. Lucas Fortnagel (Furttnagel) executed this brush-drawing at the Reformer's deathbed, February 18/19, 1546.

dead man, depicting the peaceful look on Luther's face in his final hour. The portrait was intended to display not only to family and friends but above all to posterity the countenance of a blessed death.

Luther's body was accompanied from town to town by an honor guard, and after two days of traveling the funeral procession reached Wittenberg, the cultural capital of the Electorate of Saxony. Hordes streamed by wherever Luther lay in state. The first memorial addresses were full of stunned grief, untainted as yet by the later mixture of scholarly pedantry and Protestant hagiolatry.

A messenger sent by Justus Jonas to announce Luther's death arrived in

Wittenberg on February 19, three days before the funeral procession. The town and university were totally unprepared for the news. It was early morning and, as usual during the semester Philipp Melanchthon, Luther's longtime colleague and comrade-in-arms, stood in the lecture hall explicating St. Paul's Epistle to the Romans for his students. In the middle of the lecture the messenger burst in with the news of Luther's death. Melanchthon struggled for control, unable to speak, but finally—his voice faltering—told his students what had happened, breaking out in anguish with Elisha's horrified cry as he saw the prophet Elijah ascending to Heaven in the chariot of fire: "The charioteer of Israel has fallen"—"Alas, obiit auriga et currus Israel" (2 Kings 2.12).

History in the Shadow of the Last Days

Elisha, by taking up the prophet's mantle, had also taken up Elijah's post and task, but no successor stood ready to fill the monumental gap left by the Reformer's death. Luther's charismatic greatness had given the Reformation dynamism and momentum; now it cast a dark shadow on the future of the Evangelical movement. It was not carelessness or self-complacency that had kept Luther from planning for a future without him; instead he was convinced that the power of the rediscovered Gospel would be strong enough to make its own way, even in the turmoil he often predicted would follow his death. His fears that the tumults preceding God's final victory would deeply unsettle an unruly Germany through dissension and civil war were well-grounded.

After Luther's death there was no indication that the Reformation had any chance of survival. The papacy, startled out of its passion for the Italian Renaissance, was finally mobilizing all its forces to face the ecclesiastical crisis. Pope Paul III made a momentous decision when he approved Ignatius of Loyola's plan to use the Jesuit order to regain the educational edge that had been lost to Protestantism. Then, for the first time in centuries—since Pope Innocent III had called the Fourth Lateran Council (1215)—a multinational papal council was convened at Trent in 1545. As time went on bishops assembled from all over Europe, and the council successfully impressed its reforms on Catholic Christendom. Three weeks after Luther's death a premier—and still surviving—cornerstone of Roman Catholic doctrine was laid in Trent, which was then just inside German territory. The council decided to accept both Scripture and ecclesiastic tradition with "equal reverence" and declared that "the Holy Mother Church"—the Roman mother church that had condemned Luther's reformational discovery—had the sole right to interpret the Bible.

The pope's most powerful ally in opposing the Reformation—Emperor Charles V—was also on the verge of a decisive victory. In July 1546, not many months after Luther's death, civil war broke out in the German empire between the politico-military alliance of the Protestant estates and the emperor and his allies. The devastating blow Charles dealt the commander and leader of the Protestant Schmalkaldic League, Elector John Frederick of Saxony, was made possible by the "Judas of Meissen," the Protestant Duke Maurice of Saxony. The "traitor" crossed over to the emperor's side, betraying his cousin the elector. At Meissen the Catholic cathedral chapter celebrated the imperial victory at Mühlberg with a Te Deum. When on that very day the steeples of the cathedral were struck by lightning and burned down, the townsfolk interpreted it as God's judgment.

The emperor was at the height of his power. At the Diet of Augsburg (1548) he was able to force the defeated Protestants to accept the Interim, a religious dictate aimed at stifling the Reformation that was supposed to remain in force until a church council made a binding decision on reform. This was a crippling blow to the flourishing Reformation in the cities. Resistance was quickly eliminated, first of all in the imperial towns of southern Germany, and obstinate Protestants were driven out. The Protestant imperial city of Constance dared to reject the Interim; the emperor responded by stripping it of its status as a free city and reimposing Catholicism. On May 19, 1547, fifteen months after Luther's death, Wittenberg capitulated. Its protector John Frederick lost his electoral office and most of his territories; he was left with only the Thuringian regions around Weimar, Eisenach, and Gotha.

The road to reformation via internal ecclesiastical politics had already been cut off. Cologne played the central role in an attempt to win the bishops over to the cause of the Reformation—which would have resulted in the founding of a German national church. All eyes were on the elector and archbishop of Cologne, Hermann von Wied, who had become Evangelical. One year and one week after Luther died, he had to yield to the emperor's superior strength and renounce his bishopric and electorate: his successor reinstated the old faith in Cologne. Ducal treason, imperial dictate, papal decree—what future could remain for a reformation in Germany?

On February 22, 1546, Melanchthon held a Latin funeral oration in the name of the university. The words of farewell were forthright: Luther had been a "strict healer," "God's instrument for renewing the Church." There was no trace of the mendacity to which even the most honest may succumb when standing over an open grave, anticipating the Last Judgment, judging the harvest of a life. Melanchthon did not neglect to mention Luther's sharp tongue and heated temper, even though it was a time when profound sorrow called for the comfort of unadulterated praise.

Nevertheless, Melanchthon, one of the outstanding scholars (and men) of his period, evoked an image of Luther that has survived into our day. Whether acclaimed or decried, this image has impeded access to the Reformer as he experienced and understood himself. "Strict"—indeed. This was a trait Melanchthon had experienced firsthand. But "healer," no. "God's instrument"—that is how Luther saw himself. But "renewal of the Church" was something he did not envisage. Only a year after Melanchthon's tribute the retrospective view had turned out to be false: it was evident to everyone that the power of the "instrument" had waned. Though the doctor's crucial operation had been a success, his patient the Church was in agony and closer to death than ever before.

Finally in 1555, owing to a further act of duplicity on the part of Duke Maurice, an end to the misery of the war seemed to be in sight: a treaty was concluded at the Diet of Augsburg. His pact with the emperor had resulted in his becoming Elector of Saxony after the Schmalkaldic War; but in 1552 he turned against the emperor, wresting victory from him and forcing him to flee Innsbruck. Whether farsighted or crafty, wise or wicked, Maurice practiced a double deception which, apart from any moral judgment, had an enduring effect: having first destroyed the Protestant estates' tempting prospects for establishing themselves as the earthly executors of God's Reformation, he went on to ensure the survival of the Reformation in the empire. The peace achieved in Augsburg was not a Protestant victory, nor was it a religious peace; it was primarily a compromise among princes.

The protective rights over the Church in the German empire, for which territorial rulers had been striving for over a century, were now established by law. The compromise between the quarreling parties consisted in allowing each sovereign to decide the religion of his subjects: "Cuius regio, eius religio." But outside the empire, and not only in Hapsburg territories, Protestants remained exposed to persecutions that all too often ended in the galleys or at the stake. When Justus Jonas, Luther's lifelong friend and witness to his death, himself died on October 9, 1555, two weeks after this "religious peace," the "renewal of the Church" had been reduced to—and ensnared in—the reform of regional and territorial churches. Jonas was forced to watch Luther's Reformation evolve into Lutheranism.

1526
VIVENTIS·POTVIT·DVRERIVS·ORA·PHILIPPI
MENTEM·NON·POTVIT·PINGERE·DOCTA
MANVS
AD

Albrecht Dürer, Philipp Melanchthon

Not until 1648, when the Thirty Years' War finally ended, could a broader religious settlement be extracted from pope and emperor, at least for Europe north of the Alps and Pyrenees. Not only Lutherans and Roman Catholics but Calvinists, too, were included in the princely compromise. Though the peace was negotiated in Münster and Osnabrück, it ensued from the political strength of Scandinavian Lutheranism in the north and militant Calvinism in the south and southwest—both unplanned offspring of Luther's Reformation.

Later generations have differed sharply on 1648. Some label the Reformation "schismatic" and mourn the resultant weakening of Christianity, while persistently ignoring the far earlier schism between Greek Orthodoxy in the East and Roman Catholicism in the West (1054). The opposing view asserts that the settlements of 1555 and 1648 were milestones along the way to religious emancipation. And they did in fact allow Luther's voice to remain alive and the man to be rediscovered in his works, which survived intact despite papal and imperial wishes. Friend and foe alike can, however, agree on one thing: the Thirty Years' War was a scourge that swept over Germany, paralyzing, if not totally destroying, the widely held hopes for a revival of faith and culture, piety and education. And perhaps far worse, this war decisively delayed the spread of the Enlightenment to Germany—with consequences that can still be felt today.

The means employed both to persecute and defend the Reformation have left deep, indelible scars. But joy for the renewal and grief over the schism obstruct access to Luther as he saw himself and his task. He never set himself up as healer of the Church and never regarded the renewal of the Church as his task. Effective resistance to the Reformation would neither have surprised nor dissuaded him. But disappointed he would have been had he suspected that the final return of God, Christ's Second Coming, would be so long in arriving that his own five-hundredth birthday would have to be celebrated on earth.

Luther's measure of time was calibrated with yardsticks other than those of modernity and enlightenment, progress and tolerance. Knowing that the renewal of the Church could be expected to come only from God and only at the end of time, he would have had no trouble enduring curbs on the Evangelical movement. According to Luther's prediction, the Devil would not "tolerate" the rediscovery of the Gospel; he would rebel with all his might, and muster all his forces against it. God's Reformation would be preceded by a counterreformation, and the Devil's progress would mark the Last Days. For where God is at work—in man and in human history—the Devil, the spirit of negation, is never far away.

To understand Luther, we must read the history of his life from an unconventional perspective. It is history "sub specie aeternitatis," in the light of eternity; not in the mild glow of constant progress toward Heaven, but in the shadow of the chaos of the Last Days and the imminence of eternity.

CHAPTER I

A German Event

The Enigmatic Elector Frederick

The Venetian ambassador is exasperated by the halting progress of the Diet of Augsburg in the summer of 1518: "Incredible, these Germans!" Here, he reported to his superiors in Venice, are princes and diplomats with the public good at stake, struggling to achieve a settlement between emperor and sovereign princes, while in the corridors the rumormill confounds their best efforts, and the seeds of mistrust are sown. And all because of trivialities—a theologians' dispute over indulgences. The ambassador did not even have to rely on vague hearsay: he could name the adversaries—a monk called Luther and a certain professor from Ingolstadt, Johannes Eck. Ridiculous, to let indulgences distract one from reality! Quickly, he steered his account back to political matters.

Vital interests were at stake for the proud Republic of Venice, a financial, commercial, and maritime power that lived from free access to all parts of the Mediterranean. The crusade penny, a general imperial tax for the Holy War, was on the diet's agenda; it had to be paid by the German lands and above all by the flourishing cities if the West were to defend itself properly and effectively counteract the threat from the East.

Constantinople, once the leading power in the struggle against the Turks, had fallen half a century earlier, in 1453. Now Greece and the Levant, Venice's traditional trading partners, were inadequately protected against the Ottoman onslaught. Moreover, Venice was a neighbor of the aggressively expanding Papal State, and was thus passionately interested in seeing the pope diverted from Italy and tied down by a war in the East. An emperor and a pope occupied by a crusade against the Turks were the best guarantee of an independent republic.

ON AUGUST 28, 1518, Emperor Maximilian I signed a truce in Augsburg that was intended to put an end to his bitter conflict with Venice and free him for a crusade against the sultan. But the decisive point was whether the estates of the empire would grant the taxes necessary to wage war, for Maximilian was at the limits of indebtedness, almost to the point of state bankruptcy. But he could count on Rome's complete support in the question of the "Turkish penny."

Pope Leo X had dispatched to the diet as legates two high-ranking members of the college of cardinals: one was Matthäus Lang, son of an Augsburg burgher family and intimate of the house of Hapsburg; the other, called Cajetan after his birthplace, Gaeta, had traveled up from Italy with instructions to help overcome the emerging resistance to the crusade tax. The Italian did not come to Augsburg empty-handed. On August 1, 1518, he solemnly—and gratis—bestowed the insignia of cardinalship on young Albrecht, elector of Brandenburg, archbishop of Mainz. Nor was Matthäus Lang forgotten. On behalf of the pope, Cajetan confirmed Lang's candidacy for Salzburg, one of the most important German archbishoprics. Finally, on the evening of this ceremonial day, the emperor, too, was honored—and put under obligation—when Cajetan presented him with the consecrated hat and sword, symbols of the Christian crusader.

But on August 5, when the cardinal finally came to the point in his Latin speech before the diet and tried to enlist support for the Turkish crusade, these papal honors remained without effect. The representatives of the empire did not feign politeness; they vehemently poured forth long-felt grievances, voicing the complaints of the German nation, above all against the Church's taxation policy, Rome's encroachment on the sovereignty of the estates, and the curia's endless tampering with the positions and revenues of the German church: all career roads led to Rome!

Frederick the Wise, sovereign of Saxony, was at the forefront when it came to throwing off the yoke of ecclesiastical power. This meant more than a battle against continual curial infringements on the sovereign rights of princes; it also included curbing the local bishops, who were vying with the sovereigns for power. Princes were still compelled to fight for what many free imperial cities already had: independence from the temporal supremacy of the Church. In 1518 the Luther issue, which had thus far attracted little attention outside Germany, was only one of the many ecclesiastical conflicts to arise in Augsburg. At stake was the status of the Church in German territories.

It fell to the Roman legate, Cardinal Cajetan, to find a solution to the Luther problem that would safeguard the ecclesiastical supremacy of Rome without provoking the Saxon elector. And so between October 12 and 15, 1518—after the diet had ended—Martin Luther underwent the first and only interrogation to which he was ever subjected. Cajetan had promised the

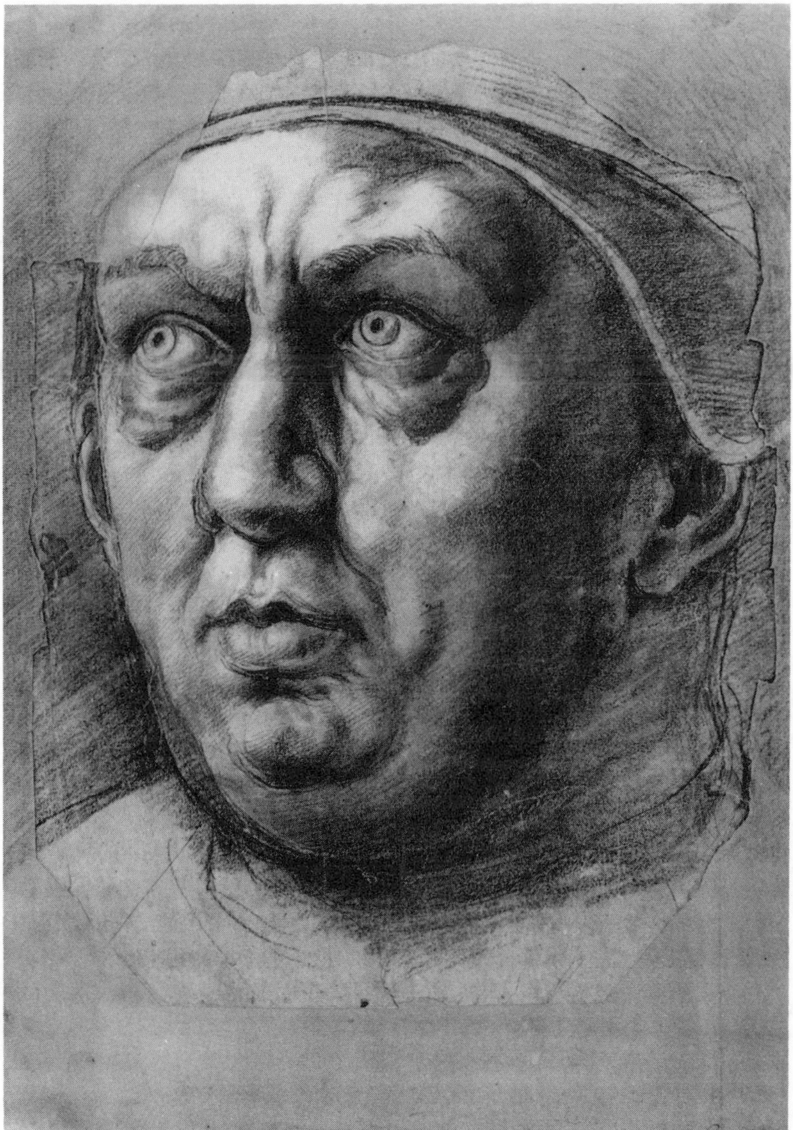

Pope Leo X (1513–21) excommunicated Luther in 1521.
Attributed to Sebastiano del Piombo.

elector to proceed as a "father" and not like a "judge," but all his efforts were in vain: reasoning with Luther was as ineffective as harsh commands. In the end the legate could only conclude that the monk must be regarded as a heretic unwilling to recant and bow to the Church.

For Cajetan that was the end of the matter. Despite the monk's intractability, the legate, as promised, had not had the man arrested, but as ordered by the pope, he did pronounce judgment. He emphatically urged Frederick: "I exhort and beg Your Highness to consider Your honor and Your conscience and either to have the monk Martin sent to Rome or to chase him from Your lands. Your Highness should not let one little friar (unum fraterculum) bring such ignominy over You and Your house."[1]

The Venetian ambassador and the papal legate were equally astonished that a German diet could allow itself to be influenced by such trivialities, or that an elector could let himself become so distracted by a monk's ludicrous chatter that the necessities of politics were forgotten. Typically German—inconceivable anywhere else!

"Typically Roman"—thus the response from the German side, venting its irritation: here come those wily Latins, trying again to take advantage of us naive Germans for their own purposes. Like every individual elector, the diet as a whole bore responsibility for the political interests of Germany, not those of Rome. As the imperial estates saw it, emancipation from the curia was among the essential national grievances that had to be met.

The reigning princes, especially Frederick, understood politics in a wider sense than we do today. Politics was not restricted to temporal welfare; it was also concerned with the prerequisites and conditions for the eternal salvation of the citizenry in town and country. That is why Luther's *Address to the Christian Nobility of the German Nation* (August 1520) could become his most effective political treatise. Here the worldly authorities could find the biblical justification for their long-practiced commitment to the well-being of the region and the regional Church. He who submissively left the welfare of the Church to the "courtiers" of the Roman curia was violating his obligations as a Christian prince.

It was not especially prudent of Cajetan to appeal to Frederick's ancestors, for the ruling house of Wettin had already taken action against the legal claims of the ecclesiastical hierarchy before the division of Saxony in 1485. Long before October 1517, when Luther in his ninety-five theses questioned the rights of the pope in such a seemingly revolutionary way, Frederick II, an Elector of Saxony, had seriously restricted the pope's right to sell indulgences within his domains. When Pope Calixtus III offered a Turkish indulgence in 1458, Frederick II intervened forthwith. The Roman legate had to agree to surrender half the proceeds to the electoral treasury. The measures taken to ensure that the earnings were divided fairly between pope and state show how little the sovereign trusted the legate: The money was kept in a large "confession box" equipped with two locks, and the keys were entrusted to town councilors. To guarantee that all funds really reached the indulgence boxes, the prince assigned the papal legate an inspector, whose reports fully confirmed the prince's suspicions.[2]

At the beginning of the sixteenth century, when Saxony had been divided for seventeen years, the sovereigns, Elector Frederick the Wise and Duke George the Bearded, had repeatedly succeeded in protecting their interests when indulgences were at issue. When a Turkish indulgence had again been offered in 1502, the two princes had ordered the funds confiscated as soon

The electors of Saxony, Frederick the Wise and his brother John the Steadfast

as it became clear that once again the crusade against the Turks would fail to materialize. Such occurrences help to explain why "the little friar" did not simply vanish from the German scene. Yet why did Frederick—known as "the Wise"—support Luther's cause to the extent he did? His "no" to Cajetan linked Electoral Saxony so closely with the Reformation in the following years that ultimately his nephew John Frederick lost his electoral dignity when, on May 19, 1547, he signed the Capitulation of Wittenberg—the result of his crushing defeat in the religious war against the emperor.

The simple but crucial answer is that Frederick was acting as a Christian sovereign. Religious conviction did not allow him to compromise, and proved itself to be a mighty political factor. And the very factor that originally made the Reformation possible in Electoral Saxony was also the major cause of the ensuing military catastrophe. Because John Frederick had given Sunday worship priority over military service, on April 24, 1547, the emperor's troops were able to surprise the elector at Mühlberg. With all the elector's sentries withdrawn and in prayer, they had managed to advance to the bank of the Elbe unobserved. This pious picture of a praying prince, who trusts himself and his army to the protection of God, finds its exact parallel in the attitude of Frederick the Wise during the Peasants' War: On April 14, 1525, barely a month before his death on May 5, the aged elector informed his impatient brother Duke John: "If it is God's will that the common man shall rule, then so be it. But if it is not His divine will and [the revolt] has not been undertaken to glorify Him, things will soon be taken care of."[3]

Such passive submission to Providence runs counter to Luther's beliefs. His harsh tracts concerning the peasants not only condemned the bloodshed caused by the peasant hordes; they also censured the princes for acting casually and irresponsibly. Trusting in God's control over the course of history and in His judgment is, after all, a matter of faith; it does not relieve sovereigns of their obligation to fulfil their duties and to render loyal service to the world to the very end, short as their time on earth may be.

Wherever Frederick's religious beliefs come to the surface, their divergence from the Reformation is apparent, and Luther openly assailed them. Not long after the indulgence controversy broke out, he stood up against a false, and to his mind egotistical, veneration of saints,[4] directing some of his sharpest barbs against Frederick's most valued possession, the relic collection in the castle church of Wittenberg. In 1523 Luther went on publicly to embarrass and upbraid his sovereign when, at the end of his draft for a new liturgy, the *Formula Missae,* he spoke of the accursed financial interests of the prince, who, with his collection of relics, debased the castle church—called by Luther "All Saints, or rather All Devils"[5]—by exploiting it as a source of

The Castle Church of Wittenberg. Here Luther posted his theses on October 31, 1517. Title page of Wittenberger Heiligtumsbuch *(Wittenberg, 1509), illustrated by Lucas Cranach the Elder, the catalogue of relics that Frederick and John had collected in the Castle Church of Wittenberg out of concern for salvation. It provided detailed information on each of the indulgences available there.*

income. No doubt Luther did Frederick an injustice—and blocked the future appreciation of the Elector as a "Christian sovereign."

It is astonishing that though repeatedly and severely attacked by Luther, and despite the commotion provoked by the controversial professor and the indignation aroused by many a radical defender of the Reformation, Frederick continued to uphold and guarantee Luther's freedom of action. On his deathbed Frederick publicly testified to his departure from the old faith when, contrary to papal doctrine, he had the Sacrament administered with bread and wine, in keeping with Christ's institution—and Luther's teachings. It cannot have been a violation of Frederick's last wish when the outlawed heretic was asked to rewrite the funeral liturgy in accordance with the principles of his reformed rite, and to preach the funeral sermon. Thus Frederick the Wise was laid to rest on May 11, 1525, with more innovations than he had been willing to approve during his lifetime.

The generations that followed found the Elector as enigmatic as had his own contemporaries. Reserved and shy, dilatory to the point of indecision, unwilling to commit himself, let alone permit himself to be committed, as he lay dying he made a gesture that heralded an irreversible change. Who was this man? His personality is not easy to grasp, as it recedes behind his political posture. Historians must rely on the image that the prince carefully cultivated as an instrument in political conflict. Here we meet a late medieval German prince who was by no means an absolute ruler. Yet he had such a sure and strong sense of duty that neither the Roman curia nor the imperial court nor even a Doctor Luther could shake his understanding of the temporal welfare and eternal salvation of his subjects. Again and again he stressed that as a layman he could not stand in judgment over Luther's theology, while at the same time making it quite clear that excommunication by the pope did not constitute proof of the doctor's guilt. In the battle between the factions, Frederick was the complete Christian prince, acting in the interests of his subjects' welfare and salvation. The supreme ecclesiastical authority of the German prince was not a result of the Reformation, as often claimed: it preceded the Reformation and provided the cradle for its early emergence and ultimate survival.

The State of the Nation

Luther described Frederick as the great hesitator—though admittedly in retrospect, and always in comparison with the outspoken support he received from Frederick's successors, John the Constant and especially John

John Frederick the Magnanimous, Elector of Saxony, Luther's protector. He was to lose his electorate in 1547 for the sake of the Reformation. Woodcut by Lucas Cranach the Elder, ca. 1533.

Frederick the Magnanimous. But it was this very hesitation that enabled Electoral Saxony to bridge the difficult years of threatening isolation within the empire and the Reformation to survive without the support of the German imperial estates.

Without Frederick and his councilors, Cardinal Cajetan's interrogation of Luther would have taken place in Rome and not on German soil. Without the Elector's perseverance, the evangelical movement would have come to an end in 1518, to remain at best a dimly remembered chapter in church history. Luther the reformer and charismatic genius would never have existed, only Luther the heretic, who for a time enjoyed a certain degree of notoriety when, like the Bohemian Jan Hus and the Florentine Girolamo Savonarola, he protested against the secularization of the Church. Luther would ultimately have become so inconsequential as to allow an unperturbed Roman curia to magnanimously reconsider his case today.

But this is not how it was to be. From the beginning the court of Electoral Saxony did not believe in an impartial investigation of Luther by the Roman "courtiers" and mendicant friars; Frederick was not at all convinced that the theology professor from the Saxon University of Wittenberg had taught heretical doctrines. Besides, any attempt to "settle" the Luther question in Rome, outside Germany, was considered an infringement of the sovereignty of electoral judicial authority. Luther, recognizing the risk this policy entailed for Saxony, made the elector a politically attractive proposal: to leave Saxony so as not to compromise the prince and thus to restore the sovereign's freedom of political action. So close had the hour of Luther's exile come that on December 1, 1518, his Wittenberg friends were assembled to bid him farewell. Luther and his guests were "in good spirits" when a message arrived: "If the Doctor is still there, he should under no circumstances leave the land; the Elector has important things to discuss with him."[6] Luther had become a factor in national politics.

The electoral chancery was able to retreat to a position of neutrality without any elaborate declarations of principle. The doctoral oath of the University of Wittenberg, which Martin Luther had sworn on October 19, 1512, not only prohibited the dissemination of heretical doctrine; it also granted full academic freedoms and privileges, which expressly included the right of a doctor of theology to discuss freely and unhindered questions of scriptural interpretation. In their declaration of December 1518 the University of Wittenberg had confirmed that this applied to Luther's ninety-five theses.[7] When the delicate problem of pontifical authority was to be debated in Leipzig, Luther and his opponent Johannes Eck, his first and lifelong German adversary, were in total agreement over this basic principle of academic freedom. With the support of both parties the ruler, Duke George (Leipzig belonged to Ducal Saxony after the division in 1485), was able to push through this debate, overriding both the veto of the responsible bishop and the timidity of Leipzig's theological faculty.

From the start Elector Frederick treated the Luther affair as a legal case, avoiding anything that might have been interpreted as partiality. He never met Luther personally and never expressed an opinion on the contents of the new theology. Up to the Edict of Worms (May 26, 1521), which placed Luther under imperial ban, Frederick was able to maintain his impartial stance. Public support could not have provided more efficient protection for the professor from Wittenberg.

Just as effectively, Frederick the "hesitator" acted by his inaction after Luther was condemned by the pope. On June 15, 1520, Pope Leo issued *Exsurge Domine,* the bull announcing conditional excommunication. It listed forty-one statements from Luther's works and condemned them as "heretical, offensive, and false." Luther had sixty days to submit. As this period passed without recantation, he was officially excommunicated on January 3, 1521. By signing the bull of excommunication, *Decet Romanum Pontificem,* the pope had finally settled the Luther question—or so it appeared. After the conclusion of the ecclesiastical trial, only the administrative sequel remained: Luther was to be turned over to the secular authorities and subsequently executed.

Why, then, were the demands of imperial and ecclesiastical law not met? After all, since the Augsburg diet of 1518, a great deal had happened to undermine the success of Luther's cause. In his report on his "fatherly exhortation," Cardinal Cajetan had set aside the crucial argument of the right of free debate with a single sentence: "Although Brother Martin has put his opinions in the form of theses for academic disputation, he has nonetheless put them forward as firm results in sermons, and even, as I have been told, in the German language"[8]—within earshot of everyone, even the common "stupid people"! He had abused his academic privilege of free disputation and thus forfeited it; henceforth only the assessment of the doctrinal contents of Luther's theses should decide.

But Cajetan had been too hasty in rendering his verdict. A curious redundancy was to weaken his case: Luther's theses "are partly in violation of the teachings of the Holy See and are partly heretical."[9] Not only from the modern vantage point of the present-day Holy Office is this double justification peculiar. Clearly Cajetan had accepted Electoral Saxony's insistence on scriptural evidence: Luther's theology was contrary to Scripture, and thus to be condemned as heretical—a second and altogether independent point was the matter of papal authority. Precisely this biblical line of argumentation might well have ended fatally for Luther.

The Elector's reply to the cardinal was that there were many erudite scholars in Saxony who would not join in a condemnation of Luther. Without outside pressure, he, the ruling prince, would with God's help know what to do, in accordance with his honor and his conscience, were Luther actually found guilty of heresy.[10]

But what would happen if Luther really were convicted of heresy and then no longer could depend on anti-Roman sentiments in Germany? What the Elector wrote was anything but the declaration of a cautious diplomat who promises nothing and leaves all possibilities open. From our modern perspective the Reformation was still in its early stages in 1518, and a commitment of the sort the Elector showed vis-à-vis Cajetan thus seems astonishing.

But the Elector's contemporaries saw the same events differently: for them the investigation and interrogation of Luther was merely the most recent chapter in one hundred years of reform effort which had been keeping the Church in suspense and Germany seething ever since the Council of Constance (1414–18).

Decisions cannot be put off forever; the reply to Cajetan was that of a confident sovereign who was well aware that a crucial moment in the struggle over Church reform had come, and who was thus acting within his authority as a Christian prince: if Martin Luther were convicted as a heretic, he should be condemned; but if the curia only wanted to get rid of an irksome reformer, he should retain his position as university professor and teacher of the Church.

Luther grasped the significance of the Elector's answer as soon as his friend and pupil, Georg Spalatin, privy councilor to the Elector, showed him a copy: "Ultimately even Cajetan will have to learn that secular power also comes from God. . . . I am happy that the Elector has shown his patient and wise impatience in this matter."[11]

Election Victory for Charles

If the elector's influence had not grown substantially overnight, Luther's cause would never have become a German event; it would have remained a local Saxon affair and easily been brought to an undramatic end in the summer of 1520, at the very latest. But the death of Emperor Maximilian I on January 12, 1519, drastically changed the political situation in the empire. At the Diet of Augsburg—his last—Maximilian, already seriously ill, had championed his grandson Charles as Roman (German) king. The emperor's death and the intrigues that followed hard upon it, the diplomatic and not so diplomatic wrangling over Maximilian's succession, which had not been conclusively established in Augsburg, aborted the "normal" run of the Luther affair. Only now, in the wake of the ensuing electoral campaign, did the Roman heresy case become a German issue.

Frederick's shrewd, self-confident, but by no means disrespectful answer, which Cajetan immediately dispatched to Rome, was his final opportunity to defer the matter. After a condemnation by the pope the Elector would no longer have been able to protect the monk and, in keeping with his own stated principles, would no longer have wanted to, once the highest ecclesiastical authority had made its decision.

But with the emperor's death, the situation changed for Rome, as well as for the empire. The interregnum resulted in a power gap which allowed the German electors to gain importance far beyond the borders of their own territories. The imperial law of the Golden Bull of 1356 had decreed that the German king was to be elected by seven princes, who in consequence of this right were called electors: they included the archbishops of Mainz, Cologne,

Emperor Maximilian I. *Drawn by Albrecht Dürer at the Diet of Augsburg in 1518.*

and Trier, and the secular sovereigns of Bohemia, the Palatinate, Brandenburg, and Saxony. On August 27, 1518, toward the end of the Diet of Augsburg, Maximilian had succeeded in winning over the majority of the electoral college for his grandson. Only Trier and Saxony had not yet been prepared to commit themselves: the archbishop of Trier's unwillingness was probably due to his very close French ties; the Saxon, on the other hand, had cited the electoral regulations of the Golden Bull, and this may well have been his true motive: no advance commitment should restrict his free vote.

Portrait of the dead Emperor Maximilian I. The emperor had left instructions for his body to be scourged, his hair shorn, and his teeth broken out. He wanted to appear before God as penitent.

This is as far as historical reconstruction can go. As a matter of course, little of the maneuvering that went on behind the scenes after the emperor's death ever reached the records. There is solid evidence that gifts, that is, bribes, were handed out by the candidates competing for the throne, but new discoveries suggest that we do not know even half the story with regard to these financial machinations. What is certain is that after a passing involvement by King Henry VIII of England, and then a Saxon interlude when the pope wanted to induce Elector Frederick to become a candidate, there were only two serious competitors left: King Francis I of France and Charles I, duke of Burgundy, king of Spain and Naples-Sicily, and, together with his brother Ferdinand, heir to the lands of Austria. Charles' election would mean a new powerful emperor with a hitherto unknown compass of power. Under these circumstances his candidacy would inevitably challenge both pope and French king, and make them allies for a long time to come, when the election would be but a distant memory.

The amount of money invested to elect one or the other candidate exceeded anything before. The house of Hapsburg spent almost one million gulden, most of which was financed by the Fugger bank. The exact French figures are not known, but the French expenditures appear to have been considerable. Maximilian had already shown in Augsburg his consternation at the sizable investments the French were making to bribe the electors. The pope, too, was distributing money liberally and making generous offers of ecclesiastical privileges and promises of cardinals' caps and bishoprics.

In the spring of 1519, when the electoral struggle was threatening to lead to a stalemate, the government of the Hapsburg Netherlands proposed a compromise that stood a real chance of smoothing Germany's way into the modern era, because it took into account the incipient development of a Europe divided into nations: not the many-titled Charles but his younger brother Archduke Ferdinand, who would in fact have been acceptable to all parties as German king, should become Maximilian's successor. But Charles indignantly rejected this solution—the "defense of Christendom" demanded a strong, universal empire.

Indeed, it was not a mere craving for power that impelled Charles to seek the crown of the Holy Roman Empire; after all, he kept his promise to share the regency with Ferdinand at his earliest convenience. Twelve years later, in 1531, long before his abdication (1555), Charles saw to it that his brother, Archduke Ferdinand, was elected king of the Romans—over the protest of the Saxon elector, who stayed away from the election. It was exactly these twelve years that led up to Ferdinand's elevation which proved to be decisive for both Germany and the Reformation.

IN JANUARY 1524 a German solution to the quest for reform of the Church seemed imminent. The third Diet of Nuremberg decided to convene a national council, a "general assembly of the German nation,"[12] in Speyer on St. Martin's Day, November 11, 1524, in order to resolve the Luther problem. It is easy to understand why the Roman curia opposed the diet's decision, since a council of this sort increased the danger that the Germans might transform their church into a national church independent of Rome. In France the pope had just barely managed to prevent this late medieval independence movement through a generous concordat with King Francis I. When King Henry VIII succeeded in establishing the Church of England in 1534, ten years after the resolution of the Diet of Nuremberg, the curia was no longer in a position to counter this secession successfully. Had it not been for the emperor, the solution of a national church would have stood as good a chance in Germany as it had in England.

The decision to convoke a national council was in everyone's interest and was advocated by all the imperial estates, even by Archduke Ferdinand. It united supporters and opponents of the new doctrine, including the

Bavarian dukes, who were as anti-Hapsburg as they were anti-Luther. But Ferdinand, regent of the Austrian dynastic lands, could do little more than recommend the plan to his brother the emperor. Yet from faraway Burgos in Spain Charles issued a curt instruction forbidding the proposed council. The road to a united German church was closed.

As in the case of the earlier imperial election, there were two reasons why Charles had no alternative. For one thing a national solution would have undercut the strength of the house of Hapsburg, and—the crucial point—the policy of dynastic power served the idea of a universal empire. As emperor Charles had to override particularist interests in order to maintain and protect the unity of Church and empire in the Western Christian world.

The prohibition of the German national council was a direct result of the imperial election of 1519. Of course the German princes could not have predicted the precise implications of their vote for Charles, but in all likelihood they suspected or feared the worst. The decision to swear in the emperor on a German constitution, the "Electoral Covenant," was not based simply on the vested interests of narrow-minded territorial dignitaries. Charles not only had to confirm the princes' rights, their "sovereignty, liberties, privileges," he also had to swear to appoint "none but native-born Germans" to imperial offices and himself to take up "royal residence, pretence, and court in the Holy Roman Empire."[13]

But such a legal commitment could not possibly negate historical reality as created by the imperial election. A French-speaking, Spanish monarch had been chosen. Though a Hapsburg, he was no German. The extension of Hapsburg power from the Turkish border in the East to the New World in the West led to a subordination of German interests to the demands of dynastic politics, which would of necessity degrade the old empire to a province at the edge of a world empire. In his effort to achieve universal rule Charles could ascribe to the Reformation only as much importance as to any other German event. It was an irritating obstacle on the imperial high road, and thus only the remedies against it varied, ranging from patient attention to brusque rebuffs, from temporary ceasefires to open warfare. Whatever the means, Charles doggedly pursued his goal: the extirpation of the Reformation, on the imperial agenda since the Diet of Worms in 1521, was going to stay there.

In fact, the evolution of Hapsburg policies did more to further the Evangelical cause than the political future of Germany. In France, England, Switzerland, and then the Netherlands, national identities began to burgeon. But Germany's development into a nation lagged behind, not as is often argued, because territorial factionalism forestalled the emergence of a common identity, but because all resources for national cohesion were sacrificed to a medieval imperial dream. And that process had already been going on for three generations of Hapsburg emperors—from Frederick III through his son Maximilian I to the latter's grandson Charles V.

And yet another point must be considered. A national council might have meant the end of Luther's cause. If a German church assembly had actually taken place in Speyer in 1524, the explosive force of reformation would in all probability have been channeled into a reform program and thus defused. Priests would have been granted permission to marry and laymen to receive the chalice. Church taxes would have been nationalized, and Rome most likely excluded from ecclesiastical jurisdiction in Germany. Of course all this would have been no more than the treatment of symptoms, in the Erasmian spirit of peaceful piety and communal concord. The Gospel of the Cross, which Luther had discovered for a Church persecuted, would have been silenced in the ensuing atmosphere of reasonable compromise and pious reform zeal. Yet it was the emperor's religious policy that—contrary to its own objectives—enabled the powers Luther had unleashed to bring about radical change in theology, the Church, and the balance of power in Europe.

The Spanish Factor

An exclusively German view of the early years of the Reformation confines the historical perspective. These were the years when Emperor Charles was devoting himself to Italy, Spain, or Burgundy. Yet the imperial diets from which the emperor absented himself were not the only important ones; there were also those that owed their results to his presence. This is certainly true for the Diet of Worms, which Luther made famous and which made him famous. In the face of the Wittenberg theologian's courageous words—"I cannot and will not recant. . . . God help me. Amen."[14]—the emperor's equally momentous declaration has unjustifiably been forgotten: "I have decided to mobilize everything against Luther: my kingdoms and dominions, my friends, my body, my blood and my soul."[15]

Nine years later, in 1530, Charles once again presided over a diet, this time in Augsburg. And once again it was the emperor who lent this diet its significance beyond Germany's borders. It was he who had invited the opposing religious factions to express their views in Augsburg; it was to him that the *Confessio Augustana*, the Lutheran confession of faith, was addressed; and it was in his name, not the pope's, that the *Confutatio,* the decisive theological rejection of Reformational doctrine, was issued.

It is not true that Germany was left to its own devices without Charles' political leadership, thus permitting the Reformation to spread unrestricted. Of course, the "German nation" was no longer in a position to determine the Roman emperor's goals, nor had it been even in Maximilian's time. But for Charles not even a European view was encompassing enough to grasp his policies.

Even a brief glance at Spanish accounts of that time demonstrates how very differently political events look from that perspective. For them the national rise of Spain under Charles placed the country center-stage in the battle against the enemies of the Church. Spain broke the ground for Christian renewal and spearheaded the Crusades—against the Turks in the Mediterranean, the pagans in the West Indies, and the heretics in Germany.

For two hundred years Spanish literature was shaped by this myth of crusade and mission, a myth which, however fabricated it might have been, clearly brings out the other political perspective. Martin Luther and Hernando Cortes, it was recounted again and again, were born on the same day of the same year; one a terrible German monster who led astray thousands of souls, the other the great Conquistador, who converted an incomparably larger number of Indians.[16] In reality Luther's and Cortes' birthdates are one or even several years apart, but the legend illustrates an awareness of the shifting geopolitical balance during Charles' reign. Evaluating the Reformation in the light of world politics means giving up the German, even the Western European perspective: from the vantage point of the Hapsburg world empire, losses in the Old World were more than compensated for by conquests in the New.

When Charles was elected in 1519 the conquests of Mexico and Peru still lay in the future; he could not know the extent to which the interests of Spanish politics would be changed by the growth of an American empire. Born in Ghent on February 24, 1500, Charles grew up in the tradition of the illustrious Burgundian empire. There was not so much as a hint that the young duke would transcend the late medieval role of a Burgundian knight to gain the stature of a Spanish world ruler. He was christened Charles after his great-grandfather Duke Charles "the Bold." When the imperial chancellor Mercurio Gattinara congratulated the newly elected German king on June 28, 1519, on having acquired a basis of power hitherto "possessed only by Your predecessor Charlemagne,"[17] he was not indulging in flattery; he was formulating a political program. His reference to Charles the Great—

Barend van Orley, Emperor Charles V, *ca. 1520.*

rather than Charles the Bold—stemmed from a very realistic appraisal of Spain's future and shows the political farsightedness with which the election of the emperor was pursued. Europe was on the way to modern times and the development of sovereign states just as the medieval dream of a universal empire seemed to be becoming reality. And Charles I of Spain was just the ruler to dedicate himself to the vision of such a Christian world monarchy. Too much, too late.

World Monarchy and Reformation

According to nationally oriented German historians, Charles' only rival, the French king Francis I, was so much a foreigner to the country that he could count only on those who were fickle, bribable, or had succumbed to the enticements of the pope. Among France's partisans—originally Trier, the Palatinate, and Brandenburg—Joachim, elector of Brandenburg, was considered particularly contemptible because his monetary demands were so exorbitant. Even Charles' offer to marry his sister Catherine to the elector was only accepted on condition that the emperor guarantee him thirty thousand gulden. Here, too, the Fuggers were to act as financiers.

Historians of every stripe have found only one statesman thoroughly praiseworthy: Frederick the Wise. A German and a man of integrity, he is considered to have been a staunch representative of the interests of the empire in a sea of corruptibility and national betrayal.

The dismal picture of an empire in decline is correct in so far as the centralist state realized by the French king was difficult to reconcile with the German ideal of a federation of relatively independent states. The very suggestion that a French monarch might accede to the throne of the empire made most of the imperial estates fear for the continued survival of "German liberty." But the historical construction of the French "foreigner" as antagonist to a "native" Hapsburg presupposes cultural and political ties to Germany that Charles never possessed. On the contrary, since succeeding to the Spanish throne he had turned even further away from the old empire and devoted himself increasingly to the new one. There were only two suitable candidates for a "German" solution: Ferdinand, the Spanish king's brother, and Frederick the Wise, who was unencumbered by rivalries and quarrels over Hapsburg lands in southern and southwestern Germany. The one possibility was blocked by Charles, the other failed because the Saxon

At the Fugger banking house in Ausgsburg:
Jakob Fugger and his bookkeeper Matthäus Schwarz

house was not strong enough. Frederick would by necessity have become too dependent upon the other princes and their support.

When six electors and an emissary of the seventh, the king of Bohemia, met in Frankfurt on June 27, 1519, on the eve of the election, only Saxony's vote appeared to be unsold. A later report goes even so far as to claim that Frederick had been able to obtain four votes including his own and had thus de facto been elected Holy Roman Emperor—but only for three hours, until the Hapsburg election commissioners forced him to abdicate. This is pure speculation. The official record of the election proceedings reports a "briefly deliberated" and unanimous election: the electors had "all and unanimously agreed and approved, named and elected His Most Serene Highness, most powerful Prince and Lord, Carolum, Archduke of Austria, King of Spain and Naples, etc. Roman King and future Emperor in the name of Almighty God."[18]

Herewith had been reached a momentous decision which would profoundly shape the course of the Reformation. Frederick kept his preference secret to the very last, and so his vote was courted to the end. Although the result was certain on the eve of the election, and one opposing vote would have made no legal difference, Charles evidently had the emphatic wish to be elected unanimously and particularly to receive Frederick's vote. This interest in Saxon support cannot simply be inferred from the fact that money flowed into the coffers of the Saxon state treasury. Money did change hands in 1523, but it may well have been in repayment of a debt still owed by the Hapsburgs for loans made to Emperor Maximilian.

It was probably not money that prompted Frederick to cast his vote for the king of Spain, especially since Saxony's flourishing silver-mining industry made it one of Germany's richest territories. What did matter were marital plans, even if Frederick officially dismissed the implication of any such connection with his electoral vote. The case in point was the engagement of Charles' sister, the Infanta Catherine, who had previously been offered to the Brandenburgs but was now to be married to John Frederick, nephew of Fredrick the Wise, prince of Saxony, and heir apparent to the electoral dignity. Only in May 1524 did Charles annul the marriage contract that had been negotiated secretly before the imperial election and had become legally binding only after the election, with the signatures of both sides.[19]

The marriage was notarially validated at the beginning of the Diet of Worms, on February 3, 1521, in the presence of the elector and Gattinara, the imperial chancellor. That it made the emperor and the prince in-laws is of great importance with regard to Luther. Charles confirmed that, having returned to Spain, he would immediately send the infanta, who was now eighteen, to her groom in Germany for the consummation of the marriage.[20] To the regret of Frederick the Wise and his brother Duke John, father of the groom, this never happened. Nevertheless, the alliance did have full legal validity for almost four years. (Only in 1525, after the contract had been abrogated, could Catherine—yet again in the service of her brother's European strategy—marry King John III of Portugal.) There is no need to speculate about the course Reformation history might have taken had this marriage become a physical reality, forming a dynastic bond between the emperor and the elector. The two were allied by the unconsummated legal marriage when imperial and canon law should by all rights have long made them opponents.

The Luther Issue in Worms

The imperial election continued to affect the Hapsburg relation with Saxony until cancelation of the marriage in May 1524. The Roman curia, on the other hand, saw no reason to show further consideration for Frederick after the election. Now there was nothing more in the way of a quick end to the Roman trial of Luther. In the summer of 1520 the time had come: Luther was condemned as a heretic. But once again things took an unexpected turn. Instead of being handed over to the secular authorities for execution of the death penalty, Luther was summoned to the diet in Worms. The emperor had been most reluctant to agree to such a public interrogation, but on March 6, 1521, the invitation was issued, personally signed by "Carolus": "Honorable, beloved, and devoted [Luther]. Since we [the Emperor] and the estates of the Holy Empire . . . have proposed and decided, to obtain information from you about your doctrines and books, we give you safe-conduct . . . with the desire that you should set out, and that under our protection you will appear here among us and not stay away."[21] It does not sound as if a heretic were being summoned but an "honored, beloved, devoted" man; an invitation was being extended to the professor from Wittenberg, and his safe-conduct to the diet and back was being guaranteed. The emperor would never have made this concession without Frederick, who had once again exercised his influence to keep the Luther question from being settled too quickly.

Contemporaries did not know that only one month earlier Frederick had collected on the electoral debt of the emperor through the notarial validation of the Hapsburg-Saxon marriage. Luther's protector in Worms was not a minor sovereign or insignificant prince: Frederick was a monarch with whom Charles sought to establish dynastic ties, to whom he was indebted—for more than financial reasons. This cannot have been clear to most of those assembled in Worms. What a majority of the imperial estates knew and did not doubt, however, was the legal basis for the summons, namely the emperor's electoral oath, by virtue of which no citizen was allowed to be placed under imperial ban without a hearing. For the Germans the legal situation was clear; what the emperor had signed in July 1519 had to be applied to Luther: "We shall and wish to . . . under no circumstances permit anyone, whether of high estate or low, elector, prince, or otherwise, to be placed under ban and double ban for any reason without a hearing."[22]

Hieronymus Aleander, the resolute and initially successful papal legate, held the contrary legal view: from January 3, 1521 on, the last day for submission, Luther was to be considered an incorrigible, notorious heretic and to be placed under ban automatically, according to canon and imperial law. After the wild merriment of Carnival, Aleander used Ash Wednesday (February 13) as a day of reflection to remind the estates assembled in Worms with all eloquence of this bond between Church and empire, which had been held sacred for centuries. His speech made so great an impression that Gregor Brück, chancellor of Electoral Saxony, personally translated it into German and the Saxon elector's delegation carefully inserted it among the official documents.

The well-informed nuncio seems to have realized that time was pressing and that the situation was becoming increasingly critical: "How much evil and harm Martini Luther's agitation and rebellion has caused, how much misery he has brought upon the Christian people, what further damage he daily inflicts, is as clear as day; that is why it is necessary and crucial to see to it that his subversive sect be wiped out forthwith, and without any further postponement."[23]

As early as 1520, well before the public debate in Worms, Luther's call to Reformation could no longer be treated as just any case to be tried in a papal, imperial, or local court and thereby nipped in the bud. So many people had become familiar with his theology and recognized their own criticisms of pope and Church in his writings that the name *Luther* had taken on an unmistakably public profile all the way down to the so-called common man. Luther was undoubtedly right to view the protective custody provided by the elector two weeks after Worms as unnecessary solicitude, for if he had had to

Hieronymus Aleander, papal nuncio at the Diet of Worms

bear witness to and pay for his beliefs with his life, the Evangelical movement would not have been stopped, but rather have gained ground even faster.

WORMS: for contemporaries and future generations alike it was a German event, the triumph of spirit over force, of German character over Latin cunning. For Luther, too, Worms was a German event, but in the worst sense of the word: the emperor "should have assembled one doctor or fifty and defeated this monk with arguments."[24] Instead of searching for the truth, they had ordered him to recant.

What had happened to make Luther report so bitterly to his friend, the famous painter Lucas Cranach, in Wittenberg? On April 16, 1521, Luther arrived in Worms; only one day later, the first hearing took place in the "Bishop's Court." There, in the presence of his imperial majesty, the electors and princes—all the estates of the empire—Johann von der Ecken, chancellor of the bishop of Trier, asked Luther two questions:

> Do you, Martin Luther, recognize the books published under your name as your own?
> Are you prepared to recant what you have written in these books?

The Saxon delegation had taken the precaution of providing Luther—who was, after all, a monk and professor of theology—with an experienced lawyer, his friend and colleague from Wittenberg, Hieronymus Schurff, professor of canon and imperial law. Schurff immediately objected to the first question: "The titles of the books must be named." When this had been done, Luther acknowledged each of the works mentioned as his own. For Aleander this was already confirmation enough of the heretic's mendacity: the "stupid monk" could not possibly have written all those books and obviously was covering up for the clever men behind the scenes.

Now everyone waited with bated breath for the reply to the second question: Would the monk recant? Those who expected a clear "no" were disappointed. Luther requested time to think. He was granted one day, until April 18, but not without the justified rebuke that he should have been prepared for after a question of this sort.

The following day promised to be an exciting one, and it was. Luther once again refused to give a direct answer. Some of my books, he said, are neither sharp nor polemical; they deal with nothing but faith and the Christian life in accordance with the Gospel. Even my opponents will be able to find nothing objectionable in them. Other writings are directed against the papacy, which is ruining the Church, weighing down the human conscience, and oppressing the empire. "If I now recant these, then, I would be doing nothing but strengthening tyranny."[25] He admitted that some of his tracts were polemical and sometimes "un-Christian" in tone, but even there he must remain firm unless errors could be pointed out.

Luther was permitted to finish his speech, but he had been asked for a response "without loops and holes." And that is what emperor and empire got: "Unless I am convinced by the testimony of the Holy Scriptures or by evident reason—for I can believe neither pope nor councils alone, as it is clear that they have erred repeatedly and contradicted themselves—I consider myself convicted by the testimony of Holy Scripture, which is my basis; my conscience is captive to the Word of God. Thus I cannot and will not recant, because acting against one's conscience is neither safe nor sound. God help me. Amen."[26]

After Luther's appearance before the diet, it became clear that the courteously formulated imperial summons had been deceptive. The diet was not to obtain "information" but to accept a recantation or impose a ban. This was the emperor's plan, and Johann von der Ecken was there to see that it was carried out. Luther did not need many words to summarize the events of Worms for Lucas Cranach: "Are the books yours? Yes. Do you want to re-

Luther before the emperor and the electors in Worms. At Luther's side stands Hieronymus Schurff, professor of law in Wittenberg, here as his legal advisor. In handwriting on the woodcut: "Intitulentur libri" (The titles of Luther's books must be named) and "Hie stehe ich, ich kan nicht anderst, Got helffe mir Amen" (Here I stand, I can do no other, Amen).

cant or not? No. Get thee hence! O, we blind Germans, how childishly we act and allow ourselves to be mocked and fooled by the Romanists."[27] As so often before, the empire had let itself become the lackey of Rome—this too was a German event.

Historical distance shows that Luther's evaluation of the interrogation at Worms must be amended and at the same time upheld, though not on his grounds. Worms was indeed a German event, but this time it was not the Germans who had been made fools of. Where else in Western Christendom would it have been politically viable to protect a rebellious monk from being extradited to Rome—as in the autumn of 1518—and to obtain a public hearing for a notorious heretic—as now in the spirit of 1521?

The media of the time, the pamphlets and "private" letters written for publication, saw to it that Luther's speech to the diet was circulated far and wide. In the Bishop's Court in Worms sat the whole of Germany, not just the emperor and the imperial estates. In fact, the nation heard even more than its rulers—namely the impressive final statement that can be found only in the published version of Luther's confession: "Here I stand, I cannot do otherwise. God help me. Amen."[28]

The German "follies" at Worms and before had kept the Luther issue alive too long for a ban from above to stifle it.

"Wake up, wake up, o German nation"

After the collapse of the Third Reich in 1945 the patriotism that had accompanied the Reformation movement in Germany was suddenly shrouded in silence. Understandably so, since a perusal of the Luther literature produced during the years of Nazi terror leaves the distinct impression that the Reformation was Luther's gift to his beloved Germans: I, the "German prophet," seek not my own but German redemption and salvation.[29] Not a word is said about the fact that Luther presented his prophecy as an accusation: "Every German will come to regret that he was born a German and is recognized as one everywhere."[30]

One aspect of the nationalistic interpretation is correct: Luther was no European, not even of the Hapsburg variety of his time. He saw himself as a German and was courted by the new national mood that was to confront and vex Emperor Charles everywhere—from Alsace to the Burgundian Netherlands, wherever hometown and homeland sought to shake off foreign rule.

Although discredited by the abuses of nationalism, the national-patriotic features of Luther's thinking and their influence on his conception of a reformation should not be obscured. The connection between Reformation and national consciousness cannot be overlooked and should in fact be kept in mind, if only to enable us to resist the legends of a "German Luther" and a "German soul" that have distorted and still distort Germany's view of itself to the present day. Indeed, in this respect the Reformation was to become a German event.

A year before the Diet of Worms the professor from Wittenberg had made an unmistakable appeal for national solidarity: "The time for silence is over, the time to speak has come"! With this allusion to Ecclesiastes (3.7), Luther began the dedication of his first political pamphlet, *Address to the Christian Nobility of the German Nation.*[31] At first he only intended to write a brief, one-page handbill printed as an open letter to "Charles and the Nobility of All Germany,"[32] directed against the tyranny and wiles of the Roman curia. But by June 1520 the letter had developed into a full-length, fiery manifesto. Though it was ninety-six pages long, four thousand copies were printed and virtually torn out of the hands of the Wittenberg publisher Melchior Lotter. Only a few days later a second edition had to be printed in Wittenberg, and editions of the tract were soon published in Leipzig, Strasbourg, and Basel. Even the usually reticent Elector Frederick expressed his approval in his very own way, by sending Luther a splendid piece of game.[33]

But Luther's friend Georg Spalatin, Frederick's privy councilor, and the loyal Augustinian friars Johannes Lang and Wenzeslaus Linck were worried; after so virulent an attack on the foundations of the papal system, any attempt at a compromise with Rome was pointless. The diatribe had been written in great agitation; its feverish prose, disjointed thoughts, and repetitions trembled with outrage and concern over the future of the aberrant Church and the oppressed empire. In this pamphlet Luther's voice has echoed through the centuries. Here is the speech he would like to have given in Worms half a year later, had he been allowed.

"The time for silence is over"—when had Luther had such a time? Not lately! Particularly in the first half of 1520, he had assailed the abuses of his time so frequently and so stridently that his best friends had become alarmed. Nonetheless, the biblical paraphrase at the beginning of the tract accurately does justice to a new situation. The audience Luther was addressing had changed. The earlier German writings were pastoral works for laymen, advising them what to do and expect in the confessional, in prayer, as godparents at a christening, at mass, and not least when in mortal danger. The Latin treatises, on the other hand, with their scholarly style of argumentation and detailed exegetical proofs, were aimed at a specialized audience, for colleagues a chance to change, for students a chance to learn. But the official, academic world had not wanted to listen to him. By February 1520 the universities of Cologne and Louvain launched their condemnations of Luther's theology. Oh, wrongheaded academics!

It was not, however, just out of a sense of disappointment at the attitude of the universities that Luther turned to the general public. His reform manifesto for the German nation is not the continuation of the academic debate via other means; it is the result of his shattering realization that the Antichrist had made deep inroads into the Church.

There are two events which, taken together, reveal the new dimensions of what was probably Luther's most effective polemic tract. In February 1520 he was deeply shocked to read Ulrich von Hutten's edition of Valla's (†1457) treatise, which showed the famous Donation of Constantine to be a forgery. This very document had been invoked for centuries to prove the transfer of sovereignty over the Western world from the Roman Emperor Constantine to the pope; the so-called Donation of Constantine had been the Roman claim to supremacy over the Western world. Lies—all of it, nothing but Roman cunning! No longer could Luther suppress the conclusion that the Antichrist, the final adversary traditionally expected to appear during the Last Days, had already started his attack on the Church.[34]

WHILE LUTHER still hesitated to air publicly this awful sense of foreboding, a second event made it plain that his premonition was based on fact. In early June 1520 a tract written in 1519—the *Epitoma responsionis ad Lutherum*—claiming to be a concise refutation of all Luther's fundamental errors, reached Wittenberg. Luther was well acquainted with the author of this *Refutation,* the Dominican and highest-ranking curial theologian Silvester Prierias, for it was his expert opinion that had served as grounds for Luther's trial and had been enclosed with the official summons to Rome in August 1518.[35]

The crucial theological argument upon which Prierias' 1519 response to Luther hinged was the same as in 1518: the Church means the Church of Rome, headed by the pope, who is infallible and thus more authoritative than councils and even the Holy Scriptures themselves. There is no authority higher than the pope; and he cannot be deposed, "even if he were to give so much offense as to cause people in multitudes . . . to go to the Devil in Hell,"[36] as Prierias quoted from canon law.

†Throughout the text dagger precedes a death date.

Luther was appalled at this papal doctrine: "I think," he wrote to his friend Spalatin, "that everyone in Rome has gone crazy; they are ravingly mad, and have become inane fools and devils."[37] Lies are passed off as truth and, as in the case of the Donation of Constantine, even codified into law, and Scripture subordinated to papal authority—this is the ultimate anti-Christian perversion of the teachings of the Church.

This discovery left Luther no choice but to address the general public: The time of silence was over! Now he had to proclaim the state of emergency. In his response to Prierias, published in June 1520 "for the information of all Christians," he warned of the god-awful consequences that would arise from Rome's suppression of the Gospel. His every word vibrates with fear and trembling before this gaping threat of the final perversion of all order and virtue. No later Protestant will ever be able to imagine the full intensity of Luther's anguish: "So farewell, ill-fated, doomed, blasphemous Rome; the wrath of God has come over you."[38]

In the greatest of haste he completed his political manifesto, *Address to the Christian Nobility of the German Nation.* The empire had to be roused; its assistance was needed if reforms were finally to be carried out so that the people's pent-up rage would not vent itself in the form of an unbridled, bloody uprising. Rome, it must be remembered, has a dual function here: firstly, it is the usurper of temporal rights, in particular with respect to the Holy Roman Empire. The horrid consequences of the Donation of Constantine[39] are sarcastically spelled out: "In name the empire belongs to us, but in reality to the pope. . . . We Germans are given a clear German lesson. Just as we thought we had achieved independence, we became the slaves of the craftiest of tyrants; we have the name, title, and coat of arms of the empire, but the pope has the wealth, power, the courts, and the laws. Thus the pope devours the fruit and we play with the peels."[40]

But Rome is also the gateway through which the Devil forces his way into the Church to launch his last campaign against Christ. The truth is turned against Christ, the office of the pope as the servant of servants is changed into the power of a ruler over rulers. However, the victorious Christ at God's right hand needs no vicar, for the ruler of the world in Heaven "sees, does, knows and is capable of all things"—without the pope. It is the suffering Christ who seeks representation on earth through "working, preaching, suffering, and dying";[41] this kind of vicar is called for. Where these two offices, sovereignty in Heaven and service on Earth, are interchanged, all Hell breaks loose, and the vicar of Christ is transformed into the Antichrist.

The worldly usurper is to be contained and combatted, if necessary by force. It is for this purpose that the temporal ruler is armed with the sword.

But only prayer and penance can overcome the Antichrist. Only God can protect the Church now, for the Last Days have begun. We can kill and wash our hands "in blood," but we will no longer be able to achieve anything trusting in our own strength. The introductory sentences of the *Address to the Christian Nobility* are the political consequence of this vision of history, a view which had to be thoroughly repugnant if not totally incomprehensible to the German nationalists among Luther's early supporters:

> Our first concern must be that we fully realize the seriousness of the situation: we should not undertake anything trusting in our strength or inventiveness—even if all the power in the world were ours. For God does not desire nor tolerate good works when begun through trust in one's own strength and reason. He strikes them down, there is nothing to be done, as Psalm 33(:16) says: "A king is not saved by his great army; a mighty man is not delivered by his great strength." For this very reason, as the historical record shows, our beloved Emperors Frederick I and II and many other German emperors feared around the world were so pitifully trampled on and forced down by the popes; they may well have relied on their own power more than on God: that is why they had to fall. And I am afraid that in our time that bloodthirsty warrior Julius II could get away with murder, because France, the Germans, and Venice relied upon themselves. The children of Benjamin destroyed twenty-two thousand Israelites because these had relied on their own strength (Judges 20–21).
>
> If this is not to happen to the noble blood of Charles, we must realize that we are not dealing here with mere men but with the prince of Hell, who likes to fill the world with war and bloodshed but can not be overcome by them.[42]

Thus Luther censures the very German emperors who were hailed by the young humanist movement as symbols of national identity. It is no coincidence that at this time the Hohenstaufens Frederick I and Frederick II receive particular attention. Barbarossa, who in thirty-five years of imperial rule unified the empire as was never to happen again, was especially popular.

The spread of the Renaissance to Germany had strengthened its national fervor. Now medieval historical sources were being scrutinized so that Roman-Italian arrogance could be matched by pride in Germany's own history. Had Luther taken control of this national movement, he would have become the personal symbol of the struggle for freedom from Roman exploitation and oppression. And the Reformer did in fact awaken such expectations: "The liberation of the Germans is in Luther's hands!" Or so thought Ulrich von Hutten, champion of the national movement, as he strove to mobilize town and country. The strident tone of his commentary on the papal bull against Luther is unmistakably nationalistic:

> Here, you Germans, is the Bull of Leo X, with which he attempts to hide the Christian truth that has now come to light again. He wants to restrict and stay our freedom, so that it cannot recover and be revived in all its strength—our freedom, which after a long period of oppression is finally showing signs of life again. We will resist anyone who undertakes such a thing. Yes, we will publicly take steps long in advance to keep that person from succeeding and accomplishing anything in his restless passion and waywardness. By Immortal Christ, when was the time ever riper, when was there a better opportunity to do something worthy of a German? Everything indicates that there is more hope today than ever before of stifling this tyranny, of curing this disease. Pluck up your courage and you will achieve it! After all, it is not a question of Luther but of everyone; the sword is not raised against this one man alone, we are all of us under attack. They do not want their tyranny opposed, they do not want their deceit exposed, their strategy uncovered, their fury defied, and limits set to their wicked dealings.[43]

Luther did not go Hutten's way of German liberation through national mobilization. Exactly the same reason which later would make him reject the knight's revolt (1522) and the Peasants' War (1525) made him in 1520 already a critic of the young patriotic movement: *non vi, sed verbo*—not by force but by the power of the Gospel!

Later interpreters have concentrated on Luther's assault on the "walls of the Romanists" in the preface, and thus turned attention away from the national program in the main body of the pamphlet. Luther's primary concern, however, was his German manifesto; challenged to answer Prierias, he prefaced his treatise at the last moment with a program of theological principles, to show that the "Romanism" of Prierias blocked all reform of Church and empire.

> The Romanists have skillfully drawn three walls around themselves with which they have thus far protected themselves so that no one can reform them. Through this, the whole of Christendom has fallen into misery. The first: whenever pressed by worldly power, they raised the claim that worldly power has no legal hold over them, but that the spiri-

> tual is above the worldly. The second: if one tries to call them to reform on the basis of Holy Scripture, they counter that no one but the pope has the right to interpret the Scriptures. The third: if one threatens them with a council, they pretend that no one but the pope may convene a council. Thus they managed to steal the three rods of discipline so that they could stay unpunished within the secure fortifications of these three walls, at liberty to indulge in all manner of knavery and evil, as we see today. . . . May God help us and hand us one of the trumpets with which the walls of Jericho were toppled; thus we can blow down these straw and paper walls and loose the Christian weapons to punish sins, to expose the Devil's deceit, so that through punishment we may straighten out and regain His favor.[44]

Though the language of Luther's programmatic *Address to the Christian Nobility* is belligerent, its militancy is that of biblical truth which, once revealed, will bring down the walls of Rome. Here is not a hero speaking, but a prophet of repentance, leading the nation not to victory but to the confessional, to see to it that through chastisement we are "reformed."[45] Punishment leads to the expiation of sins, and reform means the reestablishment of justice in Church and world—in a Church that listens obediently to the Word of God, in a body politic that casts aside "what is against God and harmful to man's body and soul."[46]

The German event is not the achievement of national glory, but rather repentance and reform. Could so radical a Reformation have any hope of succeeding, could it ever prevail politically? Without any undertone of resignation, Luther's answer was "no." His concern was not the possible, but the necessary. And necessary is now, above all, sober enlightenment through the Scriptures, "and for the Christian nobility of the German nation, true spiritual courage to succor the poor Church." For "this is what the Scriptures are all about, that in spiritual matters concerning Christians and Christendom, the only thing that counts is God's judgment; never has any Christian concern been approved and supported by the world, but its resistance has always been too great and strong."[47] This is certainly not the inspiring manifesto of a national hero, nor that of a prophet promising success.

The Reformer has two reasons for keeping his distance from the national movement. Weapons cannot liberate Germany! The great emperors did not achieve their goals and failed to accomplish their historical duties because they trusted in their armies and not in God. And furthermore: the national future is already past! History has progressed so far that the Last Days are quickly approaching and the future can thus bring victories only in the form of blood and tears. To the end of his life, Luther clung to this view; his national program for "his beloved Germans" was one of repentance, repair, and reform, with no prospect of a golden age until after the Second Coming.

Like innumerable contemporaries, Ulrich von Hutten had above all heard Luther's call to liberation and did everything in his power to make it come true. He thought he had virtually reached his goal when he was able to report to Luther in late 1520 that the weapons were at the ready to support and advance their common cause.[48] The effect of Luther's rejection of the German movement can hardly be overestimated. The national cause had united so many patriots; Hutten, a highly original thinker and well-informed writer and poet with a talent to rouse people from their political apathy, was only one of many distinguished men.

The patriotic movement was not a child of Luther's time. At the beginning of the century, the "German arch-humanist" Konrad Celtis (†1508) had already extolled the Roman historian Tacitus as a farsighted visionary who had created a monument to the Germans with his *Germania.* Hence Italy was not alone in possessing an ancient history, Germany had one too! By discovering the German Middle Ages and trying to link the virtues of the ancient Germans with the illustrious history of the German emperors, the humanists tried to lay the foundations for a historically based sense of national pride. All that was missing was a war of independence and a rousing national hero to personify the ideals of unity and freedom for a burgeoning nation. Martin Luther could have become a German William Tell, Joan of Arc, or George Washington had he only chosen to. How momentous the welding of national uprising with religious war in a single figure could be is well demonstrated by William of Orange, the Netherlands' champion of independence and autonomy.

It is impossible to tell whether Luther as a hero of national liberation could have provided and preserved the necessary sense of national cohesion in the face of such powerful counterforces. There were indeed massive obstacles in the way of the German cause: even in the sixteenth century it was clear that a German national state with the ambitions of a medieval empire was a danger to European stability. Moreover, the Hapsburg imperium lived by the grace of a loose federation of many different peoples and would not have stood for the homogeneity of one nation at its center. And further, the federal structure of an empire demands from those dedicated to a national vision greater education, farsightedness, and patience than is required in a centralized monarchy like France.

Ulrich von Hutten, champion of the German patriotic liberation movement. Woodcut.

Decisive for Luther's long-range influence was his refusal to accept the widely desired alliance of St. Paul with Tacitus, of a renewal of faith with the birth of a nation. Programmatically and prophetically, he tried to urge his "beloved Germans" into a unity of faith and purge them of that nationalism which dreams of the union of religion and blood. With his catechism and Bible, he taught the people to pray and write in German, not to propagate the uniqueness of the "German spirit" but to set an example for the many nations of Christendom to imitate. The national council Luther demanded in 1520 would have assembled in Speyer in 1524—on November 11, the day of his baptism—had the emperor not explicitly forbidden it. Never had a German national church been so close to realization. The Reformer would, however, have condemned any identification of Church and nation as running counter to the will of God: equating God's people with a state or nation, be it Germany or Rome, not only perverts the Gospel, it also threatens world peace. For us Luther is "modern" insofar as he promoted an ecumenical pluralism and warned against resolving spiritual questions by government pressure, let alone by armed force.

In his own time there were many who thought him outdated. And indeed: as a political prophet in the war council of the rebellious knights or in the camp of the revolutionary peasants, he would have become a national leader. In the short term, imperial unification under this kind of national hero would have benefited Germany most at the dawn of the modern era. But it would have been a betrayal of the Reformation. Luther as a German was a hindrance and burden for a nation trying to find its identity. He refused to become a folk hero, and by refusing became himself a German event.

CHAPTER II

A Medieval Event

Reformation and No End in Sight

The word *reformation* was as popular in the Middle Ages as *democracy* is today—and it meant as many things to as many people. Everyone was for it, as all the sources attest. But that did not explain how *reformations*—today we would speak of *reforms*—were to look and how they could be implemented. Nonetheless *reformation* was not a cliché. It was more of an irritant and an admonition, often accompanied by ire and indignation but also filled with hope and longing. It could challenge the Church as such or seek to stir up a religious order. Then *reformation* meant return to original ideals. The Church was to emulate the model of the early Christian community, to be united again in love; or a monastic community was to regain sight of the original, authentic principles of the founder of their order.

With regard to the individual *reformatio* stood for the renewal of man and woman; they were to wake from the coma of sin and, once in peace with God, regain the original innocence. Mysticism understood this peace as the indescribable experience unique to the union with God: the person loses himself in God, or the desires of the mystic become identical with the will of the Lord. Hence reformation touched the Christian in his very innermost self; it was an expression of the yearning for lost ideals and a proclamation of the hope that Church and society were moving toward a better future. In the Middle Ages those who demanded reformation never considered a "return" to the origins and "progress" toward a better future as mutually exclusive. Thus the opposite of reformation was not "restoration" but "deformation": corruption, estrangement from God, going astray en route to the Last Judgment.

Like many other cultural phenomena, reform movements spread across Europe in waves, from the Mediterranean to Germany and Scandinavia. In the eleventh, twelfth, and thirteenth centuries Italy and southern France were moved by the ideal of "apostolic poverty" and the attendant criticism of the wealthy established Church. In this case *reformation* meant repentance and a return to Christ's way of life. Though such protest groups as the Albigensians and Waldensians were persecuted by fire and sword, they could only be effectively subdued after the mendicant orders were approved by the pope and allowed to live a life of poverty within the Church—vicariously for rich prelates and laymen.

The year 1329 was one of critical decision. Pope John XXII condemned the ideal of radical poverty by denying the biblical foundations of the mendicant movement—the thesis that Christ and his apostles had lived in absolute poverty, devoid of possessions. This not only meant censure of the left wing of the Franciscan order, a group particularly critical of the rich Church, it also discredited a deeply rooted European conviction, for even those who knew only little of the Christian faith were at least acquainted with Jesus' call to poverty: "If thou wilt be perfect, go and sell what thou hast, and give to the poor, and thou shalt have treasure in heaven" (Matt. 19.21).

In those days, poverty and perfection belonged together. Shunning the things of this world was an outward characteristic of monastic life, and the imitation of Christ in poverty was the sure way to Heaven. Of the three monastic vows—obedience, poverty, and chastity—it was especially poverty which demonstrated that to remain in the world meant making un-Christian compromises. Outside the monastery one was very far from fulfilling the "evangelical counsels" the Lord had given his disciples to enable them to lead a truly perfect life.

All Christians had an obligation to obey the Ten Commandments. That was difficult enough. But the three monastic vows were even more exacting. Whoever fulfilled the "evangelical counsels" belonged to the religious elite and could pray and intercede for the common Church Christian, giving him spiritual support to at least keep the commandments. It was therefore in the vital interest of all Christians that the elite, under whose protection the simple believer lived, really meet the standards set by Christ. Consequently, the reformation of the monasteries concerned the whole of society.

It therefore stood to reason that Pope John XXII's condemnation of the mendicant movement would cause a greater stir than many of his other provocative decisions. Here was confirmation of the long-harbored suspicion that the Church had forsaken its Lord, the Christ of poverty. It gave sad evidence that the courage of the persecuted Christians in the Roman Empire had led not to the collapse of paganism, as had been believed for centuries, but rather to the Constantinian Church. The martyrs had sacrificed their possessions and their lives while the prelates acquired wealth and power!

The clever solution of the canon lawyers was morally less than convincing. They sought to eradicate the problem by drawing a subtle distinction: The followers of St. Francis, the Franciscans, are legally poor because they have no property but only possessions: they possess only the right to use the effects of their monasteries, whereas the Church as a whole, not bound by Christ's injunction to poverty, owns these effects, not the order.

Some of the Friars Minor agitated against this legal distinction and insisted on absolute poverty as demanded by St. Francis. Though the radical friars were unsuccessful even among their own order, their ideal was never forgotten and remained influential in the time to come.

The Struggle for Monastic Reform

One of the important consequences of the fourteenth-century poverty dispute was the emergence of the Observant Movement in all of the mendicant orders. They strove for reformation as a return to the original rule of their respective orders. Later criticized as rigorists, Observants regarded themselves as the green branches on the languishing tree of the Church, for Observantism means religious obedience in strict accordance with the rules. Thus, the youngest of the three major mendicant orders, the Augustinian Hermits, founded in 1256, had no alternative but to accept a series of reformed monasteries in Italy and Germany uniting in the fifteenth century to form a "congregatio reformata," in total disregard for the boundaries of the official provinces of either Church or order. The Observant congregations succeeded in securing more and more privileges, the most important of which was the right to elect their own representative, who as vicar general was subordinated to the general of the order in Rome yet was increasingly able to gain complete independence from him. These constitutional aspects of monastic reform are so important because this chain of command in the congregation began to make conceivable an ecclesiastical organization that, though not independent of the pope, could gain a measure of independence from Rome.

The vicar general of the reformed German Augustinian congregation, to which the Erfurt monastery of Luther belonged, had already in the fifteenth century acquired considerable independence and was no longer receiving his instructions from the general of the order in Rome. In this light it is readily understandable that sovereigns and cities—like Frederick the Wise and the city council of Nuremberg—urged monasteries in their territories to accept "Observantine reformation"; it was in their interest to eliminate external ecclesiastical interference.

At the same time, public demand for temporal authorities to introduce monastic reform stemmed from a genuine desire to guarantee that the monastic orders—the religious and moral elite of society—would lead a life of true perfection and holiness. This "guarantee" was a serious issue for society at large, because monastic reform involved more than the implementation of administrative measures. Monasteries were being promoted and protected as sites of intercession and precious resources for the social community, where reliable priests celebrated the endowed masses for the salvation of the souls of the dead, and where guidance could be found with wise pastors, and where, through special fraternities, the laymen could share in the fruits of monastic life.

In the late Middle Ages increasingly sharp criticism was leveled against the wealthy Church, and was directed with particular gusto at the impudent arrogance of the monks, especially the mendicants. Countless colorfully embellished tales of their easy, sumptuous life were spread angrily all across the country; the Observants, on the other hand, were conspicuously spared. Luther's development is closely linked with his reformed Saxon Augustinian congregation and its excellent chain of communication—an important factor in the rapid spread of Luther's writings in the early years.

Three Observant monasteries deeply influenced the course of the young monk's life. In Erfurt he joined the Observant Augustinians; in Wittenberg the monastery became the decisive sphere of his activity, a place for study and learning and later even a home for himself and his family. The monastery at Nuremberg became the spiritual headquarters of the nascent Reformation when it first started to spread to the cities of southern and southwestern Germany. Most likely Luther himself would have acknowledged that a fourth Augustinian monastery, the one in Antwerp, deserved pride of place as the cradle of the Reformation's first martyrs. But by that time, 1523, the word *reformation* had already taken on new meaning. A look at the late Middle Ages will help us to understand the crucial stages in this development.

The Hierarchical Church under Fire

Only in Germany and Italy had the Observant movement succeeded in curbing the poverty dispute, at least for a time. But for a long while in England and Bohemia there was to be no peace. It was above all two men who accelerated the process of fermentation and who stood at the forefront of events: the Englishman Wyclif and the Czech Hus. Both had been baptized "John," and were later, in allusion to John the Baptist, either praised or condemned as Luther's precursors.

Wyclif (†1384) was a professor at Oxford. Hus (†1415), in many respects Wyclif's pupil, was a professor in Prague. Both of them exerted influence far beyond the walls of their universities; and both were condemned by the Council of Constance in 1415—the one, Jan Hus, to death at the stake, and the other, who had already been dead for nearly thirty years, to posthumous excommunication.

Wyclif and Hus found their common theme in the contradiction between the Church of faith, which served the whole world, and the Church of prelates, which wanted to be served. Wyclif's theological convictions are in every respect an effort to think through and respond to the pope's doctrinal decision of 1323. His *De Dominio Divino* (Of the True Dominion) deals with the claims of the Church to power and possession of property. Only the true Church of Christ, which lives in the state of grace, is entitled to property and dominion. As the Church has quite obviously fallen from grace, it has therefore forfeited all claims to worldly power, thus giving the state the right to confiscate Church property.

Wyclif's contemporaries as well as later generations attributed the English Peasants' Revolt of 1381 to the impact of these ideas. But Wyclif's adversaries were as wrong as his historians: there had been far too little time for his ideas to be assimilated, spread, and translated into action. Nonetheless, Wyclif remained a force to be reckoned with in England. By advocating the reading of the Bible in the vernacular, rejecting celibacy, and attacking the doctrine of transubstantiation, his followers, the Lollards, kept his memory alive well into the time of the English Reformation.

But it was on the Continent that Wyclif's reform proposals were most influential. In 1382 Anne, sister of Wenceslaus, king of Germany and Bohemia, married King Richard II of England. This alliance of Continent and island had unpredictable consequences: numerous Bohemians went to England, where they became acquainted with Wyclif's ideas and then returned to disseminate them in their own homeland. The first ten chapters of Jan Hus's major treatise on the Church—*De Ecclesia*—read very much like an anthology from Wyclif's work of the same title.

Yet Hus lent his own special and dramatic emphasis to the Englishman's program. The theological doctrine that God determines every person's action and direction in advance—usually referred to as predestination—is the instrument with which the true and the false Church can be clearly separated. St. Augustine, one of the most influential Western Church Fathers (†430), had already given much thought to predestination as the biblical way to articulate the doctrine of undeserved grace: through God's election to grace, the sinner is summoned and saved; long before his birth, his name has been written into the "Book of Life." Amid the conflicts and rival claims of his time, Hus draws the following sharp conclusion: It is not obedience to Rome, but rather obedience to God which is the decisive mark of the true Church. To her belong those whom God through His eternal predestination has chosen as the obedient. With its hunger for power and property, the papal hierarchy has forfeited any right to be regarded as part of the true Church, which can be recognized by the imitation of Christ and the apostles.

OFFERING HUS A safe-conduct, Emperor Sigismund invited the Prague professor to Constance to justify his position before the council. Despite the emperor's promise, Hus was soon arrested and, after seven months in prison, burned at the stake as a heretic on July 6, 1415. He fell, yet he did not fail. As a martyr he took on a new life and remained a living memory into the Reformation period. For Luther St. Hus-the-martyr was very much alive; Luther was convinced that the prophecy Hus had made before his execution applied to the Reformation: "Holy Johannes Hus prophesied about me when he wrote from his Bohemian prison that they might now be roasting a goose (for Hus means goose), but in a hundred years they will hear a swan sing, which they will not be able to silence."[1]

Although Reformation thought and Hussite theology were not identical, Luther totally rejected the verdict of heresy brought in by the Council of Constance: "If he is supposed to be a heretic, no real Christian has ever been born on earth."[2] Luther, however, did not try to conceal the differences between himself and Hus, but sought instead to point them out by distinguishing between life and doctrine: "Life is as evil among us as among the papists, thus we do not argue about life but about doctrine. Whereas Wyclif and Hus attacked the immoral lifestyle of the papacy, I challenge primarily its doctrine."[3]

Certainly this assessment is not completely accurate, though true in its decisive aspects. It is not correct insofar as doctrine was of the utmost importance to both Wyclif and Hus—the doctrine of the dominion and property of the hierarchy: the Church has a right to property only as a gift temporarily

On October 31, 1517, Frederick the Wise, Elector of Saxony, had a dream foreshadowing Luther's posting of the ninety-five theses

granted by God's grace. Such a gift is not automatically placed in the hands of priests and prelates because of their office, but is given only to those who practice obedience according to God's providence. This is undoubtedly an explosive theological doctrine, with a cutting edge aimed at a Church that for a long time—and quite apart from the Papal State—had been one of Europe's largest property owners.

Wyclif, Hus, and their followers in England and Bohemia carried on the old poverty controversy, though by new means. God had predestined the obedient for salvation, and it was they who constituted the Church. The hierarchy, on the other hand, had turned against Christ and was therefore reprobate and no longer part of the Church.

Luther's view of the Bohemian reformation as being restricted to "life" is not accurate. Both Wyclif and Hus sent shock waves through the Church, challenging its power structure and attacking its doctrines. And yet there was a fundamental difference between the Bohemian and the Wittenberg reformations. Because of the public moral scandal the Church flaunted, Wyclif called upon the secular authorities to confiscate all ecclesiastical property and administer it themselves. Hus urged taking the sacraments—confession and communion—only from priests who did not openly live in sin. Luther was by no means indifferent to the general decline of morals, but moral rearmament is not the primary goal of his reformation. Luther had precisely this difference in mind when he formulated the statement found so objectionable through the ages—to his contemporaries and today's Catholics and Protestants alike: "Life is as evil among us as among the papists." The heart of the Reformation is the recovery of sound doctrine—only true faith will lead to the renewal of life.[4] Here Luther reveals his own vision of "reformation"—as unusual in his own day as it is troublesome for modern times.

The Pursuit of the Millennium

Luther's disconcerting view of reformation can be clarified when seen against the backdrop of the poverty dispute. The principal issue in the great debate over the true intentions of St. Francis of Assisi was the interpretation of the saint's first rule and his last will. Pope John XXII initially questioned, then rejected and condemned a strict interpretation of the rule of poverty laid down in both documents. From that point on, not only was the Church's proper Christian way of life at issue, but also the much further-reaching question of papal authority and the foundations of a hierarchically structured Church. Thus the storm of indignation caused by the pope's condemnation in 1323 did not solely concern his repudiation of the strict ideal of poverty.

In his testament of 1226, St. Francis had unmistakably precluded any relaxation of the principle of strict poverty: "The Brothers must beware not to accept church buildings, or poor dwellings, or anything else else built for them when not in accordance with holy poverty . . . ; they should occupy these places only as strangers and pilgrims."[5] The pope's refusal to respect this last will corresponded precisely with the "new" way the uncompromising wing of the order, known as Fraticelli or Spirituales, read history. The "depraved" papacy is soon to be replaced because the great reformation, the millennium of peace, is about to begin. The fact that Pope John XXII is battling St. Francis and his devoted followers is not surprising at all; it is the final desperate attempt to delay by any means the inevitable fall from power.

The struggle for poverty was connected with the hope for the millennium. More than a century before Pope John XXII's condemnation, the Cistercian abbot Joachim of Fiore had already interpreted chapter 20 of the Book of

Revelation to mean that the promise of the millennium would come true within the course of history and not just at the end of time, after the world had ended.

> And I saw an angel come down from heaven, having the key of the bottomless pit and a great chain in his hand.
>
> And he laid hold of the dragon, that old serpent, which is the Devil, and Satan, and bound him a thousand years,
>
> . . . .
>
> And when the thousand years are expired, Satan shall be loosed out of his prison,
>
> And shall go out to deceive the nations which are in the four quarters of the earth . . .
>
> (Rev. 20.1–2, 7–8)

According to Joachim's calculations, history ran on a trinitarian scheme: the age of the Father, the history of the Old Testament, was followed by a second era, the age of the Son and the clerical Church, which began with the birth of Christ. The middle of the thirteenth century would mark the dawn of a new epoch, the age of the Spirit and the spiritual Church—the "ecclesia spiritualis." This third age would last a thousand years and put an end to the rule of laymen and priests, to pretended celibacy, to hierarchy and papal rule. The Church would be governed by those who dedicate their lives to meditating on the mysteries of God—in short, the time of the friars would come.

From the outset the implied subversion of the hierarchy was bound to evoke resistance. That priests were ranked higher than laymen was generally accepted, but the view of monks as the ruling estate of the spiritual Church could only be offensive. Up to now the reverse had been true: the hierarchy of priests, the bishops, and the popes had securely held the reins of ecclesiastical power. The very expectation of a time when the ruling hierarchy would no longer exist was a basic challenge to the papacy. This dream spoke loud and clear: contrary to all claims, Rome is not the foundation of the Church for all times. The New Age of the Spirit will build upon new foundations and put an end to the rule of the successor to Peter!

"Spirituales," the honorary title of the strict Franciscans, points to the heritage of the abbot of Fiore. Their critical stance toward the hierarchy is obvious, though surprising considering that it was the Franciscans who accorded Pope Clement V (†1314), John XXII's successor, the attribute of infallibility when he supported the implementation of the ideal of poverty. The doctrine of papal infallibility was their contribution to Christian thought, even though it remained a controversial point in the Roman Catholic Church until declared dogma by the First Vatican Council (1870–71).[6] Only when the defenders of the poverty ideal realized that they had been deserted by the pope was the legacy of Joachim of Fiore recovered. In the tradition of Joachim, Petrus Johannes Olivi (†1298), a Frenchman from the Languedoc and one of the most important Franciscan Bible scholars, composed a loaded commentary on the Revelation of St. John. In 1326 it also was condemned—by Pope John XXII—with lasting success.

Olivi was blotted so totally from memory that his commentary, the *Postilla super Apokalypsim,* could not be reconstructed until a few years ago. The manuscripts that have survived tell an eventful tale. In the course of the later Middle Ages Olivi's commentary on the Apocalypse was often copied but constantly modified in accordance with the respective faction in power, or depending on the stance of the scribe toward the papacy.

Olivi's hope for a new age is based on his conviction that Francis of Assisi had ushered in the era of the Spirit just as John the Baptist had prepared the era of Christ. As Christ's authentic successor St. Francis had received the eternal Gospel, the "Evangelium aeternum," from God and proclaimed it to all men of good will. The pope, curia, and prelates of the now obsolete part of the plan of salvation were trying to outstay the time God had allotted them, but their opposition to the prophets of the Spirit transformed them for all to see from servants into enemies of Christ. It was equally obvious that the Friars Minor were the harbingers of a new "reformation," preparing for the new millennium, the thousand years of peace. This was the unique mission of the Franciscan order: to serve as vanguard of the third kingdom, the kingdom of the Spirit.

Chiliasm—the idea of a thousand-year kingdom of peace (from the Greek *chilia eté,* "a thousand years")—became a major factor in medieval criticism of the Church and Rome. Alien to Joachim of Fiore, speculation about a prospective crisis was to become crucial: the kingdom of the Spirit does not develop organically out of the kingdom of the Son but against powerful resistance; it is accompanied by severe upheavals and will break out as a catastrophe. The expectation Olivi had in common with Joachim, on the other hand, that monks would be the inaugurators of the new age, fell victim to the growing criticism directed at monasteries and the monastic life.

Where chiliasm could ally itself with the ideas of the two condemned "heretics," Wyclif and Hus, it was able to reach large parts of Europe. But the recipients of the Spirit were, in chiliastic Wycliffism or Hussitism, no longer the monks but the humble and true "Friars Minor" in town and country, the simple servants and handmaids upon whom the Lord would pour out His Spirit when peace would come to Israel, as prophesied by the prophet Joel:

> And it shall come to pass afterward, that I will pour out my spirit upon all flesh; and your sons and your daughters shall prophesy, your old men shall dream dreams, your young men shall see visions;
>
> And also upon the servants and upon the handmaids in those days will I pour out my spirit.
>
> And I will shew wonders in the heavens and in the earth, blood and fire, and pillars of smoke.
>
> The sun shall be turned into darkness, and the moon into blood, before the great and the terrible day of the Lord come.
>
> And it shall come to pass, that whosoever shall call on the name of the Lord shall be delivered: for in mount Zion and in Jerusalem shall be deliverance, as the Lord hath said, and in the remnant whom the Lord shall call.
>
> (Joel 2.28–32)

After Olivi's days, criticism was no longer just leveled at the wealth of the Church, but increasingly at wealth as a sign of a Church poor or even barren in spirit. As critics of the official Church were subjected to ever greater persecution, concern grew into suspicion and suspicion into the conviction that in Rome the harbingers of the Antichrist had invaded and taken over the leadership of the Church. It was not so much the Plague, the devastating epidemic that swept Europe in waves between 1348 and 1352, as it was the great Western schism of 1378 to 1415 that gave impetus to chiliasm and allowed wandering preachers of repentance access beyond the "common man" to the more educated circles.

Since 1378 it had seemed evident that the Church of the priests must be in its final throes. One pope in Rome and another in Avignon, each denouncing the other and using excommunication and interdict to call the Devil down upon his opponent! The Council of Pisa was summoned in 1409 to put an end to the havoc, but instead of fulfilling hopes and restoring Christian unity, it bestowed a third pope on Christianity. It is true that the Council of Constance succeeded in reuniting the Western Church in 1415, but hopes of a new age, of the millennium of peace, remained a dream pursued well into the sixteenth century.

Initially, Martin Luther was well received among chiliasts. They welcomed him as a prophet of transition to a new era and defender of the "new

Begetting the Antichrist. Woodcut from Der Antichrist, *Strasbourg, ca. 1480.*

age," the age of the Spirit and of peace. But he disappointed them, for his reformation did not seek to transform society in order to prepare the way for the millennium. Bitterly, the militant "champions of God" turned away from him. Preeminent among them was Thomas Münzer, who had a large following of chiliastic prophets, all of them driven by the will to extirpate the "godless" in order to ensure that the reformation would be in place in time for the Day of Judgment.

Luther's reformation was not oriented toward a "new age" in their sense. He was not a chiliast, nor was he heralding the millennium.

The Alien Luther

It would be premature for the reader to breathe a sigh of relief, thinking that he could now leave these obscure medieval speculators behind and turn to a modern man in Luther. Such a divide is artificial and misleading, for all the historically important social and political ideals of Western civilization grew out of the expectation of this messianic reign of peace, even though the preparations were to exact a high price, particularly from the "godless" on the opposing side.

Disparaging talk of "utopias," which are to be found "nowhere" (from the Greek *u tópos,* "no place"), misses the point. From the United States to the Soviet Union experience is shaped by the hope, and sometimes the unshakable conviction, that one day this kingdom of peace will be established and flourish; or even that it has already become reality in God's own country, wherever that may be, and however imperfect as yet. These are medieval ideas of reformation which, in secularized form, influence the modern world, seeking fulfilment in communism, American populism, or international pacifism. This belief in progress becomes an empty, materialistic shell or a dictatorship devoid of respect for humanity when the renewal of society is no longer sustained by the vision that, however dark it may be, the present can be endured as the birthpangs which mark the coming "reformatio."

THIS MEDIEVAL heritage is not of specifically Christian origin but is part of an ongoing Judaeo-Christian tradition. The hope that the millennium will come has undeniably been one of the mainsprings of Judaism all the way through to the present state of Israel. The Israeli chief rabbinate has approved a prayer for the state of Israel as the "beginning of redemption"; Orthodox and non-Orthodox Jews alike say and repeat it: "Our Father in Heaven, Rock and Redeemer of Israel, bless the state of Israel, the beginning of the sprouting of our redemption."[7]

There is good reason to believe that this close association of the state of Israel with the messianic kingdom was born out of the horrid experience of bloody "coexistence" with Christians in a Christian world.

But there are also genuine Christian roots in the Christian world's desire to prove itself a credible vanguard for the kingdom of God, and there lives the hope that a new age can be ushered in by means of social progress. Thus a vital element of the Middle Ages became a structural element of the modern world. In this important respect, Luther is not our contemporary.

We encounter here the alien Reformer, who was no longer medieval, but neither had he become modern. To capture this alien Luther in modern categories, we would have to call him an "anti-Zionist." Yet this is not to say that if he were alive he would necessarily be an opponent of the state of Israel, let alone argue for its annihilation. On the contrary, the very existence of Israel would have forced him to re-think his presuppositions in consideration of his oath to be the first to be circumcised should the Jews ever again succeed in establishing a state[8]—so impossible did the idea seem to him. His brand of anti-Zionism did not concern a state but an ideology, that fundamental evil in which mankind has entangled itself since time immemorial. Luther rejected all endeavors to establish a kingdom of God on earth. According to his promises, God himself will be the center of His kingdom on Zion, in the New Jerusalem. In Luther's view Zionism is the impatient effort

The Last Days have come to an end, graves open, and trumpets herald the Last Judgment.
Woodcut from Der Antichrist, *Strasbourg, ca. 1480.*

to implement God's plan and launch the future kingdom oneself: such aspirations make everyone, whether Jew or Christian, into a Zionist—and Zion is everywhere.

The "modern" Zionists of Luther's time were the bishops and popes who placed their trust in temporal power in order to establish a papal state. Even more serious, the Roman curia claimed to be Zion, the unshakable foundation of God's kingdom on earth. From Luther's perspective, "Zionist reformation" meant the subjugation of all nations and empires under the dominion of Rome, a claim the papacy indeed adhered to until well into the sixteenth century.

Since, Luther insists, reformation does not entail domination, but service to the world, Rome falls strikingly silent. Popes, priests, and prelates are all equally keen to put off the necessary reform measures until the Day of Judgment. In response to the major reform program of Pope Hadrian VI, presented at the Diet of Nuremberg on December 30, 1523, Luther interpreted the curia's efforts with laconic irony: in Rome it takes two men for a reformation, "one to milk the billy goat, the other to hold the strainer."[9]

The City of God as Utopia

Very much counter to the temperament of his age—and of later, "modern" times—Luther took a vigorous stand against all efforts to wrest from God His timetable, and to force—with sword in hand—the coming kingdom of peace. Contrary to the hopes of the party of national liberation, he opposed the rebellious imperial knights who wanted to terminate the regime of the self-serving prelates and princes.

Even more problematic is his stand against the peasants who had for so long been demanding their rights and were now gathering to fight for the rights of God as well; Thomas Münzer was making one flaming appeal after another to put an end to the rule of the godless, and Huldrych Zwingli, that proud, pious citizen of Zurich, was uniting Europe to combat the Hapsburgs and thus do battle for the Kingdom of God.

From differing perspectives, later generations considered these various groups and movements to be heralds of the future and of "progress": after all, the courageous knights dared to confront the princely clan; the oppressed peasants kindled the early proletarian revolution; Thomas Münzer, the protagonist of peasants' rights, was martyred for decrying the rule of the aristocracy; and finally Zwingli, the reformer of Zurich, advocated the estab-

Peasants torturing an indulgence preacher named Rychardus Hunderlist. Pen-and-ink drawing by Niklaus Manuel Deutsch.

lishment of democracy in Church and state. Were it not for Martin Luther, the history of the Reformation could have become the glorious story of Germany's advance into the modern era.

Though certainly impressive as a religious figure, from the point of view of progress Luther seems an unworldly, if not demonic figure: Why do we not finally let this man, with his curious sense of God and the Beyond, pass into history? After all, are not five hundred years enough?

No matter how resolved we might be to leave Luther in the past, an enigma remains. If his reformation was indeed so unrelated to the concerns or needs of this present world, how was it that his message could break out of the monastic cell, and his voice evoke such a politically powerful movement throughout and far beyond Germany? Had then all his students and disciples misunderstood this monk? But perhaps his contemporaries understood Luther perfectly well and were indeed no longer convinced that it was in the service of God to draw the sword with the knights of the empire, to hurl a firebrand with the peasants, to call to arms like Thomas Münzer, or, like Zwingli, to plot a European campaign. Had the means of force been the way of God, the history of salvation would have been simpler—and bloodier. There would have been no need for Jesus Christ to die—he could simply have invoked the protection of the legions of angels. But his reply to Pontius Pilate rejected such recourse to violence: "My kingdom is not of this world: if my kingdom were of this world, then my servants would fight" (John 18.36).

Luther's view of reformation was shaped by this testimony of Jesus before Pilate: even if the joyous assembly of God's children on Mount Zion were to be close at hand, this climax of history could be brought about only by God. Luther had to look far back into Church history, past Hus and Wyclif, Petrus Olivi and Joachim of Fiore, to find witnesses for his vision of the reformation to come. He turned to Bernard of Clairvaux, the great twelfth-century reform preacher, and Augustine, the fifth-century Church Father. Here he found a true rendering of the New Testament evidence of what would happen in the Last Days, as well as an adequate interpretation of these events.

As has so often been the case in the history of the Western Church, it was again a work of Augustine that proved to be of decisive help: this time his most mature work, the *City of God.* Augustine wrote at a fateful juncture in the history of both the Roman Empire and the Church. The long-feared "decline of the West" was setting in. The Visigoth chief, Alaric, had conquered the "eternal" city of Rome in 410, thus striking a blow at the spiritual foundations of the empire. It was as if the world had to hold its breath: Rome, symbol of civilization and peace, had fallen and was now at the mercy of barbarians. Bitterly, contemporaries tried to find reasons for the catastrophe. Could it have been Christianity? That the barbarians could destroy the pride of the empire and that Rome had fallen must be punishment for deserting the gods of their fathers.

But the Christians also were bewildered, and puzzled over how to interpret the events. How was the disintegration of Roman law and order to be understood? How could there be a future without Rome? For them, too, the world was falling apart. How could God allow the Roman Empire to fade and pass away when He had led it to the baptismal font through the Emperor Constantine?

Augustine did not evade any of these questions, trying instead to dispel the dreams of believers and non-believers alike about classical and Christian Rome. The pagan empire—what more was it than a band of thieves? And Christian Rome—is that what an outpost of the kingdom of God was supposed to be like? No, because the time between the first coming of Christ Incarnate and His return will not run along the imperial lines of a kingdom of God on earth. The Thousand Years between the first and the final coming of Christ will see states and cultures come and go; Rome is not to be an exception. Only the City of God will endure; but as an unarmed community of true Christians, without earthly power. At the end of the thousand years the eschatological prophecy of Revelations is to be fulfilled: "He [the Devil] must be loosed a little season" (20.3). Then Christianity will experience an unparalleled time of terror. The present threat from barbarians and pagans is nothing in comparison with the tribulations at the end, when Satan will seem to overcome God, when the Gospel will be forced underground and the Christian message of strength and consolation will have to be preached in secret.

Augustine's only uncertainty concerned the exact nature of the final battle: would the Antichrist emerge from within the Church, or would he found an Antichurch? There was, however, no doubt that the City of God would be shaken to its very foundation. This is St. Augustine's Christian utopia.

The Antichrist and His Designs

Luther's way of speaking about the Antichrist has become alien to us. Usually it is explained in terms of "angst" and widely felt insecurity, so typical of the waning of the Middle Ages. Yet the fear of the Antichrist is not just the product of a particularly superstitious and phantasy-ridden time. It has much deeper roots in the Christian tradition.

Christ driving "all them that sold and bought" (John 2.14ff) out of the temple. Woodcut from the pamphlet Passional Christi et Antichristi *(1521), illustrated by Lucas Cranach the Elder.*

Luther was certainly not untouched by the fears of his age, which may well explain why he was able to address them so effectively and capture the attention of such a wide audience. Yet the decisive factor in his way of coping with this mood was its use as an incentive for the intensive study of St. Augustine, whose interpretation of history and vision of the Last Days he learned to employ in deciphering the events of his own time.

Luther's view was not, however, shaped by Augustine alone. A lasting influence was Bernard of Clairvaux (†1143), who was for Luther one of the last Church Fathers and for modern historians the mystical reformer and protagonist of the Crusades. Bernard had taken up Augustine's concept of the Last Days and adapted it to developments in medieval history.

When Luther first raised his voice against indulgences in his lectures during the summer of 1514, the sense of urgency in his attack was derived from St. Bernard's periodization of world history into three epochs spanning the thousand years from the birth of Christ to the end of time: at the beginning,

The Vicar of Christ "deals" with indulgences. Woodcut from the pamphlet Passional Christi et Antichristi *(1521), illustrated by Lucas Cranach the Elder.*

in the first epoch of the Holy Fathers and Martyrs, the Church had suffered bloody persecutions when martyrs had to sacrifice their lives for the sake of their faith. Then followed the age of the heretics, whose attacks on Christian doctrine represented a far more subtle and thus a far more dangerous threat to the Church. However the most serious and radical peril to Christianity developed in these last days, here and now: no longer did the mortal threat come from the outside, but—much worse—from the very bosom of the Church itself. Bernard warned emphatically against this corruption from within: what threatens us now is the unimaginable seduction of the simple believer by the great and terrible adversary—"that is the Antichrist, the deceitful liar . . . whom only the Lord Jesus can kill with the flaming spirit of His mouth, and whom He will destroy at the time of His glorious return."[10]

In the summer of 1514 Luther was not yet prepared to accept Bernard's diagnosis that the Church was "incurably" ill. But he did invoke Bernard's epochal sequence to mobilize all defensive forces since "exactly these times of external peace and glittering prosperity are extremely dangerous to the Church." Now the threat is coming from within: the Church has made its peace with the world, settled comfortably, and gone for striking it rich. Today it is even selling protection against God's salutary punishment by means of indulgences.[11]

Three years before posting his theses, Luther had already come to regard the sale of indulgences as proof of the grievous extent to which the Church had gone astray. Cautiously, but in retrospect clearly adumbrating the battle to come, Luther warned his students of the perils of an anti-Christian perversion within the Church itself. He found the signs of the Last Days spelled out with precision in St. Matthew's Gospel:

> But he answered them, "You see all these, do you not? Truly, I say to you, there will not be left here one stone upon another, that will not be thrown down."
>
> As he sat on the Mount of Olives, the disciples came to him privately, saying, "Tell us, when will this be, and what will be the sign of your coming and of the close of the age?"
>
> And Jesus answered them, "Take heed that no one leads you astray.
>
> For many will come in my name, saying, 'I am the Christ,' and they will lead many astray.
>
> And you will hear of wars and rumors of wars; see that you are not alarmed; for this must take place, but the end is not yet.
>
> For nation will rise against nation, and kingdom against kingdom, and there will be famines and earthquakes in various places:
>
> All this is but the beginning of the birth-pangs.
>
> Then they will deliver you up to tribulation, and put you to death; and you will be hated by all nations for my name's sake.
>
> And then many will fall away, and betray one another, and hate one another.
>
> And many false prophets will arise and lead many astray.
>
> And because wickedness is multiplied, most men's love will grow cold.
>
> But he who endures to the end will be saved.
>
> And this gospel of the kingdom will be preached throughout the whole world, as a testimony to all nations; and then the end will come."
>
> (Matt. 24.2–14; the *New Oxford Annotated Bible*)

From the very start it was clear to Luther that Jesus' prophecy of the Last Days fully applied to the situation of the Church in his time. With Bernard's warnings in mind he concluded already in 1514: "The way I see it, the Gos-

Albrecht Dürer, Apocalyptic Dream, *1523*

pel of St. Matthew counts such perversions as the sale of indulgences among the signs of the Last Days."[12]

In the following five years—from 1514 to 1519—Luther found his fears increasingly confirmed, and out of concern grew consternation. This insight into the tradition preceding Luther—St. Matthew, St. Augustine, St. Bernard—allows us to grasp his sense of urgency in preaching the Gospel. This urgency breeds impatience, and impatience an uncompromising stance against all opposition. We should not expect from him a cool and dispassionate analysis of the persons and events of his day. For him, time was not just running—it was running out. The unleashing of the Devil, which Augustine had expected in the distant future and which had drawn close in the days of St. Bernard, has now come about. Once the Church invokes canon law and papal might to put its full authority behind indulgences, there can no longer be any doubt: the Antichrist is begotten, the Last Days have begun.[13]

For this reason the time for curial cures and half-hearted reforms is over. It is no longer just a matter of clearing up abuses and scandals; the Church is being threatened to its very foundations. Even our best reforms fall short of the Great Reformation which God Himself is to implement on the Last Day.

When, after 1518, the Gospel was once again being preached in its true spirit and without human distortion, Luther never claimed this would bring the long-expected cure, but rather the fulfillment of Jesus' prophecy: "And this gospel of the kingdom shall be preached in all the world for a witness unto all nations; and then shall the end come" (Matt. 24.14). Luther never expected the Gospel to repulse the Adversary, but to provoke instead intensified attacks on the faithful people of God. Those are the "afflictions of the Last Days," as the Scriptures have foretold.

What are the implications of this new understanding of Reformation? In all our handbooks and in keeping with all standards of historical scholarship, the Reformation precedes the Counter-Reformation. But according to Luther's eschatological interpretation of history, exactly the reverse applies: the Reformation is preceded by the counterreformation. Luther's public proclamation of the message of the cross is usually described as the "Reformation." For Luther this is certainly God's work and gift of solace for His persecuted Church. It is not yet the Great Reformation but rather the prelude to the counterreformation. For him there can be no pursuit of the millennium, since neither sweat nor sword can ever advance the messianic kingdom. In this crucial respect nothing but strict pacifism is expected from the Christian: enduring, persevering, waiting—publicly proclaiming the Gospel, openly beseeching God to intervene. "Thus the only thing that can comfort you in this last stage is the Day of Judgment and your faith that the lord rules in Eternity—ultimately all the godless will vanish." [14]

The other dimension of Luther's reformation is directed toward order and improvement in the world. Let us return to the Wittenberg lecture hall in the summer semester of 1514 to hear Luther's warnings against the peddling of indulgences. This whole indulgences issue, this selling of insurance as protection against the wrath of God is the appalling consequence of Rome's assiduous efforts at securing inward and outward dominion over the people of God. The Papal State must be expanded and holy wars must be fought for the honor of God and the growth of the Church—thus runs the shameless propaganda. Luther's comment: "Never before has the Church been so desolate." [15]

In the following years Luther increasingly stresses the political consequences of curial power politics: never before has the *world* been so badly off. The prince of darkness will not content himself with the collapse of the Church, he wants to rule the world as well, so that—as he planned from the beginning—he can destroy God's creation and produce chaos again. Now that the Last Days have actually come, not only is steadfastness of faith

Abſag/ oder vhed brieff / Des
Helliſchen Furſten Lucifers/ Doctor Martin
Luther izt zu geſandt.

The Devil proclaims the opening of his feud with Luther

"Never has the world been in such a state": red biretta (probably Cardinal Albrecht of Mainz) and black cowl (probably Johann Tetzel) peddling indulgences. The "bigwigs" and cunning usurers relieve the "common man" of his money.

called for, survival in the world is at stake as well. It is of lasting significance that Luther's rejection of all historical utopias did not entail abandoning the Church and the world to chaos: Christians are threatened but not helpless, under attack but not defenseless. Where the Gospel is preached, Satan's destructive assaults can be survived. Where Christian teachings tear the authorities from the clutches of the Antichrist, the world can once again come into *its* own. Luther regarded this emancipation of the world, the restoration of its secular rights and its political order, as both necessary and possible. But for this dimension he used the sober, secular, practical, temporal, and above all relative term *betterment* rather than the glorious *Reformation.* In short: Reformation is the work of God, betterment the task of Adam and Eve.

"Repentance is better than indulgence"

Luther's criticism of indulgences was by no means novel or unprecedented; reform Catholics both then and now could and can emphasize and take his stance. Even within his own order, which had so vehemently championed the cause of papal authority, voices had been raised against Roman indulgences. Around the year 1452 the Augustinian Gottschalk Hollen had put it suc-

Lucas Cranach the Younger, The Contrast between Christ's True Religion and the False Idolatry of the Antichrist. Left half: *Luther preaching Christ's sacrifice; among his audience, John Frederick, Elector of Saxony, carrying a cross.* Right half: *Satirical representation of the Roman Catholic Church, with St. Francis looking down in horror upon, among other things, the Pope peddling indulgences. Colored woodcut, ca. 1544.*

cinctly: "Repentance is better than indulgences." Let us consider this comprehensible but at the same time peculiar statement for a moment. Were indulgences to be granted without repentance and sinners permitted to spend good money to avoid examining their consciences? Certainly not; there was no way around the confessional. Only through the sacrament of penance could the contrite sinner be sure that God had forgiven his sins and remitted the *eternal* torments of Hell. What remained, however, were the *temporal* punishments which the person, absolved from sin, nonetheless had to expect, be it here on earth or in purgatory. It was at these temporal punishments that indulgences were aimed.

The Church can wholly or partially remit the penalties imposed upon a contrite penitent for his sins. Thus repentance is a necessary condition for the remission of penalties. And yet the Augustinian monk's warning was not unjustified. There was a special, particularly sought-after type of indulgence that went well beyond the remission of temporal punishments. Plenary indulgences, which only the pope could offer, promised the complete remission of punishment *and* sin, so that though a visit to the confessional was still

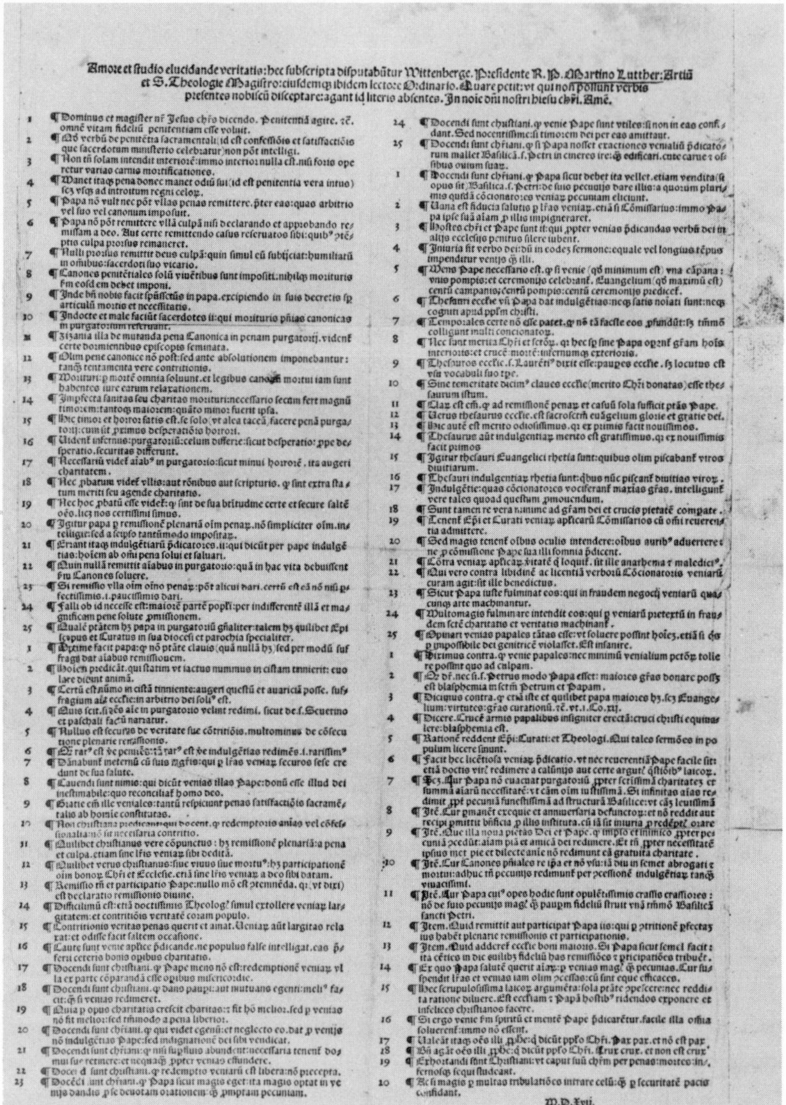

Amore et studio elucidande veritatis: hec subscripta disputabuntur Wittenberge. Presidente R. P. Martino Luther: Artiũ et S. Theologie Magistro: eiusdemq; ibidem lectore Ordinario. Quare petit: vt qui non possunt verbis presentes nobiscũ disceptare: agant id literis absentes. In noĩe dñi nostri Iħesu Chŕi. Amẽ.

M.D.Xvij.

Luther's ninety-five theses, printed in Nuremberg in 1517

necessary, contrition, the condition for forgiveness of sin, could be proven by the possession of a plenary indulgence.

Luther could have used words similar to Hollen's to formulate his objections to the theory and practice of the remission of punishment. But in one decisive point Luther went beyond late medieval criticism of indulgences. The motto of his ninety-five theses of October 31, 1517, ran parallel but in contrast to Hollen: Good works are better than indulgences.

> Christians should be taught that he who gives to the poor or lends to the needy performs a better deed than if he buys indulgences. (Thesis 43)
>
> Christians should be taught that he who sees someone needy but looks past him and buys an indulgence instead receives not the pope's remission but God's wrath. (Thesis 45)

Mending one's ways is the best penance, but it is directed toward life in the world and is thus contrary to allegedly holy withdrawal from the world.

> Christians should be taught that he who has but a limited income should keep the money necessary for his family's needs and under no circumstances invest in indulgences. (Thesis 46)

Luther always advocated the necessity of good works: "I should be called Doctor bonorum operum, the Doctor of good works." By 1516 at the latest, he no longer considered good works as necessary to gain God's favor, but he stressed them all the more as indispensable for service to the world and its needs. This insight would become the heart of his program in the years to come. During his early years as a professor in Wittenberg, he had been a prophet of repentance. In 1520, when his writings carried his voice beyond the walls of the monastery, and he had become a presence in the public arena, he proved to be adept at the ways of the world, and fully aware of its needs.

This cannot be taken for granted. The Middle Ages saw many preachers attracting mass audiences—ascetic figures with the gift of the word, who called for conversion and reform. Their common theme was the appeal to turn away from the world and live according to the ascetic model of monastic ideals. A life lived solely in the service of holiness never failed to make an impression. In 1533 the adult doctor looked back on the pupil Martin, who had once marveled at a holy man in Magdeburg:

> When I was in my fourteenth year and attending school in Magdeburg, I saw the Prince von Anhalt with my own eyes . . . who in the coarse

habit [of a Franciscan friar] was begging for bread in the main street and carrying his sack like a mule, so that he was bent to the ground. . . . He had fasted, kept vigil, chastised himself so much that he looked like death, nothing but bones and skin; and he soon died. . . . Whoever saw him gaped in devotion and had to feel ashamed of living a secular life.[16]

Lucas Cranach's 1520 engraving of Martin Luther the Augustinian Hermit (frontispiece) shows precisely these features of a monastic preacher and holy man: the Savonarola of Wittenberg, the antithesis of a gluttonous monk. By remaining within the framework of monastic holiness, Cranach's portrait misses the real Luther. Luther's new morality was not ascetic or unworldly. It was directed toward the world—not to transform it into a monastery but to let it remain the world and become what it was, God's good creation. Though he accorded jurists and their jurisprudence nothing but biting derision all his life, he hailed secular courts which sentenced according to imperial law. He defended the humanity of such jurisdiction, which "is better, more comprehensive, more sensible than canon law."[17]

AT THE end of October 1520 Luther published his manifesto *The Freedom of a Christian,* which deals with man's salvation as the gift of liberty, the new freedom for faith and action. "A Christian is a free master over all things and subject to no one."[18] Freed from the constraints of the law, the believer has become heir to Christ's holiness, justice, and piety. "Is this not a joyous exchange—the rich, noble, pious bridegroom Christ takes this poor, despised, wicked little whore in marriage, redeems her of all evil, and adorns her with all his goods?"[19] What is this "joyous exchange"? It is liberation from enslavement to the anxious craving for salvation. Now the "poor, despised, wicked little whore" can herself start to hand out the riches she has received for free. Since Christ has filled our needs, we can serve our neighbor "in his wants and for his betterment."

Christian freedom is received for free and freely shared with one's neighbor. That is why "a Christian is a servant of all and subject to everyone."[20] Luther had treated social reform, the collective dimension of this service, two months earlier in his address to the German "King, Princes, Nobility, Cities, and Communities,"[21] as the original title has it. Ostentatious luxury, "through which so many noblemen and wealthy people are impoverished," must be curbed; trade must be regulated so that "German money [cannot] leave the land"; usury is "the greatest plague of the German nation. . . . Should it last another one hundred years, it would not be possible for

Germany to keep one single penny." Business monopolies are equally immoral: "The Fuggers and their ilk should be brought under control"; and finally, "Is it not wretched that we Christians continue to allow public whorehouses"![22]

These practical reform proposals are not intended to compete with the historically very attractive medieval utopias of reformation. There are worlds between the *Address to the Christian Nobility* and the dreams expressed in medieval reform treatises, with their hopes that society would be transformed through an angel-pope or peace-emperor. Nor does Luther's program call for militant saints of the Last Days, who, without regard for losses, "straighten paths in the desert" for the Lord. He does not present his points of reform in the tone of finality characteristic of a theocrat who wants to make the world finally and forever comply with the laws of God. Luther's reform catalogue lacks any claim to eternal validity; it comprises, as he says, no more than the suggestion of a theologian who recognizes the problems of his time without having a clear view of all the practical aspects. Reformation as "betterment" does not require a final, authoritative, ideological blueprint; it demands political experience and expert factual knowledge.

Luther never styled himself a "reformer." He did not, however, shrink from being seen as a prophet; he wanted to spread the Gospel as an "evangelist." He called himself preacher, doctor, or professor and was all of these. Yet he never presumed to be a reformer, nor did he ever claim his movement to be the "Reformation."

He didn't and he couldn't—because "reformation" is God's ultimate intervention. On the rare occasions Luther employed the common term *reformatio,* he meant corrective action. But even when this is clear, we should beware of making him into the inspiring idealist who mounts a promising offensive for moral rearmament on the threshold of the modern age. Luther was proclaiming the Last Days, not the modern age. Though historically seen as the last days of the Middle Ages, for him they were the beginning of the end of all times. "We shall overcome"—but not by gradually containing sin, war, and misery. Against these, he raised hell.

Though often misunderstood, Luther's suggestions for improvement should not be regarded as Christian ethics in the sense of timeless directives. Luther did not leave governments and societies an unalterable plan for all times and all centuries, a "Handbook of Public Life" or a binding program of Christian politics. His ethics are "survival ethics in dangerous times." In the context of chaos and danger they are admittedly vital, down-to-earth, practical—not legalistic but adaptable to the changing plights of mankind. Faith shatters any claim to eternal validity, opening instead the eyes of the faithful for what is the most needed service to others. The Christian living between the rage of the Devil and the wrath of God, between the power of chaos and the coming judgment, must make the most of the time that remains and must staunchly protect creation, our living space. God entrusted the world to man and woman, and they must discharge their duties to the very last; in this and this alone can they be of help to God. "Yes, He can probably do it alone, but He does not want to; He wants us to act with Him and honors us by carrying out His will with and through us. If we do not desire this honor, He will help the poor by Himself."[23]

Those who refuse will not be able to escape God's judgment, no matter how many masses they have offered, pilgrimages they have undertaken, or heretics they have fought: how can leaving home and family behind to chase after one's own salvation really be considered a good work? The Devil will laugh because we are harming God and helping Satan to bring about the chaos he loves.

Luther horizontalized Christian ethics: he transferred its goal from Heaven to earth. Good works are not required for salvation but crucial for surviving in a threatened world.

Luther's proclamation of the reformation-to-come, as well as his call to reform and betterment, are presented in a medieval vocabulary and can only be understood against the background of the Middle Ages. Yet it is exactly this background which allows us also to discern the uniqueness of his vision. This entails above all the rejection of any attempt to transform the world, whether it be advanced by the disciples of Joachim, by Pope Innocent III, or by the sixteenth-century peasants rebelling for their God-given rights. Luther can be seen as a follower of Bernard of Clairvaux—but then a radical follower, because the situation since the days of St. Bernard had so deteriorated that the crusade now to be launched is no longer aimed at the liberation of the Holy Land but of the Holy People, the Church itself. Because of the advanced time of world history, these crusades can no longer be waged by armies. Only one weapon is left: the preaching of a powerless Christ, and Him crucified.

Hence it is not a question of Luther initiating or bringing on the reformation. From his point of view, all he or any Christian can do is to initiate reforms to better the world to such an extent that it can survive until the moment when God will put a final end to our chaos. This view of life-during-the-Last-Days makes Luther so difficult to understand for people in the modern world; he virtually provokes an interpretation that permits the old opponents to write him off as "medieval" and the modern supporters to style him as a spokesman for progress.

The fact that Luther cannot be classified either as medieval or modern may also explain his special gift of presenting anew the original Christian message of the imminent dawning of the Kingdom, vivid and vital, real and realistic for the people of his time. From today's perspective, his linguistic skills were sketchy, and he lacked the necessary scholarly tools. But in his ability to show how to live a Christian life between-the-times, he was centuries ahead of today's most advanced theological scholarship.

CHAPTER III

An Elemental Event

Enduring Influences: Father Hans

Glory to Luther! Eternal glory to the esteemed man to whom we owe the recovery of our most precious treasures and on whose good deeds we still live today! It would be unseemly to complain of the limitations of his views. The dwarf who stands on the giant's shoulders can indeed see farther than the giant himself, especially if the dwarf puts on his spectacles. But not withstanding our broader perspective, we miss that lofty intuition and giant heart, which we cannot acquire.[1]

This, too, is Martin Luther, whom the enlightened cosmopolitan Heinrich Heine holds up as a mirror for his own times. The modern dwarf who has been so fortunate as to escape the darkness and doom of the Middle Ages is contrasted with the towering giant of the past. So great an act of liberation could have been accomplished only by a "giant heart," a completely unique, brilliant, and ultimately inexplicable figure.

It is the task of the historian to oppose stubbornly and with all his might the poet's adoration of Luther as a genius. Poetic intuition that divines the mighty "secret of Luther's heart" will not stand up in the high courts of psychology and social history. It must be possible to uncover the sources and resources of this person, at least to get closer to him by analyzing modes of experience and patterns of behavior. Evidence that would enable us to answer all such questions is extremely scarce; but for that very reason, no helping hands may be disregarded—and all suspicions against psychohistory must be put aside.[2]

As his earliest environment and the basis of his development in childhood and youth, Luther's home and family deserve particular attention. Luther was born in the center of the county of Mansfeld, in Eisleben, a small town with a population of no more than four thousand, situated about seventy

Luther was no stranger to the peasants' way of life. Daniel Hopfer, Bauernhaus und Bauernschmaus *(Farm and Feast)*

miles southwest of Wittenberg and some sixty miles northeast of Erfurt. Luther always considered himself a Mansfelder, remaining attached to his home soil even in his final role as mediator between quarreling princes.

Luther once unequivocally gave 1484 as the year of his birth: "I was born in Mansfeld [in the county of Mansfeld] in 1484, that is certain." But as in the case of Erasmus of Rotterdam, Luther's early chronology is not that clear at all. He might be assumed to have known the year of his birth, but not even his mother was sure of it; accurate records were not yet being kept about human life—except perhaps in Heaven. His younger colleague and biographer, Philipp Melanchthon, resolutely insisted on the year 1483, basing his date on the horoscope he had worked out for Luther. How often Melanchthon's confidence in the art of astrology exposed him to his older friend's ridicule! But a great deal speaks for the fact that the "stargazer" was right this time, and that Luther was born on November 10, 1483 and baptized—as was usual at the time—on the following day, St. Martin's Day. And so he came to be named Martin.

A year after Martin, their second son, was born, the Luder family moved to the town of Mansfeld, some seven miles from Eisleben and only half as large (circa 2,000 inhabitants). Luther's father had started as a miner and

A medieval mine. Luther's father, Hans Luder, was originally a miner.

had been able to take advantage of Mansfeld's flourishing copper-mining industry and there to become a *Hüttenmeister,* the lessee of one pit in the copper mines belonging to the counts of Mansfeld. Hans Luder hailed from Möhra near Eisenach in the Thuringian part of Electoral Saxony. He was of peasant stock but as a *Hüttenmeister* had already attained a position of respect and a good income shortly after Martin's birth, and this despite the fact that copper mining was susceptible to the fluctuations of the economy and required considerable investment.

Hans' father, Heine Luder, had been a relatively independent farmer with only a modest annual tax to be paid to the elector of Saxony. By marrying a Ziegler, grandfather Luder allied two of the most prosperous peasant families in the village of Möhra; from then on the Luders had a good deal of land to call their own. Though Martin Luther was never a farmer himself, his family background afforded him insight into the conditions of the peasantry. Thus he realized that many of the peasants' grievances were justified, as made clear in 1525, when he tried to mediate in the Peasants' War: "What good is it if a peasant's field yields as many gulden as stalks and kernels but the authorities take all the more, increase their luxury continuously, and squander what they have on clothes, food, drink, buildings, and the like, as if it were chaff?"[3]

Despite this social critique it would be wrong to equate the situation of the peasants in central Germany with that in the southwestern part of the empire, in Alsace, the Upper Rhine valley, or Württemberg, where most peasants were serfs and exploitation virtually forced the impoverished tenants to take up arms. After all, the peasants in Möhra owned their farms, shared with the inhabitants of the surrounding villages a form of self-government and a community treasury, and enacted their own local laws. They observed the prudent prohibition against dividing up farms. It was always the *youngest* son of a peasant family who inherited the property; the other children either had to marry into another family or try to earn a living in other trades. And thus Martin's father Hans Luder had to move away from the farm. There was not much that a young man from the country could do. After all, it is unlikely that he could read and write, for Möhra had neither a parsonage nor a school. So he took his chances in the prospering copper industry in the county of Mansfeld.

Two corrections are called for in this success story of the frugal father who, without any outside help, worked his way up the social ladder from poor peasant's son to independent entrepreneur. In the first place, his success was neither immediate nor continuous. Entering the copper-mining industry involved substantial risks to which Hans Luder was not immune. For years he owed the sizable sum of several thousand gulden to the copper-processing company, which not only financed the extraction and smelting of the copper but also set prices and did the actual selling. There were extended periods during which Luder was completely dependent on the company, and he remained in debt until one year before his death. Nonetheless, he proved to be good for his debts, and when he died in 1530 he left the not inconsiderable fortune of 1,250 gulden, a sum more than ten times the salary earned at that time by an average professor at the University of Wittenberg.

These changing fortunes in business make it likely that Martin heard at an early age about financing and interest on loans, and about problems with the trading company. In any case, Luther's later treatment of the far-reaching influence of large companies was knowledgeable, critical, and surprisingly unacademic. The Luder family experienced all the vicissitudes of a small business. Though they were not poor, thrift had to be a part of their way of life. Late in life Luther was still to remember that his early years had been anything but luxurious. His mother had had to struggle to feed her large family. How many brothers and sisters Martin had is not quite clear; all we know for certain is that of a total of probably eight other children, only his brother Jacob and three sisters reached adulthood.

Portraits of Luther's parents, Hans and Margaret (Hanna) née Lindemann, by Lucas Cranach the Elder, 1527. Over Hans Luder's picture appear the words: "On the 29th day of June in the year 1530, Hans Luther, father of Dr. Martinus, died a Christian." (He actually died in May.) Over the painting of Margaret: "On the 30th day of June in the year 1531, Margareta Lutherin, mother of Dr. Martinus, died a Christian."

It was by no means a foregone conclusion that Martin could go to school, but finally the family did raise the money for his education in Magdeburg and Eisenach. We know that Luther felt deep gratitude toward his father for enabling him to attend school. In 1501, at the University of Erfurt, Luther was no longer regarded as the son of poor parents, since he had been able to pay his enrollment fees in full. The spelling of his name was now embellished with an "h" to suit the more elegant, academic usage: the student named Luder was entered in the university register as "Martinus Ludher ex Mansfeld." From 1518 on he spelled his name "Luther," but in one of his last letters he again spoke of "my beloved Frau Ludherin."

In 1507, when Martin, who had by this time become an Augustinian monk, celebrated his first mass as a newly ordained priest, his father galloped into Erfurt with twenty riders and bestowed on the monastery the truly generous sum of twenty gulden: Father Hans was obviously a man of means. Lucas Cranach's painting of Hans and Margaret Luder shows them in 1527 as self-confident burghers at the end of an industrious life. Both of them have the alert sparkling eyes that also mark their son's face. The young Reformer resembles his father to a striking degree; the mother's features will be found again in the old Luther.

Martin Luther was born into a modern world. At the family table he heard the story of the budding mining industry and became aware of the problems of the entrepreneur. Thus, early in life, he learned about the impact of early capitalism in practice and not just in theory.

Mother Hanna: Old Witch and Grand Lady

The second correction in Hans Luder's traditional success story digs deeper. It concerns the social status of Luther's mother Margaret, called Hanna by her family. Accurate information about Hans Luder has always been available: he was resolute, farsighted in his planning, ambitious, and he strove for independence, according to the motto "A free peasant is nobody's slave."

But what information do we have about Margaret Luder? In fact only the portrait painted of her in old age plus whatever may be taken for granted in connection with the mother of a large family. Work filled her days, and economizing was a necessity; she gathered the firewood for the kitchen herself, for there were no servants in the Luther household when Martin was a child. Honesty was a matter of course, and when little Martin once filched a nut, he received a thrashing that "drew blood," as the adult Luther still remembered.[4] Reminiscences of this kind were pieced together to create the story of a woman of humble circumstances, tough, bent with work, simple in her superstitions, and perhaps a bit stolid in manner. The verses that Martin so often heard from her do indeed sound rather somber:

> None is well-disposed to us;
> that's the fault of both of us.[5]

A mother who punishes her son so severely as to draw blood and burdens him with her own fears—what a perfect case history for an anxiety-ridden, depressive son! Yet this view has not gained acceptance. It was Luther's relationship to his father that has attracted all the attention. Margaret Luder disappeared in the shadow of a much more impressive husband who so thoroughly tyrannized his son that the Reformation came to be explained as an act of self-defense, a protest against merciless fathers, be they called Hans, the pope, or God. That the mother might also have had an influence on the boy seemed inconceivable or at least irrelevant. For this reason the features of Margaret Luder have remained pale and undefined: a simple woman, uneducated and superstitious, nothing more.

There is good reason, however, to be skeptical about this portrait of

Luther's background. Diagnoses of this kind are not only subject to changing scholarly trends but also owe part of their impact to the psychologizing mood of our times. In the sixteenth century, when the father fixation had not yet been invented, the mother played a decisive role. Even the Reformer's opponents bear witness to this fact, albeit in their own way. For them too Margaret was an impressive figure—but as a whore not a wife, for his father's name was not Hans but "Devil." No self-respecting psychohistorian would stoop so far as to treat seriously such scurrilous allegations as that Luther's mother had had intercourse with the Devil in the bathhouse of Eisleben and that Martin was thus not genuinely human but a child of Satan. But late in life Luther still mentioned this attempt to strike at his person: "If the Devil can do nothing against the teachings, he attacks the person, lying, slandering, cursing, and ranting at him. Just as the papists' Beelzebub did to me when he could not subdue my Gospel, he wrote that I was possessed by the Devil, was a changeling, my beloved mother a whore and bath attendant." With the irony that was his preferred weapon against the Devil, Luther concluded: "As soon as he had written that, my Gospel was done for and the papists had won."[6]

This is Luther's belated reaction to a tract written by Johannes Cochlaeus in 1533. The satanic defamation even found its way into diplomatic dispatches. When Pietro Paolo Vergerio was still curial nuncio and not yet a Protestant professor at the University of Tübingen, he informed Rome about his meeting with Luther at the Castle of Wittenberg on November 7, 1535. The meeting had been arranged to discuss Protestant participation at a council recently announced by the pope and called to convene at Mantua. Vergerio, too, believed he could explain the Reformer's disturbing personality with the theory that the Devil was his father: "On the basis of what I have found out about his birth, I am quite inclined to assume that he is possessed by a demon."[7]

The rumor survived obstinately into the nineteenth century, when waning belief in the Devil robbed the legend of its impact and credibility—from Luther's perspective a process with a negative side as well, for as superstition fell victim to sophistication, so did the awareness of Satan's threat. The Devil's concern, Luther knew, was to overcome the Gospel, not the honor of a simple virgin. If Luther's sense of the Devil is at all related to anything he learned from his mother's superstitions, then it is precisely in reaction to any such underestimation of God's most powerful opponent.

But Margaret Luder is interesting even without scandalous bathhouse stories. She did not come from peasant stock, as has been assumed up to

Christ, Judge of the World. The Virgin Mary and St. John intercede for the imperiled faithful. To the just, the Judge is saying, "Come," and to the evil, "Go"—to Hell. Woodcut from Der Antichrist, *Strasbourg, ca. 1480.*

now. As in the case of his father, Heine, Hans Luder's career began with a good match, which explains a great deal about his rise from peasant's son to respected citizen and makes the efforts to give young Martin a good education easier to understand. Through the correction of a host of errors and misunderstandings, it is now safe to say that Hans Luder married a Lindemann, who, unlike her husband, did not come from a farm but was the daughter of an established burgher family in Eisenach.[8] A Hans Lindemann is recorded as a citizen there in 1406, and a Heinrich Lindemann enrolled at the University of Erfurt in 1444–45. Another Lindemann, also named Heinrich and a student at the University of Erfurt as well, went on to be a member of the town council in Eisenach for twenty-three years, and was even elected mayor in 1497. In Luther's time we encounter two cousins, the sons of his mother's eldest brother, whose name we do not know. The elder cousin is Johann Lindemann from Eisleben (†1519), doctor of law and electoral councilor in Saxony; his younger brother Kaspar (†1536) received his degree of doctor of medicine after studying in Leipzig, Frankfurt on the Oder, and Bologna. He became the personal physician to Elector Frederick and to his successor John and treated Luther occasionally. During the last four years of his life Kaspar Lindemann was professor of medicine in Wittenberg.

Now a whole series of events begins to make sense, or at least starts to appear in a new light. That Hans Luder settled in Eisleben was no coincidence, for Margaret's eldest brother lived there. The decision to give Martin an education was a well-established Lindemann family tradition. The abrupt move from Magdeburg, where Luther attended the cathedral school for a year, to Eisenach probably had family reasons as well. No, Martin was not a poor lonely boy being pushed from one strange town to another; he was Margaret's son, who had uncles and aunts in Eisenach to look after him and who in fact went to stay there with Heinrich Schalbe, a friend of the family. Luther owed a great deal to Schalbe, himself a town councilor and ultimately mayor of Eisenach. Later Luther was to speak warmly of the "Collegium Schalbe," which had given him so much. In early 1520 Luther was accused of having Bohemian forefathers, with the implication of having Hussite roots. He replied by pointing out that his family was from Eisenach, and it was the Lindemann, not the Luder, family to whom he refers: "Practically my whole family lives in Eisenach, they can testify for me, they also know me personally as I attended school there for three years."[9]

The step from Latin school to the University of Erfurt and the decision to have Martin study law fits in with the Lindemann family tradition, for his Eisleben cousin Johann had started as a lawyer and rose to the position of electoral councilor. Thus the educated world was not alien to Luther; he had encountered it early through his mother and her family.

His father's rapid rise from miner to lessee of a mine becomes more understandable as well. Margaret's family most likely guaranteed the otherwise inexplicable line of credit granted their son- and brother-in-law—astonishingly high credit, considering the risky nature of the copper industry. The Lindemanns were very much present in the life of both father and son; Luther's youth was not purely a man's affair, as has hitherto been assumed.

Thus Luther's social environment paved the way for his education. In his day, eleven years of schooling were a privilege. His mother's family was well aware that education opened the door to advancement, and his father, though from a simpler background, possessed enough insight to encourage the plans for Luther's enrollment in a Latin school and above all in a university.

What can be said about the religious atmosphere in the Luder home? Out of the modern debate about the "Young Man Luther" a new and noticeable resistance has emerged against attempts to deduce psychological damage from Luther's religious upbringing. These reservations are well founded insofar as there is no evidence on which to base a diagnosis of Luther as a neurotic or psychotic. On the other hand earlier research so thoroughly shielded Luther's human failings that his life story threatened to become hagiographic legend: the man-of-God dedicated only to heeding the Gospel cannot be measured according to human categories.

Luther himself accommodates efforts to explain his development in psychological terms. We must take his own statements on the subject seriously, even if no reliable scientific method has yet evolved to penetrate the person of the Reformer behind the few psychologically revealing, autobiographical fragments he left.

To start with Luther made some extremely telling comments about his upbringing. But as he does not distinguish between his father and mother, there is no way to diagnose either a father- or mother-fixation. Should one want to talk about a fixation at all, then a parents fixation; both his father's intimidating hand and his mother's thrashings lingered in his memory. Luther's father seems once to have struck him so hard that it took the frightened boy some time to find his way back to a normal relationship with him. But even that does not allow us to conclude that Hans Luder was a short-tempered, pitiless man, since it also becomes evident that he was at pains not to alienate the child. It is obvious that the rod alone did not rule the Luder household.

When Luther himself became a father, it is clear that he had learned a lesson from the punishments he had experienced as a child. This was not the way he wanted to bring up his son Hans; God does not treat mankind that way either.

> One should not hit children too hard: my father once whipped me so that I ran away from him; I was upset till he was able to overcome the distance. I would not want to hit my Hans so hard, otherwise he would become timorous and estranged from me; I cannot imagine a grief worse than that. This is the way God does it: My children, I do not chastise you myself but through Satan and the world; if you come to me and invoke my help, I will rescue you and put you on your feet again! For our Lord would not want us to become estranged from him.[10]

Margaret and Hans Luder together educated their children—Luther left no doubt about this cooperation. Now it is of particular importance that in Luther's mind their style of education and upbringing—strict but not unfeeling—sparked the decision that was to change his life: "The serious and austere life they led with me later caused me to enter a monastery and become a monk; but they meant it very well indeed."[11]

Responsibility, experience with misbehavior, and subsequent punishment were all shaped into concepts which later became so central to the Reformer, and molded—or at least sharpened—young Martin's conscience. It was the way he was raised at home that brought him to the gates of the monastery—but not straightaway.

In the summer of 1505 Luther the law student started back to Erfurt after a visit with his parents. On July 2, with some four more miles to go, he was caught in a terrible thunderstorm near the village of Stotternheim. Hurled to the ground by lightning, he called out: "Help me, St. Anne; I will become a monk."[12] There is no reason to doubt that the unsuspecting traveler became terrified when confronted with sudden death. The situation as such can indeed lay claim to rarity; the reaction, however, cannot. A vow of this kind was neither exceptional nor proof of psychological instability; on the contrary, it was perfectly in keeping with the times and not abnormal for any young, unmarried man of tender conscience. This is not to deny young Luther's unmistakably individual decision; the vow to enter a monastery was not a necessary consequence of his upbringing and environment. All of the Luder children must have experienced their parents' strong hand, yet only Martin took up monastic life. Environment is an explanation in retrospect, not the determining factor from the outset.

It is nevertheless important to realize that Luther's vow corresponded with the religious climate of the time and did fit in with the ideals he had been reared with at home, school, and church. St. Anne was the patron saint of people in distress in thunderstorms as well as the patroness of miners. The cult of St. Anne had spread across central Germany before Luther's time, so it was not necessarily only the religiosity of the father that caused the son to invoke Mother Anne when he was in distress. At the church of St. Mary in Eisenach, where Luther's friend Johannes Braun was vicar, a special liturgy was sung for St. Anne. Anne was the Virgin Mary's mother, but she was venerated for more than that because through the doctrine of the Immaculate Conception, according to which Mary herself had been conceived without the taint of original sin, her mother Anne, too, participated in the miracle of the incarnation of Christ. As a reformer Luther later rejected the "doctrine of Anne" completely: "It also applies to St. Anne, whose feast is being celebrated today, that I cannot find a word about her in the Bible. I believe that God left this unmentioned so that we would not seek out new holy places, as we are doing now, running to and fro and thus losing sight of the true Savior, Jesus Christ."[13]

But on his way to Stotternheim Mother Anne was for him still the powerful patron saint. It was only after his reformation breakthrough that he discovered all believers to be saints. Though the cults of St. Anne and St. Mary were already popular in the Middle Ages, the theological concepts underlying them could not be accepted as dogma until centuries later because of their questionable biblical basis. Not until 1854 did Pope Pius IX confirm the doctrinal basis of the cult of St. Anne, insofar as from the very moment she was conceived by her mother, St. Mary was declared to have been without sin. It was only in 1950 that Pope Pius XII proclaimed the second major Marian dogma, the bodily assumption of the Mother of Christ into heavenly glory. Like the Immaculate Conception, the Assumption of the Blessed Virgin was already before Luther's time widely considered to be a revealed truth.

Luther's invocation of St. Anne and his vow to become a monk were deeply rooted in the religiosity of his age. The very normalcy of his reaction later made both his critical evaluation and his Evangelical solution intelligible, viable, and liberating to so many. If Luther clearly grasped the events and forces that led him to enter a monastery, he affords us not only an insight into his own soul but presents us with a psychogram of his time as well.

We must, of course, add that a considerable distance of age and experience lies between the actual occurrences and Luther's recollection of them. All his memories, which recall not only his parents but also flogging by schoolmasters, date from a time when he had already made his biblical discoveries. Fundamental among these is distinction between the law, with its obligations and demands for proper behavior, and the Gospel, which bestows grace and righteousness. Once he realized that the constraints of the law and the spontaneity of faith are mutually exclusive, he found the vocabulary to interpret his own history: his early years had been lived under the law.

School Days, School Days

We do not know when Martin entered school; probably he was six or seven. At an advanced age Luther thanked Nikolaus Oember from Mansfeld for carrying him to school when he was a small boy—considering the condition of the streets in places like Mansfeld at the time, this must have been a crucial help on rainy days. Although Martin attended school in his hometown for some time, only leaving at the age of thirteen, we know little more about this period in his life than that the fundamentals of grammar, logic, and rhetoric were drummed into the children by means of strict, sometimes cruel discipline. Martin's teacher did not consider him a model pupil, so it could happen that he was struck as often as fifteen times in a single morning. It was not, however, corporal punishment as such that Luther later condemned; but he felt that a teacher should be capable of distinguishing between laziness and insufficient ability.

Weekends were the worst times. One of the older pupils was appointed "lupus," wolf, and had to keep the "wolf book," registering all violations of school rules. Incorrect conjugation or declension resulted in immediate punishment; "wolf punishments," on the other hand, could wait till the end of the week. The approach of punishment day meant misery to all the younger children and all the sensitive ones.

This is not to say that Luther later believed in sparing the rod altogether. He meted out punishment to his own children—his principles do not correspond to modern educational trends. But he rejected chastisement and flogging as a means of prodding, feeling they fostered children's obstinacy and

ΜΩΡΙΑΣ ΕΓΚΩΜΙΟΝ.

uotionibus. Allusit autem ad Græcū Epigrāma, quod iocatur Grāmaticis esse, πέντε χόλη, πέντε πτώσεις καὶ πέντε κατάρας. i. quinq; genera, quinq; casus, & quinq; deuotiones, ob quinq; primos uersus Homericos, quorum primus incipit a μῆνιν, quod iram significat. Secūdus, οὐλομένην, qđ perniciē significat, habet & μυρία ἄλγεα. i. innūeros dolores. Tertius, animas mittit ad inferos. Quartus, canū laniationē. Quintus, auium, & iram Iouis. Atq; his auspicijs ingrediuntur suum munus. Epigrāma autem est libro primo Palladæ titulo huiusmodi, Ἀρχὴ γραμματικῆς πεντάστιχός ἐστι κατάρα· πρῶτος μῆνιν ἔχει, δεύτερος οὐλομένην, μεστὰ δ' οὐλομένην, Δαναοῖς πάλιν ἄλγεα πολλά. ὁ τρίτος, ψυχὰς εἰς ἅδην κατάγει. τῷ δὲ τετάρτῳ τὰ ἑλώρια, καὶ κύνες ἀργοί· πέμπτος, οἰωνοί, καὶ χόλος ἐστὶ Διός. πῶς οὖν γραμματικὸς δύναται μετὰ πέντε κατάρας καὶ πέντε πτώσεις, μὴ μέγα πένθος ἔχειν; i. Principium grammatices, quinq; uersibus contenta, est deuotio. Primus iram habet, secundus perniciosam. Et post perniciosam, Græcorum rursum dolores multos. Tertius animas in inferos deducit. Quarti aūt, tractus, & canes ueloces. Quinti, aues, & ira est Iouis. Quomō igit Grāmaticus pōt post quinq; execratiōes, et quinq; casus, nō magnū luctū habere? In φροντιστηρίοις) Aristophanes, ἐν νεφέλαις, Socratis scholā uocat φροντιστήριον, q̄si dicas solicitudinis locū, qđ illic tristes ac cogitabundi sederent. Et Socrates dicere cōsueuit, φρόντισον, hoc est cogita, hoc dicto adhortans, ad diligentē rei cōsyderationē. Asinū illū Cumanū) Is repertū leonis exuuiū, adaptarat corpori suo, atq; ita leo creditus, timebatur. Donec quidā ex auriū pminentiū inditio, sensit asinū esse, deinde fuste cōtusus, ad stabulum reductus est. Amaricinū olet.) De compositione ungenti Amaricini, quod & sansucinū uocant, uide Diascoridem in primo. Hoc Plinius in de

q; tantum diris obnoxij sunt isti, quead modum indicat epigrāma græcum, uerum sexcentis, ut qui semper famelici, sordidiq; in ludis illis suis, in ludis dixi, imo in φροντιστηρίοις, uel pistrinis potius, ac carnificinis, inter pueroꝝ greges, cōsenescant laboribus, obsurdescāt clamorib9, fetore pædoreq; cōtabescant, tamē meo beneficio fit, ut sibi primi mortaliū esse uideant. Adeo sibi placēt, dum pauidā turbā, minaci uultu uoceq;, territant, dū ferulis, uirgis, lorisq; cōscindūt miseros, dumq; modis oībus suo arbitratu, sæuiūt, asinum illum Cumanū imitantes, interim sordes illæ, meræ munditiæ uidētur, pædor amaricinū olet, miserrima illa seruit

Tyrānis ludi magistrorum.

Hans Holbein the Younger, drawing of a teacher chastising a pupil, in Laus Stultitiae *(In Praise of Folly) by Erasmus of Rotterdam*

were detrimental to their desire to learn. What he advocated from very early on was a teaching system tailored to children's needs, allowing pupils, both boys and girls, to learn "joyfully and playfully," preferably at half-day schools in the interests of working children, and ideally with female as well as male teachers.[14]

Luther thought he had learned deplorably little during those long years. His experiences in Mansfeld provided a negative model that impelled him toward radical educational reform.

Can something more positive be said about Magdeburg, the next stage on his educational path? Luther remembered strikingly little about the period. He was fourteen when Hans Reinecke, his friend in Mansfeld, took him along to the *Nullbrüder* (probably called such because of the *Nollen,* or pointed hoods, they wore), the Brethren of the Common Life. Martin must have arrived in Magdeburg in 1497, just after the bishop had permitted them to enlarge their hostel. The Brethren of the Common Life belonged to the lay branch of the Devotio Moderna, a Dutch reform movement that in the fifteenth century had spread across large parts of Europe, westward to Paris and as far south as Württemberg. The Brethren eagerly devoted themselves to housing and supervising schoolboys away from home.

A quarter of a century later, in 1522, Luther mentions to the mayor of Magdeburg that he had gone "to school with the Brethren of the Common Life."[15] The statement can easily be misunderstood. It does not mean that the Brethren maintained a school themselves, but that they lodged pupils away from home and supervised their schoolwork. This was a much more pedestrian role than, as the older thesis had it, the promotion by the Brethren of the Renaissance north of the Alps through their writing and teaching.[16] The notion that Luther must have been deeply influenced by the reform ideals of the Brethren in Magdeburg is indeed no longer tenable. Yet there is a kernel of truth in this old myth, for the Brethren, originally small-city artisans from Zwolle and Deventer, accomplished more in the way of educational renewal than is immediately apparent. The very idea of establishing hostels to enable children from outlying areas to attend good schools testifies to their concern with sound education and pedagogic reform. The Latin textbooks they wrote to replace obsolete medieval cramming methods circulated far beyond the Netherlands.

The Brethren's aim was to place learning in the service of piety. As Geert Groote (†1384), founder of the Brethren of the Common Life, saw it, the members were to practice simple piety in imitation of Christ, living in lay communities without taking vows. For this reason the movement came under suspicion of spreading anticlerical sentiments. At the Council of Constance (1414–18) the Dominicans tried to drag the Brethren into a heresy trial, and it took Johannes Gerson (†1429), chancellor of the University of Paris and a leading council theologian, to protect them from persecution. But by the time Luther attended school in Magdeburg these events had long since passed into history. Their anticlericalism, real or surmised, was a thing of the past, and when Luther criticized the elevated status of monks and priests, it was not because of the Brethren at Magdeburg.

The Brethren and their Devotio Moderna movement were important to the history of reform in the fifteenth century. Wherever they were permitted to settle, whether in monastery-type communities joined in the Windesheim Congregation, or in quiet lay groups, they demanded from monasteries and communities a vivid sense of inner mission and reform. They copied theological treatises and themselves read patristic literature, especially St. Augustine and St. Bernard. Understandably, Johannes Gerson became popular among the Brethren after supporting their cause at the Council of Constance. His life also seemed an exemplification of their ideals: though learned, he eschewed the seductive stylishness of scholarly subtleties and was able to find words for the hopes and grievances of his contemporaries. Gerson stood for gradual edification, not revolutionary reform; he was less concerned with the educated elite than with the ordinary Christian, thus embodying the Brethren's ideal of modern piety. Gerson's memory is perpetuated on the pulpit of the Church of the Brethren in Urach in Württemberg, where he is shown as a doctor of the Church in the impressive company of Saints Ambrose, Augustine, Jerome, and Gregory the Great, the four great Fathers of the Western Church.

Luther, too, valued the patron of the Devotio Moderna, calling him "Doctor Comforter." Like the Brethren, the Reformer saw him as a pastoral theologian concerned with the care of souls. As a young professor in Wittenberg Luther was already familiar with the writings of the devotional movement and quoted its most successful writer, Gerald Zerbolt van Zutphen, though confusing him with Geert Groote, the founder of the movement.[17] Luther was also acquainted with the *Rosetum,* a handbook for edification and meditation by Johannes Mauburnus, a member of the Windesheim Congregation at the monastery of St. Agnietenberg near Zwolle. Thus he had studied and appreciated several of the most widely read authors of the Devotio Moderna; but there is no indication that he took a serious interest in its program, and, if at all, then certainly not in Magdeburg, for during his one year there he was still in the middle of his primary education.

In Luther's time the Devotio Moderna was already so widespread as to have lost some of its distinctive edge. He came into contact with the movement in its final phase, a hundred years after its inception. Hence it was not the Reformation that was the cause for its decline. Around the turn of the century the Italian Renaissance was already beginning to influence Europe north of the Alps. No longer was the reform movement being advanced by artisans and the petty bourgeoisie: now a higher social stratum, with other aims and claims, was taking the initiative in the renewal of Church and society. They gathered in *sodalitates,* learned societies, met at the homes of patrician families, engaged in stylistically refined correspondence, and regarded classical rhetoric as the quintessence of true culture.

The Devotio Moderna, too, had called for a return to the sources, but all it could offer were *florilegia,* anthologies of quotations to be used as guides for spiritual growth through the imitation of Christ. Now, a new and different world was being opened up, the world of classical and Christian antiquity. In Basel, Strasbourg, and Nuremberg unabridged editions of the Church Fathers were published, allowing "true" Christian erudition to be studied. The Brethren still concentrated on devotional Bible reading without the distractions of a scholarly apparatus of text variants and linguistic elucidations. But their collections of pious proverbs could no longer provide the key for a precise understanding of the Bible; they were replaced by Hebrew and Greek dictionaries and grammars.

The era of the Devotio Moderna was over—at least for the time being. It was to surface again in new forms to take a stand against the petrifaction of "orthodoxy" and to make a renewed appeal for genuine piety. But that chapter already belongs to the history of the beginnings of pietism.

The spirit that prevailed in the sixteenth century was different; scholarship was to be linked with wisdom, not subordinated to piety. Erasmus of Rotterdam, who as a schoolboy had boarded with the Brethren in Deventer—at the end under the supervision of Alexander Hegius, the most distinguished reform pedagogue of the time—should have had every reason to acknowledge his indebtedness with gratitude. Instead he often complained bitterly about their narrowmindedness and lack of sensitivity for scholarship and the arts. During the era of humanism and the Reformation, such a condemnation of one's own education, documenting the bitter struggle for emancipation, can be found again and again. It is part of the psychogram of Luther's time and certainly not unique to the Reformer's own childhood. Luther's break with his upbringing and education was not caused by Hans and Margaret, Magdeburg or Eisenach. A whole phalanx of humanists rejected their educational backgrounds, almost as if they had agreed in advance to do so. Modern Devotion was shaken off, just as scholastic scholarship was disparaged. As so often in the history of thought, intellectual prowess laid claim to progress by proudly discounting its own ancestry.

It should not be of surprise, therefore, that Desiderius Erasmus also rebelled against his schooling. In the case of Luther, however, the time spent

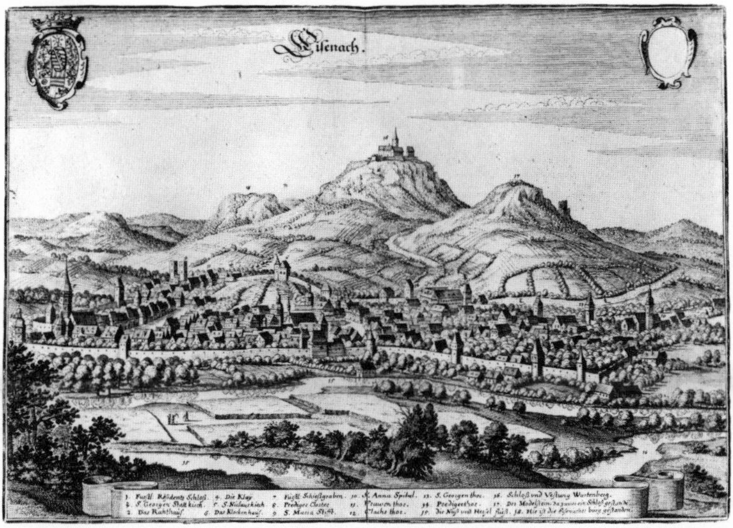

Eisenach. Wartburg Castle overlooks the town. Copperplate after Merian, 1650.

among the Brethren was too short, and their influence has been vastly overestimated. The mere fact that both of them, as young boys, lived among the Brethren—the one spending nine years in Deventer, the other one year in Magdeburg—does not suffice to ascribe common roots to Erasmus and Luther. Even their origins failed to fashion them into joint champions of a Christian Renaissance.

Preparation for Life

Fourteen-year-old Martin spent the last four pre-university years in Eisenach, where he was surrounded by a large, widely respected family to help and advise him, and at least partly replace his parents. From this period in his life dates the story of Luther as a *Partekenhengst,* collector of "Parteken," or small gifts of food. Poor little Martin has been pitied as the hungry schoolboy far away from home, with neither parents nor protection! How moving it is to hear that a widow noticed the boy because of his clear voice and took him into her home. Such experiences in Eisenach could later grow into legend in a time when people no longer remembered that on high holidays schoolchildren traditionally trekked around town and country, singing songs and expecting—and as a rule receiving—reward in the form of sweets or something more substantial. All the kind widow probably did, if she existed at all (the anecdote does not come from Luther himself), was to invite the boy in for a bite to eat.

Martin stayed at the home of Heinrich Schalbe, a friend of the family, influential town councilor, and later mayor of Eisenach. The boy received free board and accompanied Schalbe's son Kaspar to school.[18] In Luther's correspondence to Johannes Braun we have concrete evidence for the importance of the circle around Heinrich Schalbe. Ten days before Luther read his first mass as an ordained priest, he invited his older friend, a priest from Eisenach, to share this momentous occasion in a priest's life and join him at the Augustinian monastery in Erfurt on May 2, 1507. In the postscript to his invitation Luther mentioned the "Schalbense Collegium," whom he would have liked to invite as well, but did not want to inconvenience.[19] By collegium Luther could have meant the support group for the Franciscan monastery in Eisenach, with which the Schalbe family had been associated for a long while. But it is more likely that he was referring to a regular house-soirée, of which he still had fond memories years later. The school years in Eisenach were altogether more pleasant than those of "torture" in Mansfeld.

From this same period dates Luther's anecdote that, out of respect for the pupils, the school principal always took off his academic cap when he entered the classroom "because God may have destined some of you to be mayor, chancellor, doctor, or statesman."[20] The principal of St. George's school can no longer be identified with certainty. If there is anything to the story, it underlines once more the contrast between the schools in Eisenach and Mansfeld. In any case, with the same educational farsightedness, Luther later reminded the authorities of their obligation to develop a school system as the best investment in the future.

What with the Collegium Schalbe, collecting "Parteken," and a fine school, Martin's Eisenach years were happy ones. It was also a time in which he came to experience the joys of an intense friendship. Although Johannes Braun, vicar at the church of St. Mary, was considerably older—he had matriculated at the University of Erfurt in 1470—he meant a great deal to young Martin. In a second letter of invitation to his first mass, to an unidentified addressee, Luther again mentions Father Braun and calls him his "very closest friend," who would most certainly be coming to celebrate the young priest's first mass with him.[21] Luther and Braun continued to stay in touch. When two years later Luther was unexpectedly transferred from Erfurt to Wittenberg to take on teaching duties at the Augustinian study house, he apologized to his "dear fatherly friend" for not having been able to inform him about this sudden move. The first letter surviving from Wittenberg went therefore to his friend in Eisenach:

> To the most honorable Johann Braun, devoted to Christ
> and the Virgin Mary, priest in Eisenach.
> My lord, dear Father!
>
> Brother Martin Luther, Augustinian, wishes you salvation and the Savior Himself, Jesus Christ.
>
> My lord and father, whom I esteem highly but love even more—Please stop wondering why I have left you clandestinely without saying good-bye, how I could bring myself to do such a thing, as if there were not the closest bonds between us, as if ungrateful forgetfulness had blotted all memory from my heart, as if a cold, withering storm had extinguished every spark of love in me. There is absolutely no truth in this. Things did not go according to my own plans. . . . It is true that I went away; but no, in actual fact the most and best part of me stayed behind with you and will always stay with you. I am absolutely convinced that I mean enough to you, since your faith in me did not arise from my merit but only from your goodness, so that you will not allow me to lose for no reason what I received without reason. For you were never like that.
>
> Thus we are separated in space, but have come even closer spiritually. And you agree—if I am not totally mistaken.[22]

Even these few lines from a larger, moving epistle reveal the intimacy and human warmth between the two. They stand in sharp contrast to the formal declarations of friendship that had become the rule in humanist correspondence. Luther had acquired a trusted friend while in Eisenach and retained close ties with him when he became a monk. And even more important, the language of friendship found here will become Luther's vocabulary of faith and trust in God.

Luther was to find among the Augustinian brethren a second and likewise paternal friend in Johannes von Staupitz, whom he even dared to address as most beloved father in Christ, "in Christo suavissimo Patri,"[23] and from whom, like Braun, he found himself painfully separated at a decisive time, in November 1518, when the curia was demanding that Luther be sent to Rome. This experience of separation caused him such intense suffering that he dreamt of Staupitz coming to him, comforting him and promising to return.[24] Staupitz's death on December 28, 1524, left a gap that could not be filled. For seven years Luther was silent about him. Only when his own father died on May 29, 1530, did he start to talk about him again, both at the table and from the pulpit, to point out what the great Augustinian vicar had meant to him and to the cause of the Reformation.

The figure of Johannes Braun, on the other hand, was never to take on such lasting significance. Braun belonged to Luther's pre-Reformation—even his pre-academic—phase. In the years that lay between Hans Luder's parental and Father Johannes von Staupitz's spiritual care, the vicar at the church of St. George in Eisenach took over the role of fatherly companion during an important period of maturation. Should there have been an emotional rift in Luther's relationship to his father—recent psychology is inclined to explain the course of Luther's career in this light—it never hindered him from developing very close relationships with other father figures. Early in life Martin Luther proved himself to be a highly sensitive yet outgoing person, capable of genuine friendships.

"One need not paint the Devil above one's door"[25]

There is hardly any authenticated information about those first eighteen years, which led Luther to the threshold of the University of Erfurt. What we do have are memories used to illustrate and evaluate later experiences. These memories are colorful and vivid, but they are not in a real sense biographical data. As testimonies to what the older Luther looked upon as being formative for his childhood and school years, they are precious and revealing.

Sometimes apparently too revealing! Some reminiscences are rarely mentioned today, and if touched at all, are glossed over or dismissed as insignificant medieval remnants. But the legacy of Luther's parental home entailed more than a proper respect for hard work and deep erudition; it included also the at once wondrous and scary world of spirits, Devil, and witchcraft, which the modern mind has come to call superstition. It is indeed not immediately clear what one should make of Luther's account of 1533 in which he so confidently takes for granted the existence of witches and witchcraft. Yet this too is part of the historical record:

> Doctor Martinus said a great deal about witchcraft, about asthma and hobgoblins, how once his mother was pestered so terribly by her neighbor, a witch, that she had to be exceedingly friendly and kind to her in order to appease her. The witch had cast a spell over the children so

Under the spell of sensuality. Urs Graf, The Witches' Sabbath, *1514.*

that they screamed as if they were close to death. And when a preacher merely admonished this neighbor in general words [without mentioning her by name], she bewitched him so as to make him die; there was no medicine that could help him. She had taken the soil on which he had walked, thrown it into the water, and bewitched him in this way, for without that soil he could not regain his health.[26]

If this story were not virtually forgotten, it would be grist for the mills of both Luther-disparagers and admirers. The witch's tale fits perfectly into that tenacious tradition which continues to portray Luther's mother as a backward peasant woman. It is she who is purported to have introduced young Martin to a world full of demons and to have put fear of the devil into that soul already weighed down by his strong, willful father. The old bathhouse story of mother Margaret enjoying intercourse with the Devil would thus, in a new, psychological form, find its way into Luther's biography: If Martin was not begotten *by* the Devil, he was at least raised with him.

But for Protestant partisans Hanna's witch and Luther's words serve to provide wonderful proof of the need for the Reformation, for progress along the drawn-out and thorny path from late medieval superstition to enlightened evangelical faith—a path courageously paved by Luther, even though not followed by him to the end. In all modern classroom and textbook treatments of Luther, the Devil is reduced to an abstraction: be he a figment of mind or time. Thus the Evil One, as a medieval remnant, can be exorcized from the core of Luther's experience, life, and thought.

But the sources are as stubborn as Hanna and cannot be silenced. To begin with, Luther's mother cannot be held solely responsible for Luther's realistic perception of the Devil's machinations. Hans Luder thought exactly the same way, and so did the miners in Mansfeld, who, far away from the light of day, were even more exposed to the artifices of the infernal powers—spirits, demons, and hobgoblins—in the darkness of their mineshafts. Nor would Martin have learned anything different from the Brethren of the Common Life in Magdeburg or from Heinrich Schalbe or Johannes Braun in Eisenach.

Luther's world of thought is wholly distorted and apologetically misconstrued if his conception of the Devil is dismissed as a medieval phenomenon and only his faith in Christ retained as relevant or as the only decisive factor. Christ and the Devil were equally real to him: one was the perpetual intercessor for Christianity, the other a menace to mankind till the end. To argue that Luther never overcame the medieval belief in the Devil says far too little; he even intensified it and lent to it additional urgency: Christ and Satan wage a cosmic war for mastery over Church and world. No one can evade involvement in this struggle. Even for the believer there is no refuge—neither monastery nor the seclusion of the wilderness offer him a chance for escape. The Devil is the omnipresent threat, and exactly for this reason the faithful need the proper weapons for survival.

There is no way to grasp Luther's milieu of experience and faith unless one has an acute sense of his view of Christian existence between God and the Devil: without a recognition of Satan's power, belief in Christ is reduced to an idea about Christ—and Luther's faith becomes a confused delusion in keeping with the tenor of his time.

Attempts are made to offer excuses for Luther by pointing out that he never doubted the omnipotence of God and thus determined only narrow limits for the Devil's activities. Luther himself would have been outraged at this view: the *omnipotent* God is indeed real, but *as such* hidden from us. Faith reaches not for God hidden but for God revealed, who, incarnate in Christ, laid Himself open to the Devil's fury. At Christmas God divested Himself of His omnipotence—the sign given the shepherds was a child "wrapped in swaddling clothes, lying in a manger" (Luke 2.12). To Luther Christmas was the central feast: "God for us." But that directly implies "the Devil against us." This *new* belief in the Devil is such an integral part of the

Reformation discovery that if the reality of the powers inimical to God is not grasped, the incarnation of Christ, as well as the justification and temptation of the sinner are reduced to ideas of the mind rather than experiences of faith. That is what Luther's battle against the Devil meant to convey. Centuries separate Luther from a modern world which has renounced and long since exorcised the Devil, thus finding it hard to see the difference between this kind of religion and medieval witchcraft. But Luther distinguished sharply between faith and superstition. He understood the hellish fears of his time, then discovered in the Scriptures the true thrust and threat of Satan and experienced himself the Devil's trials and temptations. Consequently he, unlike any theologian before or after him, was able to disperse the fog of witches' sabbath and sorcery and show the adversary for what he really was: violent toward God, man, and the world. To make light of the Devil is to distort faith. "The only way to drive away the Devil is through faith in Christ, by saying: 'I have been baptized, I am a Christian.'"[27]

The following chronicle of his own encounter with the Devil as a poltergeist has a clearly medieval ring:

> It is not a unique, unheard-of thing for the Devil to thump about and haunt houses. In our monastery in Wittenberg I heard him distinctly. For when I began to lecture on the Book of Psalms and I was sitting in the refectory after we had sung matins, studying and writing my notes, the Devil came and thudded three times in the storage chamber [the area behind the stove] as if dragging a bushel away. Finally, as it did not want to stop, I collected my books and went to bed. I still regret to this hour that I did not sit him out, to discover what else the Devil wanted to do. I also heard him once over my chamber in the monastery.

The final passage, with its pointed formulation and its underlying expression of contempt for the Devil, was amazing at the time and is overlooked today: "But when I realized that it was Satan, I rolled over and went back to sleep again."[28] It is not as a poltergeist that the Devil discloses his true nature, but as the adversary who thwarts the Word of God; only then is he really to be feared. He seeks to capture the conscience, can quote the Scriptures without fault, and is more pious than God—that is satanical.

> When I awoke last night, the Devil came and wanted to debate with me; he rebuked and reproached me, arguing that I was a sinner. To this I replied: Tell me something new, Devil! I already know that perfectly well; I have committed many a solid and real sin. Indeed there must be good honest sins—not fabricated and invented ones—for God to for-

> give for His beloved Son's sake, who took all my sins upon Him so that now the sins I have committed are no longer mine but belong to Christ. This wonderful gift of God I am not prepared to deny [in my response to the Devil], but want to acknowledge and confess.[29]

Luther's purpose is not to spread fear but to strengthen the resistance of the faithful. Like Christ, the Devil is omnipresent. He acts and reacts, is drawn and challenged by anything that smacks of Christ and true faith. Here is found a radical deviation from the medieval concept of the Devil, according to which the evil one is drawn by the smell of sin, the sin of worldly concern. In Luther's view, it is not a life dedicated to secular tasks and worldly business that attracts and is targeted by the Devil. On the contrary, where Christ is present, the adversary is never far away: "When the Devil harasses us, then we know ourselves to be in good shape!"[30]

Many of these stories come from Luther's *Table Talk,* the collection of his conversations with dinner guests. At the table in the former Augustinian monastery in Wittenberg, God and the world were debated, current affairs discussed, and memories exchanged. Luther's recollections do not have the function of self-glorification, nor do they look back to the "good old days" of a man who is getting on in years. As a rule they have a point to make: the reporting of battles past is to instruct and prepare the younger generations for the prospect of the fierce opposition which will always threaten the preaching of the Gospel.

The same applies to tales of the Devil. They are not meant as horror stories to keep the overly audacious in line but as consolation and strength to timid and tried souls. Luther responds to the concerns of his table companions and to the questions arising from their inveterate, medieval, common fear of the Devil, irrespective of education and origin. How curious that it should still be the gullible Hanna and her superstitions which are supposed to have had such a decisive influence on Luther.

God's Word in Filthy Language

One delicate question—one that might even be unfitting for any respectable home—may lead back to Luther's upbringing. The problem cannot be ignored: if a man is so obviously preoccupied with ideas about and visions of the Devil, does he not require a psychiatrist, or might he not be at least subject to psychological inquiry? In this case it would not be a question of father or mother fixations but of his surprising response to the Devil, which enlightened people find incomprehensible as well as extremely dangerous. Belief in the reality of Satan certainly promoted the frenzy of the witch hunts that seized all denominations and delayed the Enlightenment.

Now we must listen carefully to Luther and not turn away in embarrassment. Not torture and flames but professions of faith and of scorn for the Devil are the proper weapons to use against Hell. Luther adds a coarse expression of his contempt for the satanic fiend to his avowal of Christ as the defender of Christianity: "But if that is not enough for you, you Devil, I have also shit and pissed; wipe your mouth on that and take a hearty bite."[31] Is a man who still thinks and talks like this as an adult caught in the stage of development modern psychology terms the anal stage because of mistakes made in his early upbringing? Or is it perhaps just the drastic literal expression of the proverbial call: Devil, get thee behind me? Or is Luther's age showing through; is he a boor who, in his anger and agitation no longer capable of self-control, casts off the academic whitewash and falls back into the language of his origins? That would be an explanation that could be based on his own words, for he knows: "What someone is used to and has been raised to, that he cannot conceal."[32] He often speaks of his peasant ancestors—they "were good peasants"[33]—so there might be good reason to suspect that childhood experiences broke through in the old Luther, experiences with manure and open cesspools. If this had been the case, in his old age Luther's bent toward crude expressions would have grown into pathological wallowing in scatological language.

As reasonable as all this may sound, his parents' mistakes, his primitive background, and psychological quirks do not constitute a sufficient explanation. Overlooked has been the fact that even as a young professor and monk, Luther, discussing the Devil at length for the first time, did not hesitate to use explicitly scatological language—and at a highly official affair at that. Luther had been designated to preach the ceremonial sermon before members of his order on May 1, 1515. This illustrious occasion was the assembly of the chapter, the decision-making body of the Augustinian Observants in Gotha. Luther had chosen a theme with which the Brethren were familiar, since it was treated in the constitutions of the order (chapter 44). The sin of slander, in this case called back-biting, was described in the handbook as a work of the Devil:

> A slanderer does nothing but ruminate the filth of others with his own teeth and wallow like a pig with his nose in the dirt. That is also why his droppings stink most, surpassed only by the Devil's. . . . And though man drops his excrements in private, the slanderer does not respect this

privacy. He gluts on the pleasure of wallowing in it, and he does not deserve better according to God's righteous judgment.[34] When the slanderer whispers: Look how he has shit on himself, the best answer is: You go eat it.[35]

It cannot be established whether Luther held his sermon before or after the election which put him in charge of ten monasteries in Thuringia and Saxony. But even if he had expressed himself this way before being elected district vicar, it would hardly have jeopardized the outcome. After all, the monks knew all about the Devil's affinity to cesspool and toilet. Though the sermon about the slanderer, whether monk or Devil, is drastic, it is by no means a Freudian slip by an old man with childish complexes. Considered in the light of his times, Luther's choice of words is neither striking nor offensive; such was the language used for the subject, and not only inside the monasteries. In 1521, in Luther's presence, the cardinal of Mainz and chancellor of the Holy Roman Empire acknowledged that he himself was "shit": "I know very well that without God's grace there is nothing good in me, and that I am as much a piece of useless, stinking shit as anyone else, if not more."[36] The cardinal may have been alluding to St. Paul (Phil. 3.8), but he was being more Pauline than the Apostle.

The leading humanist from Gotha, Konrad Mutian, inquired about this "harsh preacher"; the scholar appears not to have been particularly edified by Luther's cruder passages. For him the preacher was a typical monk, and his language therefore unrefined and coarse, not the height of educated respectability. Such ranting monastic preachers—soon they were to be called the Obscure Men—were all too well known and were the last people from whom a man like Mutian would have expected a renewal of the Church. Luther, on the other hand, was so pleased with his sermon that he personally arranged for its distribution and sent a copy to both his former teacher at St. George's school in Eisenach and to his friend Johannes Braun.[37]

Luther's ravings should not be suppressed out of embarrassed respect, and certainly not because they might no longer be considered proper today. Dealing so gingerly with him means not taking him at his word. Luther's language is so physical and earthy that in his wrathful scorn he can give the Devil "a fart for a staff":[38] You, Satan, Antichrist, or pope, can lean on it, a stinking nothing. When the therapist hears that Luther was already suffering from painful constipation in his monastery years, he is tempted to diagnose a psychological complex. In the total historical context, however, Luther's scatology-permeated language has to be taken seriously as an expression of the painful battle fought body and soul against the Adversary, who threatens both flesh and spirit.

Sociohistorical research clarifies a further aspect of Luther's idiom, or at least of its impact. The filthy vocabulary of Reformation propaganda was aimed at inciting the common man. A figure of respect, be he Devil or pope, is effectively unmasked if he can be shown with his pants down.[39] Luther was certainly more than just a spokesman for a social class which hitherto had no voice. The "ass the Devil pinches" is more than a drastic phrase serving agitational ends. He was not merely trying to appeal to "the people" but the Devil himself when calling his words a "pack of stinking lies."[40]

Luther used a great deal of invective, but there was method in it. As he explained in his election sermon of 1515, the Devil drags God's name and His works of justification through the mud. Here lies the otherwise incomprehensible link between Devil, "Great Swine," "Papal Ass," and "Antichrist." It is with the shocking and provocative passion of youth, not the impotent rage of old age, that Luther advocated the only appropriate retort to the Devil's dung: "You go eat it!"[41]

We find here far more than upbringing and environment. Inclination and conviction unite to form a mighty alliance, fashioning a new language of filth which is more than filthy language. Precisely in all its repulsiveness and perversion it verbalizes the unspeakable: the diabolic profanation of God and man. Luther's lifelong barrage of crude words hurled at the opponents of the Gospel is robbed of significance if attributed to bad breeding. When taken seriously, it reveals the task Luther saw before him: to do battle against the greatest slanderer of all times!

IN THE course of our account of Luther's early years neither individual persons nor particular events have emerged that would qualify as paramount influences on his development. Our possibilities of getting to know Martin Luder, the child and schoolboy, are severely restricted. The modern, psychologically probing reader who wants to discover the man behind the work will have to wait patiently until Luther discloses himself in his later actions and writings. The same dearth of sources thwarts all serious efforts to close in on young Martin via his father Hans or his mother Margaret. Of course some convictions that were later fundamental must have been rooted in experiences at home and in school, but only while he was at university and after he had entered the monastery would they take on a more definite shape when, with his "second baptism"—his monastic vows—his "second infancy" began.

What developed at home, school, university, and monastery broke through only much later, under the manifold pressures of his post as professor of biblical theology at the University of Wittenberg. Martin Luder, the descendant of peasants and burghers, was undoubtedly a sensitive child, raised with God, Devil, saints, and demons. Having a deep respect for both his father and mother, he was open to the influence of his parents and was early prepared to make good friends among peers and elders alike. Luther the man could give of himself fully in his encounter with others and could respond with intense fervor in friendship as well as in hostile clashes. There is nothing in his youth to suggest that critical independence with which he would one day scrutinize traditions, or how hard he would strike at all authority not anchored in truth. But the time came when he was forced to concede that the spiritual heritage from his home and early years proved to be too shaky and had to be left behind.

The difference a personal encounter can make in one's assessment of another person is concisely suggested in a letter Sigmund Freud wrote to Stefan Zweig. Despite the centuries between them and Luther, its contents apply to the Reformer too:

> Dear Doctor [Stefan Zweig],
> I almost wish that I had never met Dr. St. Zweig personally and that he had never behaved so kindly and respectfully to me, for I am now suffering under the doubt of whether my judgment [about the new book] may not be affected by personal sympathy.[42]

Such encounters change one, awaken doubts, and undermine established judgments, as is demonstrated by the life of the Reformer. When Martin Luder became first a student, then Friar Martinus Ludher, and finally the Luther of Wittenberg, he encountered on every page of Scripture a God of whom he had hitherto known nothing and a Devil whom he had hitherto not feared. These were encounters that shaped his future by drawing him away from the past. These same encounters deeply agitated him and took him outside of and beyond himself, so that he speaks with passionate immediacy to anyone willing to listen to him—and prepared to hear him out.

Freud's letter can also be read as advice to the psychohistorian. Meeting an author personally may not always be sheer gain. It may as easily obstruct access to his works and make it more difficult to hear what is actually being said.

two

The Unexpected Reformation

CHAPTER IV

The Road to Wittenberg

Decisions before the Reformation

Gateway to Modern Times

"What splendor when bachelors received their degree of Master: torches flamed and the celebrations were great. In my view no temporal, earthly joy can be compared to it"—so intense were Luther's feelings upon receiving his reddish-brown magisterial beret. The event took place in January 1505, probably shortly after Epiphany, but the joy still lingered years later: "That is how we should still be able to celebrate."[1]

After four years of university studies, he had become magister artium, master of the liberal arts, in Erfurt, ranking second among seventeen candidates. The excellent education he had received at the Latin school in Eisenach had evidently not quite made up for his poor schooling in Mansfeld. This can explain why Luther was only thirtieth of fifty-seven candidates in his first academic examination, the baccalaureate, in the autumn of 1502.

The years leading up to the baccalaureate were dedicated chiefly to the principles of logic, the foundations of dialectics, and the rules of rhetoric and grammar. At the University of Erfurt, as at all European universities, the Greek philosopher Aristotle—Plato's student and the teacher of young Alexander the Great—was the principal scholarly authority from the first day of lectures onward. After the bachelor's degree the students' program became even more comprehensive: now the students were introduced to Aristotle's works on metaphysics, ethics, politics, and economics.

According to the traditional curriculum the last two years were to be spent in special seminars and disputations, interpreting and debating important works of Aristotle and dealing with the quadrivium—music, arithmetic, geometry, and astronomy. Demands on the students during these final years were extremely high. They lived together in what might be compared to university residence halls, under rigorous supervision, and found little time for relaxation during the short breaks in their nearly monastic daily rhythm. At the age of twenty-one, one year earlier than prescribed by the university statutes, Luther passed his master of arts examination and had now acquired a comprehensive view of the scholarly disciplines.

The disparaging judgment—and humanist catchphrase—that all this was no more than "games of logic" is hardly apposite to the university education of that time. Logic and dialectics were taught to familiarize students with logical thinking and systematic discussion. Luther profited throughout his life from the oral debate and written argumentation required during his scholastic training.

But quick-wittedness and rhetorical skills were not enough. Academic training strove to equip students with the general ability to test the proofs and conclusions presented in various areas of scholarship and subject them to systematic scrutiny. Reason, experience, and, in theological questions, revelation formed the basis of true knowledge, and all findings were to be ordered intelligibly with the help of logical methods. Thus later work in specialized fields was built on a common educational foundation. The master of arts examination was required for all students except the monks. Then came the next step—preparation for one's future profession as a theologian, lawyer, or physician.

The leading lights at the University of Erfurt were members of the arts faculty: Jodokus Trutfetter from Eisenach and Bartholomaeus Arnoldi von Usingen were recognized authorities who were anxious to introduce their students directly to Aristotle's texts instead of relying on the existing commentaries. They interpreted "the philosopher," as Aristotle was called in the Middle Ages, with greater critical distance and more understanding than could be found elsewhere in Germany. Luther was fortunate to be able to complete his liberal arts studies in one of the most dynamic faculties in Europe.

Though Leipzig was nearer his parents' home in Mansfeld, Luther probably decided to study in Erfurt, some sixty miles away, because it was closer to his beloved Eisenach, where he had last attended school. Already a number of members of the Lindemann family had studied in Erfurt, and so had his close friend Johannes Braun. Wittenberg, which was to play such a central role in Luther's life, was not merely far away; its university was only in the planning stage, and teaching did not commence there until 1502. Thus Erfurt was an obvious choice as well as an exceedingly lucky one.

Luther's alma mater already had a proud past. It had been established in 1392, during the period when the first German universities were being founded, and was one of the oldest universities in the empire, along with Prague, Vienna, Heidelberg, and Cologne. As the "Academy of Thuringia" it soon attained high repute in the whole of Germany and rose to become one of the great universities. Around 1400 there were already more than three hundred and fifty students enrolled; a century later, when Luther began his studies, the number of students matriculated had grown to five hundred, despite competition from the large universities in Cologne, with eight hundred students, and Leipzig, with six hundred. Thus Erfurt possessed the third-largest university in Germany, an extraordinary civic achievement considering that the university was a municipal institution—and received no princely support. Erfurt was not even a free imperial city, and without political strength or legal guarantees, it was greedily eyed by Saxon electors and jealously guarded by its distant sovereign, in Luther's day the bishop of Mainz. Yet more than 15 percent of all German students were educated in Erfurt.

Why would anyone be interested in a university education in the late Middle Ages? It had certainly never been scholarship alone that drove young men into the lecture halls. And indeed the philosophical training all students had to undergo, at this time, was generally not identical with their academic goals. Universities were founded, supported, and attended because of the three "professional schools," the higher faculties of theology, jurisprudence, and medicine. Princes and town councilors were always interested in lawyers, who were needed as civil servants for the rapidly growing administrative machinery of the emerging territorial states and for the thriving imperial cities. In the field of medicine Germany was still far behind Italy and England, though attempts were being made to write more up-to-date handbooks, with the result that by the latter half of the sixteenth century perceptible progress was being made.

The theological faculties profited from this academic boom. Although a university education was not required for ordination, there was a demand, especially in towns, for academically trained theologians who were equal to the intellectual standard of the time. The mendicant orders—which in the years prior to and during the Reformation were derided as bastions of arrogant stupidity—made an enormous contribution to the cause of theological scholarship. They set up *studia generalia* with their own teaching staffs, and the various orders founded theological professorships at the universities.

This was no different in Erfurt, where the three major orders—the Dominicans (O.P.), Franciscans (O.F.M.), and Augustinian Hermits (O.E.S.A.)—had established their own chairs. Thus, theological faculties were as a rule extremely well staffed. Nonetheless, the "queen of disciplines" had to accept the predominance of the jurists and, with particular reluctance, of the leading canon lawyers. With this, however, the university merely reflected the priorities of society. Many years later, Luther—never an admirer of lawyers—still remembered the privileges they had had in Erfurt and their arrogance toward the theologians:[2] "A successful jurist is a woeful Christian."[3]

The higher faculties were not Erfurt's particular strength; one could study law very well in Tübingen or Cologne, and medicine in Vienna or Leipzig. Likewise, the theology faculty lacked a distinctive academic profile in the late fifteenth century because it was oriented chiefly to the traditions of the religious orders. The shock waves resulting from the condemnation of Johannes of Wesel, Erfurt's most renowned theologian, could still be felt. In 1479, when he was cathedral preacher in Worms and no longer professor in Erfurt, he had been hauled before the Inquisition and condemned to lifelong imprisonment for having dared to declare indulgences a pious fraud, demand that the laity, too, should receive the chalice at Communion, and insist that not pope and council but Scripture alone was the final authority of faith. All this had cast a dark shadow on the theological faculty of Erfurt—the shadow of Hussite heresy.

In the German academic world around 1500 Erfurt had only one basic academic advantage—but it was one that could not be overlooked. The philosophy training offered there provided far more than a mere foundation for more advanced studies; the arts faculty itself had a clear program and profile of its own. Although the statutes did not commit the university to a particular school of thought, Erfurt was nonetheless considered a stronghold of the via moderna.[4] The Amplonian College (also called, impressively, "Heaven's Gate"), which may have been Luther's residence hall for several years, was expressly instructed to teach according to the modern way, "secundum modernos."

From our modern vantage point medieval scholasticism may seem to have been a rigid, inflexible, backward-looking, monolithic system that came to an end with the Middle Ages and has had no effect on the development of modern thought. But in fact, scholasticism in its prime did encompass alternatives that have never lost their historical importance. The fourteenth century, with its systematic inquiry into the nature of truth and reality, established decisive precedents. There were two schools: the one was later designated via antiqua (the old way) and the other via moderna (the modern way). The representatives of the via antiqua, followers of Thomas Aquinas and Duns Scotus, were realists. They held that universal concepts (*universalia*) are more than just human tools to inventory the extramaterial world, but are the expressions of reality itself, indeed that final, higher reality behind all individuality. Men as individuals can exist only because "mankind" exists as a universal reality.

In contrast the followers of the via moderna dared to tread a new, uncertain, and controversial path: sensory perception of reality does not lead to the cognition of universal realities but to abstract thought. Universals are the result of such abstractions and are devoid of independent reality. What is real is the individual, the human person as a unique entity perceived by the senses. It is the human intellect that assembles the many perceptions of individual persons into the universal concept of "mankind." "Mankind" as a universal concept is not a real entity existing outside the human mind; it is a "name" (*nomen*) conceived by the mind and based on convention. Such names or concepts provide the scientist or philosopher with comprehensible systems for ordering the wealth of particular phenomena. Since these systems are constructs of reason and based on experience, they possess no independent reality; and being models, they always require verification—by means of the sensually perceivable reality of the particular. If abstract concepts are allowed to develop lives of their own, the link between thought and reality becomes either speculative or dangerously ideological—and usually both at once.

The nominalists, as the representatives of the via moderna came to be called, were soon decried as skeptics who dared to term universal realities mere words (*nomina*). The phrase "logical games"—so readily used to discredit late medieval philosophy—stems from the polemic arsenal of the via antiqua. Exponents of the old way reproached the nominalists for being interested in conceptual terms and not in the reality they stood for. The nominalists did, in fact, question traditional concepts in order to determine their factual validity. On the other hand, the sweeping generalization propagated by humanists, reformers, and later by representatives of the Enlightenment—that scholasticism wasted time with idle speculation—originated with the adherents of the via moderna, who accused the realists of creating mental constructs far removed from reality. These are caricatures produced in the heat of a crucial debate about a fundamental problem.

Nominalism had been firmly established in Erfurt since the mid-fifteenth century, but at first its program had no distinctive identity. The via antiqua had the advantage of clearly designated authorities: Aquinas and Duns Scotus. The via moderna, on the other hand, shunned such commitments. The Englishman William of Occam (who died in 1349 in exile in Munich) was the famous—to his opponents infamous—founding father of nominalism. But despite all recognition of his impressive achievements, he was never able to attain the prominence in his own school that the leading doctors of the via antiqua enjoyed in theirs. The via moderna had a number of spokesmen with equal claims, each of whom put forward his own solutions to innumerable specific problems. Considerable influence had been gained among the exponents of the modern way by the Italian Gregory of Rimini and the Frenchman Pierre d'Ailly, as well as by the Germans Marsilius von Inghen in Heidelberg and Gabriel Biel in Tübingen, who might be considered a second Occam. But each of them had his own mind, of which their school of thought taught them to be proud. It was not only in theological matters that their positions diverged. In the realm of philosophy, too, they laid stress on such differing aspects and opposed each other and their founding father Occam with such critical intensity that what they had in common could easily seem blurred. The nominalists had always been concerned with academic freedom, but their kind of heterogeneity was counterproductive when it came to firmly establishing their own school at any of the new universities.

Four years prior to Luther's enrollment at the University of Erfurt, two professors from the arts faculty, Jodokus Trutfetter and Bartholomaeus Arnoldi, had held a solemn disputation (1497) before the whole university, in which they had succeeded in formulating the common core of nominalism and of developing its fundamental principles into a cohesive program.[5] This can be considered a real breakthrough[6] because it consolidated nominalistic trends into one academic school. Even more important in the long run than the successful disputation was the fact that both of the Erfurt professors set about integrating their principles into their academic teaching. They wrote handbooks to introduce students to the application of nominalistic criteria. Only two years after the disputation Arnoldi published his introduction to natural philosophy (Leipzig, 1499), and Trutfetter followed suit in 1501 with his handbook of logic, which saw a large number of editions.

Again and again both of them cited one basic notion as the decisive principle and characteristic of the via moderna: all philosophical speculation about the world must be tested by means of experience and reality-based reason, regardless of what even the most respected authorities might say to the contrary. Arnoldi emphasized that this was to be no different in the case of theology: all theological speculation is to be tested by the authority of the Scriptures as interpreted by the Church.

Hence experience and Scripture were the only valid norms in the realms of philosophy and theology. Addressing the nominalist Johannes von Wesel, who, though condemned, was still quoted often in Erfurt, Usingen demonstrated how even authorities in one's own school have to be treated: "However important you are, my answer must be: Even great men are sometimes careless and negligent enough to make assertions and statements of which they are not certain."[7]

"Not certain"—that is the basic tenor, the refrain repeated over and over, the chief weapon used against Occam as against Aristotle. Such relativizing of authorities by appealing to scientific method and solid proof spelled the demise of scholasticism. But such freedom from tradition is never attained once and for all. Later academic history shows how tempting it is to accept the convictions of great scholars, enabling new "schoolmen" and new "scholastic" thinking to establish itself again and again. The discovery of the uncertainty of knowledge must be made ever anew.

Nominalism was a major factor in the advance of both the natural sciences and theology. Subordinating speculation to experience freed physics from the confining grip of metaphysical systems that transcended experience. Once experience became experiments, modern science was born, and it was nominalism—not humanism—that had paved the way. In the realm of theology the full implications were not immediately seen. Only Luther's quest for God's reliable and certain word in the Scriptures put an end to the supremacy of speculative philosophy.

The conclusion is clear: at the turn of the sixteenth century the "modern" professors of the arts faculty in Erfurt pushed open the gates to the modern age. Yet only some gates, and only somewhat modern.

Luther Becomes a Nominalist

In the spring of 1501 Luther was introduced to this challenging climate of intellectual innovation. Using the new textbooks, he learned to subject the conclusions of medieval scholarship to critical examination. Much of what he learned in Erfurt could not be applied until later, in a new context, when he himself had broken away from the philosophical theology of scholasticism and was compelled to defend his view of a scripturally based theology against highly reputed scholastic authorities. But the philosophers in Erfurt's arts faculty had done more than arm him with weapons to defend himself; they had also provided him with concepts that were to become essential to the Reformation.

First there was the nominalistic subordination of reason to experience, whereby, against all ideological speculation, experienced reality itself becomes the focus for the perception of the world. Furthermore, nominalists sought to distinguish between God's Word and human reason. In the realm of revelation, in all matters concerning man's salvation, God's Word is the sole foundation—here reason and experience do not prescribe but confirm; here they do not precede but follow.

These nominalist principles attained great significance in the context of Reformation theology: God's world, reason, and experience belong together the same way as do God's salvation, Scripture, and faith.

Modern scholars have only now begun to cast off their prejudices against the via moderna, which was superseded by the seventeenth-century scientific revolution it had prepared. There is no question that Luther was trained as a nominalist in Erfurt; but the implications of his academic training are still contested and under debate.

Luther proudly referred to himself as a member of the school of Occam: "My master Occam was the greatest dialectician."[8] But he also showed himself to be a child of new times by adding: "But it must be admitted that he could not formulate elegantly."[9] In February 1520 the universities of Cologne and Louvain condemned Luther's theology as heretical. In March he defended himself with an argument derived in both form and content from the nominalistic tradition: "I demand arguments not authorities. That is why I contradict even my own school of Occamists, which I have absorbed completely."[10]

Since the end of 1515 Luther had been criticizing his "master's" teachings on grace and justification with increasing acerbity. Though this fundamental criticism should not be underestimated or ignored, Luther's sharp attacks on his school do not imply that he now totally rejected it and distanced himself from everything he had learned in Erfurt. Such an interpretation would contradict Luther's own statements and ignore the distinction he himself made, along nominalistic lines, between the realms of reason and revelation: a poor, even a dangerous, theologian can nonetheless be an outstanding dialectician, logician, or scientist, as was the case with Occam.

With respect to his teachers in Erfurt Luther was both pupil and critic. He had no illusions about the enormity of the theological gulf between them. And yet, as Trutfetter's "deeply devoted" student he had learned to take

Scripture at its word and to subject even the most revered scholastic theologians to close scrutiny.[11] Luther formulated the idea of loyal opposition and committed it to paper in Erfurt on May 9, 1518, immediately after an unsuccessful attempt to visit Trutfetter at home. Luther had wanted to talk with Trutfetter to explain his critique of scholastic theology, but the professor had had his servant convey the message that he was ill, and Luther left disappointed. Not for us but for Trutfetter this departure must have symbolized Luther's farewell to the via moderna. It is not difficult to understand the motives for Trutfetter's rebuff. It was not Trutfetter the "Church loyalist" seeking to avoid Luther the "heretic"; in May 1518 things had not yet gone that far, although the Dominicans were already about to take up the chase and open the case against Luther. Trutfetter was not dismayed by the first confused accusations of appointed and self-appointed Inquisitors alike. He must have been dismayed by Luther's harsh attack on the very basis of his whole life's work, the significance of Aristotle.

The break between them, that point when loyalty grows into loathing, was as inevitable as it was fair and in the open. Before his programmatic attack in the Disputation against Scholastic Theology of September 1517, which was to cause a great stir in academic circles, Luther wrote to his former professor to inform him of the impending public confrontation. Luther asked his Erfurt friend Lang to pass the theses of the disputation on to Trutfetter, with the message: "Should Aristotle not have been a man of flesh and blood, I would not hesitate to assert that he was the Devil himself. My wish would be for Usingen [Bartholomaeus Arnoldi] and Trutfetter to give up their teaching, indeed stop publishing altogether. I have a full arsenal of arguments against their writings, which I now recognize as a waste of time."[12] With this one sentence the scholarly achievement of a whole life spent in the service of the university was swept aside. "A waste of time": this break was irreparable.

Luther's attack on Aristotle concerned both the via moderna and the via antiqua insofar as neither of them allowed their doctrines to be dictated by the Word of God. But it was the via moderna that had insisted on distinguishing the realms of God's Word and human reason; Trutfetter and Usingen themselves had furnished Luther with the means of opposing the via moderna's violations of this boundary. In his very attack, Luther showed himself to be a splendid pupil.

The reaction of Wendelin Steinbach, a senior colleague and successor of Gabriel Biel in Tübingen, demonstrates how easy it is for us to draw erroneous conclusions from Luther's attack on scholasticism during the early Wittenberg years. Though he had no sympathy with the positions of the type

Luther defended, he did not understand the attacks from Wittenberg as a basic break with the via moderna but rather as a revival of the radical theses of the Augustinian Gregory of Rimini.[13] Gregory was generally considered one of the most significant leaders of the via moderna, and not for a moment did anyone assume that his radical theology of grace implied a break with the moderns. This Tübingen perspective helps us to discern the Erfurt hook in Luther's Wittenberg stance of 1517. Jodokus Trutfetter and Bartholomaeus Arnoldi—who also never became a follower of Luther—had particularly highlighted Gregory of Rimini as a loyal interpreter of nominalistic principles. Trutfetter was not scant with his praise: Gregory of Rimini is an important guide both in theology and philosophy.[14]

In 1507 the still insignificant University of Wittenberg, which had been founded only five years earlier, had the audacity to offer Jodokus Trutfetter a professorship in their arts faculty—and he actually accepted. But, as might be expected, he did not stay long; only one year later he was back in Erfurt. Thus his teaching in Wittenberg remained an episode, but not an inconsequential one. In 1508 the via moderna was introduced at the arts faculty in Wittenberg, and, significantly enough, it was to be taught explicitly in line with the via Gregorii. This innovation can probably be ascribed to Trutfetter. Gregory was a fortunate choice because the Augustinian professors teaching according to the via moderna could now fall back on an authority from their own order. Luther later honored Gregory as the only scholastic who did not deviate from Augustine's theology of grace. Though this praise of Gregory does not correspond with the opinions of his teachers, it must nonetheless be noted that his years in Erfurt had familiarized him with the scholarly achievements of an era that he could never spurn as the "Dark Ages."

It is true that after he obtained his doctoral degree in 1512, tension developed between Luther and the University of Erfurt, which was not prepared to accept his move to Wittenberg. But these differences did little to diminish his love for Erfurt. The ensuing problems were finally settled and Luther was able to establish himself as a professor in Wittenberg. There was nothing to indicate the breach that would come in later years. His relationship with Bartholomaeus Arnoldi remained so close that at the age of fifty Arnoldi decided to enter the Augustinian monastery in Erfurt at Luther's advice.

Martin Luther was a nominalist, there is no doubt about that. The suspicion does arise, however, that there was a link between Luther's university training and his decision for monastic life, that it was because of Erfurt nominalism that he found his way to the Augustinians so quickly and perhaps at all. Roman Catholic Luther scholars have seen a connection here.

According to their view, the nominalists had distorted the image of God into that of an arbitrary god who vengefully, mercilessly pursued anything that incited His wrath, so that one could do nothing but flee from such a god—flee to a monastery. But if we examine the via moderna more closely, we find no trace of this arbitrary God. The fact is that proponents of the "modern way" stressed not God as the "highest being," but as "the personal God" who had revealed and displayed His will to redeem mankind.

There is nothing to indicate that if the young magister had been trained according to the teachings of the via antiqua—for example, in Cologne or Leipzig—he would have taken up the legal career his father had planned for him. Nor can the Erfurt humanists be made responsible for Luther's decision. Yet as we will see, Luther owed a lot to his encounter with them.[15]

But nothing in the program of nominalism itself directed his steps away from the world and to the monastery.

The Impact of Humanism

In Luther's time there was no conflict at all between humanism and nominalism in Erfurt. Just as in Tübingen, where the humanist Heinrich Bebel could adorn scholastic books with his poetry, so Nikolaus Marschalk, a recognized humanist and Erfurt's administrative director, recommended Trutfetter's textbooks in eulogistic verse. The success and confidence of the arts faculty, which knew itself to be in the academic forefront of the time, prevented its students from rejecting scholasticism as obsolete and welcoming the humanists as the sole heralds of a new era.

That Marschalk encouraged students to learn Greek and Hebrew did not have any immediate effect. In Wittenberg Luther began learning Hebrew systematically, using Reuchlin's grammar; and only in early 1519 did Melanchthon teach him to read and draw Greek letters. In view of the usual resentment humanist language studies evoked among theologians Luther's lack of bias is striking. In his very first lecture he went so far as to question the Latin translation of the Bible, which for centuries had been hallowed by tradition. This was probably a legacy of Erfurt: neither the name Reuchlin, the grand master of Hebrew, nor the name of Erasmus, Europe's most famous Greek scholar, were for him new, or suspect. When he entered the monastery he left almost all his books behind, but insisted on taking along his copies of Plautus and Virgil, authors he would quote all his life.[16]

It is unlikely that Luther belonged to a definite circle of humanists. He did not meet Mutianus Rufus, the central figure in Erfurt humanism, until 1515, when he had already been a professor for three years and, as district vicar of the Augustinian Observants, had already advanced to the higher rungs of a monastic career. But his friendships with Georg Spalatin, spiritual counselor to Elector Frederick the Wise, and Johannes Lang, a fellow Augustinian, offered him close contact with humanism. Both were later to become reliable allies in the Reformation movement.

Crotus Rubeanus, who collaborated with Ulrich von Hutten on the satirical, anti-scholastic *Letters of Obscure Men,* remembered his fellow student Martinus Ludher as a budding humanist in the Erfurt days. Alluding to Luther's love of classical literature, which was accessible to him only in Latin, Rubeanus justifiably draws attention to Luther's humanist tendencies.

Yet Luther always knew that he could not equal the elegant humanist artists of the written and spoken word, though this did not particularly disturb him. But in his interpretation of theological sources, the Scriptures and works of the Church Fathers, he did not have to defer to anyone, and he trod a path many of his contemporaries—whether humanists or avowed scholastics—could not follow.

From Magister to Monk

Before Luther had turned twenty-two his life underwent a radical change. On July 17, 1505, he knocked at the gate of the monastery of the Augustinian Hermits in Erfurt and bade the prior to accept him into the order. With this step he relinquished all plans for the future and hopes for a career. After his master of arts examination Martin had received money from his father, which he spent in Gotha, buying the most essential books for his law studies, among them a costly folio edition of the *Corpus Iuris,* the legal code of the Roman emperor Justinian. Just a few weeks later he returned his brand-new legal collection to the bookseller.[17] He no longer needed it because in the meantime a decision had been made that neither his father nor his friends could reverse: the decision for the monastery and against the world.

Hans Luder had gone to considerable expense to offer his eldest son a university education in preparation for a career that might take Martin as high as the post of "learned counselor" and thus to a level of influence in politics, like his cousin Hans Lindemann. But now the father had to watch his authority being disregarded and his carefully conceived plans thwarted. Martin cited a higher authority: hurled to the ground by lightning and close to death, he had pledged himself to the monastery. Even a father, who was entitled—and had a God-given right—to demand obedience from his children, had to respect a vow of this kind. Luther the Reformer would later come to view his earlier decision as a flagrant sin—"not worth a farthing"—because it had been made against his father and out of fear. "But how much good the merciful Lord has allowed to come of it!"

According to a much later report, Martin had been confronted with death once before, on his way home to Mansfeld in 1503, at the end of the winter semester. Hardly had he left the city walls when his dagger pierced his leg, cutting an artery. Only because he was in the company of a friend, who could fetch a doctor, was his life saved. Lying at the edge of the road, he tried to apply pressure to his artery to stop the bleeding till the doctor came. In his distress he implored the Mother of God to help him: "Oh, Mary, help." He was close to dying "with my trust in Mary",[18] as he later told the circle of Wittenberg friends. The critical tone is unmistakable: he should have placed his trust in Christ the Savior, not in Mother Mary!

Whether this accident happened at the beginning or toward the end of his studies cannot be ascertained. The event that took him inside the monastic walls, on the other hand, can be dated with precision. On July 2, 1505, a thunderstorm near Stotternheim brought him close to death once more, and in terror he called out, "Help, St. Anne, I will become a monk!"[19]

Many years later Luther could still recall how appalled his father had been at his vow, and how his friends had tried to change his mind. Occasionally he himself had wondered whether this vow, which had been forced out of him by fear and had thus not been made voluntarily, truly bound him to fulfill his pledge. But all remonstration was in vain, and even his own doubts did not suffice to reverse his decision. On the evening of July 16, two weeks after the incident near Stotternheim, he gave his friends a farewell party, and on the following morning they accompanied him to the Augustinian monastery. The moment of parting had arrived: "You see me today and never again." He was convinced that he was leaving the world behind him forever, as he had promised St. Anne. But things were to turn out differently: "To the world I had died till God thought it was time."[20]

There was a widely held suspicion that monastic vows were nothing more than an excuse for monks to secure a pleasant, comfortable life without having to work or to worry about where their next meal was coming from. Luther was aware of these caricatures, and for this reason he had to point out repeatedly that it was not poverty that had driven him into the monastery. His decision to become a monk had created quite a sensation because the situation in which he received his calling—thunder and lightning near Stotternheim—evoked wide-ranging associations. His friend Crotus Rubeanus

Hans Baldung Grien, The Conversion of St. Paul, *ca. 1505–07: "Suddenly there shone round him a light from heaven" (Acts 9.3). Luther's conversion sometimes was interpreted thus by Augustinians.*

as well as his monastic teacher Johannes Nathin compared Luther's experience with the conversion of the Apostle Paul. The parallel is indeed suggested by the Acts of the Apostles: "And as he journeyed he approached Damascus, and suddenly a light from heaven flashed around him. And he fell to the ground . . . " (Acts. 9.34).

Luther himself did not see his choice of the monastic life in the same light as St. Paul's conversion. In keeping with the 1504 Constitutions of the German Augustinian Observants, he was first subjected to thorough questioning by the chapter, the decision-making monastic assembly, in order to determine whether his wish to become a monk truly came "from God".[21] Only when the answers of a candidate were deemed satisfactory was he admitted to the novitiate, a trial period of one year. When Luther was questioned he must have given an account of the incident near Stotternheim, and the parallel with Damascus is bound to have struck the brothers in the chapter. But the term *conversion,* which was appropriate for Paul, did not apply to Luther; nor was he wrenched out of a life of luxury like St. Francis. He had been raised strictly and "decently." There was no question of turning from unbelief to belief. Luther was not tormented by doubts about God's existence and he was an obedient son of the Church. It was fear for his salvation that had driven him. He wanted to achieve eternal life and was filled with "fear and trembling." He was not converted from Saul to Paul but from the world to the monastery. And this was, in fact, demanded in the admission liturgy. Over Luther, the aspiring monk who lay at his feet, the prior prayed: "Oh, God, who kindles the hearts of those who have been converted from the vanity of the world to the victorious prize of the heavenly calling. . . . May they recognize that the grace of their conversion has been granted gratuitously. . . . Amen."[22]

Thus conversion meant turning away from the world and turning ascetically toward God; that was the medieval monastic tradition. What conversion meant in practice was explained very clearly to the candidate during his first questioning by the prior: killing off one's own will, meager meals, coarse clothing, hard work during the day, keeping vigil during the night, chastising the flesh, self-mortification by begging, extensive fasting, and an uneventful monastic life in one place. Only when the aspirant said yes to all this was he admitted to the novitiate. The admission liturgy as spelled out in the Constitutions concluded with the novice being entrusted to the care of the master of novices, among whose first tasks was acquainting the novice with the Rule of St. Augustine and the Constitutions of the order.

Luther engraved these regulations and precepts so deeply in his mind that his later recollections of the monastery years were still replete with monastic formulations.

Luther did not seek the monastery as a place of meditation and study to exercise a faith he had once lacked. Nor was he looking for a sanctuary of strict morals to protect him from the immorality of the world outside. He was driven by his desire to find the merciful God. And that was precisely what the order demanded of the candidate for admission, as the liturgical formula makes clear. Searching for the merciful God was a crucial part of the monastic life and was by no means a unique expression of Luther's hunger for salvation, out of step with the Community of Brethren.

Before a candidate's first questioning in the chapter house began, he was always apprised of the central condition for acceptance: his search for the gracious God. The prior asked: "What do you seek here?" The reply had to be "The gracious God and your mercy." When the aspirant's own clothing was finally taken from him and exchanged for the habit of a novice, the prior prayed: "Lord, save Thy servant . . . and grant him Thy mercy. . . . Acknowledge this Thy servant, whom we have given the spiritual habit in Thy holy name, of Thy blessing so that he shall deserve to achieve eternal life through our Lord Jesus Christ." The prior's last words to the novice at the end of the acceptance ceremony was the exhortation: "Not he who begins but he who perseveres to the end will be saved."[23] Then the novice was turned over to the novice master.

Thinking back on his time at the monastery, Luther emphasized that it was this search for the gracious God, with its attendant "trembling and fidgeting" which had driven him: "In the monastery I did not think about women, money, or possessions; instead my heart trembled and fidgeted about whether God would bestow His grace on me." The criticism is directed at himself as well as at the monastic tradition when he adds: "For I had strayed from faith and could not but imagine that I had angered God, whom I in turn had to appease by doing good works."[24]

This reproach against the monastic sanctification by works came after Luther's break with Rome, which is not to say that monastic life posed no problems for Brother Martin the Augustinian prior to that critical juncture in his life. With its impressive scope, the initiation liturgy entailed goals and demands that directly concerned the friars' everyday exercise of faith and also proved to be crucial topics to the young professor of theology. On the one hand, the monks confessed that their monastic calling was an act of God's grace, and on the other, they acknowledged their obligation to "fight" under the banner and rule of Christ to attain one day the "victorious prize." When the novice became a full member of the monastic community after his trial year, the prior once again prayed for this reward in the service of Christ: "Oh, God, may our brother sit at Thy right hand at the Last Judgment and be glad that he fulfilled his monastic vows completely."[25] These last words spelled out the mighty tension between grace as gift and as duty.

Yet a monk could count on mighty helpers both in life and later at the Last Judgment. He was as sure of the intercession of the Blessed Virgin Mary and of St. Augustine as he was of the comfort of the Holy Ghost in his battle with the Devil, the evil Adversary, in distress and temptation. Everything needed was available to him, both grace and help; now it was a matter of whether he was capable of making use of the offer and directing all his strength to the ultimate goal.

In the monastery Luther was surrounded by saintly helpers, ranging from St. Anne and the Blessed Virgin to St. Augustine, the founder of the order, but at home these impressive names did not sway the resistance. "The Devil may have had a hand in it," Hans Luder still contended when he attended his son's first mass as an ordained priest. It was, of course, well known that the Devil could produce hail and thunder[26]—but hardly to bring about such a good work as the decision for monastic life! Only with the Reformational breakthrough did the monk begin to discover the Devil's surprising interest in "good" works. But this time Satan had thoroughly miscalculated. As Luther later saw it, by taking his monastic vows he not only acted against his father and tried to take God's will into his own hands, he also caused the Devil a great deal of harm: "I became a monk by driving my head through the wall: against the will of my father, my mother, of God, and of the Devil."[27]

First there were his parents; they had quite different plans for his career. Against the will of God, because He rejects the monastic way of life, not wanting the fearful sinner to seek salvation and refuge in good works. Lastly, the Devil had come to considerable harm since it was in the monastery that the indulgence controversy started. And indeed, at least in the beginning, the weapons Luther used to combat the threat posed by indulgences were truly those of a conscientious monk.

There is one further point to be added: the monastery not only provided the spiritual vision which made Luther assail the indulgences; it also prepared him for the second stage in his career as reformer. By wearing the habit for fifteen years he was able to speak to the condition of a whole generation of nuns and monks who, though drawn by the message of Evangelical freedom, still felt in conscience bound by their vows. Luther had gone the way of Europe's highest and most subtle religion of conscience, the way of the "religious," as monks were called. He trekked years along this path before he could say: "Christ is different from Moses, the pope, and the whole world; He is not just different, He is far more than our conscience. . . . When the conscience assails you, He says: "Believe!"[28]

Piety and Politics: Cowl and Cabal

To the approximately fifty monks at the Augustinian monastery in Erfurt the young magister was an attractive but not extraordinary candidate. When Luther first set foot in the chapter house, the convent had two members who had already preceded him from university to monastery: Johannes von Paltz and Paltz's successor to the Augustinian chair at the university, Johannes Nathin; Johannes Lang and Bartholomaeus Arnoldi were to follow. Apart from Johannes von Staupitz, the vicar general, these were the men who were to be of particular importance to Brother Martinus. Luther had not entered just any monastery; this was the illustrious "Black Monastery," which now housed the *studium generale* of the Saxon Reform Congregation, the only one until a second study center was attached to the University of Wittenberg in 1504.

There has been considerable puzzling over why Luther decided for the Augustinians and not some other order. One factor might have been that the Erfurt monastery had established a fraternity in honor of St. Anne.[29] Such a fraternity allowed the monastic community to reach out to the city beyond monastery walls, through laymen who were also active members. This gave people outside the order, like the student Luther, an opportunity to get a clear picture of the Augustinian community. Moreover, Observantism, the strict observance of the rule of the order, must have attracted one who sought to make a radical break with the world. And finally there was the possibility of studying theology in an order that would not force him to abandon the via moderna, which Luther had learned at the feet of Arnoldi and Trutfetter. After all, the Dominicans were pledged to Thomas Aquinas and the Franciscans primarily committed to Duns Scotus. Though the Augustinians had decided for the via antiqua in their statutes, in practice they granted freedom of choice.

The Erfurt monastery of Augustinian Hermits had played a central role since the beginnings of the stormy history of the order. In 1256 Pope Alexander IV united a number of smaller Italian communities of monks and hermits under the rule of St. Augustine. Like the two larger mendicant orders, the Dominicans and the Franciscans, the Augustinians, too, were caught up in the fifteenth-century quest for reform. Following the Council of Basel an "Observant" reform movement was also established among them. Its objective was the return to strict adherence to the rule of the order, which had gradually been loosened to adapt to the practical requirements of life. Henceforth communal recitation of the Divine Office and communal meals were to be required again, the rule of silence was to be respected, private property—especially books—was forbidden, the habit of the order was to be uniform, the prior's permission was needed to leave the monastery premises, and all dealings with women were strictly prohibited.

When they were founded the mendicant orders served two important functions: as the Church's answer to criticism of its wealth—it had long since become the largest land owner in Europe—and as a reaction to demographic changes that confronted the Church with daunting problems. The secular clergy could no longer cope with the demands arising from increasing urbanization and found the mendicant orders an effective aid in ministering and preaching to the new urban masses. The hermits had originally settled in remote areas; now they were expressly charged with pastoral duties in the cities. Even north of the Alps there were Augustinian monasteries in many cities by the fourteenth century.

The peaceful coexistence of mendicant monks and secular priests did not last long. Rivalries and overlapping spheres of responsibility led to fierce conflicts between diocesan organizations and the heads of orders. The fifteenth-century era of reform was also an era of controversy. The mockery of "priests as dumb as beasts" and "lazy, gluttonous monks" was by no means just the product of Reformation propaganda, nor was it spread exclusively by laymen.

Thus the relationship between the regular and secular clergy was badly in need of repair. Johannes von Staupitz—appointed head of the German Augustinian Observants in 1503—had written an expert opinion in Tübingen three years earlier, admonishing members of parishes to return to their priests and underscoring the obligation to attend mass and confession at their parish church. Johannes von Paltz, in Erfurt, like Staupitz an observant Augustinian, made exactly the same point by instructing all laymen to heed the authority of the local priest as the vicar of Christ in the congregation, however dubious his conduct.[30] The fact that, as he was convinced, there was little hope that the secular clergy would reform—"unless God miraculously intervenes"—did not nullify the obligation of obedience to the parish priest.

The organization of the orders was not bound to the existing diocesan structure of the Church. Provinces were independent from the bishop, and the individual provincials, heads of the provinces, reported directly to their general in Rome. The mendicant orders' simple, efficient structure was threatened directly by the new reform endeavors of the Observants, for now a second form of organization was superimposed on the provincial system. Since 1430 Augustinian monasteries had, for the purpose of reform, been withdrawing from the provincial structure to unite into independent reform congregations with no regard for provincial boundaries.

To enable such congregations to flourish and achieve the desired reforms, popes granted them special privileges that were to lead to grave discord. The Augustinian Observants were, for example, permitted to appoint their own vicar general, who was totally independent of the provincials and subject only to the general of the order. This development went so far that vicars general could, by appealing to the pope, withdraw their obedience from the general of the order. This privilege was also written into the Constitutions of 1504. From this moment on an irreparable rift in the order was only a brief step away. Reform or unity—the foundations for this structural alternative of the age of Reformation had already been laid.

Internal but noisy quarrels between the "reformed" and the "Conventual" or non-reformed monasteries now added complications to the bitter competition among the various orders and the sharp tensions between the monks and the secular clergy. Johannes von Staupitz is often accused of having provoked the decisive clash between the two factions of the Augustinian order in 1510. But this internal strife had already commenced full force under his predecessor, Andreas Proles. Proles had succeeded in expanding the congregation, which originally numbered five monasteries, to include twenty-seven at the end of his period in office.

Expansion had taken place at the expense of the provinces, and the incorporation of hitherto conventualist houses rarely occurred without a bitter struggle. Proles was not slow to excommunicate "stubborn" monks and priors if they refused to join the reform congregation. He had secured the necessary outside pressure by gaining the support of temporal authorities like the city council of Nuremberg and of the Saxon prince, Duke William III, great-uncle of Luther's protector Frederick the Wise.

The year 1474 had seen Proles' success in winning the Erfurt monastery for the Observantine cause. When he tried to reform the Königsberg monastery in Franconia, however, it looked as if he had gone too far. The provincial categorically refused and was able to impel the general of the order in Rome, Jacob of Aquila, to intervene. Proles was removed from his post as vicar general and was threatened with excommunication should he try to add any more monasteries to the Observant congregation or ever again invoke the help of the temporal authorities.

This seemingly peripheral episode, one among many tensions in the late medieval Church, is extremely important for our understanding of the protection the electors of Saxony later afforded the Reformation. Every actor in this suspenseful play operated within a framework determined by princely politics and care for "his" territorial Church on the one hand and the concern of the Church for reform and unity on the other.[31] Duke William reacted sharply to the disciplinary measures against Proles and lodged a complaint with the Saxon provincial because the latter had dared to protest to the general against the secular authorities' help in the matter of monastic reform. William's line of argument was to set a precedent: this was, according to his complaint, one of "our" monasteries, which we have taken under "our protection."[32]

In the meantime Proles had notified the duke that his Observants, the Erfurt Patres, wanted to resist the instructions from Rome and were determined to appeal from their poorly informed general to "our most Holy Father the Pope." The duke, preferring to keep the matter under his own jurisdiction, immediately wrote to the general, requesting him to rescind his decree against Proles. The provincial then carried the controversy to an extreme. He disregarded the duke's call for restraint and put the indeed unambiguous instructions of the general into effect. The monasteries of Gotha, Langensalza, Sangerhausen, and Königsberg, where Observantism had only just been introduced, returned to the provincial association. The duke then took drastic action, issuing instructions to his officials to break the resistance to "a thorough reformation." The Conventual monks were expelled and by order of the duke could no longer count on the protection of the secular authorities.

The Conventuals were deeply aggravated about their expulsion. A notice posted on the door of the Augustinian church in Gotha read: the Observants "despise us as if they were saints." The biting mockery of this statement cannot be missed, for the man in the street knew all about monastic "saintliness"—"the more sainted, the more tainted." The persecuted faction made drastic threats—and gained the laughs for their side: since they were no longer deemed worthy to inhabit the "sainted halls" of the reformed monasteries, they would go to the bordellos and see to it that the ladies posted themselves at the monastery gates in the evening. The women could then recount their carnal experiences with these so saintly friars.[33]

The Conventuals seemed to be maintaining the upper hand in their dispute with the "saints," for all the intermediaries who went to plead the case of the reformed congregation in Rome were flatly turned back. Only with the death of the general of the order did things change for the Observants. Jacob of Aquila died in the spring of 1476; shortly afterward a new provincial was elected in Saxony. And on July 1, 1477, a compromise was negotiated that must be regarded as a clear victory for Proles and Duke William. The provincial had to give his permission for the contested monasteries to leave the province and join the reform congregation. Only the Königsberg monastery in Franconia was left to him as a token consolation. And, because as it was now decreed, the mandates and measures against Proles were infringements upon the privileges granted to the congregation by the pope, they were clearly invalid.

Yet this was not the end of the conflict. The problem was a structural one and could not be settled by compromise. A fundamental decision had to be made, a choice between the Conventuals and the Observants. The Conventuals had a "progressive" approach with what one might call "common sense," and were intent on adapting their monasteries to the demands of the time; the Observants desired "reform" and thus insisted on strict observance of the rule of the order. Then as now, one side or the other had to be supported. Even the historian, with his chronological advantage, must choose sides. As usual, value judgments are concealed in the choice of adjectives. The "power-hungry" duke and the "ruthless" Proles had split the order—that is one view of this complex situation. But the opposite one had much to support it, too: a "sincere" prince and a vicar general "imbued with a fine sense of concerned religiosity" were carrying out reforms long overdue.

Apart from the question of a fair evaluation, this history of conflict in the Augustinian order provides a precise insight into the hopes and fears of the community Luther joined in the summer of 1505. First of all, Luther found admission into a monastic congregation which was not merely on paper committed to Observantism and thus to seclusion from the world, moral austerity, meditation, and intensive study. At the same time, however, the congregation was well versed in the ways of the world and did not hesitate to pursue the political aim of asserting itself in the power triangle of prince, provincial, and pope. Above all, these conflicts between congregation and province dragged the order into the increasingly important field of battle between Roman centralism and territorial autonomy.

The tension between pluralism and unity was already an acute problem in the late medieval Church, long before the time of the Reformation. The mendicant orders failed to meet the challenge of the time because the goals of reform proved to be incompatible with the desire for unity.

Reform or Unity: The Fundamental Question of an Age

Johannes von Staupitz merely inaugurated a new phase in this old conflict when he tried to continue with different means the successful but perilous policies of his predecessor Proles. Once again we should beware of the tempting use of tendentious adjectives which abound in the literature when, for example, "fanatical" Brother Martin is found on the side of the Observants, and the "power-hungry" Vicar General Staupitz is seen plotting to unite the non-reformed Saxon province with his reformed congregation. Both the dreams and the deeds of Staupitz deserve a second look.

For the cause of the Reformation it would prove to be of singular importance that Luther did not enter a monastery somewhere on the periphery, in Frankenhausen or Sangerhausen, but the one that regarded itself as the central bastion of the respected congregatio reformata in Allemania, the German Augustinian Observants. Andreas Proles belonged to the Erfurt community; with Johannes von Paltz and Johannes Nathin, the monastery housed the leading theological authorities at the university who were at the same time the most dedicated spokesmen for radical monastic reform.

The German Observants elected as Proles' successor Johannes von Staupitz, destined to become one of the key figures of early Reformation history.

Johann von Staupitz, Luther's mentor and vicar general of the Augustinian Observant congregation. By an unknown master, ca. 1520.

Staupitz was a Saxon nobleman born in Motterwitz near Leisnig. He studied at the universities of Cologne and Leipzig, and in 1500 he obtained his doctoral degree in theology in Tübingen, where he had been prior of the Augustinian monastery since 1497. Shortly after being awarded his doctorate, he returned to his motherhouse in Munich, which he headed until 1502. His theological and monastic career, unlike Luther's, was totally unconnected with either the university or monastery in Erfurt. Except for confrontation.

In 1502 Elector Frederick the Wise summoned the approximately forty-five-year-old Augustinian prior from Munich to assist in the founding of the University of Wittenberg. Staupitz became the first dean of theology in the winter semester of 1502–03 and held the chair of biblical theology for ten years, until he handed it over to Martin Luther in 1512.

The congregation considered him an attractive candidate to succeed Proles, what with his connections with the Saxon dynasty, which were as good as his predecessor's, his academic status as a professor and founding dean, and his interest in procuring a second Augustinian *studium.* And indeed on May 7, 1503, he was elected vicar general of the Augustinian Observants, a position he held for seventeen years. The circumstances had changed substantially by August 28, 1520, when he laid his office in the hands of the Nuremberg Augustinian Wenzeslaus Linck in Luther's birthplace of Eisleben. Linck was to be the last vicar general of the German reformed congregation. In the end, the Reformation both destroyed and completed the reform work of Proles and Staupitz.

With the election of Staupitz as vicar general the Erfurt monastery fell within his jurisdiction. His presence at the monastery on July 3, 1506, is well documented. It is not certain, however, whether during this visitation Staupitz met Brother Martin for the first time. In his late (1555) account, Matthäus Ratzeberger, Luther's generally reliable biographer, may have been referring to this first encounter.

Ratzeberger relates that as a novice Luther had to do sweeping and cleaning as a "menial servant," so that little time remained for his studies. When Staupitz learned of Luther's overwhelming interest in Bible studies, he convinced the prior to assign him a duty more appropriate to a magister; the task Luther was then set was to memorize the Scriptures by heart, page by page. Luther applied himself so diligently "that Doctor Staupitz was very much impressed, and kept a special eye on him above all others."[34]

Just as during his happy school years in Eisenach, Luther once again found a paternal friend, who not only encouraged him academically but also provided him with spiritual counsel, something Luther desperately needed, for as a priest and then a professor he was soon to be confronted with duties that imposed on him a hitherto unfamiliar responsibility: the cure of souls.

Luther was ordained in the spring of 1507, possibly on Easter Saturday, April 3; not even a year had elapsed since his solemn admission as a full member of the monastic community. A month later he celebrated his first mass at the Augustinian church on May 2. When he almost ran away in the midst of the service this was not a result of agitation or stage fright but of overpowering awe at the majesty of God. The master of novices or, as another report has it, the prior, was able to persuade Luther to complete the celebration of the mass.

There is no reason to play down this incident out of fear that the suspicion might arise that Luther was religiously unstable and subject to a morbid sense of sin. Nor had he—as Luther fans prefer to argue—fallen victim to typical medieval scruples that the Reformation discovery would later help him to overcome. No, Luther had undergone what would remain one of his fundamental religious experiences. Speaking about Isaac's prayer for his wife Rebecca, the old Luther, during his last set of lectures on the Book of Genesis, described the fear and trembling he had felt during his first mass: "'And Isaac prayed to the Lord for his wife, because she was barren: and the Lord answered his prayer'" (Gen. 25.21). A prayer like this, which breaks through the clouds and reaches up to the majesty of God, is not easy. I, ashes, dust, and full of sin, speak with the living, eternally true God. This cannot but cause one to tremble, as I did when I celebrated my first mass. . . . Joyous faith, however, which rests on the mercy and the Word of God overcomes the fear of his majesty . . . and rises boldly above it."[35]

"This cannot but cause one to tremble"—a sense of the "mysterium tremendum," of the holiness of God, was to be characteristic of Luther throughout his life. It prevented pious routine from creeping into his relations with God and kept his Bible studies, prayers, or reading of the mass from declining into a mechanical matter of course: his ultimate concern in all these is the encounter with the living God.

In his years as a monk there was indeed one additional factor: Luther knew himself to be unworthy to appear before this holy God. His restless monastic life, with its intense asceticism and mortification, was informed by a conviction held throughout the Middle Ages—that only by striving for perfection could one even hope to exist before God.

Luther's invitation to Johannes Braun to take part in the young priest's first mass in Erfurt indicates this very anxiety. When Luther there spoke of the holy God—holy in all His works, including the mass—who had called him in his unworthiness to the priesthood, he was not indulging in empty phrases or pathological sentiments. Braun must immediately have understood Luther's request for support with his personal presence and prayers of intercession, so that with the liturgy of the mass Luther could, as he put it, "make a sacrifice pleasant to God."[36] The reform climate of the age had sharpened the sense of high dignity and responsibility of the priesthood. The indignation which found expression in bitter stories about arrogant monks and lazy priests given to beer and women stemmed from the ideal of the "man of God," the priest who lives a "perfect" life, the monk who takes seriously his service at the altar, on the pulpit, and in the confessional.

This was the climate of thought in which Luther lived his monastic life, the incentive for his arduous attempts to follow the Augustinian rule to the letter. The ideal of true perfection was also to determine the position he was soon to take when Vicar General Staupitz initiated the final stage of the old dispute within the order. For the moment, however, Brother Martin was still unperturbed by the controversy over Observantism. Since the summer semester of 1507 he had been devoting himself to the study of theology under the guidance of Johannes Nathin, the senior Brother, who held the Augustinian chair of theology at the University of Erfurt. Despite intensive research, nothing of significance has as yet been discovered about this theologian who must have been a real influence on Luther in Erfurt. Have all his writings disappeared, or did he really never publish anything? All we know is that he received his master's degree in Erfurt thirty years before Luther was enrolled there and that he spent four to five years in Tübingen as a younger colleague of Gabriel Biel, holding survey lectures on the whole range of theological fields.

Luther thoroughly prepared himself for his first mass with the help of Biel's comprehensive exposition of the canon of the mass, published in 1488. Now, as a student at the theological faculty, he was introduced by Nathin to the best theological textbook of the time, Biel's dogmatics, which was also a survey of the history of Christian thought. The renowned nominalist from Tübingen had, in the traditional medieval manner, laid out his voluminous tome as a commentary on the scholastic theological textbook known as the *Sentences of Peter Lombard.* Philipp Melanchthon later related that Luther had studied his Biel so intensively that the Reformer was able to quote whole pages from memory. How assiduously he pored over Biel's commentaries can still be seen from the critical comments he wrote in the margins of his own copy in earlier and later years. Even when Luther was already distancing himself from theology as he had been taught it, he still recommended Biel as a fine guide for priests hearing confession.[37]

The Augustinian monastery in Wittenberg. After Luther's marriage in 1524, it was also his family home.

In April 1508 the budding theologian was already listed as a lecturer of his order next to such experienced Doctors as Paltz and Nathin.[38] It is unlikely that Luther had much personal contact with his senior colleague Johannes von Paltz. Though still an official member of the monastery, Paltz, after a clash with his brethren, left Erfurt in a huff in 1505 to become the prior of the monastery at Mühlheim near Koblenz. Despite his physical absence Paltz was very much present through his widely read writings, which were characterized by a readily understandable, colorful type of medieval piety. He was the spokesman for the monks, extolling the monastic way of life as the sure way to salvation.[39]

But Johannes von Staupitz had already turned his attention to Luther. Not only did he encourage the young, striving monk theologically and spiritually, he also involved him in the turmoil of his daring Augustinian politics. Luther became a wanderer between two monastic factions—even literally so during the years before he obtained his doctoral degree in theology. First Staupitz summoned the Augustinian lecturer from Erfurt to Wittenberg for the winter semester of 1508–09 to lecture on Aristotle's *Ethics,* and instructed him to prepare for his doctorate in theology at the same time. In the autumn of 1509 Nathin, undoubtedly having discussed the matter with Staupitz, recalled Luther to Erfurt. This summons must have come as another surprise to Luther and most likely resulted from the death of a member of the Erfurt faculty. After rendering one and three-quarters years of service to his home monastery as a member of the theological faculty in Erfurt he was recalled by Staupitz to Wittenberg.

God's Prospective Adviser

If we are to evaluate the events of these years, it is essential for us to recall the situation in 1509. Luther was in Erfurt again and thus committed to obedience to the monastery and prior there. If opposing instructions from the vicar general would give rise to a conflict, there could be only one legal recourse—an appeal to Rome. And this is precisely what happened. First Staupitz succeeded in winning a victory in 1510 that the Observants might all be assumed to have rejoiced in: the Saxon province accepted Staupitz as their new provincial. It was an unprecedented development—the Conventuals had voluntarily chosen as their superior the leader of the "reformed" movement they had so bitterly opposed. There is no question that the personal union combining the posts of provincial and vicar general in one figure was a turn of events the majority of reform houses should have applauded.[40]

And yet it was precisely this marked success that led to the stormiest conflict Staupitz had to weather in his troubled years in office. The tragic element in this drama was that all concerned were taking their commitments seriously and pursuing goals consistent with their vows and views. Moralizing judgments scholars have also made in this case obscure the fact that the order in its quest for reform-in-unity had drifted into a hopeless situation.

Let us start with the perspective of Staupitz: Proles' successful expansion of the reform congregation led to a continuing war—interrupted by the occasional truce—with the provinces, which intensified whenever the congregation, with its power base in Saxony and Thuringia, encroached on Bavaria, Württemberg, and the Rhineland up to Bruges and Antwerp. What happened in Gotha, where expelled monks pilloried the "saintly" Observants, did not remain an exception. The records are full of the shrill voices of bitter Conventuals or Observants, depending on which faction happened to have the upper hand at the moment and was able to "hold" or "capture" a monastery. The personal union Staupitz achieved was a first, important step toward putting an end to this state of affairs and effecting pacification if not peace. Had this policy been carried out consistently, it might have led to the homogeneous reform of all the German provinces of the order. Indeed it could have shown the way to reform of all the monastic orders and hence strengthened the Church in a time of great need.

But there was more at stake than reconciliation of the two warring factions. The conflict of 1510 is so intriguing from the perspective of reform and Reformation history because, quite apart from issues of unity, it uncovers a real alternative which hitherto has been overlooked. The crucial question which drove a wedge into the reformed congregation was indeed a real one: Is Observantism the way for monks, who strive for perfection and save themselves by withdrawing from a wicked world and by forming islands of obedience in a hopelessly secularized Church? Or are the Observant monasteries launching pads for reform of the whole Church, so that the whole life of perfection is directed toward mission and the salvation of others by preaching and ministering to the lay people?

There was complete agreement on the fact that the Church was in a state of sharp decline, down to its noblest institutions, the mendicant orders. But the means for improvement were as hotly debated as the aims of a truly basic reform. Under Johannes von Staupitz this clash of principles became manifest: more than two-thirds of the congregation supported Staupitz and accepted his view that the proposed union with the province would further the Observantist cause, in that it was a way for the order to shoulder its task as nucleus of a general reformation. But seven monasteries, including the two most important ones in the congregation, Nuremberg and Erfurt, were convinced that Staupitz was putting the whole cause of reform in Germany at risk: the world once fled would break through the walls of the monastery. They thus appealed to the general and sent two friars to Rome, one of them Martin Luther. Despite intensive research, the name and origin of the other cannot be established. Their protest mission proved abortive. They stayed in the Holy City for one month, but in early February 1511 were forced to set out on their approximately six-week journey home without having accomplished a thing. Under the date of January 1511 the curial records show the laconic entry: "The Germans have been forbidden to appeal from their vicar to the pope."[41]

The question of obedience had thus been settled: Rome had ordered the monasteries to relinquish all resistance against Staupitz. At a chapter meeting in Jena in July 1511 Staupitz explained his solution, which now had Rome's explicit approval. Speaking to representatives of the seven opposing monasteries, he pointed out that the personal union would not affect any of

Wittenberg at the time of Luther's death. After a woodcut by Lucas Cranach the Elder.

the congregation's privileges. The Observants would continue to elect their own vicar general, who would only need papal confirmation in accordance with their statutes. Then their vicar general would be appointed head of the Saxon province by the general of the order. The Conventuals were thus completely outmaneuvered: there should be no fear of infiltration or contamination by the non-reformed Augustinians.

How deep sentiments were running may appear from the fact that Staupitz's arguments could not bridge the gap: even a solution guaranteeing the Observants all the rights and clear predominance could not meet with general approval. The opposition of the seven monasteries, though weakened, was not crushed. Nuremberg, a majority in Erfurt, and the other five monasteries adhered to their position. Luther, on the other hand, sent to Rome at the beginning of the year to represent the opposition to Staupitz, now left its ranks and bowed to the decision of Rome.

The so-called resistant monasteries remained unmoved and succeeded in blocking the union. As Staupitz wanted to effect reform without jeopardizing unity, he had to give up his plans in view of the surviving resistance. From 1512 on there is no further mention of a union. Staupitz was as circumspect in healing the inflicted wounds as he had been prudent—if unsuccessful—in trying to reunify Conventuals and Observants. In the late summer of 1511 Luther was transferred from the Erfurt monastery to Wittenberg. With him went his friend from the student years, Johannes Lang, who advanced to become prior in Erfurt after he earned his doctorate at the end of 1516.

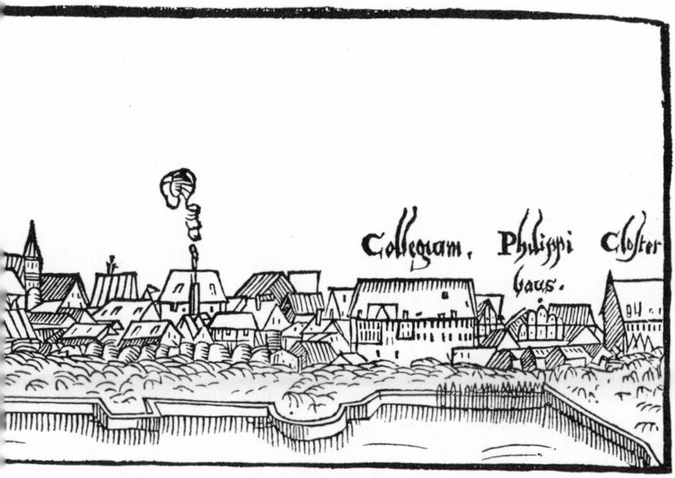

But also the relationship to Nuremberg, whose monastery and municipal council had formed the other center of resistance, got Staupitz's special attention. It was placed on a totally new footing: a special kind of religious fraternity was created, modeled after humanist sodalities. A circle of erudite monks and burghers calling itself "Sodalitas Staupitziana," or Staupitz Society, was to become a focal point of Staupitz's influence and later a distribution center for Luther's writings. Staupitz confirmed his good relations with Nuremberg during Advent of 1516: day after day he ascended the pulpit to preach God's unerring grace to large crowds of appreciative citizens. The "Booklet" with a revised form of these sermons in Latin and German versions provides us with the most impressive document of his spiritual theology, a theology shaped by the Epistles of St. Paul and the works of Augustine.[42]

On May 5, 1512, the regular chapter meeting of the congregation convened in Cologne and confirmed Staupitz in his office as vicar general. A further decision concerned Luther: he was appointed deputy to his prior Wenzeslaus Linck and put in charge of the Wittenberg *studium generale,* thus being entrusted with the academic training of the younger members of the order. On October 19, five years before he posted his theses, Luther received his doctoral degree in theology and was accepted into the university senate three days later. Now the time had come to take over the task for which Staupitz had so long groomed him: the *Lectura in Biblia,* the chair of biblical theology, which Luther was to hold until his death.

TWO IMPORTANT dates have to be added to complete the account of Luther's monastic career. At the chapter meeting in Gotha in May 1515 Luther was elected district vicar in charge of ten monasteries, including his own motherhouse in Erfurt, with its Augustinian *studium* the only study center of the Saxon congregation apart from Wittenberg. His correspondence documents how seriously he took this office. October 1518 marked a radical turning point in the life of this Augustinian who had been so long and deeply involved in all the affairs of his order. When after his unsuccessful negotiations with Cardinal Cajetan in Augsburg Luther ran the risk of being arrested on the instructions of the general of the order, Vicar General Staupitz consequently gave him dispensation from his vow of obedience. Although this cannot be equated with removal from the order and Luther thus continued to wear his habit, the stage in his life that had begun thirteen years before in the chapter house in Erfurt had now come to a close: it was obedience that had propelled him along the road to Wittenberg. To his vicar general he was indebted for the monastic platform that was to become the starting point for the Reformation of the Church. His Augustinian brethren were the ones who had not contented themselves with seeking their own perfection in Observantism, but had decided instead to fashion their monasteries into staging areas from which to reach out for the betterment of the Church and world.

Luther himself was convinced, however, that he owed the vicar general infinitely more: "Staupitz laid all the foundations." At this point we have reached the most critical juncture in Luther's theological career, a career we can from now on observe at first hand in his publications, which were to appear with breathtaking speed for the next thirty-five years. The effect of these writings was felt far beyond his order, with consequences that were more than once to alarm even their author.

Luther's most vicious antagonist, Johannes Cochlaeus, circulated the rumor that at some point after the chapter meeting in Jena Brother Martinus had betrayed his faction by changing sides and thus had "succumbed to his Staupitz." By implication he suggests that this explains the summons to Wittenberg in the summer of 1511.[43] And indeed there are still those who suspect that the doctorate was the reward for betrayal.

Is there any truth to the claim? Luther certainly did not "succumb to his Staupitz," he submitted to him, and only after the general of the order had definitely decided to support the vicar general. Luther's later criticism of the strict Observants, whom he ironically called "little saints"—one is reminded of the Gotha pamphlet—was trained at the brothers' selfish striving for saintliness without regard for the obedience they had pledged in their vows.[44]

Luther demanded obedience as district vicar and preached it as Reformer, when his subordination to the prior had become obedient faith in Christ. For Luther it is faith that fulfils the very first commandment: "Hang on to me, I will provide and help you in your hour of need"—thus the *Large Cathechism* of 1529. In this sense did the Reformation discovery transform monastic obedience into faith in Christ.

Yet there is a grain of truth in Cochlaeus' allegation insofar as Luther's steep climb in the academic world was due to the protection of Johannes von Staupitz. Though the suspicion that Luther "succumbed" or was even bribed is unfounded, especially since Staupitz's decision to have him seek the doctorate stems from an earlier time, the fact remains that Staupitz took a special interest in Luther's career. At the beginning of the winter semester of 1508–09 the young lecturer and six other Augustinians were suddenly transferred to Wittenberg. Brother Martin did not even have time to notify his friend Braun of his departure. In Wittenberg Luther immediately had to begin lecturing—every day from two until three in the afternoon. He had been assigned the field of moral philosophy, to be taught in the *via Gregorii.* He chose to leave no doubt that he would have much preferred to devote himself completely to biblical studies, for philosophy was for him a constant waiting for the real thing; he longed to get to the heart of the matter.[45] But this time there was no chance of a dispensation because the university statutes were clear: an instructor in the arts faculty, a student in the theological faculty. The first stage on the long road to the doctoral degree in theology was initiated under Johannes von Staupitz as dean on March 9, 1509. Luther was now "admitted to the Bible" and from then on had to give his students brief elucidations of scriptural texts. The next step followed in the autumn, just before he was recalled to Erfurt: he acquired the rank of *sententiarius,* which entitled him to give lectures on the doctrines of the Church. Because he was ordered back to Erfurt and then sent afoot to Rome, his academic career was delayed by a full year, as a comparison with his friend and fellow Augustinian Wenzeslaus Linck clearly shows: At the beginning Linck was only one month ahead, but in the end he received his degree thirteen months earlier than Luther.

Staupitz's decision to have Luther prepare for the doctorate must have included Linck as well; it was made well before the union dispute, quite likely in 1508. Staupitz pursued long-range personnel policies. In 1512 he could put these two handpicked men in charge of the Wittenberg monastery: Linck—already a Doctor—as prior, and Luther—not yet a Doctor, but well on his way—as subprior and director of the *studium generale.*[46]

Luther's course of action in the Observantism dispute was anything but servile and career-minded. He had been loyal to the Erfurt line in rejecting the plan for union. With this he had dared to stand and be counted against the vicar general's policies, although this was the man who had offered him an academic future. Only after all legal options had been exhausted and his party's appeal had been rejected by Rome did he side with Staupitz and thus show the vicar general the obedience that the latter now had the right to expect. This novel way of viewing Luther's behavior is completely in keeping with all we know about the Reformer's character. Throughout his life he was incorruptible and prepared to place principles before friendships. At such moments he counted neither his interests nor his inclinations.

Luther never maneuvered into higher positions of power. In fact he was given to doubt about his own abilities and was never fully convinced that he could truly fulfil people's expectations. As he remembered so well, under the pear tree in the garden of the Wittenberg monastery Johannes von Staupitz had to use all his eloquence to convince the master of arts that he should now also go for his doctorate in theology.

Luther argued that he was fully occupied with his Aristotle lectures and did not feel equal to the burden of studying theology at the same time: "I shall not survive that for long." Staupitz's reply: "The Lord has big plans. He needs good and wise people who can assist Him in heaven as well. When you die, you will there have to be His adviser."[47]

The Fool in Rome

"I, too, was so foolish as to carry onions to Rome and bring back garlic."[48] For a sixteenth-century peasant this was a bad deal: "shit for shillings." Luther had hoped to gain spiritual strength through his visit to the Holy City, but he left Rome with mixed feelings. The Augustinian cause that had brought him there plays hardly any role in his later recollections; there is no suggestion there of an inner involvement in the issue he has to bring to the general's judgment—he simply does not mention the matter. His journey to Rome was a business trip, concerning the affairs of his order. His personal involvement concerned a different aspect of Rome: incredible opportunities of furthering the cause of salvation for others and himself as well.

The indulgences offered for sale in Germany were only poor imitations of what could be purchased in Rome. There was first of all the opportunity of a general confession, which he wanted to seize to unburden his soul, making it as clean as it had been after baptism. But his own salvation was not his sole concern. He celebrated mass in Rome daily; at the altar of St. Sebastian, he once even said several in a single hour. He caught himself regretting that his parents were still alive: "for I would have loved to deliver them from purgatory with my masses and other special works and prayers." But priests from many European countries rushed to the altar with similar wishes in mind, so that it was difficult to put his pious intentions into action: "There is a saying in Rome: 'Blessed is the mother whose son celebrates a mass in S. Giovanni in Laterano on a Saturday.' How I would have loved to make my mother blessed there! But the waiting line was too long and I did not get a turn."[49]

Because Luther wanted to free his grandfather—Lindemann or Heine Luder—from purgatory, he scaled the Santa Scala on his knees, with an Our Father on each step, for by praying this way it was said one could save a soul. When he had arrived at the top, however, skepticism overtook him: "who knows if it is really true."[50] Despite such misgivings on these steps he was nevertheless deeply awed by the rich variety of opportunities for an enterprising pilgrim to earn all sorts of merit. His flash of doubt is certainly not indicative of the emergence of a 'new skepticism' and the onset of the Enlightenment; his kind of skepticism rather arose from the conviction that God would not allow Himself to be pinned down in this way. It was this sense of reverence, typical of his faith and piety from the start, which stayed with him on the road to reformation.

His experiences in Rome were ambivalent. He was convinced he would be able to find salvation in abundance in this center of Christendom and was thus determined to make the most of the unique opportunities being offered everywhere. For Luther Rome was and would remain the glorious city of the steadfast martyrs, where the apostles Peter and Paul and the first Christians had witnessed to their faith with their blood. But noticing how much blasphemous behavior went on in the Holy City disturbed him deeply. "Where God builds a church, the Devil puts a chapel next door"[51]—would that this saying applied to Rome! But, as people put it, Rome was worse: "If there is a Hell, then Rome is built on it." This saying would later take on a new significance when the monk became the reformer, unmasking the pope's alliance with the Devil.[52]

Luther's criticism of Rome was not a result of his excommunication by the pope. Later he remembered clearly the shock and horror he had felt in

View of the Roman Forum through the Titus Arch

Rome upon hearing for the first time in his life flagrant blasphemies uttered in public. He was deeply shocked by the casual mockery of saints and everything he held sacred. He could not laugh when he heard priests joking about the sacrament of the Eucharist. In Erfurt his first mass had set him shivering with awe; now in Rome he had to stand by while servants of God thought it funny to blaspheme the most sacred words of institution: "Bread thou art and bread thou shalt remain; wine thou art and wine thou shalt remain."[53]

In their anger and outrage others, unquestioned in their loyalty to Rome—including Erasmus and Adrian Floriszoon (later Pope Hadrian VI)—could execrate the city and its priests. Luther's tone was more quiet but probably also more dismayed: "Well, I was a serious and pious young monk who was pained by such words."[54] The "pain" echoes again and again. The rampant immorality he saw and heard about shattered his ideal of Rome; the saying that was in the mouths of so many contemporaries also proved true for him: "The closer to Rome, the worse the Christians." But his belief that the Church in which he had been raised was the true Church remained unaffected.

Luther was by no means alone in his criticism. Erasmus of Rotterdam, who had journeyed to Rome five years earlier, wrote as unambiguously: "With my own ears I heard the most loathsome blasphemies against Christ and His apostles. Many acquaintances of mine have heard priests of the curia uttering disgusting words so loudly, even during mass, that all around them could hear it."[55]

Ten years later Ignatius of Loyola, founder of the Jesuit order, was advised against going to Rome—because of its stupendous depravity. It was Pope Hadrian VI who officially admitted the deplorable state of affairs. He had his nuncio read out a confession of guilt to the Diet of Nuremberg in January 1523: "We know that for years there have been many abominable offenses in spiritual matters and violations of the Commandments committed at this Holy See, yes, that everything has in fact been perverted. . . . The first thing that must be done is to reform the curia, the origin of all the evil."[56]

But it was not the moral decay, the vice and immorality at the center of the Church, that made Luther start to doubt whether the pope was indeed the vicar of Christ. Luther had been a "fierce papist," and for that reason later hesitated to publish his early writings, which were still "loyal to the pope." His misgivings began with the indulgence controversy in 1518–19, when he had to recognize that God's grace was for sale in Rome. Even after the papal excommunication had driven a wedge between Wittenberg and Rome, the Reformer never claimed moral superiority. It is not the profligacy of the

Church of Rome that divides us, "there are just as many bad Christians among us as under the pope."[57] It was not Rome the proverbial cesspool of vice that gave birth to Luther the Reformer.

Luther's reminiscences of his trip to Rome are an invaluable aid to understanding why the Augustinian monk started on that lonely journey which would ultimately bring him to the reformation breakthrough. The question he posed at the top of the Santa Scala—"Who knows if it is true?"—was gradually transformed into the fundamental quest for the reliable basis of all Church doctrine. Long after the event, in August 1582 Luther's son Paul reported a conversation with his father about the experiences in Rome: My "dearest father" told me that when he was climbing up the Santa Scala and praying at every step he suddenly remembered the words of St. Paul: the just shall live by faith. Thus his prayers were answered and from then on he considered the Epistle to the Romans his "highest authority."[58]

Historically the account is untenable; we know nothing of a "breakthrough experience" in Rome. And yet it is illuminating to see Luther's trek to Rome in light of later events. Any serious search for salvation is subject to the question: who knows if it is true? For Luther, God's promise became the only life-sustaining answer that could provide certainty: the just shall live by faith.

CHAPTER V

The Reformation Breakthrough

Discoveries along the Way

Eighteen months after his return from Rome the master of arts and monk became a doctor of theology and professor in Wittenberg. From the critical perspective of his time Luther now joined the ranks of those stupid monks who endlessly argue about anything and nothing, who set themselves up as guardians of piety and proper doctrine, yet are unable to count their own toes. Learned theologians in his own country and ecclesiastical authorities in Rome at first dismissed the questions Luther raised as typical monkish bickering. There was as yet no way to predict that a man had appeared on the scene who was seeking the truth in the mazelike roads to salvation offered at the time.

It is crucial to realize that Luther became a reformer who was widely heard and understood by transforming the abstract question of a just God into an *existential quest* that concerned the *whole* human being, encompassing thought and action, soul and body, love and suffering. The search for salvation was not reserved for the intellect alone. Nor did Luther liberate himself from scholastic theology by retreating into his private self; it was not the battle of heart against head that drove him to raise his voice and take a more critical view of medieval theologians whom his own teachers still regarded as authorities. It was not that he found them too scholarly for the delicate business of faith, but rather that he did not find them scholarly enough. For Luther careful heed to the Scriptures was the only scholarly basis for theology and thus the reliable standard of truth.

Much in the development of this ascetic monk and Bible scholar seems obscure at first. As no writings by his professor of theology in Erfurt, fellow Augustinian Johannes Nathin, have surfaced as yet, there is no way of knowing what Luther might have learned at his feet. Luther cannot have spent more than a few months living under the same roof with Nathin's predecessor, Johannes von Paltz, before the approximately sixty-year-old Paltz became prior of the Augustinian monastery in Mühlheim, where he died in

March 1511. And Luther never devoted so much as a line to Paltz's vast oeuvre. He makes clear that for him there was only one Johannes in his monastic world, Vicar General Staupitz. He knew how great a debt he owed Staupitz. Writing only a year before his own death, Luther praises him for "first of all being my father in this doctrine, and having given birth [to me] in Christ."[1]

When this "rebirth" took place is uncertain. Even Luther recognized the decisive turning points only in retrospect. As the exact dates are so hotly disputed, what can be said about the whole matter? At the end of the road to becoming a reformer stood the discovery that the Scriptures confirmed what he had sensed, sought, and seen with increasing accuracy by living with the God of the Scriptures. With the intellectual and emotional inquisitiveness that was always to characterize him, he analyzed the Scriptures to determine the truth of what Johannes von Staupitz had taught him. The only obstacle still in his way—as he put it in his 1545 *Rückblick*, an autobiographical fragment referring to 1518 and 1519—was the central text in St. Paul's Epistle to the Romans: "For therein [in the Gospel] is the righteousness of God revealed" (Rom. 1.17).

A series of discoveries that proved only retrospectively to be steps in the same direction freed him from the fundamental notion common to all medieval schools of thought: the righteousness of God is the eternal law according to which He who is unattainably holy will judge all men on doomsday. Then justice will be done, and punishment or reward meted out.

But did the Middle Ages know nothing about the righteousness that Christ grants as a gift? Had no one read the apostle Paul before? Was not Luther's answer that the faithful participated in Christ's righteousness identical with the answer that St. Augustine had given in *Spirit and Letter?* Thus twentieth-century critics have tried to dismiss Luther as "superficial" and an "ignoramus." At best, they would, in their ecumenical generosity, grant that he had discovered "for himself" what had always been plain to every good Catholic.

These critics are right in that St. Paul was generally regarded as "the" apostle in the Middle Ages and that St. Augustine had been thoroughly assimilated in biblical commentaries. But both of them were always understood to say that the Church distributes Christ's righteousness like the talents that can be increased by hard work and good investment. Christ's justice does not make a man righteous before God; it puts him in the position to become righteous. At the Last Judgment the righteous God will decide if the faithful have used and truly done justice to Christ's gift. What is completely new about Luther's discovery is that he sees God's righteousness as inseparably united and merged with the righteousness of Christ: already *now* it is received through faith. That is the reason all the faithful will be able to stand the test: "That is the long and the short of it: He who believes in the man called Jesus Christ, God's only Son, has eternal life—as He himself says (John 3.16): 'For God so loved the world, that he gave his only begotten Son, that whosoever believeth in him should not perish, but have everlasting life.'"[2]

Why did Luther become more than an original thinker and a fascinating witness to a vanished world? He was able to become the Reformer of the Church because he was prepared to test his discovery against the Scriptures and ultimately to anchor it there. Only thus could it achieve lasting value for him and lay claim to validity for the whole Church. The "Gates of Paradise" were opened to him and a flood of knowledge swept over him once he had succeeded in grasping the passage (Rom. 1.17) in which St. Paul quotes the prophet Habakkuk: "The just shall live by faith" (Habakkuk 2.4).

"I am not good and righteous, but Christ is."

Three Versions of the Central Reformation Discovery

Now this alone is the right Christian way, that I turn away from my sin and want nothing more to do with it, and turn alone to Christ's righteousness, so that I know for certain that Christ's goodness, merit, innocence, and holiness are mine, as surely as I know that this body is mine. In his name I live, die, and pass away, for He died for us and was resurrected for us. I am not good and just, but Christ is. He in whose name I am baptized, receive the Holy Sacrament, study the Catechism—He will embrace us if only we trust in Him.[3]

The expression "righteousness of God," said D. Martinus, used to hit my heart as a thunderbolt. For when under the papacy I read: "Deliver me in thy righteousness" [Psalm 31.1], item: "in thy truth," I immediately thought righteousness was the grim wrath of God, with which he punished sin. I hated St. Paul with all my heart when I read: "the righteousness of God is revealed in the Gospel." But afterward, when I saw how it went on, that it is written: "The just shall live by faith," and also consulted St. Augustine on the passage, then I became glad, for I

> learned and saw that the righteousness of God is His mercy through which he regards us and keeps us just. Thus was I comforted.[4]
>
> As much as I had hated the expression "righteousness of God" before, I now loved and treasured it. Thus this passage from Paul became truly the gate to Paradise. Later I read Augustine's treatise "Spirit and Letter," where I unexpectedly found the same interpretation of God's righteousness as the righteousness with which God clothes us by making us righteous. And although it is still imperfectly formulated and does not clearly explain everything connected with God's imputation, I nonetheless was pleased to find him teaching the righteousness of God as that righteousness through which we are made righteous.[5]

It was a matter of life, not of thought, study, reflection, or meditation, but of life in the most comprehensive sense of the word. From now on the life of the Church and the life of Christians in the world would be the theme that guided and shaped all he did and wrote.

Luther's discovery was not only new, it was unheard-of; it rent the very fabric of Christian ethics. Reward and merit, so long undisputed as the basic motivation for all human action, were robbed of their efficacy. Good works, which Church doctrine maintained as indispensable, were deprived of their basis in Scripture. This turnaround touched on more than individual faith and righteousness; the totality of life was affected and thus had to be reconsidered. Throughout the coming years of confrontation and conflict, there was only one objective: to unfold the implications of this discovery and to see to it that they gained a wide hearing.

The Devil and the Cloaca

Luther's autobiography, which appeared in 1545 as the preface to the first edition of his Latin works, has been the subject of exhaustive scholarly research. Nonetheless, Luther is not yet heard out, and his urgent admonition and warning has been missed: "Reader, be commended to God, and pray for the increase of preaching against Satan. For he is powerful and wicked, today more dangerous than ever before because he knows that he has only a short time left to rage."[6]

"Today" means that Luther not only discovered the Gospel but also roused the Devil, who is now raging terribly and gaining an unprecedented power of absolutely new satanic proportions.

This is no longer the Devil who, in a triple alliance with "sin" and "world," seduces the voluptuous flesh of man against his better "self." The medieval poltergeist is virtually harmless in comparison with this adversary, who, armed with fire and sword, spiritual temptations and clever arguments, has now risen up against God to prevent the preaching of the Gospel. As long as the righteous God reigns far away in Heaven, waiting for the end of the world, the Devil, too, will remain at the edge of world history. But the closer the Righteous One comes to us on earth through our belief in Christ, the closer the Devil draws, feeling challenged to take historically effective countermeasures. The Reformation symbol of Christ's presence is not the halo of the saint, but the hatred of the Devil.

Transforming Luther into a forerunner of enlightenment means dismissing this warning of the Devil's growing superiority as a remnant of the Dark Ages. But that would be to deprive Luther's life of the experience of the Devil's power, which affected him as intensely as Christ's. Take away the Devil and we are left with the Protestant citadel, the "better self," the conscience, which thus becomes the site of the Last Judgment, where the believer, confronted with the laws of God, acknowledges that he is a sinner and declares himself at the same time to be righteous by virtue of Christ's sacrifice.

It is precisely this conventional, conscience-oriented morality that man's innermost self struggles to fulfill, and that Luther, to the horror of all well-meaning, decent Christians, undermined. The issue is not morality or immorality, it is God and the Devil. This patent encroachment on conscience desecrates the very thing that elevates man above the beasts—his knowledge of the difference between good and evil. The two great turning points of the Reformation age, the Lutheran and the Copernican, seem to have brought mankind nothing but humiliation. First man is robbed of his power over himself, and then he is pushed to the periphery of creation.

"The Spiritus Sanctus [Holy Spirit] gave me this realization in the cloaca." If this is the site of the Reformation discovery, man's powerlessness is joined by ignominy.[7] Must the trail of the Reformation be followed this far? There is a dignified way out: by cloaca Luther did not mean the toilet, but the study up in the tower above it. That, however, would be to miss the point of Luther's provocative statement. The cloaca is not just a privy, it is the most degrading place for man and the Devil's favorite habitat. Medieval monks already knew this,[8] but the Reformer knows even more now: it is right here that we have Christ, the mighty helper, on our side. No spot is unholy for the Holy Ghost; this is the very place to express contempt for the adversary through trust in Christ crucified.

Christ in the privy helping one to resist the Devil is certainly anything but genteel. In their propriety later centuries recount only how Luther hurled his inkwell across the room at Wartburg Castle. If the Devil must be mentioned, then at least with decorum. There is no truth in that polite legend, and it masks the actual situation. Bluntly quoting Götz von Berlichingen (immortalized by Goethe in this form: " . . . er kann mich im Arsch lecken" [*Faust,* act 3]), Luther attests to the birth of Christ in the filth of this world.[9] The Son of God was truly born into the flesh, into the blood and sweat of man. He understood men because He experienced—to the bitter end—what it meant to be human.

As powerful as the Devil is, he cannot become flesh and blood; he can only sire specters and wallow in his own filth. The manger and the altar confront the Devil with the unattainable. Both the demonic, intangible adversary of God and the Son of God are present in the world, but only Christ the Son is corporeally present. Anyone who goes further, making the Devil into a living being, is superstitious. The cloaca is a revealing place. It unmasks the Devil's powerlessness as well as man's. Although far removed from propriety, it is also a place of faith, the Christian's place in life.

Thus the final sentence in Luther's *Rückblick* cannot be ignored without suppressing a facet of his belief. Wherever the Gospel is preached and bears fruit, the Devil is there to get in the way—that is his nature, "today" more than ever! Fear of the Devil does not fit in with our modern era, for belief in the Devil has been exorcized by attractive ideologies. But in the process our grasp of the unity of man has been lost: living with the real Christ in one's faith means being a whole person as opposed to an intellect that subscribes to a mere idea of Christ.

The Devil will readily help theologians to "elevate" the zealous, fighting, wrathful, loving God of Israel into the philosophical concept of an "Omnipotent Being."

For Luther the disembodiment of God into an impressive idea is one of the Devil's decisive misdeeds. Satan may be no doctor of theology, but he is very well trained in philosophy and has had nearly six thousand years to practice his craft. All the encouraging victories of God which occur prior to the Last Judgment melt under the Devil's glare. Arguments are of no help against the Devil; only Christ can come to our aid. Satan's wisdom is thwarted by the statement "the just shall live by faith"[10]—faith not in an idea but in a God who, under the banner of the cross, is fighting for a world the Devil, too, is trying to win. Satan's power is not unlimited; he must stay within specified bounds, but until doomsday they encompass the whole world.

The Devil's filth personified: the "birth" of the Pope and his curia

The Born Reformer

There is a further misinterpretation of Luther's *Rückblick,* one deriving not from an omission but from a twisting of his words. Luther describes his strenuous road to the Reformation, warning twice—at the beginning and at the end of the account—that the first volume of his collected early writings is still deeply embedded in the papacy. "The reader must take into account that I am not one of those who suddenly, out of nowhere, achieve perfection and penetrate the Scriptures."[11]

A true theologian is made by life, with its tribulations and struggles, not by philosophizing and speculating. But despite this frequently expressed warning, the popular image of Luther ignores these experiences, struggles, successes, hopes, and fears, and reduces his development to two stages: first the desperate monk and then the self-confident Reformer from the moment he—suddenly—grasped the true meaning of verse seventeen of the first chapter of St. Paul's Epistle to the Romans.

Even specialists in the field cannot escape the temptation of depicting the professor from Wittenberg as so much of an ivory-tower scholar that he seems to have been engaged in a systematic research program, as if all he had had to do was to arrange his various exegetical discoveries and after a brief analysis draw the appropriate conclusions that led him directly to the Reformation. Finding the correct approach or starting point is then viewed as the crucial factor, and Luther was evidently successful in that regard: he had to test scholasticism by the standard of St. Augustine and then to find his way from St. Augustine to St. Paul in order to acquire the key to the Scriptures.[12] Thus armed, Luther was ready to enter the indulgence conflict and from there to proceed "logically" to a repudiation of the pontifical Church.

But not even an ordinary academic career runs so smoothly, and not even Luther was in a position to advance according to plan. Discovering the Scriptures was a process fraught with surprises and not infrequently with perplexities. He kept finding new passages that spoke to him in the voice of the living God. Scholarship alone would neither have provided this challenge nor would it have been able to cope with it. The Divine Office and the confessional, meditating and reading the Bible, uncertainty and doubt, fasting and keeping vigil to the very limits of his physical powers—all these accompanied his first attempts to unseal the Scriptures for his students and to test the viability and persuasive power of his exegetical conclusions in academic disputations. The simultaneous struggle of religious experience, practical life, and scholarly penetration was intensified in the beginning conflict over the Church. Luther once mentioned that St. Augustine was only able to testify to the apostle Paul's message of the gift of Christ's righteousness because of the violent provocation to which he was subjected in his clash with the Pelagians, the opponents of God's grace.[13] Here personal experience is speaking.

With Augustine against Aristotle

The name of Augustine of Hippo, one of the Church Fathers, is the first definite clue to Luther's development. In 1889 and 1890 serendipitous finds in the Ratschul Library in Zwickau provided insights into Luther's beginnings that had hitherto been hidden from scholars and would not have been so comprehensively available even to his own contemporaries. What came to light were a number of books Luther had studied as a young monk. They were filled with his own underlinings and marginal notes.

Thanks to the Zwickau discovery we can date his study of Augustine as far back as the autumn of 1509. One of the surviving books from the Augustinian library he used in Erfurt is an edition of various writings by Augustine, printed under the title *Aurelii Augustini opuscula plurima* in Strasbourg in 1489. Luther had noted on the title page: "St. Augustine died in the year of our Lord 433. Now, in the year 1509, that is 1076 years ago."[14] The date of death is incorrect—Augustine died in 430—and shows how poor Luther's knowledge of historical facts still was. But the comments he wrote in the margins of the book in 1509 prove that by studying Augustine he had discovered the contrast between the Church Father and Aristotle, and had begun to work out a theological position of his own.

The marginal notes do not yet register all the implications of the contrast; they probably only dawned on him gradually. Not until the great disputation against scholastic theology in September 1517 was this early interest in Augustine to bear fruit. That was where the battle cry "contra Modernos," "contra Aristotelem"—against the moderns, against Aristotle—could be heard.[15] But the early notes on Augustine already point out the confusion that arises when the boundaries between scholarship and wisdom, between human speculation and divine revelation, are no longer respected. Then theology *and* philosophy suffer: "Augustine can even use reason to prove that the whole of philosophy is foolishness. Imagine what that means!"[16]

At about the same time, meaning in the 1509–10 winter semester in Erfurt, Luther annotated Augustine's two most extensive late works, *De Trinitate* (*The Trinity*) and *De Civitate Dei* (*The City of God*), about the inner nature of God and the history of the Church. These comments, too, end in critical dismay: "I find it more than astonishing that our scholars can so brazenly claim that Aristotle does not contradict Catholic truth."[17]

Luther immediately integrated what he read in Augustine into the survey lectures in theology he was preparing at the same time. He inveighed against the scholastic doctors, using the Holy Scriptures more pointedly and systematically than had hitherto been the case. Philosophy can never grasp man's true nature, namely that he is God's creature.[18] It cannot comprehend the meaning of the biblical definition of the soul as "the image of God" (Gen. 1.27): "There I rely on Scripture against all rational arguments and say with Paul: If an angel—that means a Doctor of the Church—descended from heaven and taught differently, he should be damned."[19]

What an unknown monk in an inconspicuous monastic cell in Erfurt was committing to paper here would one day lead him to the historic pronouncement on the political stage of the Diet of Worms: "Here I stand, God help me, amen"—a statement that was not an affirmation of himself but an expression of his loyalty to the Scriptures, a loyalty conducive from the very start to generating clashes, even with the authorities. Even if an emperor came down from heaven!

The question of how many angels could dance on the head of a pin was soon being cited by the humanists to demonstrate the stupidity of the scholastics. Luther, too, took an interest in this seemingly abstruse problem, not in order to solve it but in order to point out that faith dwelt in a realm of its own. The question is not as ridiculous as the answer: as with the soul, all we know about angels is what is revealed in Scriptures: "Everything that is added to faith is certainly only imaginative speculation"[20]—unfounded and thus uncertain, pure invention.[21]

This is an adumbration of the principle of the new Wittenberg theology that Luther would formulate seven years later "against the whole of scholasticism": "The whole of Aristotle is to theology as shadow is to light."[22] Contemporaries immediately recognized the import of the attack, as Aristotle, who had become academic theology's great authority in the course of the thirteenth century, had provided the terminology and categories used to establish the central concepts of the Holy Scriptures and Church doctrine: God is the "prime mover"; the soul, as "form," determines the human being; justification takes place through the "infusion" of "the power of grace"; the sacrament of the mass transforms the "substance" of bread and wine; man is "free" to decide between good and evil. Gaining a critical grasp of all these basic notions and finding new biblical terms for them was to cost Luther years.

The knowledge that there was an infinite, qualitative distance between Heaven and earth became an established principle for Luther as early as 1509: all human thought, as noble, effective, and indispensable as it might be to solve problems in the world, does not suffice to fathom salvation because it cannot reach Heaven. Questions of faith must be resolved through the Word of God or not at all. The temptation—or compulsion—to sanctify the words of man and believe in them is satanic. When God is silent, man should not speak; and what God has put asunder, namely Heaven and earth, man should not join together.

Thus not even Augustine, especially Augustine the neo-Platonist, could become the new, infallible authority, because that would merely have been replacing one philosophy with another, substituting Plato for Aristotle. Augustine was the exemplary scriptural exegete, who, since 1509, had given Luther the means to demonstrate the extent to which theology had degenerated into a mouthpiece for Aristotle.

The alternative is clear: whatever transcends the perception of empirical reality is either based on God's Word or is pure fantasy.[23] As a nominalist Luther began making a conscious distinction between knowledge of the world and faith in God,[24] but through Augustine he realized that his school lagged far behind its own basic principle: Scripture was being violated by philosophy.

Prior to 1509 Brother Martin had been given "not Augustine but Scotus" to read.[25] Augustine was not a compulsory subject of study under the Augustinian rule. Thus, as Luther wrote in October 1516, one year before he posted his theses, his enthusiasm for Augustine did not stem from loyalty to the order: "I do not defend Augustine because I am an Augustinian; before I began reading his works he meant nothing to me."[26] But once he had discovered Augustine he was so enthralled by all the new ideas he encountered there that he did not read Augustine's works, he "devoured" them.[27] This enthusiasm bespeaks the joy of discovery, not an uncritical attitude.

Thus the year 1509 prepared the way for an unusual medieval alliance between Augustinianism and nominalism. Before Luther recognized the Church Father as a fighter against the "enemies of God's grace" and came to appreciate him as a reliable interpreter of the apostle Paul, the nominalistically trained magister could already welcome him as an ally in the battle against philosophy overstepping its bounds.

The First Lectures in Wittenberg

We must keep in mind that Luther had already put forward the Holy Scriptures as a program and the decisive standard of faith prior to his trip to Rome in 1510. Looking back on his long journey, Luther mocked himself as a "mad monk." But the "mad" pilgrim was not nearly as naive as he appeared in retrospect. Luther's ironic recollection is, however, a reminder that criticizing scholasticism, even in connection with central problems, did not yet constitute a Reformational turning point. The pursuit of the righteousness of God did not end in the discovery of the "Scriptural principle"; it really only began there.

Luther was twenty-nine when he was offered the chair of biblical theology in Wittenberg as Johann von Staupitz's successor. The lectures he held on the Psalms from 1513 to 1515 were probably his first as a full professor. The independence that had already been so striking in 1509 once again came to the fore. Luther probed one text after the other, hour after hour, trying to get through the words to the Word. The thrilled expectation of discovering God's Word in the Scriptures could become reality only through the interpreter's inner dedication in prayer and meditation combined with intensive scholarly work on the text.

Arriving at indisputable theological positions entails more than overcoming inner resistance; there are textual ambiguities to deal with as well. Careful analysis reveals how extensively Luther used the scholarly aids at his disposal and studied the biblical exegeses of the Church Fathers and medieval authors.[28] His efforts to learn Hebrew in order to get as close to the original text as possible were no less thorough, though the Vulgate, the Latin version of the Bible, remained his exegetical basis throughout his life. And this was as it had to be, for a doctor of theology had a commitment to the Church, not to himself. Because of the public responsibility of the office, the familiar text had to be used to render theological results generally intelligible.

The crucial obstacle to understanding the Scriptures, however, is man's inner resistance to the Word of God. The objective scholarly interpreter must become an affected listener. For Luther that meant first becoming a sinner, confessing his true condition, for the Word of the Scriptures unmasks all men as sinners (Rom. 5.12) and thus as enemies of God (Rom. 5.10). That makes "humility" so important. Exercising humility means justifying God—that is Luther's unprecedentedly bold claim. The justification of God means conceding the truth of His verdict: all men are sinners. Admitting God is right is what Luther calls the "obedience of faith" that must precede all righteousness by faith.

This obedience is the central theme of his first course of lectures on the Psalms: by judging himself and humbly submitting to God's judgment here, man anticipates God's Last Judgment. It is still the monk who is the prototype of the true Christian as long as he corresponds to the traditional ideal and is truly "in the condition of repentance," without wanting to improve on God's judgment. Thus the very thing Luther does *not* mean is "sinner," yes, but in my humility just a bit righteous too.

Despite the monastic orientation of his theology of humility and despite the fact that his students were primarily monks, Luther never lost sight of the Church as a whole: exegesis is done in the service of preaching.

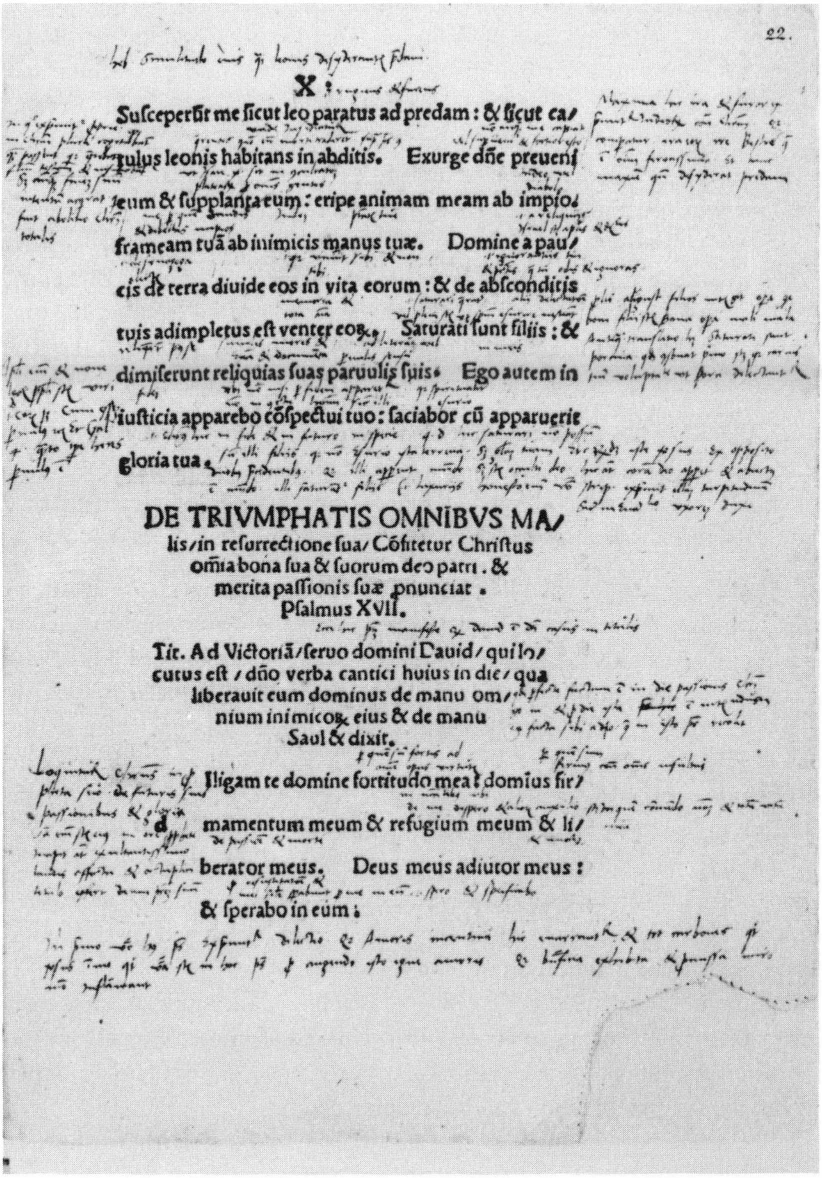
22.

X

Susceperūt me sicut leo paratus ad predam: & sicut ca/
tulus leonis habitans in abditis. Exurge dñe preueni
eum & supplanta eum: eripe animam meam ab impio:
frameam tuā ab inimicis manus tuæ. Domine a pau/
cis de terra diuide eos in vita eorum: & de absconditis
tuis adimpletus est venter eoꝝ. Saturati sunt filiis: &
dimiserunt reliquias suas paruulis suis. Ego autem in
iusticia apparebo cõspectui tuo: saciabor cū apparuerit
gloria tua.

DE TRIVMPHATIS OMNIBVS MA/
lis/in resurrectione sua/ Cõfitetur Christus
omīa bona sua & suorum deo patri. &
merita passionis suæ ꝓnunciat.
Psalmus XVII.

Tit. Ad Victoriā/seruo domini Dauid/qui lo/
cutus est/dño verba cantici huius in die/qua
liberauit eum dominus de manu om/
nium inimicoꝝ eius & de manu
Saul & dixit.

Diligam te domine fortitudo mea: dominus fir/
mamentum meum & refugium meum & li/
berator meus. Deus meus adiutor meus:
& sperabo in eum.

Luther's handwritten interlinear commentary to psalms 16.12–17.3a (Vulg.). Page from the manuscript of his first lectures on the Book of Psalms (1513–15).

One of the central issues of religious life at that time was the question of repentance, confession, and punishment. That Luther made this particular topic his own is evidence that his theology was rooted in the preaching and ministry of the Church. Luther opposed self-complacency and "slaving away" at good works as well as the breathless pursuit of self-justification when he taught repentance as the basic form of every Christian's life and not just an occasional emergency measure for the sinner. It was not a tedious "Church obligation" to which a Christian had to subject himself at least once a year; it was the constant profession of humility: only God is righteous.

The ideas Luther developed in his two major courses of lectures, the first on the Psalms and the second directly afterward on the Epistle to the Romans, are summarized in the first two of his ninety-five theses of 1517:

1. When our Lord and Master Jesus Christ said, "Repent" [Matt. 4.17], he willed the entire life of the faithful to be one of repentance.
2. This word is misunderstood if it is taken to refer to the sacrament of penance that is received from time to time.[29]

At the beginning of 1516 his two-semester lecture course on the Epistle to the Romans—November 1515 to September 1516—had probably reached chapter three. In his marginal notes to verse twenty he interpreted the righteousness of God as he was to describe in 1545: a liberating discovery.[30] Although he did not yet appreciate all the consequences, the conclusion he immediately drew was that being a sinner, man could achieve nothing before God but could be justified by grace alone: "ergo sola gratia justificat."[31]

This grace could be obtained only by faith—"sola fide"—trusting in the Word of Christ.[32] The voice of the now "Reformation" exegete still sounds unpracticed, and a series of discoveries still remain to be made. The experience of inner contrition, what Luther called "plowing oneself," was still the precondition for justification by faith.[33]

Not until the beginning of 1518 would faith be understood as such great trust that the Christian as confessant could and should rely totally on the word of absolution. Henceforth he was encouraged to disregard his inner state; the last precondition had been eliminated.[34]

The printed commentary to St. Paul's Epistle to the Galatians completes the development Luther outlined in the autobiographical *Rückblick* (his recollection of his Reformation breakthrough) with which he prefaced his collected works.[35] It is the year 1519; the Reformation "discovery" of justification by faith has been clearly expressed and worked out. Humble self-judgment has, it is true, not been eliminated, but now it is understood as a condemnation of the conscience: as a total sinner, I can only rely on God, who has committed Himself to my salvation.[36] The new righteousness cannot be proven because it "is not based on our works: it is founded on the promise of God, who does not lie."[37]

Faith is no longer chiefly obedience, it is trust in the reality of God's unshakable love. God is just because He can be taken at His Word and will remain true to His promise.[38]

Luther's own *Rückblick* furnishes the clearest account of how he succeeded in understanding the central sentence: "For [in the Gospel] is the righteousness of God revealed" (Rom. 1.17).

> I hated the expression "righteousness of God," for through the tradition and practice of all the doctors I had been taught to understand it philosophically, as the so-called "formal"—or, to use another word, "active"—righteousness through which God is just and punishes sinners and the unjust. But I could not love the righteous God, the God who punishes. I hated him. . . . I was very displeased with God, if not in secret blasphemy, then certainly with mighty grumbling, and said: should it not be enough for miserable sinners eternally damned by original sin to be oppressed by all sorts of calamity through the law of the Ten Commandments? Must God add suffering to suffering even through the Gospel and also threaten us with His righteousness and His wrath through the Gospel too? . . . I pondered incessantly, day and night, until I gave heed to the context of the words, namely: "For [in the Gospel] is the righteousness of God revealed, as it is written: 'The just shall live by faith.'" Then I began to understand the righteousness of God as a righteousness by which a just man lives as by a gift of God, that means by faith. I realized that it was to be understood this way: the righteousness of God is revealed through the Gospel, namely the so-called "passive" righteousness we receive, through which God justifies us by faith through grace and mercy. . . . Now I felt as if I had been born again: the gates had been opened and I had entered Paradise itself.[39]

This terse, vivid account makes it all too easy to overlook the new discoveries Luther was continually making both before and after the great turning point in his life. Luther's theology cannot be reduced to a single point; his work was invigorated and stimulated by the joy of discovery. But this joy was more than mere intellectual satisfaction because questions of life and death were at stake. Between 1513 and 1519 he experienced a series of breakthroughs of this kind, although none as significant as that of the understanding of God's righteousness and justification by faith.

Yet, as Luther pointed out at the beginning of his professorial career and at the end of his life, all his discoveries could not exhaust the wealth of the Scriptures. In his early Psalm lectures he said: "If you, O human being, cannot grasp some scriptural passage completely and are capable of unveiling the concealed truth only in part—be it as large as it may—then know that there is witness there that points past you and will only be revealed to you or others in the future."[40] One might assume that this was a beginner exercising the humble restraint befitting a monk and that the expert, the Reformation Luther, would overcome it. But that was not the case. A note in Latin was found next to Luther's deathbed; he wrote it two days before he died:

> No one can understand Virgil in his Bucolics and Georgics unless he has spent five years as a shepherd or farmer. No one understands Cicero in his letters unless he has served under an outstanding government for twenty years. No one should believe that he has tasted the Holy Scriptures sufficiently unless he has spent one hundred years leading churches with the prophets. That is why: 1. John the Baptist, 2. Christ, 3. the Apostles were a prodigious miracle. Do not profane this divine Aeneid, but bow to it and honor its vestiges.

This is followed by the statement "We are beggars" in German, and in Latin again, "That is true."[41]

A doctor of theology for thirty-four years, practiced in the translation and exegesis of Scripture—notwithstanding all this experience, he had to admit that he was overwhelmed by the depth and wealth of the Scriptures, which no man would ever fathom in a single lifetime.

In view of Luther's life-long struggle to clarify the Scriptures in questions crucial to salvation, his "last words" may sound like a confession of resignation. This, however, is misleading. The point is rather that to study the Scriptures is like a journey—full of surprising discoveries. He once compared his scriptural studies to a walk through a forest: "There is hardly a tree in this forest that I have not shaken and obtained apples or picked berries from."[42] Certainly his statement did not lack pride, but neither did it make any claim to his having finished with the Scriptures.

During his last, ten-year(!) course of lectures on the Book of Genesis (1535–45), Luther took another extended walk through the woods and gathered the fruits of his roamings into concentrated summaries of his theology. Although these lectures deserve to be used as an introduction to

Jacob's dream (Gen. 28.10ff.): the dream becomes reality. Woodcut from Luther's translation of the Old Testament, 1523.

Luther's world of faith, they have nearly fallen into oblivion owing to the prevailing interest in the young Luther as well as to the complex history of how they have come down to us.

The theme throughout is the wild rage of the Devil, who seeks unceasingly to destroy the Son of God everywhere: "He is his target,"[43] because His birth and death are the agents of divine redemption. The Devil's battle against Christ makes the "walk through the woods" necessary and divests it of its arbitrariness. Luther's single-mindedness is demonstrated in his interpretation of the story of Jacob's ladder. Jacob was fleeing from his brother Esau. One night he dreamt of a ladder that reached into Heaven, with angels of God ascending and descending it (Gen. 28.12–14). Luther was able to illustrate the whole of his Reformation theology by means of Jacob's dream at Beth-el: through God's Word and spirit, Christians are led up to Heaven and, in their faith, united with Christ. Christ Himself, however, descends to lead Christendom. The ladder connecting Heaven and earth is the incarnation of God; it is what the Devil hates most and is perpetually fighting against. The Devil wants to tear the faithful away from Christ, their ladder to Heaven.[44]

Luther had long been a master in finding ever new and graphic ways of combining the various realms of God's work—in Christ, in justification, in the Creation—into a single vision. Now the kingdom of the Devil had received sharp contours as well. Thirty years earlier "sin, world, and Devil" had still formed the traditional medieval phalanx of evil. To escape the Devil one had had to avoid the world and seek salvation where there was no room for sin—most safely at a monastery. But now the Devil was the opponent of the world created by God, seeking to destroy all the forces involved in protecting God's creation: family and economy, state and Church. Luther's walk had taken him out of the monastery and into the world.

"Today you have the Bible"

The objection has been raised that as an exegete Luther was not scholarly enough and that his erudition could not compare with that of an Erasmus or a Melanchthon. The Reformer's biblical exegeses are accused of being "overrun by dogmatism and edification."[45] Luther would have protested vehemently against being compared with Erasmus: scriptural exegesis is far more than philology and historico-critical method. He would, however, have acknowledged Melanchthon's erudition, and in fact did: apart from the Holy Scriptures, Melanchthon's textbook of theology, his famous *Loci communes,* was the most important work for a Christian to read. "I can find no book under the sun in which the whole of theology is so excellently arranged."[46]

Luther was extremely critical when it came to judging the value of his own books. The commentary on the Epistle to the Galatians (1531–35), the exposition of the Book of Deuteronomy (1523), and his sermons on four chapters of the Gospel of John (1528–29) he thought worth preserving because they were his only works really to contain theological teachings. He found the rest of his writings interesting solely from a historical point of view; they enabled a reconstruction of his laborious quest and the course of the whole conflict. The person who wants to become a theologian today, he wrote, has "a major advantage: he has the Bible."[47]

Luther did not simply mean the books of the Old and New Testaments; they had, after all, long been familiar and—at least to theologians—freely accessible. Luther was pointing out that laymen now demanded that theologians furnish biblical grounds for their statements. They had to be experienced in Scripture-based argumentation and to have acquired criteria to assess the relative significance of various biblical passages. The conversance with the Bible that Luther had attained and exercised was what he wanted to pass on to posterity.

Luther laid his exegetical foundations in his first lectures on the Psalms and continued to perfect his interpretations throughout his life. As a good nominalist he first concentrated on the manner of expression *characteristic* of Scriptures; this enabled him to acquire a grasp of their *particular* subject matter on the basis of linguistic usage[48] and obviated the alien mediation of Greek philosophy. His criticism of scholasticism did not culminate in the common reproach that its line of argument was too formal, logical, or dialectical. What made his own tradition suspect to him was its belief that Aristotle's philosophy offered a timeless, comprehensive system of interpretation that even provided a key to the Scriptures. But the Holy Ghost has His own language; one must become His student, learn to spell, and then, going out from the individual word, gradually acquire the whole vocabulary. A single misconstrued word can distort the sense completely. The concept of the "righteousness of God" is a striking example and not an exception; Luther had to toil away at other passages with equal intensity before he could penetrate the meaning of the words.

Luther knew that a good translator had to be bilingual. "Spelling" did not imply a slavishly literal, word-for-word rendering; it was the thorough comprehension of the linguistic usage of the Scriptures. That is the secret of the originality and power of the Luther Bible. Command of one's own language and the ability to use it to its best effect presupposes listening to the way the common people speak: "One must ask the mother at home, the children in the street, the man at the market, and listen to how they speak, and translate accordingly. That way they will understand and notice that one is speaking German to them."[49]

One of the Saxon princes once asked Luther to explain what the well-known scholastic "ways" or schools and the "school conflict" were actually about. Luther provided him with a very lucid answer, not missing the opportunity to interpret the "way" of Wittenberg as a reformed "via moderna." What linked the "terminists," the old and new nominalists, was attentiveness to linguistic usage.

> "Terminists" was the name of one sect of the university to which I, too, belonged. They take a stand against the Thomists, Scotists, and Albertists, and were also called Occamists after Occam, their founder. They are the very latest sect and the most powerful in Paris, too. The dispute was over whether "humanitas" [humanity] and words like it

> meant a common humanity, which was in all human beings, as Thomas and the others believe. Well, say the Occamists or terminists, there is no such thing as a common humanity, there is only the term "homo" [the concept "human being"] or humanity meaning all human beings individually, the same way a painted picture of a human being refers to all human beings.
>
> But your Princely Highness must [know]: in these matters those men are called terminists who speak of a thing in terminis propriis [appropriate terms] and do not interpret words in an alien and wild way; and in this way it is called reality speaking of the thing. When I speak to a carpenter, I must use his terms, namely angle bar and not crooked bar, axe and not hatchet. So one should also leave the words of Christ alone and speak of the sacrament in suis terminis [his terms], ut "hoc facite" [as "that does"] should not mean "sacrificate" [sacrifice], item "corpus" [likewise, "body"] cannot mean "of both kinds," as they now torment the words and want to stray from the clear text.[50]

But becoming a "modern" terminist is only one side of translating. First one must become a student of the Holy Spirit and listen with care to His language. Despite all the differences between the Old and New Testaments, between the Evangelists Luke and John, between Paul and Peter, the Holy Scriptures are homogeneous in that they testify to the God who is unknown to philosophers. What kind of a God can it be who has to do battle against the Devil, who suffers and is crucified?

The reproach is plainly directed at far more than just "Aristotle" or "scholasticism." Since the Fall every man has been a philosopher, for he has taken his experience of the world and his knowledge of reality—which he has succeeded in describing scientifically—as a standard by which to measure God. But the intellect does not suffice to grasp the God of Abraham, Isaac, and Jacob; He must be apprehended through the Scriptures. The "God" created by man is a false god of his own making.

Even before Luther mastered Greek he took pains to determine the sense of certain key words like "spirit," "strength," or "repentance" in Greek. As laborious as the work was, the only way he could get to the core of the New Testament was by cutting through the historico-philosophical and -legal tradition that had for centuries been linked with the Latin "spiritus," "virtus," or "poenitentia." He discovered the verbal structure typical of the Hebrew language: when the Old Testament speaks of "the Word of the Lord," an action, namely the action accomplished by the Word, is implied at the same time.

The great linguistic event of his time, the rediscovery of the original biblical languages, provided the means to probe the Vulgate and take the first steps toward modern Bible scholarship. Luther seized the opportunity as soon as it arose: the moment Erasmus' edition of the Greek New Testament became available in Wittenberg in the middle of the summer semester of 1516, he immediately set about familiarizing himself with this new tool, so shocking for Latin-oriented Christians. While he was engaged in the exegesis of chapter nine of the Epistle to the Romans, he drew—the word "write" would be inappropriate—Greek letters in his lecture manuscript for the first time to point out a translating error in the Latin Bible.

Scholars may, and must, argue about whether humanistic or nominalistic impulses were at work here. But Luther's conviction that the Scriptures contained something radically new and contradictory to man's expectations indisputably went far beyond either of the two movements. Luther the Reformer could still recall an incident far back in his days as a university student. Either at the Erfurt university library or his college library he had chanced upon a Bible chained to a lectern, as valuable folios generally were. He opened the unfamiliar volume to the First Book of Samuel and elatedly read the story of Hannah and how her son Samuel was chosen to be a "man of God." At that time he had already wished that he could possess and study such a Bible one day.[51]

During those early years everything was still taking its preestablished course according to the plans of the father and the son, yet the student's "curiosity" about the Scriptures had already been awakened. Why this curiosity, this formative factor in Luther's future development, arose defies scholarly explanation.

"Today you have the Bible," source of life, God's original testimony, and thus both foundation and standard of all ecclesiastical authorities, be they Church Fathers, councils, popes, or learned doctors. Scripture and Church belong together, but not as though the Scriptures were the letter and the teaching Church the spirit that breathes life into it. The Church is the creation of the Word, but the Word can never be the creation of the Church.

The Scriptures reveal the Word. But that is precisely why they are not the book of truths that might constitute a complete, irrefutable textbook of theology, and why they do not need any further truths added, for example, in the form of new dogmas. The Bible contains only one truth, but it is the decisive one: "that Jesus Christ, our God and Lord, died for the sake of our sins, and was resurrected for the sake of our righteousness."[52]

Whether from a medieval or a modern perspective, this is a revolutionary reduction and concentration of faith. Comprehensive medieval systems and remarkable speculative models of the modern age seem to know far more and have far more to say about God than the Scriptures. Luther's reply to Erasmus applies to both: "Through the Crucified One, the Christian knows everything he has to know, but he now also knows what he cannot know."[53]

Concentrating on Christ crucified was directed against the tangle of medieval theology and was at the same time an attempt to reunite what the foundation of the theological faculties at the universities had divided. The flourishing monastery schools of the twelfth century, with their combination of scholarship and piety, had not been able to hold their own in the face of the new competition. But for Luther this model of theological study in the liturgical context of prayer and meditation was the ideal and remained so even after he had renounced his monastic vows (November 1521). Everything the new disciplines required in the way of linguistic and historical scholarship needed to be incorporated into this system of studies. The repeated reforms at the University of Wittenberg were endeavors to recreate the monastery school model, but—complained Luther—they never succeeded. His repeated appeal to use monastic endowments to found schools for boys and girls of all classes are well known. The Reformer reminds us again and again that the old monasteries, with their combination of piety and scholarship, "have now been caused by the Devil to fall into a deplorable state, so that they are dens of iniquity . . . to the detriment of Christendom."[54]

The reproach that Luther was a scholar without true erudition who jeopardized the objective exegesis of the Scriptures as a result of his "edifying interests" is justified only—if at all—from the standpoint of a complete separation of faith and scholarship. But where the Holy Ghost affects the reader's rational faculties and seeks to win his will, where the Scriptures are holy because they are life-giving, "edification" and "biblical exegesis" cannot be played off against one another without ruining both. Yet that is exactly what happened.

A further factor must be taken into account to understand Luther as an interpreter of the Word and defender of the "scriptural principle." The Bible is not a book, it is a whole library of writings extending across two millennia. Despite its variety, however, there is a center from which and toward which it must be interpreted. Luther's definition of this center was soon very popular among Evangelical theologians: "What proclaims Christ" is the point of reference for exegesis. Luther himself clarified this eloquent formula: what impels you to Christ *crucified* is at the heart of the Scriptures—the apostle Paul's principle in the First Epistle to the Corinthians: "We preach Christ crucified, unto the Jews a stumblingblock and unto the Greeks foolishness" (1 Cor. 1.23).

Since a number of Luther scholars have begun dating the Reformation breakthrough relatively late, in the vicinity of spring 1518, the first Psalm lectures (1513–15) have stopped being of central interest. This is warranted insofar as nothing of *The Freedom of a Christian* as a consequence of justification by faith can yet be felt in these lectures. Luther apologizes in his 1545 *Rückblick:* the gates of Paradise were opened to him much later. But the early lectures on the Psalms are irrefutable proof that Luther expected to see the Word of God crystallize out of the words of the Scriptures, a concept that goes far beyond the establishment of a scriptural principle. The precept that the Scriptures alone formed the foundation of theology was already familiar to medieval scholastics, who provided it with a methodological basis and argued about the consequences the principle would have for ecclesiastical tradition. But the scriptural principle could become scriptural practice only once the Bible was discovered to be more than a collection of various kinds of truths and proofs, when it was recognized as having its own message, one which decided about life and death, and thus had to be interpreted out of itself, out of its center.

The risks involved in paying careful heed to the Scriptures, in finding the thin line between using and abusing, were described unmistakably by Luther in a sermon he preached in 1515 on the anniversary of his baptism:

> Whoever wants to read the Bible must make sure he is not wrong, for the Scriptures can easily be stretched and guided, but no one should guide them according to his emotions; he should lead them to the well, that is to the cross of Christ, then he will certainly be right and cannot fail.[55]

Designating the cross of Christ as the standard of exegesis is evidence of Reformation decisions made prior to the turning point.

In the first ten years, he recounts, he read the Bible through twice a year. His growing understanding of the Scriptures led to differences over correct interpretations, then to the theologians' and prelates' dispute, and finally to the conflict in the Church. The clash of opinions had not been provoked by the printed pages alone. The Reformation reached the people because of a surprising conclusion Luther drew from the scriptural principle he had known for so long: the Scriptures must be preached! Because heresies threatened the living apostolic message, it had to be recorded in a book to protect it from falsification. Preaching reverses this process of conservation again, allowing the Scriptures of the past to become the tidings of the present.

Luther's opponents ridiculed

So the Bible is a necessary evil! It is necessary because without it man's spirit will claim to be holy and there will be no way of proving him wrong. Scripture becomes "evil" when, as a hollow pontifical document, it petrifies in holiness instead of being publicly proclaimed in the Church as the living Word. The Gospel has been committed to lifeless paper; fresh words can transform it into glad tidings again.[56]

CHAPTER VI

The Reformer Attacked

The Persecution of Christians "Today"

Total immersion in the Scriptures is a dangerous undertaking, for the unprecedented Word of God is anything but "credible." Because the Word contradicts common sense and morals, it gives rise to doubts and fears. These are the tribulations, the diabolical temptations that plagued Luther throughout his life. They are so integral a part of his nature, of his personality structure, that we must go beyond Luther the author to come face to face with Luther the man. The Devil's assaults are well aimed and effective, striking the victim down, robbing him of all joy in God and man, producing temporary loathing for God and himself. Luther was sometimes assailed by such spiritual torments for one or even two days. The alarming thing about this state is that the days seem to last an eternity. There is no way out, no end in sight.

In his *Grosser Katechismus* (1529), Luther places Satan's attacks through temptation at the core of his explanation of the sixth petition of the *Lord's Prayer:* "And lead us not into temptation." His elucidation revises the medieval notion that the Devil leads every man into temptation through his carnal instincts.

> "Not to lead us into temptation" means that God gives us the strength and power to resist. But it does not mean that the spiritual distress is removed and done away with. No one can avoid temptation and enticement as long as we live in the flesh and have the Devil around us; and this will not change: we must bear tribulation, yes, even be in the midst of it. But that is why we pray not to fall into and drown in it. That is why it is different to feel spiritual distress than to accept temptation and say "yes" to it. All of us must feel it, though it may not be of the same type for everyone, but greater and heavier for some: youth is primarily tempted by the flesh, then those who are adult and aging by the world; but the others, those who deal with spiritual matters, that is, strong

> Christians, by the Devil. But as long as this feeling goes against our will and we would rather be rid of it, it cannot harm anyone; for if one did not feel it, it could not be called temptation. But accepting it means that one hands over the reins to temptation, does not fight it and pray against it.
>
> Temptation should protect us from false self-confidence. That is why we Christians must be prepared and aware every day that we are constantly being tempted. So no one can go his way with certainty and carelessness, as if Satan were far from us; we must instead be ready for his tricks and ward them off. For even if I am now chaste, patient, friendly, and of firm faith, the Devil can in this very hour pierce my heart with an arrow that I can hardly survive. For he is the kind of enemy that never desists and tires; when one form of tribulation ceases, ever different and new ones arise. That is why there is no counsel or consolation except to run here to seize the Our Father and to speak to God from the heart: "Dear Father, Thou hast commanded me to pray; do not let temptation push me back into sin, shame, and unbelief."[1]

Luther's catechismal explanation transmits a piece of medieval monastic wisdom that had already made its way from monastic cell to parish a century earlier. But spiritual distress now receives a new, Reformation interpretation, and its inescapableness is impressed upon *all* the faithful. This Reformation recasting seems to have a medieval flavor at first because, as usual, the Devil plays an exceedingly dangerous, omnipresent role. That is why everyone is acquainted with tribulation. The young are plagued above all by the temptations of the flesh while older people suffer under the miseries and anxieties of the world. The Devil takes care of "strong Christians," as Luther calls those who, like himself, perform spiritual duties. For everyone, young and old, spiritual and layman, the statement holds that God does not cause distress, but He countenances it to make Christians realize that God alone helps, self-help can only fail.

Tribulations transform abstract theological principles into good news because the professing of "by grace alone" or "by faith alone" becomes an inner experience only for the victim of the Devil's attacks, who discovers that he lives without stability of his own, but by faith alone, and survives only by virtue of grace. God is one's sole refuge, prayer one's sole protection. Thus Satan, as dangerous as he is, does not have a free hand; he is set to work schooling Christians in faith. He will have no trouble finding them, for God is not the only one who reads Luther's catechism every day—the Devil knows it by heart, too.

What Luther is teaching here is eloquent testimony to his own spiritual crises. His experiences are rooted in a fundamental form of spiritual temptation: is my penitence in the confessional great enough to permit me to receive absolution, forgiveness of sins? Confessional scruples were such a widespread problem in the Middle Ages that a number of handbooks and guides dealing with scrupulosity and giving instructions on how to deal with the affliction appeared on the market.[2]

Confessional distress was of so grave a nature that mitigation of a basic sort was called for. The solution advocated by Franciscan theologians, above all, was to demand no more than "minimal penitence" from a confessant. The priest, by virtue of his office, would then transform this penitence into true contrition when he granted absolution. But that was simply to dislocate, not dispel, the problem, for how could the confessant be sure that he had genuinely achieved the requisite minimum of repentance? No demand would ever be so minor that it could not remain unfulfilled.

The distinctive features of Luther's tribulations stand out prominently against this background. He, too, knew these scruples and the doubts over whether he had perhaps not even accomplished what might justifiably be expected of him if he only tried hard enough. Luther's response was a specifically Reformation one: the fears attendant on temptations are not diminished if demands are lowered. God and God alone produces certainty. His "accomplishment" on the cross was on behalf of us all, and His promise will hold good for all times.

All of the Devil's attacks are directed at certainty of salvation, that fundamental article of faith. All temptations, whatever sort they may be, are aimed at awakening doubts in God's reliability. Not only Luther the fearful monk but Luther the professor and "reformer," too, felt singularly affected by these "critical doubts." Although he never called himself a reformer or saw himself as one—only Christ is the Reformer, only Judgment Day will bring "reformation"—the fact remains that "he began the whole movement," he rediscovered the Gospel. He regarded himself as an instrument of God; he could term himself "prophet" or "Evangelist." But the cruelest of the Devil's challenges—because it was the most obvious—concerned this role: "Do you think that you alone possess wisdom?" Would God have allowed so many generations of Christians to die in ignorance of the truth?

Luther spoke freely of the fear these objections evoked in him and thus gave neither contemporaries nor future generations occasion to glorify him as a mighty hero and unerring deliverer of Church and empire. In an age that dismissed renewal as relapse and branded change as heresy, to question his vocation could not help but shake him thoroughly. He "who alone wishes to possess wisdom" has prepared Hell for himself and is tormented by the guilt of having driven masses of followers into the arms of the Devil. Whenever he felt the Devil breathing down his neck in this way, there was only one answer left: God alone is absolute certainty, even if the Church at times is lost in a cloud of unknowing.

Even when the faithful were led into "Babylonian captivity" and had to suffer papal oppression, they could fall back on the imperishable, divinely conferred "treasures of the Church": Scripture and sacraments, creed and Lord's Prayer. The challenge "Do you think that you alone possess wisdom?" occasions not only alarm but joy at the signs God has given that truth is unconquerable even in the darkest centuries. But the Scriptures provide the sole mainstay; only the truth can overcome the Devil. Luther's proclamation before the emperor in Worms, "Here I stand, God help me, Amen," is a trenchant expression of his certainty that contrary to his wishes and plans, God had made him His instrument.

Linked as they are to person and time, challenges to his status as prophet and Evangelist apply to Martin Luther in his unique historical situation. But all Christians are subject to two other forms of diabolical temptation: on the one hand, despair over moral unworthiness and on the other, uncertainty over whether God has not already excluded one from salvation for all eternity—what theology terms predestinational anxiety.

Even the earliest sources demonstrate Luther's awareness of God's holiness and His wrath at unholiness and sin. Luther's reminiscences permit one to conclude that he was the very sort of person to fall into the fearful self-doubt the handbooks described as the sickness of scrupulosity. A man with these proclivities should not have become a monk and certainly not an Observant mendicant monk, one would assume today. But in Luther's time the contrary was the case: so unsettled a person, it was thought, should choose the safe path and enter a monastery. Luther was really able to try out the salutary and salvational methods of his time, to the point of desperation. He endeavored to observe the Augustinian rule by means of extreme self-discipline, fasting, prayer, study, and vigils. When he had done what he could to be a worthy recipient of the sacraments of penance and the Lord's Supper, God would not deny him His grace.

The discovery that he who lives by faith is truly just before God was accompanied by a reevaluation of spiritual distress. The new interpretation manifests itself in two conclusions: tribulations are not a disease, so there can be no cure for them. They are a characteristic condition of Christian life. Only firm faith in God's unalterable promise enables spiritual crises to be withstood—not overcome. God's law shows with frightening clarity what has become of man; everyone is exposed in his unworthiness. God's law is the Devil's proof: there is no salvation! Yet precisely at this point it becomes clear that the mercy of God is the only refuge.

Luther's spiritual crises escalate in intensity. The Devil himself appears on the scene and will not content himself with simple "temptations," as Luther termed the seducer's arts. The Devil drives a person to doubt his election, and seduces the doubter into wanting to penetrate God's hidden will to find out whether or not he is really among those chosen by God. This undertaking must fail and the ensuing uncertainty leads to fear, blasphemy, and hatred for God, and finally to doubts about the existence of God altogether. What the Devil would most like to do is to push all Christians to the brink of revelation, tempt them to try to penetrate God's nature, and then let them fall where he himself fell: into the void. With this the Devil discloses his most ardent desire: he is "not only a liar, he is also a killer."[3]

Luther's own theological and personal turning point became a momentous breakthrough for Church and society with his public call to resist the Devil in the spiritual and temporal realms, to unmask him as a liar and brand him a killer. It was typically medieval that Luther had to abandon the world. The end of the Middle Ages drew near when he would not let the world go to the Devil, instead sounding the battle cry for its preservation and improvement. The world, which had previously been the wide gate and the broad way to Hell, and partner to a pact with the Devil, now disclosed itself in the Reformation view to be the world God had ordained and preserved, an environment in which plants, animals, and man could flourish. Whereas good works had once been done for God's sake, to comply with His high righteousness, they were now redirected to earth for the sake of man, in the service of life and survival until doomsday. Reformation of the Church will be God's work—at the end. Improvement of the world is the reformation's work—now.

Mysticism and Life: Tauler and Staupitz

The upheavals in Luther's soul, which he described as hellish torments, had far-reaching consequences. The Reformer went his own perilous way, not only as a biblical theologian but also as a psychologically experienced minister. His inner tension could easily have broken him, or, conversely, he might have sublimated it. There was a genuine risk that the monk would become so entangled in his own self-analysis that he would end by fettering himself: his creative power and extraordinary intelligence might have fallen victim to his native sensitivity. He was preserved from this fate by his mentor, his "Father in Christ," Johannes Staupitz: "Through Staupitz, the Lord Jesus repeatedly uplifted and strengthened me in the most wonderful way."[4]

The other possibility would have been to go the way of speculative mysticism, something the young Luther did actually try for a time: a soul craving for God seeks to leave the world behind, to cast off earthly fetters, to attain heavenly spheres, and—finally—to find peace in the joyous union with God. Reading the young Luther, one keeps expecting a clear profession of mysticism. And it comes, but in an unanticipated form and tenor, without the goal of ascending to God. Luther was enthusiastic about Johannes Tauler and the *Theologia Germanica,* of which he supervised an incomplete printed edition in 1516 and a complete edition in 1518; but he read Tauler and the *Theologia Germanica* as striking examples of genuine, personal, living theology, not as exponents of mysticism. Tauler became a signpost in Luther's search for life by faith in the world.

Johannes von Staupitz was the decisive figure. He preceded the young monk and professor on the road to faith. Staupitz, as Luther later saw it, showed him the way that led him to the crucial turning point or—as his opponents would have said—onto the precipitous path of heresy. We have already met Staupitz as vicar general of the German Augustinian Observants, summoning Luther to Wittenberg from Erfurt and deciding that Luther should undertake doctoral studies. But there was far more than order or university connecting the two. Both were trained scholastically, though according to different schools, and both were subsequently inspired by St. Augustine and St. Paul to develop a biblical theology. Man's sins, God's grace, and justification through Christ were themes central to the theology of both teacher and student.

Luther was more the scholar, Staupitz more the pastor and preacher, but both combined the duties of teaching with the preaching of the Gospel. The differences between them are evident, too: Luther came from artisan and burgher stock, Staupitz was an aristocrat; Staupitz was not only Luther's superior, he was also fifteen years older. When Luther received his doctorate in 1512, Staupitz was forty-five, at the height of his career and, after overcoming the crisis in his order, at his most charismatic. Luther "studied" with Staupitz, as both a theologian and a minister.

Luther had a special affinity for Staupitz's sense of humor, though Luther's own jokes were more aggressive and less genteel. Theirs was not black humor; their laughter derived from the human foibles that demonstrate themselves to be all too human when viewed from the perspective of infinity. This gift of self-irony is illustrated by an anecdote told about Staupitz as a young preacher. The Augustinian prior had embarked upon a series of sermons on the Book of Job at the monastery church of Tübingen in 1498. When he had "come as far as the tenth or eleventh chapter," he realized that the stilted analysis from the pulpit "was tormenting [Job] more than his wretched boils." And so Staupitz broke off the sermons, concluding with the words: "I am stopping. Job and I are both glad!"[5]

The sermons on Job are of such great relevance because they discuss the problem of Satan's power and the sense of Job's torments and tribulations. The extant manuscript breaks off after thirty-four sermons—and Staupitz had just reached chapter two. He never even managed the ten chapters mentioned in the anecdote; that would have taken years. The arrangement of the sermons in a succession of main parts, discourses, sub-parts, and sub-chapters is so complicated as to render the text of the sermons extremely unwieldy. Staupitz later changed his style radically. His riveting book on the election and justification of the faithful, published in 1517 from Advent sermons given in 1516, is free from ponderous academic formalism.[6]

The anecdote about Staupitz and his Job sermons evinces a Protestant slant when it concludes: "The foundations of the Christian faith, so he said, were still hidden from him at that time." But the heart of the matter is that Staupitz genuinely purged biblical exegesis of cumbersome erudition. Luther's recollection of Staupitz's instructions that only the Bible was to be read in the monastery (probably meaning in the refectory during meals) is in keeping with this.[7] More changed than style when Staupitz put aside the discussions of Gregory the Great and Thomas Aquinas and reached for the Scriptures. What remained was the subject: God's mercy, the refuge Job seeks in his suffering. This divine mercy becomes even more palpable and develops an exceptionally personal appeal in Staupitz's principal work, the 1516 Nuremberg Advent sermons. Christ, who suffered and was crucified, is the guarantee for a merciful God. "I" can see from Christ, who died "for me" and lives "in me," that God has turned his countenance to me.

Staupitz can root his theme of God's comfort and consolation in spiritual distress firmly in this foundation of the cross of Christ. Job, he told the congregation in the Augustinian church in Tübingen, survived the assaults of the Devil, the world and the flesh by virtue of God's grace and mercy[8]—but he could never be certain of a future with God.[9] In his Nuremberg sermons Staupitz adopted a completely different tone: Christ owes the elect succor through grace! Staupitz's response is an impressive attempt to master the trials of a troubled time fearful of God's inscrutable ways; instead of staring toward a fate unknown to them, the tormented should look to Christ, where they can find safety. That is what Staupitz meant when he forbade the desperate Luther to speculate about God's wrath: "Our Father is too high. . . . Attach yourself to Christ, then everything will turn for the good"—"Providence can be comprehended and found in the wounds of Christ—and nowhere else."[10]

Staupitz did not help the frightened monk by simply giving him the first confessional counsel that came to his mind; he spoke out of the fullness of experience. The theology of temptation was his specialty. Through his counsel Staupitz delivered his fellow Augustinian from deep distress, for Luther was close to despair: Am I among the elect? Is my name written in the Book of Life? Had Staupitz not come to his rescue, Luther later confessed, he would either have succumbed to despair or he would have hardened himself against all fear of God in arrogant indifference.[11]

Christ's wounds assure us of God's love, which precedes all penitence—that is Johann von Staupitz's discovery. Both Staupitz and Luther must have read the works of the Erfurt Augustinian Johannes von Paltz, whose *Himmlische Fundgrube* (*Heavenly Treasuretrove,* circa 1490) was very widely read and saw nearly twenty editions in thirty years. The work attested plainly to what contemporaries were striving for. They were holding out for a tangible forgiveness of sins. Like Staupitz, von Paltz emphasized Christ's wounds, but he was worlds away from Staupitz. The *Fundgrube* is a guide to meditation: one should submerge oneself in the five sacred wounds and school oneself in this way to overcome the world, kill off the flesh, and drive away evil thoughts. Meditating devoutly on Christ's Passion would inspire such intense love of God that the meditator would become capable of true contrition for his sins.[12]

That is the very advice Staupitz does not take over, nor would it have been of any help to Luther: if I have not been elected by God since all eternity, meditating on the Passion can only be additional torment. The way of Staupitz is a bold, almost impudent, one: he obliges Christ to redeem those who believe in Him. The motto Staupitz adopted was a programmatic demand: "I am thine, save me" (Ps. 119.94). Christ is not a means or a helper enabling man to fulfil the demands of God's righteousness, he is the executor of God's mercy and thus the proof and pledge for God's election.

If Luther is viewed as a solitary discoverer, leaving behind his time as he progresses, Staupitz seems a ship that passes in the night, someone who merely crossed his path. This is why the differences between Staupitz and

Luther have been stressed to the present day. And there are differences, as later decisions plainly show. In the critical spring of 1521, when Luther, already excommunicated by the pope, had little difficulty imagining what he might expect from the emperor and empire, he sent a distressed letter to Staupitz:

> I dare to write to you so openly because I fear you will be caught between Christ and the pope, who, as you can see, are feuding bitterly. But let us pray that with the spirit of His mouth, the Lord will destroy this son of evil shortly. If you do not wish to follow me along this path, let me go and obey God's guidance. . . .
>
> Truly, your submission has saddened me greatly. It has shown me a completely different Staupitz from the one who so courageously preached grace and the cross. . . .
>
> Wittenberg on the day of St. Apollonia 1521
> (9 February)
> Your son Martinus Lutherus.[13]

Warning Staupitz of the dangers of "submission" had no effect. With papal permission Staupitz abandoned the Augustinian order in April 1522 and was elected abbot of St. Peter's Benedictine monastery in Salzburg on August 2. Luther felt deserted, even betrayed, and expressed his disappointment openly. Nonetheless, Staupitz always remained his "revered" father, the first person to have discovered and embarked on the road to reformation. The vicar general and doctoral supervisor had done more than allay tormenting fears of predestination; he had, Luther felt, "helped him out" by providing basic, biblical, and thus unimpeachable answers. This was Johannes von Staupitz's enduring contribution to Luther's theology.

The genuine divergences between Luther and Staupitz did not stem solely from contrary decisions in life. What they had in common masked considerable dissimilarity: for Staupitz, the Devil did not threaten the harmony of the world; like Job, the "just" are only "temporarily" exposed to enemies. God's omnipotence reduces the realm of the Devil's activity to a narrowly restricted area. In his last letter, which he wrote to Luther shortly before he died, there is the intimation that he suspects the Devil has led the Church into captivity, but he does not share Luther's view that the Last Days, with their cataclysmic unleashing of chaos, have already dawned.

The year 1520 saw the publication of Luther's treatise *The Freedom of a Christian,* in which he presented his doctrine of justification in the form that was to make history. The "joyful exchange" emerges as the central event in a

Christian's life. As bride and bridegroom exchange possessions in a marriage, so the sinner receives justification from Christ, and Christ takes over the Christian's sins. Luther later found an image for the joyful exchange in Jacob's ladder: Jacob's dream has come true; Christ descends from Heaven, and the Christian ascends to be united with God.[14]

Staupitz, too, spoke of the joyful exchange whereby Christ takes over guilt, thus becoming "unjust and a sinner" Himself—a concept that immediately provoked pious indignation.[15] But the conclusion Staupitz drew was different from Luther's: liberated from the burden of sin, the faithful will now find perceptible peace. The new condition of righteousness can be experienced; it is a sweet foretaste of eternity.[16]

Luther, on the other hand, experienced the growing power of the Devil, who, challenged by the Gospel of the joyful exchange, directs his attacks at the faithful. The Devil cites Moses and his Ten Commandments against the "alien" righteousness of Christ; he breeds scruples, insists on good works, and relentlessly drives the conscience to assuage the wrath of a just God. The "joyful exchange" of which Luther speaks does not lead to the sweet experience described by Staupitz, for in the battle with the Devil there is no rest, no peace, and no visible success.[17]

Through Christ's exchange the faithful Christian is "simultaneously sinner and just"—"simul peccator et iustus."[18] He is a sinner because self-love and inner resistance against God remain unconquered; he is just because he has been given the righteousness of Christ, which is valid before God. Luther found the language and the model for a graphic description of this state of dual existence in Tauler and the *Theologia Germanica.* The soul is taut with groaning over the burdens and sins of creation; it is beyond earthly cares when it experiences the joyous union with God. In mysticism groaning and rapture characterize the beginning and the end of the road from painful separation from the world to joyous union. For Luther "groaning" and "rapture" are experiential terms for the simultaneity of peace and misery: peace is interspersed with the cruel reality of the Devil's power—"simul gemitus et raptus."[19]

Luther's encounter with Augustinian theology through Staupitz and with mystical experience through Tauler encouraged and confirmed him on his way to a new piety and a new way of thinking. Both of these central experiences, tribulation and mystical ascent, diabolical remoteness from God and joyous union with God, are no longer typical of the spiritually ill and the spiritual elite, two marginal Christian groups. All parts of the true Church suffer spiritual distress and are at the same time united with God. Thus the

Church of martyrs is no obsolete stage in Church history. The Church is the community of the faithful and must thus remain the community of those afflicted by the Devil.

Luther's phraseology and imagery—"joyful exchange" and "Jacob's ladder"—are totally devoid of any trace of abstract academic sterility. They express life in process and not a static condition; they originate from the living experience of faith in a life between God and the Devil, not from theological theory.

> I did not learn my theology at once, but had to seek ever deeper and deeper after it. That is where my spiritual distress led me; for one can never understand the Holy Scriptures without experience and tribulations. . . . If we do not have such a Devil, then we are nothing but speculativi Theologi, who handle their thoughts badly and speculate about everything with their reason, that it must be like this and like that; just like the way of the monks in the monasteries.[20]

Thrice Excommunicated

It was August 7, 1540. As so often, there were guests at the table when the master of the house mentioned the special significance of the day: "It is twenty-two years ago today that I was condemned in Rome."[21] Luther spoke energetically and often about his road to Reformation because he knew that the rising generation had no idea of what it meant to grow up under the papacy. Certain dates and events were etched in his memory, consolidating over the years to form a history of his life and the Reformation. The dates were not always correct, for though Luther had an astonishing memory for the written word, he did not have a head for numbers. But this time he was right; the date of his *first* condemnation had impressed itself firmly on his mind.

Excommunication was always a prominent subject in his recollections. The curia had publicly handed the doctor of the Church over to the Devil as a heretic and enemy of God. He had reacted with perplexity, which he subsequently tried to hide under the cloak of irony. "They dealt with my poor self in so pontifically fine a way that I had already been condemned in Rome for sixteen days before the citation reached me [on August 7, 1518]."[22]

He had been able to anticipate the outcome of the trial in Rome and what kind of judgment would be forthcoming, for the first opponent to speak in

Rome was both Luther's accuser and his judge:[23] Sylvester Prierias, defender of absolute pontifical power and thus vehement defender of indulgences. But Luther, too, considered himself a defender of the pope and believed that respect for the power of the Holy Father in Rome meant taking a stand against the abuses resulting from indulgences.

Well into the indulgence controversy Luther still regarded himself as loyal to the pope—indeed, even as an ardent and submissive papist. Luther had been raised to obedience—to his parents and teachers, prior and pope—so condemnation by Rome must have wounded him to the very depths of his soul. Now, he was being excommunicated again, for the second and decisive time. Only the dread suspicion and then the terrible certainty that the papacy had opened Rome to the Antichrist enabled him to bear the blow of a papal ban.

On December 10, 1520, even before the papal bull threatening excommunication, "Exsurge Domine," arrived in Wittenberg, the students organized what we might call a "happening" and burned books by scholastic authors near the east gate of the city, the Elstertor. Luther joined the students at the bonfire, where he consigned the papal bull and the Church of Rome's ecclesiastical law to the fire to express his terrible discovery: Rome had led the Church into the Babylonian captivity. Trust in the pope had given way to the certainty that there was a great "change" approaching and that God Himself was going to intervene. Despite his experiences in Rome and all the criticism of the curia that was circulating, his trust in the papacy had long remained unbroken. How very much the pope had been the center of the Church to him can be seen in his appalled conclusion: the successor to Peter was no longer in a position to "strengthen his brethren" (Luke 22.32). Now it was clear—the Last Days had begun.[24]

His break with the past was not sudden, nor did it concern the papacy alone. From a spectator's vantage point Luther seems to have severed all ties and resolved to undertake a heroic struggle for freedom. He himself experienced the dramatic years between 1518 and 1521 very differently: he had not turned away; he had been turned away, excommunicated three times—by his religious order, by the pope, and by the emperor. He experienced this triple blow as a painful process of separation. The misery of isolation made a lasting imprint on his memory: "In the year 1518 Staupitz released me from my vow of obedience to the order and left me alone in Augsburg. Then the pope cut me off from his Church and finally the emperor from his empire. But the Lord took me up."[25] This is an allusion to the Twenty-seventh Psalm: "When my father and mother forsake me, then the Lord will take me up" (Ps. 27.10). Luther did not see himself as a man going his own way but as a man forsaken; that is how he experienced and understood the beginnings of the history of the Reformation—lonely but not alone.

Do Not Indulge in Indulgences!

A historian can only call Luther's behavior intrepid—he did not evade condemnation by Rome and the empire. But the picture remains incomplete until we establish what produced and sustained this man. He was malleable, anything but rebellious, impulsive, sensitive, and open to new influences. The question inevitably arises: why did he not recoil from the concentrated power of the empire in Worms, how could he bear to be condemned a heretic by Rome and damned as the Devil's spawn? Any attempt at an answer must take into account Luther's own response: fear of the Lord controls thought and action. Anxiety and fear engendered by temporal powers and ecclesiastical pressure pale in comparison.

There is nothing in Luther's development to point to a craving for recognition or ambition to gain public approval. Who knew Doctor Ludher from Wittenberg when he set out in October 1517? University professors in Germany were, it is true, beginning to wonder about him, and the vicar general obviously expected a great deal from him, but that was all within a small, restricted world. He was not even a famous professor, and in the crucial early years his bitter opponent, Johannes Eck, who was approximately the same age, had far better connections and a much more forceful public personality.

At the beginning it seemed a most remote possibility that this monk would ever leave his comfortable niche at the University of Wittenberg and set pope and emperor alike against him. Luther did not speak up publicly until the preacher of indulgences Johannes Tetzel (†1519) became active in the Brandenburg territories near Wittenberg in the spring of 1517. Tetzel was equal to his task. He knew how to make the business of salvation so appealing and urgent that people from Wittenberg with money to spend were also crossing the border to purchase indulgences. In the confessional Luther soon heard what they had to relate upon their return. What they told him of Tetzel's preaching appalled him more than the actual indulgences they brought back with them. Drafts of such sermons probably written by Tetzel have survived; they show that the Wittenberg purchasers of indulgences had listened carefully to their indulgence preacher: "All of you, run for the salvation of your souls. . . . Seek ye the Lord while He is near." While the indulgence peddler is near!

> You priest, you nobleman, you merchant, you woman, you virgin, you married woman, you youth, you old man, go into your church, which, as I have said, is St. Peter's, and visit the hallowed cross that has been put up for you, that incessantly calls you. . . . Remember that you are in such stormy peril on the raging sea of this world that you do not know if you can reach the harbor of salvation. . . . You should know: whoever has confessed and is contrite and puts alms into the box, as his confessor counsels him, will have all of his sins forgiven, and even after confession and after the jubilee year will acquire an indulgence on every day that he visits the cross and the altars, as if he were visiting the seven altars in the Church of St. Peter, where the perfect indulgence is granted. So why are you standing about idly? Run, all of you, for the salvation of your souls. Be quick and concerned about redemption as about the temporal goods you doggedly pursue from day till night. "Seek ye the Lord while he may be found . . . while he is near" (Isa. 55.6); work, as John says, "while it is day," for "the night cometh when no man can work" (John 9.4).—Do you not hear the voices of your dead parents and other people, screaming and saying: "'Have pity on me, have pity on me . . . for the hand of God hath touched me' (Job 19.21)? We are suffering severe punishments and pain, from which you could rescue us with a few alms, if only you would." Open your ears, because the father is calling to the son and the mother to the daughter.[26]

Tetzel, a Dominican monk, faithfully repeated the official Church doctrine concerning indulgences: indulgences availed only those who were penitent and had confessed. But the proof of penitence—which was demanded—was the willingness to accept penance, and possession of an indulgence constituted proof of this willingness. A great many priests were ready to give absolution on the basis of such evidence.

A confessant must first convince the priest that he is contrite, then confess his sins, and finally accept the penance prescribed by the priest. Together these three elements form the sacrament of penance. Only the third part of the sacrament, the actual punishment, can be replaced by indulgences. Was Tetzel making a mockery of indulgences? No, because his rendering was based on the instructions that his archbishop, Cardinal Albrecht of Mainz, had issued on indulgences, and the cardinal in turn derived his interpretation from Pope Leo X's bull on indulgences.

What Luther did not know was that Albrecht, of the noble house of

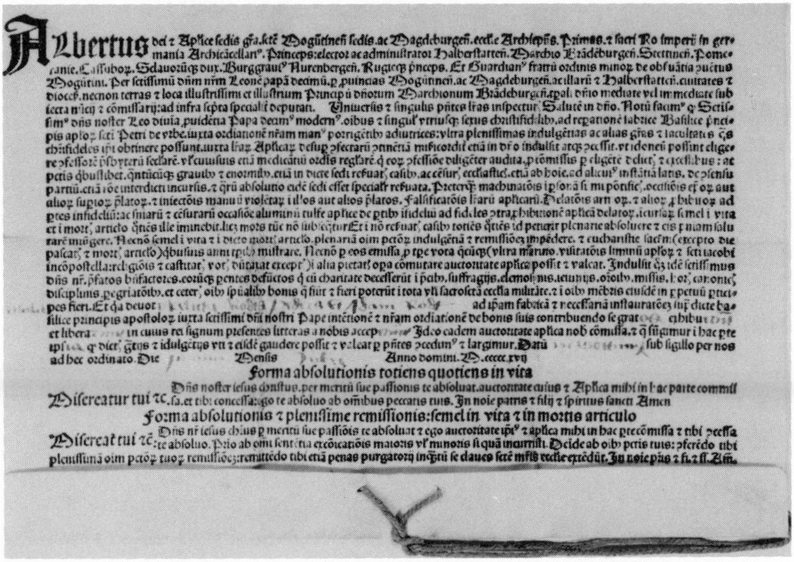
Forma absolutionis totiens quotiens in vita

Forma absolutionis et plenissime remissionis: semel in vita et in mortis articulo

Letter of indulgence for the rebuilding of St. Peter's in Rome, printed in Mainz, 1516/17.

Hohenzollern, was caught in a political dilemma. The archbishopric of Mainz had long been a lucrative source of income for the curia. When the Hohenzollerns wanted their Albrecht, archbishop of Magdeburg and administrator of the see of Halberstadt, as archbishop of Mainz as well, the curia was quick to draw attention to the difficulties. Money was the only way of atoning for violating the prohibition against accumulating posts and benefices. The curia was, however, very helpful. They permitted Albrecht to keep half of the proceeds of the indulgence for the rebuilding of St. Peter's to repay the money he had borrowed from the Fugger bank in Augsburg, which had provided him with the necessary funds to obtain Rome's consent.

In popular histories of the Reformation (and with admirable self-criticism in the modern Catholic version), Tetzel and Albrecht appear as the guilty parties, sharing the blame for Luther's Reformation. The one had hawked indulgences and thus misrepresented them completely; the other, a wily ecclesiastical prince, had ill-used the pope for his own purposes. Indeed Luther spared neither of them, but his revolt was not a personal vendetta and it concerned far more than dubious formulations and the business transactions of the Church. He had begun his exhortations against indulgences some three years before: what can be so seriously abused in practice must undergo fundamental correction. The search for grace cannot be satisfied by purchasing indulgences; its fulfilment comes from the preaching of the Gospel.

On the eve of All Saints' Day, October 31, 1517, Luther posted the ninety-five theses, which he had composed in Latin, on the door of the Castle Church of Wittenberg, according to university custom.[27]

Luther directed these theses against the system of indulgences, but not by citing the unfortunate, exaggerated statements of overzealous purveyors of indulgences and making them look ridiculous. What he explicitly opposed was the advertising slogan: "A penny in the box, a soul out of purgatory." Half a year later the theological faculty in Paris likewise repudiated the slogan, even condemning it as "false, scandalous, and untenable."[28] But that was not Luther's main point. He wanted to stress true repentance and thus make the limited value of indulgences clear: they profit only the living, not the dead in purgatory, because indulgences can only commute punishments imposed by the Church. The profound consequences of sin, namely fear and insufficient love of God and one's neighbors, cannot be removed by indulgences but only by the Gospel:

62. The true treasure of the church is the most holy Gospel of the glory and grace of God.
63. But this treasure is naturally [merito] most odious, for it makes the first the last. [Mark 9.34; Matt. 20.16]
64. The treasure of indulgences, on the other hand, is very acceptable, for it makes the last the first.
65. Therefore the treasures of the Gospel were the net with which one once caught the wealthy.
66. The treasures of indulgences are now the net with which one catches men's wealth.[29]

How well composed the ninety-five theses are is evident from the fact that the conclusion can already be deduced from the first thesis: "When our Lord and Master Jesus Christ said 'Repent!' (Matt. 4.17), he willed the entire life of believers to be one of repentance." But, as Staupitz had impressed on his student, true repentance is love, a response to the love of God, and not fear of Hell.[30] And true repentance leads through temptation, death, and Hell, for it is the path in imitation of Christ, which no one may spend money to evade. *Penance* is a misleading word, for genuine repentance is not imposed; it is granted as a gift.

Thus it is already obvious that the ninety-five theses were criticizing more than indulgences. Luther went one bold step further in his thoughts about the Church and the treasures of the Church: "Every true Christian participates in the treasures of the Church, even without letters of indulgence" (thesis 37); "this treasure is the Gospel of the glory and grace of God" (thesis 62). In the ensuing controversy over the Gospel of grace, this guiding principle became an actuating force.

Barely two weeks after being posted, the theses had circulated all over Germany, Luther reported; and understandably so, "for all the world is complaining about indulgences."[31] According to university records there was a disputation on the theses in Wittenberg, as Luther had desired. But against his wishes they were translated into German and printed in Nuremberg. No copy of this edition has survived. Luther affixed a handwritten "list" to the church door and only then sent a second version of the Latin theses to the printer, first in Wittenberg and then in Nuremberg, Leipzig, and Basel.[32] Luther later described the echo he found as a depressing success: "The publicity did not appeal to me. For . . . I myself did not know what an indulgence was, and the song was getting too high for my voice."[33]

Three years earlier, in the autumn of 1514, Luther had already denounced indulgences in the university lecture hall, terming them proof of the nadir Christendom had reached. There were Christians who thought money and a sigh would get them to heaven: "It is dangerous to believe that we can draw on the treasures of the Church without adding anything ourselves."[34] He had thus recognized the threat to true repentance as early as 1514, though good works still constituted the treasure of the Church for him at the time. But Luther's 1514 deprecation of indulgences demonstrates that the ninety-five theses had two faces, one looking backward, and the other, directed to the reevaluation of repentance and the treasures of the Church, looking into the future. Contemporaries will not have found it easy to distinguish between them. For most people Luther's manifesto was chiefly a bold formulation of criticism that had long been common. It is thus understandable that the theses were passed from hand to hand and "posted in many places," as Duke George of Saxony, who was later to become Luther's inexorable foe, was at this point still pleased to report.[35] On October 31, 1517, a question had been raised; the Church itself was not in imminent danger.

And it was not the ninety-five theses themselves that had such a revolutionary effect on posterity. The decisive event was the subsequent debate on the question of the fallibility of councils, the supreme power of the pope, and the right to admonish the Church, on scriptural grounds, to change its ways. The dispute revealed a rift that could not be mended later. The *Sermon on Indulgence and Grace,* which was written at approximately the same time as the theses but only appeared in February 1518, already belonged to this intensified phase. The inquiry of October 31, 1517, had become a call to repentance: this was the right way of preaching indulgences. The sermon became the first bestseller of the Reformation; it was published all over the empire and reprinted more than twenty times in two years.[36]

The Wittenberg program was now being publicly developed in a manner accessible to the layman. Two key sentences marked the minimal platform Luther urged the Church to accept: "It is a grievous error to think that one could make amends for his sins, as God forgives sins without recompense, out of unlimited grace at all times, and demands nothing in return but living a proper life from then on." Contravening the scholastic doctors, he concluded with the unshakable principle behind all eighteen articles of the sermon: "In the points listed I have no doubts: they are clearly attested to in the Scriptures. So you should have no doubts either and let Doctores scholasticos be scholasticos."[37]

Two of the three principles of the Reformation have now been combined: "unmerited grace" and "pure Scripture," sola gratia and sola scriptura. The sermon written for laymen attests to these principles as basic coordinates of a Christian's life before God's countenance and in the service of a "proper life" in the world. Barely four weeks later, before Easter of 1518, Luther adds a third Reformation principle: sola fide, God demands and wants faith alone. There is no specific level of contrition necessary to obtain the forgiveness of sins. Trust in the divine Word "Your sins are forgiven" is what counts before God—"cum sola fides iustificet."[38]

Only in the following years and in the course of events throughout his life would Luther discover what a "proper life" meant in the day-to-day world. Christian life on the basis of the Gospel looks very different from life under canon law. Disregarding one's own, ever uncertain inner state and putting one's trust in God's unshakable promise liberates the believer from brooding, all-consuming self-analysis. Good works are not repudiated, but their aim and direction have been radically "horizontalized": they have moved from Heaven to earth; they are no longer done to please God but to serve the world.

Scripture or Pope

On October 31, 1517, Luther sent his ninety-five theses, and probably the first version of the *Sermon on Indulgences and Grace,* to Cardinal Albrecht of Mainz, for whom Tetzel was working. Hieronymous Schulze, bishop of Brandenburg, to whose see Wittenberg belonged, was also informed of the contents of the theses and sermon. Instead of replying, Archbishop Albrecht forwarded the documents to Rome in December 1517: His Pontifical Holiness will know how "such error" is to be countered.[39]

"Error"—today no one, regardless of denomination, would use that word for Luther's criticism of indulgences. The charge that grace was being commercialized was justified. But the question remained: was purchasable grace merely an abuse, or was it a symptom? Was the peddling of indulgences no more than a blunder that could easily be put right, or was it perhaps an indication of a deeper aberration? The year 1518 was to bring the answer.

The Dominican Sylvester Mazzolini from Prierio, the papal court theologian and later judge at Luther's trial, provided the response to the Reformation challenge. It took Prierias—as he was called after his birthplace—only three days to unmask Luther's ninety-five theses as heretical. Prierias' *Dialogue Concerning the Power of the Pope* is so illuminating because his ideas were far ahead of papal theology, which had been stagnating for a century. The four points underlying his *Dialogue* anticipate the results of the First and Second Vatican Councils.

According to Prierias the pope is the highest authority and foundation of the universal Church. He is infallible "when he makes a decision in his capacity as pope." His doctrine is "the infallible rule of faith, from which the Holy Scriptures too draw their strength and authority." A council may be mistaken at the start, but not at the end, when the pope has authorized the council's decisions. Though the doctrine of papal infallibility had already been developed in the late thirteenth century—in radical Franciscan circles[40]—it was still severely limited by the majority of canon lawyers of the time. Prierias' simple, unambiguous doctrine of infallibility is understandable as an Italian reaction to the fifteenth-century "conciliar" councils, which were not governed by the pope, undermined the concept of centralism, and fostered hopes of reform in the Church. But in Germany his brand of papalism had never been heard before. It was this papal doctrine that would determine Luther's "no" to Rome.

> As I [Prierias] intend to sift your doctrine thoroughly, my Martin, it is necessary for me to establish a basis of norms and foundations. . . .
>
> Third foundation:
>
> He who does not accept the doctrine of the Church of Rome and pontiff of Rome as an infallible rule of faith, from which the Holy Scriptures, too, draw their strength and authority, is a heretic.
>
> Fourth foundation:
>
> The Church of Rome can make decisions both in word and deed concerning faith and morals. And there is no difference except that

> words are better suited. In this sense habit acquires the force of law, for the will of a prince expresses itself in deeds which he allows or himself arranges to have done. Consequently: as he who thinks incorrectly concerning the truth of Scriptures is a heretic, so too he who thinks incorrectly concerning the doctrines and deeds of the Church in matters of faith and morals is a heretic.[41]

In his "conclusion" Prierias draws the ultimate consequence: "Whoever says that the Church of Rome may not do what it is actually doing in the matter of indulgences is a heretic." Prierias had now proclaimed not only the doctrine but also the deeds of the Church, here the sale of indulgences, to be infallible.[42]

On the basis of these axioms he would not even have needed three days to condemn Martin Luther, and with him all Christians who dared to oppose the teachings or practices of the Holy Church of Rome on scriptural grounds: heretics! That is all the *Dialogue* did, nor did it need to do more: the *Dialogue* truly made all dialogue superfluous. Luther demonstrated his opinion of the papal theologian's work plainly as soon as it arrived in Wittenberg: he had it printed—without comment. But he used more than Prierias' own voice to counter Prierias' words; he also composed a reply and took only two days to do it, one fewer than Prierias, as he emphasized. The same publisher simultaneously issued both Prierias' *Dialogue* and Luther's reply in Leipzig.

Evidently the idea of using prefatory axioms to establish an unequivocal position made sense to Luther, and he countered Prierias' four foundations with three of his own. The first had long been obvious to him and consisted of the two biblical texts that had been in his mind and heart since the autumn of 1509: "Prove all things; hold fast that which is good" (1 Thess. 5.21); "Even if an angel descend from heaven and preach a gospel contrary to that you have received, let him be accursed" (Gal. 1.8).[43]

Luther drew the second and third foundations from ecclesiastical tradition and ecclesiastical law. He quoted Augustine and canon law to prove that the Church had expressly acknowledged the Bible as the only standard of faith and morals. Thus Prierias' foundations contradicted Church doctrine, for they were not—this was the decisive point—based on Scripture, nor were they rooted in the Church Fathers or the law; and they were, moreover, bereft of reason: "It is thus my right, that means my Christian freedom, to reject and dismiss you and your *Dialogue*."[44]

The Luther affair could have been concluded with this exchange of blows. The two parties had nothing left to say to each other. Luther's copy of

Prierias' *Dialogue* had been accompanied by a summons to Rome—he was to appear for interrogation within sixty days. It did not take the gift of clairvoyance to predict the outcome.[45] Before the grace period had expired the decision was made in Rome to take Luther into custody. The papal legate in Augsburg was instructed to have Luther, who was already designated a heretic, arrested if he refused to recant. Two days later, on August 25, the Saxon provincial was ordered to have Luther seized and imprisoned, "bound hand and foot."[46]

THE VERY interaction of religion and power politics for which Luther so vehemently reproached the Papal States now enabled him to survive. The Turks were influencing the course of events, as they would do more than once in the sixteenth century.[47] Once Egypt fell into the hands of the sultan, the coasts of Italy were no longer secure; then, Hungary had good reason to fear an invasion, and planning and financing a European crusade against the Turks took on prime importance.

In early May of 1518 Cardinal Cajetan was dispatched to the diet in Augsburg to gain acceptance, with Emperor Maximilian's approval, for a crusade indulgence and a crusade tax. As the curia was aware of the "indulgence climate" in Germany, it was prepared to make concessions from the start. The imperial estates were to appoint a committee to supervise the indulgence funds so that no one could suspect the proceeds of being misappropriated: "If we disappoint the requisite trust in this matter, one would justifiably not believe another word of ours in future"—thus the pope's instructions to his legate.

But the imperial estates would not negotiate. Elector Frederick spoke so scathingly of the "false, blasphemous indulgence" that the subject was dropped. The only thing authorized after several turbulent meetings was a much reduced Turkish tax.[48]

The association of the indulgence for the building of St. Peter's with the now futile offering of a crusade indulgence began to bring Luther's name to the attention of political circles. For the moment his differences with Johannes Eck, the professor from Ingolstadt, which had already grown into an academic feud in Germany, played only a marginal role. In Rome all arrangements had been made to silence the troublemaker noiselessly. In view of the recalcitrant imperial estates and the dangerous Turkish campaigns, the German tirades against Rome could no longer be passively condoned. Emperor Maximilian had already agreed to execute the ecclesiastical condemnation with an imperial ban. Luther's sovereign was to be placated by being awarded the Golden Rose of Virtue, as Pope Leo announced to the consistory. Furthermore, the elector was to be permitted two new indulgences for the Castle Church of Wittenberg. That was how they expected to win the relics collector for their side and induce him to abandon his protection of Luther.

The plan was a good one. Had it been carried out, Luther would have been put in the Church of Rome's custody on the first anniversary of the posting of his theses. In Wittenberg new letters of indulgence pinned to the doors of the Castle Church would have conveyed the message that no theses had ever been posted.

The situation changed when the pope learned of the plans Maximilian and a majority of the electors had to elect the king of Spain as the emperor's successor. Frederick the Wise, who turned a deaf ear to the emperor's election plans, became a political figure to be reckoned with. The elector's value to the curia had suddenly risen steeply. Thus the Saxon was successful in having the venue of Luther's interrogation changed to German soil, to Augsburg. The pope empowered Cardinal Cajetan to decide Luther's guilt or innocence after talking to the accused: disputation was to be avoided at all costs.[49]

Luther's trip to Augsburg was carefully organized by the electoral court. He was provided with sufficient traveling expenses, his lodgings were arranged for, and he was furnished with sound legal counseling. The Saxon Luther was not to be at the mercy of the ecclesiastical judge in Augsburg. When Luther stopped at the Augustinian monastery in Nuremberg on his way, he was warned that his life was at stake: it was to be feared that the interrogation would be followed by arrest. The Roman order to take him into custody had leaked out! He truly expected the worst, as can be seen from the message he sent to Wittenberg, which was formulated as a will: "May Christ live, may Martinus die—like every sinner."[50]

Luther traveled to Augsburg convinced that he would suffer a martyr's death if he did not recant. "Now you must die"—"Oh, the disgrace I shall bring down upon my parents" were the thoughts incessantly with him.[51] The road to Augsburg was a trip to a sure fate. He knew: it was over.

He remembered one thing about the interrogation in the Fugger house particularly: "Recant," Cajetan had demanded again and again. "But I could not bring myself to say those six letters, REVOCO ['I recant']!" This was certainly not fair to the cardinal legate, who had made himself far more independent of the pontiff's instructions than one would have dared to expect. A conversation between the two actually took place; at least there had been an opportunity for an exchange of arguments.

Cajetan had thus made an important contribution to the clarification of

Luther's position. Up to that point Luther had cited not only the Scriptures and reason in his defense but also the Church Fathers and canon law. Now, however, it became clear to him that tradition and law could be ambiguous: the cardinal had confronted him with Pope Clement VI's regal bull "Unigenitus." It claimed to establish that the treasures of the Church were at the pope's disposal for the purpose of remitting punishments. Thus criticism of indulgences led unavoidably to conflict with the pope and his judicial office.[52]

The outcome of the Augsburg interrogation was portentous: Cajetan doggedly demanded a recantation, but Luther insisted on scriptural proof. This led to the first excommunication, as he later called it. Vicar General Johannes von Staupitz, his mentor and comrade-in-arms, released him from obedience to the Augustinian order: "I absolve you from obedience to me and commend you to the Lord God."[53] The papal order for Luther's arrest could thus be postponed by legal means; at least Staupitz was now relieved of the obligation to take action against Luther. Without an official farewell to the cardinal, Luther left Augsburg hastily, after nightfall on October 16, 1518, riding an unsaddled horse with which he had been provided.

Against Pope and Emperor

What had been demanded of Luther after the dissolution of the imperial diet behind closed doors at the Augsburg Fugger house became a public spectacle in Worms. Luther traveled to Worms as he already had to Augsburg—with fear and trembling. On the way he was stricken with such a high fever that his companions feared for his life. What the emperor's safe-conduct was worth was most uncertain—memories of Jan Hus warned against any kind of overconfidence. Opinions at the electoral court were divided; it was left to Luther to decide whether he wished to go to Worms or not. There is resolution and realism in the letter Luther sent ahead from Frankfurt to his friend in Worms, the electoral confessor Georg Spalatin: "We shall enter Worms, even if all the gates of Hell and all the powers of Heaven try to prevent it. . . . There the task is to chase away the Devil."[54] In his own letter-book Spalatin noted: "He wants to come to Worms. Even if there be as many Devils there as tiles on the roof."[55]

Luther's famous statement has circulated in this (abbreviated) form ever since. The words sound so refreshingly hopeful, the language so vivid and graphic, that one can almost see the roguish little devils cavorting on the roofs of Worms. Things did not look so picturesque to Luther.

Worms was anything but a theatrical backdrop. Luther had managed to

Albrecht Dürer, Kaspar Sturm, *1520. Kaspar Sturm accompanied Luther to Worms, providing him with imperial safe conduct.*

scrape through in Augsburg, but now in Worms he had to face the consequences and defend himself against the concentrated power of the Devil. He felt he was being subjected to a three-fold attack. First, the Devil had assaulted his body, wanting to weaken him through illness. Even more dangerous was the assault on Luther's soul: he was plagued by despondency and haunted by fear. Obviously the Devil was trying hard to drive him to apostasy. Luther did not travel through Germany to Worms in a mood of stoic equanimity and unshakable resolve, exultant in the imposing escort of the bold imperial herald Kaspar Sturm. It was Luther's contemporaries who turned his journey into a triumphal procession, much to the annoyance of the papal legate Aleander.

It is to Aleander that we owe the eyewitness account of Luther's arrival in Worms:

> I had already concluded my letter when I gathered from various reports as well as the hasty running of the people that the great master of heretics was making his entrance. I sent one of my people out, and he told me that about a hundred mounted soldiers, probably the Sickingens, had escorted him to the gate of the city; sitting in a coach with three com-

> rades, he entered the city [at ten in the morning], surrounded by some eight horsemen and found lodgings near his Saxon prince. When he left the coach, a priest embraced him and touched his habit three times, and shouted with joy, as if he had had a relic of the greatest saint in his hands. I suspect that he will soon be said to work miracles. This Luther, as he climbed from the coach, looked around in the circle with his demonic eyes and said: "God will be with me." Then he stepped into an inn, where he was visited by many men, ten or twelve of which he ate with, and after the meal, all the world ran there to see him.[56]

It was neither a triumphant victor, nor a demon or miracle worker who had come to Worms; the monk who stepped down from that coach was a sorely tested man.

On his first day before emperor and empire Luther was so intimidated that his statements could hardly be understood. The same evening the papal nuncio Aleander wrote to the pope's vice chancellor in Rome: "The fool entered with a smile on his face and kept moving his head back and forth, up and down, in the presence of the emperor; when he left he no longer seemed so cheerful."[57] Aleander felt nothing but contempt for him: a laughing fool! Rarely has a "smile" been so totally misinterpreted. The enormous tension and almost intolerable pressure Luther had been subjected to became evident once more when the questioning was over. In keeping with old German tournament custom, he threw up his hands, shouting, "I have come through, I have come through!"[58]

He had been awed by the weight of the situation and the presence of the princes of the empire. But there was more to it than that! He had known since he had made his first attempts at theology in 1509 that true belief must curse the angel that preaches a different Gospel (Gal. 1.8). He had marked out his boundaries with regard to the "Jews" and "Greeks," to Moses and Aristotle; he had taught, written, and preached against undermining the Gospel with laws and entangling it with philosophy. Now he himself was up against a wall. Contrary to his expectations, the pope and curia had not taken his side, the side of the Gospel. He had been sure that "the pope would damn Tetzel and bless me. . . . But when I expected blessings from Rome, I received instead thunder and lightning."[59] Within a very brief period he had had to reorient himself—in fact, he had had to leave everything behind that he was familiar and at home with.

In Augsburg the positive function of canon law had become doubtful to him. Less than a year later the public disputation in Leipzig had witnessed

Bernhard Strigel, Emperor Charles V

the collapse of a further axiom. Confronted with his opponent from Ingolstadt, Johannes Eck, he had been forced to come to the conclusion that councils, too, could offer no guarantee against the Devil, an appraisal that cost him the support of Duke George of Saxony. What could he now expect in Worms?

On the afternoon of April 18, 1521, the decision was to be made: would the empire, too, "excommunicate" and expel Martin Luther? He was being pitted against the full force of hallowed tradition. "Martin Luther," the Trier official Johann von der Ecken asked on the emperor's behalf, "do you perhaps wish to defend all of your books?" This was the most terrible challenge Luther had ever experienced. Here was the Devil's question being asked officially, by the empire: Do you alone possess wisdom, against so many centuries—against the Holy Church, against councils, decrees, laws, and ceremonies that our forefathers and everyone around us have upheld up to the present day?

On the previous day he had asked for time, "so I can give the correct answer without doing injury to the Word of God and endangering my soul." Now there could be no more evasion, meditation, mitigation, or examination. Ecken could not refrain from ridiculing the temporizing monk: anyone may be expected to be in a position to bear witness unequivocally and fearlessly at any time; all the more in your case, you famous, experienced professor of theology! The Trier official did his job with such ironic mastery that nuncio Aleander recommended that the curia reward him generously for his performance.[60]

Luther made good use of the time he had; his unemotional, explanatory speech before the diet went to the heart of the problem: I am not arguing about my life but about the teachings of Christ. And so I am not free to recant because by virtue of this recantation tyranny and godlessness would be reinforced, and they would rage all the harder. What a recantation puts at stake is plain: not only peace of mind but the welfare of the empire; not only redemption but the preservation of the world. Where the Gospel is denied, the common weal is imperiled.

But this is at best a well-meaning program; reality looks different. The Gospel that the monk from Wittenberg propagates counter to all tradition does not bring peace and harmony; it brings conflict and controversy. That is Luther's view of the Gospel's effect: it gives rise to disputes and arguments. But where it is rejected, there is nothing to keep violence at bay. This is how he spoke before the Diet of Worms:

> From this, I think, it is apparent that I have sufficiently considered and weighed the arguments and dangers of scholarly disputes that have been aroused in the world as a result of my teachings, because of which I was so sharply and forcefully admonished yesterday. It is my nature to see the positive side of things—that because of the Word of God, zeal and disputes arise. For that is the course, the manifestation, and the effect of the Word of God; as Christ says: I came not to bring peace but the sword: for I am come to set a man at variance against his father, and so on. That is why we must bear in mind that God is wonderful and terrible in his counsel, so we will not strive to smooth out differences if by doing so we contemn the Word of God. Through this a flood of insufferable evil will most likely pour over us.[61]

What confused nonsense he seems to be talking, certainly nothing the diet could make any sense of. Quarrels and dissension arise if the Gospel takes its course unhindered; wickedness and violence break in on the world if it is suppressed. Peace is imperiled whatever the diet decides.

Whether the representatives of the empire were aware of these tensions is a question that will have to remain open. From Luther's point of view the presumed contradiction does not exist. Where the Gospel is preached, the

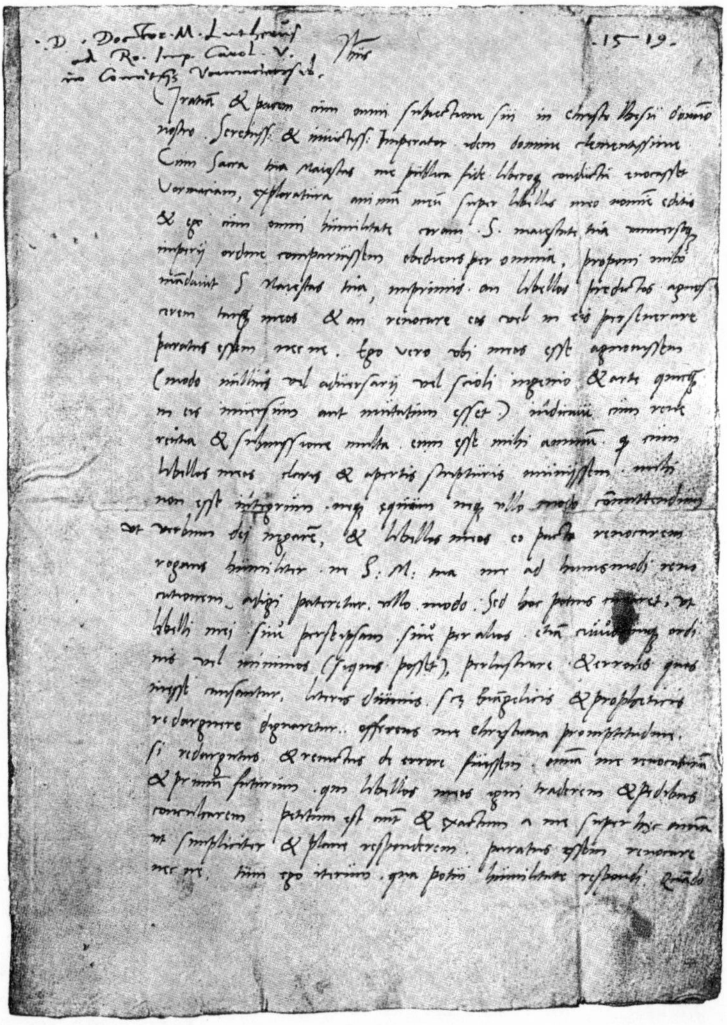

*Letter to Emperor Charles V in Luther's own hand, written after the Diet of Worms, 1521. Luther once again lists the reasons why he cannot submit to the judgment of the Pope. The fragment ends with a central statement: "As long (*quando*; last word, bottom right) as my conscience is captive to the Holy Scriptures, which have furnished evidence for all my books, I cannot recant if I am not proven wrong"*

(Weimarer Lutherausgabe, Abt. Briefe, *2: 307–10)*.

Der Römischen Kaiserlichen Maiestat
Edict wider Martin Luthers Bücher vnd leere seine anhenger
Enthalter vnd nachfolger/vnd etlich ander schmeliche schrifften. Auch gesatz der Truckerey.

Wir Karl der fünfft von gottes gnaden. Erwelter Römischer Keiser zu allen zeitē. Merer des Reichs. &c. In Germanien/zu Hispanien/bei der Sicilien/Jherusalem/Hungern/Dalmacien/Croacien. &c. Künig/Ertzhertzog zu Osterreich/Hertzog zu Burgūdi. &c. Graff zu Habspurg/Flandern vnd Tyrol. &c. Entbieden allen vnd ietlichen Churfürsten/Fürsten/Geistlichē vnd weltlichen/Prelaten/Graffen/Freien Herren/Rittern/Knechten/Hauptlüten/Landtfögten/Vitzthumben/Vögten/Pflegern/Verwesern/Landtrichtern/Schultheissen/Schöffen/Burgermeistern/Richtern/Röten/Burgern/vnd gemeinden. Auch Rectorn vñ Regenten aller gemeinē vniuersitetē/vñ sunst allen andn vnsern vnd des Reichs/auch vnsern erblichen Fürstēthūm vnd land vnderthonē vnd getrüwē/in was wirdē/statz/oder wesens die sein/den diser vnser Keiserlicher brieff od glaublich abschrifft/die durch ein geistlichen Prelaten od offenbarn Notari/verfertigt ist/davō fürkumpt od gezögt würt vnser genad vñ alles güt. Hochwirdigē vnd erwirdigen/hochgebornē/wolgebornē/ersamen vñ Edlen/liebē fründ/Neuen/Oheimen/Churfürsten/Fürsten/Andechtigen vnd getrüwen.

The text of the Edict of Worms, in which Luther is banned, signed May 26, 1521

battle with the adversary inevitably follows. As the Devil wants to subjugate the world, to battle against the Devil is at the same time to serve the common weal.

THE INTERROGATION concluded with Luther's answer "without loops and holes," a succinct series of statements ending with the impressive words: "My conscience is captive to the Word of God. Thus I cannot and will not recant, for going against my conscience is neither safe nor salutary. I can do no other, here I stand, God help me. Amen."[62]

Aleander and everyone else present immediately realized that Luther had taken back nothing of the scathing attack that had shaken the Church of Rome. He had, after all, unequivocally declared that popes and councils frequently erred and contradicted themselves! The foundations of medieval belief were being rejected as inadequate, and not on the grounds of "principle" or a "loftier standpoint" but on the basis of verifiable historical experience. Pope and council had demonstrably erred repeatedly.

The emperor had no trouble reaching a decision: Luther was a dangerous and destructive force, undermining the foundations of faith in the empire. He must be placed under "ban and double ban." On May 26, 1521, the emperor promulgated the Edict of Worms: We enjoin you all "not to take the aforenamed Martin Luther into your houses, not to receive him at court, to give him neither food nor drink, not to hide him, to afford him no help, following, support, or encouragement, either clandestinely or publicly, through words or works. Where you can get him, seize him and overpower him, you should capture him and send him to us under tightest security."[63]

Luther's appeal to conscience as the highest authority made an extraordinary impression on later generations. Out of the understandable desire to declare Luther as the forerunner of the Enlightenment, the statement "Here I stand, I can do no other" was reinterpreted as the principle of freedom of conscience.

But that is missing the whole point. Appealing to conscience was common medieval practice; appealing to a "free" conscience that had liberated itself from all bonds would never have occurred to Luther. Nor did he regard "conscience" as identical with the inescapable voice of God in man. Conscience is neither neutral nor autonomous: hotly contested by God and the Devil, it is not the autonomous center of man's personality, it is always guided and is free only once God has freed and "captured" it. What is new in Luther is the notion of absolute obedience to the Scriptures against any authorities; be they popes or councils. The way Luther dislodges the Christian conscience from its individual, immediate proximity to God and integrates it into the obligation to heed reasonable worldly and historical experience is innovative. *Faith* is not founded on reason: God's omnipotence transcends reason and the cross of Christ contradicts it. *Actions,* on the other hand, must be able to stand the test of reason and experience because their sole objective is service to one's neighbor; there is no room here for self-justification or self-sanctification.

Luther liberated the Christian conscience, liberated it from papal decree and canon law. But he also took it captive through the Word of God and imposed on it the responsibility to render service to the world. That is why in all realms of life, be they marriage and sexuality, civic duties or obedience to the temporal authorities, the Word of God must be heard anew; it must be applied with the standard of practical reason and directed at how life is to be lived. Satan availed himself of ecclesiastical law to enslave man in all spheres of life, in faith, morals, and politics. The "grievances of the German Nation," the complaints about the exploitation and tyranny of the Church of Rome, are the evidence that the lives of both individual and community are threatened and in urgent need of external reform.

Looking back on Worms, one can understand the wish, somewhere between dream and dismay, so well expressed by Leopold von Ranke:

> One could almost be tempted to wish that Luther had for the moment stopped there [the attack on papal abuses]. It would have strengthened the whole nation in its sense of unity, and it would have furthered national cohesion, if under Luther's leadership it had risen up against the worldly rule of Rome. The answer, however, must be: the power of this spirit would have been broken had he been fettered by considerations

> not wholly religious in content. He had gone out not from the needs of the nation but from religious conviction, without which he would never have achieved anything and which certainly got him further than would have been either necessary or useful for that political struggle. The eternally free spirit moves along its own path.[64]

If Luther had been "moderate" and castigated only curial infringements, the German nation might have awakened and achieved unity by doing battle under his leadership against the temporal rule of Rome—long before Bismarck.

It is a dream, and such an understandable one that it affected even a man of Ranke's stature. But he then succeeded in shaking it off on the grounds that Luther's horizon did not encompass politics.[65] If "politics" is equated with "strategy," and if its goal is to establish the City of God on earth, then Ranke is right. But politics as a means of preserving the world until doomsday is something Luther propagated to the very end of his life and even became actively involved in where he could; the last days of his life were spent at the negotiating table.

Though no professional politician, Luther was an eminent political mind.[66] He had an enduring influence on the politics of his time. The grievances of the German nation, which had been occupying princes, bishops, and imperial diets for almost eighty years, had resulted in a *White Book* against Rome in 1521.[67] Independent of their attitude toward the Evangelical movement, the imperial estates emphatically demanded that the emperor put a halt to the damage being done by Rome. Luther provided legal foundations for these grievances by disqualifying canon law as foreign, papal law, and providing a scriptural basis for the temporal authorities' right to self-determination.

There were, however, considerable gaps in the new legal foundations, which various groups, not all of them marginal, tried to turn to their own advantage: under Sickingen, knights revolted against clerical rule on the Rhine (1522);[68] rebellious peasants destroyed monasteries and robbed monastery property (1524–25); and princes pursued a course of "secularization," which was nothing but a redirection of Church property and funds into their own coffers (1526–27). Grievances were once again in order, this time to prevent the aristocracy from establishing its rights at the expense of the public welfare. In the struggle against all these efforts to promote personal interests in God's name, Luther became more than a political issue, he became a politican.

The example of the Papal States and episcopal principalities revealed the

Devil's basic strategy to him: the power of faith is to be undermined and the world to be ruled by means of ecclesiastical might. Luther's fierce resistance to this perversion emerges from his epoch-making discovery that only when the crippling fear of not being saved and the anxious egotism of achieving one's own salvation have been overcome by faith does the welfare of the world come into view. The gift of justification releases man from his greed for rewards and enables the believer to be truly pious "for nothing"—not from fear of punishment and Hell but to the greater glory of God and "to the benefit of one's neighbor."[69]

three

The Reformation in Peril

CHAPTER VII

Life between God and the Devil

Driven and Drawn

Nineteenth- and early twentieth-century accounts of Luther portray him as a simple workman's son from Mansfeld who, by studying hard in Erfurt and Wittenberg, succeeded in cutting through the tangle of medieval Church doctrine and finding his way back to the Holy Scriptures. Defying persecution and threats, he defended his discovery undaunted, resolutely following the path he knew to be his, and mesmerized the masses with the power of his preaching. That is how he made history.

Much of this heroic interpretation of Luther's bursting genius is beyond dispute. A chain of major decisions in Luther's life, from becoming a monk to the rapid succession of events in the complex controversy over the Church, must be deemed momentous also by posterity. In the interest of faithful Christians all over the world, he had to decide again and again—sometimes on the spur of the moment—in how far he could with good conscience make allowances for pressure from Rome, from the princely court, and, until about 1519, from his fellow monks in the German Augustinian congregation.

Luther saw his life and work from a different perspective, one uncommon, even alien, to the modern historian and enlightened cosmopolitan: he was led, indeed driven. From the first disputes over his indulgences theses to his final retrospective view of the road to the Reformation, Luther consistently maintained that his "career" was neither the product of a natural predisposition nor a plan engendered by personal ambition.

That he considered himself absolutely unequal to the task of a reformer was not simply pious modesty. The monk and university professor had to overcome two major handicaps in order to achieve mass appeal. At the beginning of the sixteenth century monks competed with university professors for the lowest rankings in public esteem; viewed as sanctimonious and pseudo-erudite, they were roasted with equal glee in the local pub as at the patrician's table. Both had long since become figures of public ridicule.

Luther thus had what seemed to be the worst possible qualifications for a popular reformer—an opinion shared by Hieronymus Aleander, the special papal legate dispatched to the Diet of Worms in 1521 specifically to deal with the Luther problem. Aleander thought Luther incapable of electrifying the masses and far too stupid to have authored such erudite writings. The monk was nothing but a straw man for the person really pulling the strings. And there was only one person ingenious enough to initiate such an effective, dangerous campaign against Rome: Erasmus of Rotterdam, a biblical scholar as perfidious as he was learned.[1]

Luther, too, saw himself as an instrument, but of a totally different type. It was not intelligence or determination that was shaping the course of his career; God was driving him on and sweeping him along. He had no illusions about his abilities. Others had superior talents and education, and Erasmus, the great humanist so feared by Aleander, far surpassed Luther in the art of oratory and knowledge of languages. Luther lacked an air of cool superiority when dealing with people who did not share his views; he flared up and lost his temper. Even his writings were undisciplined; it was not only his early works which he would have preferred disappear from circulation. He recommended that the Holy Scriptures, not his works, should be read; and if anything else was to be consulted, then rather the *Loci communes,* Melanchthon's concise work on Evangelical doctrine first published in 1521.

Luther's self-assessment might be taken for the last vestiges of monastic humility, but it was a humility with a hard core: service to the Word—Luther had not sought it; the post of a professor—he had not desired it; the mission of an evangelist—he would have liked to avoid it. As he saw it, he entered the monastery under compulsion, blinded by fear; his doctoral studies had been imposed on him against his will by his Augustinian superiors. Instead of fighting and becoming entangled in feuds, he would have liked to devote himself to study and meditation. Time and again Luther offered to cease his activities if only the Gospel became public property. But again and again he was overwhelmed, led where he did not wish to go, by a God who, irrespective of obedience or disobedience, steers the course of history.

Hardly had his indulgence theses become public knowledge than his opponents in Germany and Rome condemned him as a heretic, and his inquiry into the danger of being misled by purchasable indulgences as heresy. Their arguments so obviously contradicted the Scriptures and faith in Jesus Christ that only one interpretation was possible: the heresy-hunters were blind and obstinately refused to hear the Word of God. They, too, were evidently being driven . . . but not by God!

This public outcry was the overture to the Reformation. What we encounter in Luther is not the medieval battle cry "God wishes it"—*deus vult,* but "God does it"—*deus facit.* Luther's exposure of curial abuses of power and the Scriptures was as impossible to suppress or retract as the discoveries of a Columbus before or a Copernicus after him. Remaining silent would have constituted, as he understood it, the spiritual murder of the faithful, who for centuries had been deluded into trusting in the authority of the Church.

The indulgence controversy was only the beginning. Again and again, after every new incident, every new turn of events that linked Luther's life with the history of the Reformation, he declared in his table talk and letters: "Here I was driven by God, here I was hurled from the beginning to the outcome."

LATER GENERATIONS liked to speak of "divine guidance" and "providence." Luther, on the other hand, preferred a phrase drawn from the mystical tradition: "I was swept along," an expression less of a destiny guided by a remote Almighty than of the intervention of a present, all-powerful God. Man does not appear in the light of his self-determination, but in the light of his need for guidance from God's overwhelming power. Modern man shrinks from the thought of such direct divine intervention. With the coming of the Enlightenment God retreated into the distance, at best comprehensible now as the primal architect of the cosmic world machine. Perhaps modern man understands "divine providence" as the harmonious world he longs for, or it may simply be a symbol of a still-to-be-discovered natural law. Above all, he suspects "guidance" of being a projection of one's own wishes or at most a defense ex post facto of unpopular decisions: Luther must have confused his own mind with God's counsel!

Luther and Enlightened Humanism

Not at all! Luther could never regard Providence as a private court of appeal or as justification for his own actions. Augustine affirms that the God who is closer to me than I am to myself creates, guides, and drives the life of the individual exactly as He does the world history of all.

IN *De servo arbitrio* (*Bondage of the Will;* December 1525), his polemical tract against Erasmus—and "modern" men of all eras—Luther took up and emphasized the subject of the distant and the present God. Contemplating the real tension between God's sovereignty and human responsibility, he unlocked the doors to his own life history, incorporating his own experiences as a "reformer in spite of himself" and scrutinizing them in the light of central scriptural passages.

But the suspicion that personal experience dictates scriptural interpretation may be a modern prejudice. Luther may well have started from the opposite end: from listening first to Scripture and then applying it in the light of daily life. Faith in God and experience in life were so intimately linked for Luther that the beginning cannot be distinguished from the end. That is also why Luther's "life between God and the Devil" must deal with his view of his own life as well as with his interpretation of how things stand in the lives of all. Luther's reply to Erasmus is considered too complicated and strangely abstract. Scholars have rejected the tract as unsuccessful or exaggerated, the "liberal" view has rendered it innocuous, and the "pastoral" one has tried to put it right. Luther was unquestionably being provocative: "Free will in man is the realm of Satan"; "God Himself does evil through those who are evil." His response to Erasmus seems to have deteriorated into contempt for man and a profanation of God. And yet, as ill structured as it is, it is not in the least a failure; it is ruthlessly direct and clear. Were these the only pages of his writings to have survived, we could deduce from them the total scope of Luther's thinking.

The tract was entitled *The Bondage of the Will* in direct response to Erasmus's preceding treatise *De libero arbitrio* (*The Free Will*), but it could much better have been called "The Majesty of God." That would immediately have revealed what was at stake, while rendering it less shocking.

Luther's dispute with Erasmus had already begun several years earlier, though neither publicly nor directly. Luther saw no advantage in confrontation; the preaching of the Gospel would suffer as much harm as scholarship and the arts. And yet he was divided against himself. While desiring the compromise of silence, he wanted to debate the issue. It was the otherwise reticent Erasmus who allowed himself to be thrust into open confrontation, not only by critics, who unjustly distrusted him, but also by his patrons among the nobility, who rightly admired him: King Henry VIII of England and Duke George of Saxony.

In early September 1524 the time had come: Johannes Froben in Basel published *De libero arbitrio Diatribe sive collatio.* In it Erasmus took up the thesis of the unfree will, which Luther had long formulated openly. The question, as the humanist emphasized, was one which scholastic theology had already found extremely perplexing. The Holy Scriptures were evidently not unequivocal, and even if Luther were right, it would be inadmissible for an assertion of this kind to be made in public, from the pulpit. Where would the normal Christian be if, at the mercy of "fate," he were relieved of all responsibility for his own moral improvement! The thesis of the unfree will would lead the ordinary believer to moral abuse without helping the theologian to attain the certainty of knowledge.

It was of the utmost importance to Luther to keep discussion of this fundamental issue from being the reserve of theologians. What he wanted was to present his basic ideas plainly in preaching and teaching, so as to make them intelligible to his less educated contemporaries, and even to do it in German. He had always rejected the idea of an educated elite. The problem was one that has stirred reflective people of all eras and educational levels: if God is the supreme ruler—and there was no quarrel between Luther and Erasmus on that point—the question of how to reconcile the cruel, ruthless, and apparently blind course of history with God's mercy will inevitably arise. It is only a short step from this challenge to a nightmarish conclusion: God is merely the past hope of generations that wanted to believe, He is the projection of a society in search of an ultimate design and purpose. Heaven is empty; we stand alone.

Luther's reply to Erasmus is modern in that it already reflected these consequences in the form of questions. As he battled with the problem, he did not take Erasmus the man and programmatic reformer into account; he suspected the Dutchman of being the first Christian atheist. All the characteristic aspects of Luther's thinking and beliefs can be found here: God's grace and human works, the dark power of the Devil and the viability of human beliefs.

Erasmus had made a pertinent observation and drawn a reasonable conclusion from it: the best minds of scholasticism had spent centuries comparing biblical passages and had nevertheless been unable to agree on how much freedom man could have in a world ruled supremely by God. It was therefore his advice to draw the appropriate consequences from the situation and to counter any claim to absolute, ultimate solutions with scholarly skepticism. God is so far above us that we can never grasp more than a part of His truth; for the truly pious, that is enough.

This must have sounded like sweet music to the ears of many; it was the unmasking of a blind, academic theology alienated from its historical sources. Modern Bible scholarship in the sixteenth century, with its rediscovery of Hebrew and Greek, the languages of the Old and New Testaments, called into question the authority of the Latin text of the Bible, on which the whole of scholasticism had been based. But conservative theologians in Cologne, Louvain, Rome, and Paris stubbornly adhered to the Vulgate, the Latin translation sanctioned by the Church. These "obscurantists" and "sophists," who prided themselves on their pseudo-education, had succeeded in having the great German Hebraist Johannes Reuchlin condemned in Rome less than four years earlier (1520); now they were endeavoring to silence Erasmus, whom they had long considered suspect, as well. He was impugned as Luther's guide and mentor, though from Erasmus' standpoint Luther was anything but a disciple. With his trust in the potential of theology Luther seemed to be quite the child of scholasticism, incapable of bearing the insecurity of scholarly research. For the scholastic from Wittenberg the adventure of open inquiry could be nothing but a bold attempt to undermine the Church.

This would, however, be a misrepresentation of Luther, as he was unquestionably one of the theologians who could appreciate what humanist scholarship had achieved: without knowledge of ancient languages there could be no reliable exegesis of the Scriptures! When Erasmus published his edition of the Greek New Testament in December 1516, Wittenberg hailed the work as revolutionary. The first copy available there was received with great ceremony. In contrast to Erasmus, Luther even numbered among the first—of the humanists of his time, among the few—who used Reuchlin's works to study Hebrew. Thus Luther recognized that the mastery of ancient languages was a necessary tool in accomplishing a clear textual interpretation of the Bible.

SCHOLARSHIP LEADS TO various results and divergent points of view. Using his own exegetical work as an example, Luther demonstrated to his students again and again that a text or part of a text or just a single word could be translated in very different ways; he showed that decisions must be left open not only where he was uncertain but also where he himself thought matters were clear.

This relativist attitude of groping and searching can be described as scholarly detachment and skepticism; such skepticism is an integral part of modern scholarship. But when doing research, it is equally important to approach and grasp straightforward matters with an open mind, not governed by given authorities, not deferring to sanctioned traditions. The Scriptures do not contain only obscure texts, where "skepticism" would be apt; there are also clear, self-evident passages that can be translated unambiguously and must therefore be interpreted accordingly. Clear scriptural passages seem obscure only when earlier, established interpretations are not taken as preliminary versions but become pre-judgments that judge—without allowing themselves to be judged—because the reader or listener has a closed mind.

The most stubborn and effective of these preconceptions are based on a "clear" and "general" consensus of what is "self-evident." "Common sense" knows precisely what deserves to be termed moral, how true piety manifests itself, and how a righteous God must behave. But there are straightforward passages in the Bible that are in such marked contrast to our sense of what is morally self-evident and to our natural image of God that only God's spirit can bring clarity and awaken in us the readiness to listen to the text with an open mind and then to accept it.

THOUGH THE questions Erasmus and Luther labored and clashed over seem to be lofty ones, they were to become basic issues throughout the course of the Reformation and modern intellectual history as a whole. Erasmian "skepticism," as liberal and liberating as it appeared to be, would, as Luther anticipated, lead believers astray in one of two ways. On the one hand the Scriptures would be elevated to "Holy Scriptures" and locked away with seven papal seals that could be broken only by the "Holy Church." With that the book on which the Church was founded would become a Church Book, shrouded in mystery, deriving its authority and power from the pope, as the Roman theologian Silvester Prierias summarized the claims of the curia as early as 1518—seven years before Luther's dispute with Erasmus. The Bible could no longer be read with a critical eye on pope or Church, since its message would then be limited to proofs for the authority of the papacy, to passages which, according to the claims of the curia, might properly be interpreted only by and from the vantage point of the pope.

The other consequence, too, would result in a sealed book, but this time final judgment would be left not to the pope but to biblical scholars. Today that would mean the systematic theologians above all—who, like the "sophists," the scholastic theologians, so complicate the Scriptures that the "uninitiated" Christian can no longer find any solid ground in which to root his faith.

"The Holy Ghost is not a skeptic," says Luther; He does not lead us into the semi-obscurity of conflicting views on basic questions that, true to the spirit of scholarly detachment, should be left unanswered. There is, after all, one fundamental truth in the Bible about which there can be no arguing, for it has been revealed: God Himself became a man, suffered, and will rule for all eternity. The message is unequivocal; it is the reader who equivocates, who cannot approach the text objectively and without preconceived ideas. He is man in conflict, who does not want to accept God's judgment over him. "Remove Christ from the Scriptures and there is nothing left." Through Christ, God and His design were rendered accessible to everyone, even though there may be passages, statements, and concepts that are obscure to us and for which we need scholars. But that does not apply to more than isolated problems. The Gospel is plain and must therefore be taught and preached simply and without skepticism.

It would be totally wrong to declare Erasmus defeated by this argument. He has certainly never been driven from the field—up to the present day. He was, after all, not interested in skepticism as such, but in an attitude that, with its academic reticence and struggle for objectivity, would serve peace in the Church and the world. It is unquestionably easier to live with Erasmus than with Luther, not so much with Erasmus the man—who was vain and over-sensitive to criticism and contradiction—but with his ideas, which have appealed to the cultural elite throughout the centuries.

That is one side of Erasmus, the side that corresponds to our present-day temper. But the modern aspect does not constitute the whole: as a rule, the Renaissance is associated with rebirth and energetic new departures; but in his conflict with Luther, Erasmus presented a totally different picture, one of weariness, disappointment, and disillusionment at the end of a long era of seemingly secure values and firm convictions. It was in his confrontation with Luther, his diatribe on the free will, which generations have interpreted as humanism's programmatic repudiation of the Reformation, that the outstanding Bible scholar was more scholastic and medieval than ever before. His treatise was oriented toward the past; it was extremely conservative in its rejection of public discussion of unauthorized, untried, and hence unacceptable solutions and biblical interpretations.

Unlike Luther, Erasmus was, however, modern in that he placed his hopes in a long future. He believed there was enough time for a re-education of the elite to produce a gradual ethical change; the medieval "mirrors for princes"—the political "textbooks" of that time—would have to be rewritten to suit governmental and cultural leaders of a bourgeois society. Erasmus pinned his hopes on the progress of time and the educated man, the best defender of the loftiest interests, whose innate, ineradicable striving for self-actualization is purified by God and then finds consummation in true piety.

From Erasmus' perspective Luther was impatience personified, a monk who would listen to no one, who had not learned from history and threatened the cause of piety and education by casting doubt on man's moral dis-

Hans Holbein the Younger, Erasmus of Rotterdam

position and perfectability. A thing done well cannot be done quickly, as the saying goes.

But Luther had no time to wait. There could be no thought of either a long-term educational policy or a step-by-step subjugation of peace-imperiling barbarism. Of course he regarded the founding of schools and universities as "a thing done well"; that was one of the absolute obligations of a Christian regime in Church, state, or city, so that people could learn to use reason in adapting themselves to their world and would not become the pawns of the powerful. But there would never be an educational program with the means of transforming a society so as to give political shape to the longed-for kingdom of peace and justice.

What Luther saw on the horizon were the dark clouds of divine judgment gathering over a world nearing its end, a world fettered and enslaved in a thousand ways, that insisted on self-determination before God, that dared to speculate about the "meaning of history" and to speak of freedom of the will without being able to free itself from the paralyzing primeval fear of being trapped helplessly in the cage of an impenetrable world history.

Luther and Erasmus—two realities: not the Middle Ages versus the modern era, but two interpretations of man and history drawn from divergent perspectives and experiences, neither of them indisputably "obsolete" or "progressive."

Man as a Mule

Luther's break with Erasmus was bitterly divisive to the Evangelical camp. If the Peasants' War was the external crisis of the Reformation, Luther's falling-out with Erasmus was its internal one. Sympathizers were faced with a choice they had never dreamt of. The preceding years had seen a wave of popular pamphlets proclaiming the rediscovery of the Holy Scriptures as the Reformation cause. Now the time had come for a liberation from the unholy "appendices," from the "wisdom" of ecclesiastical law, which had numerous provisions to regiment Christian life and threatened to stifle it completely.

At that time Erasmus and Luther were still considered allies, champions in the common struggle against the repression of conscience, the half-knowledge of impudent monks, and the Roman exploitation of Germany through direct and indirect taxes, through crusade funds and indulgence peddling. Neither excommunication by the pope nor the emperor's ban could extinguish this sweeping protest movement. Luther's excommunication had only limited effect because the moral authority of Rome had reached its nadir all over Europe, and curial theologians were evidently not in a position to respond to the religious issues of the Reformation in their fight against Luther. The effect of the imperial ban imposed in the 1521 Edict of Worms was contrary to expectations. Instead of protecting the traditional order, it made Luther's program for the reform of Church and empire even more of a national issue and prevented the Reformation from sinking into the oblivion of a local theological dispute, as had so many other late medieval renewal movements. Nor was the peasants' revolt that had struck terror in the hearts of the Germans since spring 1525 able to inhibit the Reformation, although in all centers of European power Luther was now being decried, feared, and fought as a violent revolutionary and public danger.

Erasmus provoked the great spiritual crisis, the lasting and powerful historical challenge to the Reformation when, finding the central point of Reformation theology, he exposed the appealing alliance of Renaissance and Reformation as only a temporary coalition. He succeeded in pinning Luther down to a statement that coming centuries would read as a symbol and summary of the whole of the Reformer's theology and that was often taken as sufficient grounds for neglecting the reasons that had induced the Reformer to raise his voice. The horrible diagnosis: man is the battlefield between God and the Devil.

When God had long paled into an uncertain hypothesis and the Devil was no more than a medieval vestige and a childish memory of times past, Luther's slap in the face of humanist progress was still remembered: for Luther, man is *not* the mule that, stupefied by ignorance, cannot decide between two haystacks—education could help that mule. No, the condition of man does not depend on the breadth of his education but on his existential condition as a "mule," ridden either by God or the Devil, but with no choice in the matter, no freedom of decision, no opportunity for self-determination.

This proclamation of man's total impotence on the eve of man's greatest scientific discoveries and enduring cultural achievements could only eliminate Luther as a point of spiritual orientation in the tumult of modern times. It is true that the linguistic accessibility of his German writings gave rise to so broad and deep-rooted a Luther tradition in Germany that the Reformer could not simply be discounted in favor of the Erasmian vision of erudition. But Luther's principal effect was as a beacon of freedom in the confessional struggle from the age of the Counter-Reformation to the late nineteenth-century *Kulturkampf;* his continuing popularity did not imply agreement with the contents of his works. The experiences of the Third Reich ultimately robbed this Luther of his credibility, too. "Anti-Semitism" and "submission to the authorities"—these became the catchwords of a "new" Luther interpretation.

The loss of heroic status led to a perceptible cooling of admiration for Luther in Germany and promoted a more critical evaluation, which discounted as medieval the view of man as a "mule." This is where the dialogue, having reached an impasse, will have to be taken up again, for it is through this needle's eye that all the threads of the Reformation discovery run: justification by faith alone (*sola fide*), the preaching of God's Word alone (*sola scriptura*), and trust in God's grace alone (*sola gratia*).

Luther and Fundamentalism

We can encounter Luther only where he was convinced he stood and not where he approximates the temper of our time. And that, as he plainly says in the concluding remarks of his treatise against Erasmus, is in the recognition of man's powerlessness before God. Luther concedes that Erasmus more than any other opponent had realized that this, and not the indulgence controversy or purgatory, was the central question of the Christian faith. Yet to call it a central question" is already misleading; this is not a problem to be solved, since this issue in the Scriptures is crystal-clear.

In 1521 Luther had not been willing to recant before the emperor in Worms without factual refutation, but now his tone was even more strident, leaving no opportunity for a counterargument: "This is what the Scriptures teach . . . and so do I. Here I can yield to no one." He goes on even more pointedly: "Whoever teaches otherwise denies Christ and faith." So whoever contradicts the Reformer here rejects him totally. How inconceivably bold it was of Luther to venture such an assured, conclusive judgment on a problem the Greek philosophers and scholastic theologians before him—and many others after him—had tried in vain to solve. Who has ever succeeded in overcoming the basic conflict between God's omnipotence and man's freedom without opening an even greater abyss? Luther's answer is short but not immediately clear: the testimony of the Holy Scriptures is his legitimation.

For us in the twentieth century, his answer cannot be convincing, because application of the Reformation principle of *sola scriptura,* the Scriptures alone, has not brought the certainty he anticipated. It has in fact been responsible for a multiplicity of explanations and interpretations that seem to render absurd any dependence on the clarity of the Scriptures. In the eighteenth and nineteenth centuries post-Reformation Protestantism tried out many variants of "fundamentalism" to counter the trend, often declaring the letter of the Scriptures sacrosanct. But even desperate rescue missions cannot breathe new life into a motto that was once so persuasive: as God truly became incarnate in Jesus, so His spirit became inerrant truth in the Holy Scriptures.

That this motto had fallen into disuse would be no loss from Luther's point of view. He started from a different and, in fact, contradictory principle, which was to be ignored in the Protestant longing for a "paper pope": "God and the Scriptures are two different things, as different as Creator and creature."[2] This historically innovative principle forms the surprising basis of his response to Erasmus, in which we can also find a new and crucial point of departure for present-day theology. It is this principle that distinguishes Luther from the biblicism of both his own and later eras.

IN THE early days of the Reformation the principle of the Scriptures alone (*sola scriptura*) was such a convincing battle cry that it must be numbered among the factors that enable us to understand how a scholastically trained monk from a university at the edge of civilization could, despite these obstacles, find such enthusiastic acceptance. The thesis of the sufficiency of Scripture alone had the immediate ring of truth, quite different from the two more complicated, equally explosive concepts: by grace alone—by faith alone (*sola gratia—sola fide*). Even untrained readers of Reformation pamphlets in areas where Evangelical preaching was not yet permitted could immediately grasp that God's Scriptures were the decisive authority, which could liberate one from the shackles of tradition.

In villages and cities, inns and market squares, peasant leaders had long been speaking of a return to the "old law." Since Luther had appeared on the scene, there was an additional demand: the old law was to be interpreted and framed according to the Word of God. And it was not only in the country that the call for the law of God found a receptive ear. In the cities, too, people were demanding a reintroduction of the old laws; freed from clerical tutelage, citizens wanted to mold their lives according to Scripture. To the leaders of the urban Reformation, who had attended the only recently founded Latin schools and had been appointed to their newly established preaching posts by a city council—not a bishop!—the discovery of the Holy Scriptures as the sole Christian rule signified the great Evangelical turning point.

Many of the urban Reformers, from Luther's older Wittenberg colleague Andreas Bodenstein von Carlstadt to John Calvin, a member of the second generation of the Evangelical movement, had legal training. They applied the new methods that accompanied the renaissance of jurisprudence to theology: the standard for every just judgment was the literal sense of the law; not traditions and learned interpretations, but the text alone was the final

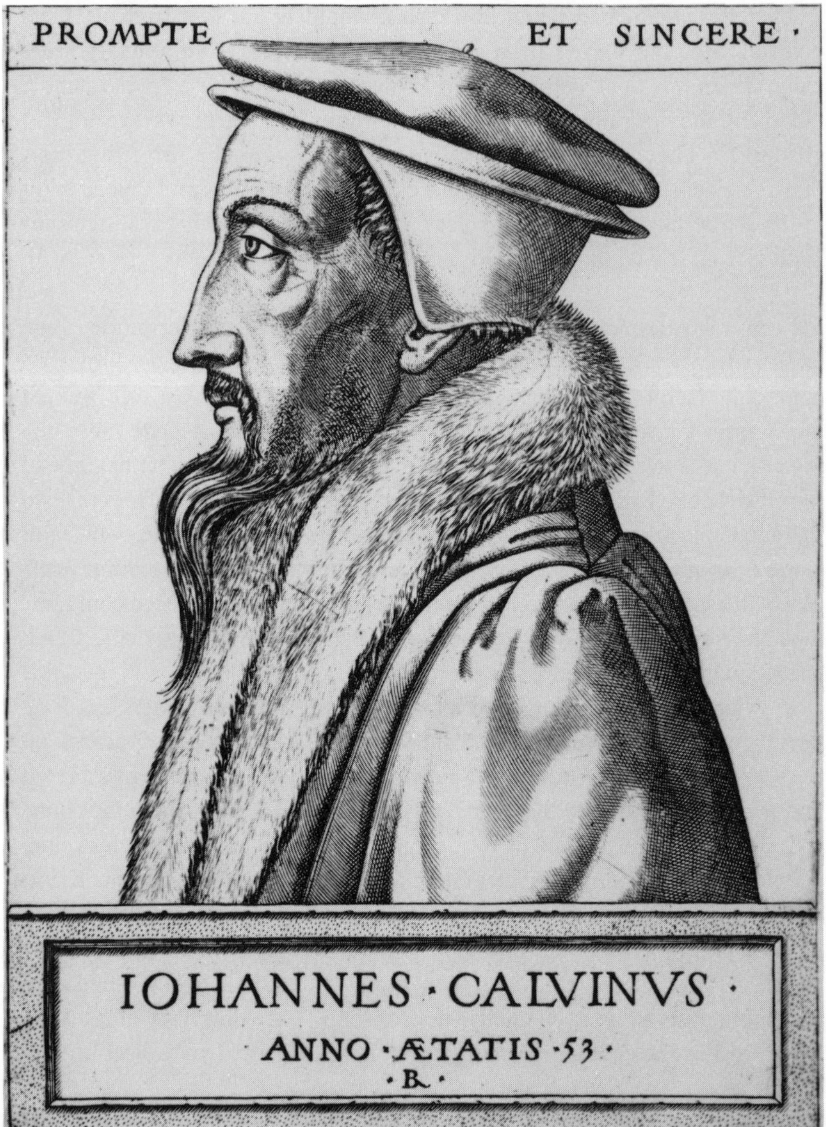

The Geneva reformer, John Calvin. By René Boyvin

arbiter. Analogously, the Scriptures, not the Church Fathers or scholastic doctors, constituted the norm in matters of Christian faith. The Bible, not the pope's canon law, should judge and regulate Christian life. For these legally trained reformers the heart of the discovery of the Gospel consisted in the principle that the teachings and preaching of the Church must prove themselves by Scripture and Scripture alone.

This does not, however, apply to Martin Luther, at least not in this form. The exclusive authority of the Holy Scriptures was not part of his Reformation discovery—a fact that gave rise to tensions in the sixteenth century and has caused misunderstanding to the present day. In his early works, which according to Luther himself belonged to his "papist" phase, he already presupposed the Scriptures to be the obvious sole source of faith. Later he explained this early insight: in 1518 he had successfully participated in the great academic disputation of his order, the Augustinian Hermits, in Heidelberg; there he had been allowed to introduce his new theology to members of the order and guests in a learned debate of thesis and criticism, question and answer.

On his way back from Heidelberg he stopped in Erfurt, where he had spent his first university and monastery years. He wanted to visit his revered teacher Jodokus Trutfetter and explain in person the program for theological and Church reform that actuated him. But in vain. He was denied access to the house; Trutfetter's servant dismissed Luther with the excuse that the professor was indisposed.

As soon as Luther reached the Augustinian monastery in Erfurt, where he was staying the night, he wrote his former teacher a moving letter, pleading for understanding and reminding him that Trutfetter himself had been the one to teach his students to have faith only in the Holy Scriptures and to judge all other authors critically, as not only Augustine but even St. Paul and St. John had demanded.[3]

To name Trutfetter was not a tactical apology. As a student Luther had indeed been helped by Trutfetter to find this crucial key and made his professor's scriptural principle his own. In Luther's earliest known works the normative authority of the Bible is never called into question; it is put to use against speculative scholastic teachings not determined by the Scriptures and where necessary even against the Church Father and founder of his own order, Augustine. His quest did not concern the authority of the Bible, which was self-evident to him; he wanted to know how this authority could be properly expressed, how the Word of God could be ascertained among the wealth of scriptural testimony.

The term *authority* as a description of Luther's understanding of the Bible could be misleading if—as happened before and after him—the Scriptures were taken for a collection of objective truths that had to be compared and rearranged in ever new systems, depending on the issue in question. The principle Luther dictated to his students in his first lecture series on the Psalms already leads beyond this "scholastic" use of Scripture. The exegete should treat a difficult scriptural passage no differently than Moses did the rock in the desert, which he smote with his rod until water gushed out for his thirsty people (Exod. 17.1–7). The rod is faith, under which Scripture unfolds, and faith is the confident hope of hearing the voice of God from the pages of this book and of being addressed directly. But for a biblical text to be really penetrated by it, the rod of faith must be wielded with the help of scholarly aids, particularly of linguistic research. Conceptual and grammatical clarity are and remain the basis and the regulating mechanism of theological exegesis.

The development of young man Luther's theology can indeed be traced by the way he spurns the centuries-old symbolic interpretation of Scripture in his own works, for otherwise the text threatens to become intellectually inflated and the spirit of God is put at the mercy of the ingenious exegete.[4]

Once Scripture has been dealt with down to its language and grammar, what does it reveal to man in his yearning for knowledge of himself and the world? The diagnosis is frightening: man cannot redeem himself; he is only a heartbeat away from death and on the way to nothingness. Where it is a question of salvation, decisions lie not with the free will but with God alone, on whom man is dependent from his first sigh to his final breath. Man must be driven forward by the Word and grace of God and held fast in his faith to the very last moment; without divine mercy he collapses into himself and back into nothingness.

But where it is a matter of shaping the world, man, even the wicked, godless man, has the duty and the ability to use his reason and good judgment to act freely and steer the course he chooses.[5] This distinction between man and world, between person and achievement, is undoubtedly less than what "Erasmians" and "fundamentalists" expect from the Scriptures. What they are seeking there—whether in the laws of the Old Testament or the Sermon on the Mount—are specific instructions that enable the new man to enforce God's supremacy on earth.

"GOD AND the Scriptures are two different things"—Luther's distinction sounds as alien and bold to the medieval man as to his descendants in the age of the Renaissance and Reformation. Reform and renewal, the best any age has to offer, was always—whether for Bernard of Clairvaux, Desiderius Erasmus, or John Calvin—inspired by the Holy Scriptures and directed toward enforcing God's law in Church and society, in monastery, study, and town hall. Luther, on the other hand, dared to stress the distance: two different things—like creator and creature. The clarity of the Scriptures leads to the recognition of man and his indestructible dependence either on God the Redeemer or Satan the corrupter. There is no third alternative. But the Scriptures do not lead to a disclosure of the majesty of God's dominion, and they do not reveal His plan for the history of the world, in which the new man can simply take his place as the vanguard of freedom and progress.

The Bondage of the Will of the year 1525 is directed against the most important representatives of the Renaissance north of the Alps—but not only against them and their followers then and now. It is aimed equally at the fundamentalists, who have taken up the cause of the Reformation and promoted it under the motto of *sola scriptura.*

It is a very narrow path Luther is walking. Following him means being initiated into life between God and the Devil, the vital problem of his theology, where Scripture, grace, and faith—the three basic Reformation concepts—interpret and clarify one another.

CHAPTER VIII

Discord in the Reformation

The Sacrament of the "Ignorant"

Once the "time for silence" had drawn to a close in early 1520, the new study of the Bible began generating a host of problems which now had to be solved in accordance with Scripture but without recourse to canon law. Baptism, the Eucharist, penance, marriage, and authority were the central topics Luther would be dealing with in the coming years. The construction of a new Christian worldview would call out not only old adversaries but opponents from Luther's own ranks, who had learned to use the Old and New Testaments as a basis for theological debate—and dispute.

In what Luther later came to see as the darkest days of his life, he gave us the best example of what the crucial term *Anfechtung* means and described his way of coping with it: "The Prince of Demons himself has taken up combat against me; so powerfully and adeptly does he handle the Scriptures that my scriptural knowledge does not suffice if I do not rely on the alien Word."[1] The "alien Word"—this alienating concept goes to the root of the conflict. The "alien Word" is the Gospel, which is not "my own," but which I must hear spoken "to me." The Christian can be justified in the sight of God only through trust in the extraneous righteousness of Christ and not through his own righteousness. Likewise, a Christian can only be promised absolution, the Word of forgiveness, "from outside." He cannot trust his own conscience, and the confusion will only increase in view of the fast-approaching end.

"My scriptural knowledge would not suffice if I did not rely on the alien Word." What an odd statement from a professor of theology, especially one who can refer to himself as Evangelist and insist on the authority of Scripture with such conviction that no other authorities, no matter how respected or hallowed, can compete. It is at this point that we encounter the crucial difference between confidence and certainty, between truth and the assimilation of truth. Luther describes the distinction in terms not of a theory but of the existential dimension of the Reformation doctrine of justification: "I have saved others; I cannot save myself,"[2] because I cannot free myself from my despair, because my own visible righteousness vanishes before my very eyes, and my own conscience forsakes me. That, Luther feels, is why I need the other, why I am dependent on the intercession and community of the Church.

Trust in the alien Word determined the way Luther experienced, interpreted, and defended the sacraments of baptism and holy communion. The Devil, that master of subjectivity, lurks in the heart and the conscience, but he is powerless in the face of the alien Word. Baptism and communion are the pledge that God is present in the turmoil of the fight for survival against the Devil. These two sacraments constitute the visible, tangible prop that makes it possible to resist the Devil in God's name. Thus baptism and holy communion are the solid ground on which the certainty of a Christian's faith rests. It is therefore clear that there can be no greater danger than the undermining of these two sacraments. Making baptism and communion into the work of man destroys the foundation of Christian life because it makes God's truth and reality dependent on the powers of persuasion of the individual, subjective conscience.

Of this very thing Luther repeatedly accused both the papacy and also those Reformation groups he liked to call Anabaptists and Sacramentarians. Baptism already had become a central theme in the major Reformation writings of 1520. For Luther it was the visible sign of unmerited justification through God's grace. Baptism performs the "joyful exchange" through which a sinner receives the righteousness of Christ and Christ takes over his sins; and all this is not simply "cheap," it is free. The gulf between Luther and the Church of Rome becomes obvious when Luther, criticizing the commercialization of the Church, makes an easily comprehensible comparison between God's free "baptismal grace" and the pope's expensive "indulgence grace."[3] Precisely because baptism is "democratic," granting everyone the justification of Christ, it also gives all believers sacerdotal status, for everyone "who comes crawling out of baptism has thus been consecrated a priest, bishop, and pope."[4]

In late 1521, when Luther had already been in hiding at Wartburg Castle for nine months, Philipp Melanchthon reported the first signs of a movement that was soon to spread everywhere the Reformation succeeded in gaining a foothold. Today this movement is usually designated the "left wing of the Reformation" or "radical Reformation," a collective term used to subsume a variety of groups. From Luther's point of view these Baptists and social

Lucas Cranach the Elder, *Martin Luther as Junker Jörg, 1521*. This is the disguise Luther adopted while he was in hiding at Wartburg Castle.

revolutionaries, antitrinitarians and spiritualists had one thing in common: they were "fanatics."[5] Restless, roaming spirits, separatists with no sense or feeling of responsibility for Church and society, disobedient to the temporal authorities and the Holy Scriptures—that is how Luther saw them.

His first encounter with Anabaptist currents in 1521–22 influenced his attitude toward all reformers who were not Wittenberg-oriented: peasant leaders and Sacramentarians, Zwinglians, urban reformers, Schwenckfeldians, and whatever else they might be called, they threatened the Reformation cause because together they formed a common front repudiating Church and society. The case was clear: a simultaneous threat to the Church and the world was proof that the Devil himself was at work here; the fanatics were his henchmen, so there was little to distinguish them from the "papists."

As productive as Luther's "medieval" battle against the Devil was, its limitations now become evident as well. The vision of a world pervaded by the Devil has appalling effects if it leads to collective judgments. When papists, Jews, and so-called fanatics are condemned as groups, individual differentiation becomes impossible. The individual human being disappears behind a uniform foisted upon him.

In the tumult of the Last Days individual qualities are lost in collective judgments and "all who are not with us are against us." Yet herein lies the paradox, for there is a genuine grain of truth in these collective condemnations, which is easy to overlook in our time. It is for the sake of this timeless truth that Luther's voice must be heard—however reluctantly. To comprehend this, we must look at his understanding of infant baptism.

From Luther's point of view the command to administer baptism found at the end of the Gospel of St. Matthew puts an end to any debate about the sense or nonsense of baptizing children. The task is clear: "Go ye therefore, and make disciples of all nations, baptizing them in the name of the Father and the Son and the Holy Ghost" (Matt. 28.19).

Baptism only becomes a sacrament, a visible pledge of God's fidelity instituted by Christ, through the promise He made (for Luther always one of the central pillars and unmistakable "clear places" of the Scriptures): "He that believeth and is baptized shall be saved; but he that believeth not shall be damned" (Mark 16.16).

When Melanchthon wrote to Luther from Wittenberg that the Zwickau Prophets were citing precisely this text to challenge infant baptism, Luther answered on January 13, 1522, with a detailed exposition of his opinion on the subject that closed with the words: "I have been waiting for Satan to attack this sensitive spot—but he decided not to make use of the papists.

Now he is making efforts in and among us Evangelicals to produce the worst conceivable schism. May Christ quickly trample him under His feet."[6]

Why this dramatic talk of the Devil and of the Church breaking asunder? Baptism was not being called into question, only infant baptism rejected! The reason is that for Luther this constituted a denial of a decisive point. Infant baptism revealed the meaning of baptism. From Luther's standpoint one could not genuinely preserve baptism while repudiating infant baptism, for it was in the child to be baptized that the meaning of Evangelical faith became visible: trusting only in the "alien" justification granted by God; acting out of the "alien," the new conscience; and living on the intercession of others. Where one's own faith begins to waver, the alien faith appears on the scene. And this is the exact situation of the "infant," for whom the Church, godparents, and parents believe vicariously. The baptismal font is the reservoir of alien righteousness surrounded by alien belief.

For enlightened Protestantism, which has developed faith into a rational system and eliminated the Devil from it, this belief is not alien, but alienating and peculiar. Luther, however, insists on this very alienation when faced with the menace of an intellectualization of faith: if the Devil is to be withstood, intercession is indispensable; "loners" are defenseless against his threat and subject to his tyranny. A good Christian is always an infant in his dependence on God and in the way he is bound up with Christ and His Church.

In the *Grosser Katechismus* (*Large Catechism,* 1529), Luther summarizes the meticulous theological reply he gave Melanchthon to produce a more widely comprehensible survey of his theology as a whole. He plots a course bypassing medieval sacramental faith and modern subjectivist beliefs: baptism was instituted and ordained by God—proof enough that it is "no trivial matter . . . like putting on a new red dress."[7] God's own work is performed by man, for baptism is conferred in God's name, in the name of the Father, the Son, and the Holy Ghost. To be baptized is to receive an "inexpressible treasure," deliverance from "sin, death, and devil." We have run all over to acquire an indulgence; shall we now not know how to appreciate this true and great gift?

The Baptists call baptism with water an "outward thing" and ask: how should a handful of water help the soul? But the external is not empty, because God "attached" his Word to the baptismal water. Through this corporeal gift, God provides a powerful mainstay that can be perceived by the senses.[8] A Christian does nothing but receive; he must, however, spend a lifetime dealing with this treasure. Man's "ignorant" nature cannot grasp it.

But on the basis of baptism, it can contradict tribulation and reason: I shall be saved body and soul.[9]

Baptism thus functions as both redemption and certainty of redemption. The argument against infant baptism, that infants cannot believe because they do not have the rational faculties to grasp the Christian message, distorts the sacrament, transforming it from the work of God into the work of man. The "ignorant" child is not baptized because of its faith but because of God's promise. "We bring this child here in the belief and hope that it will have faith and pray to God for faith. But not for this do we baptize it, only because God has commanded it. . . . His Word can neither err nor lie."[10]

Penance is closely linked with baptism and is thus not a separate sacrament. It does not reestablish baptismal grace that has been lost; it is a return to baptism, a return to the beginning that God made there! Baptism grabs the Devil by the throat and the old Adam by the collar; wherever we turn, baptism marks us throughout our lives.

Protestants have often pointed with glee to the obscure, magical interpretation of the sacraments in the Middle Ages. Luther indeed opposes magic and superstition when he consciously and pointedly speaks of "ordinary water" that can only become operative when combined with God's promise. But criticism of magical superstition is not a specifically Reformation trait; its origins are pre-Reformation. Luther could fall back on his scholastic training for it.[11] What he here attacks so vehemently is not the superstitious overestimation of baptism, but its faithless undervaluation in Christian life in favor of penance and penitential good works. This made it perfectly reasonable to call entering a monastery, when novices dedicate their lives to penance, "second baptism."[12] Rejecting infant baptism and demanding adult baptism of the converted and of penitents is thus not "radical Reformation" but "radical Middle Ages."

The widespread influence of the Anabaptist movement in the face of bloody persecution fits the tenor of the time: the new layman is the old monk.

MODERN RESEARCH is once again directing its attention to Anabaptist criticism. It knows that early Christendom was silent on the subject of infant baptism and has recognized that Luther's central biblical passage, the baptismal commandment, was added to the Gospels of St. Matthew and St. Mark only later. The baptismal commandment is a teaching of the early Christian community.[13] But if it is—rightly—not baptism "in itself" that is called into question but only infant baptism, Luther's inquiry remains valid: shifting the emphasis to an adult's conscious decision to be baptized confuses God's gift with a human act. The problem is not adult baptism but the arguments against infant baptism.

An age that thrives on concepts like self-determination and credibility demands adult baptism. "Self-determination" is genuinely necessary to a profession of faith, especially in a post-Christian world. To withstand the test of self-analysis and the ensuing diabolical accusation, however, infant baptism is the rich sacrament for the empty-handed. The statement "We are beggars, that is true" does not suddenly become valid when a person is on his deathbed. It marks the way life begins.

Divided over the Sacrament of Unity

"Before I would have mere wine with the fanatics, I would rather receive sheer blood with the pope."[14] In 1520 Luther had already objected that the medieval doctrine according to which the eucharistic elements, bread and wine, were transformed into the body and blood of Christ was arbitrarily based on Aristotelian tenets. The Fourth Lateran Council (1215) had affirmed that the substance was converted while the accidents, the outer appearances of bread and wine, remained. But the Holy Ghost, according to Luther, knows even more than Aristotle. At Christmas human nature was not "transformed," for in Christ both natures, the nature of God and of man, were fully retained. This might outstrip the philosopher's understanding; the believer can grasp it.[15]

Despite his criticism of the medieval doctrine of transubstantiation, Luther remained faithful to tradition in leaving untouched the concept of the real presence of Christ in the sacramental elements. Not even his sharp attack on the focus of the mass, the sacrifice the priest offers to an angry God, changed anything about that. The "Sacramentarians" or "sacramental fanatics," on the other hand, repudiated the doctrine of Christ's corporeal presence in the bread and wine. Instead of letting themselves be invited to the "Lord's Supper," they invited the Lord—so Luther suspected—to a commemorative meal of bread and wine.

Why did the controversy arise? What was so embittering as to make Luther's university colleague Andreas Carlstadt into his opponent and to set a series of important southern German and Swiss reformers—Zwingli in Zurich, Oecolampadius in Basel, and Bucer in Strasbourg—against him? Only a few simple words were at issue, Christ's words instituting the Eucharist: "This is my body." (Matt. 21.21; 1 Cor. 11.24). Plainly the statement is essential to the faith and piety of the Church, and Carlstadt, Zwingli, and Luther each read the sentence with different eyes, finding the key to its interpretation in a different word.

Carlstadt was of the opinion that Jesus had referred to himself at his last meal: he says "this" and means his own body. Thus the words do not denote bread and wine, but Jesus the man, and the words of institution become a prediction of the Passion: I am the body which will be sacrificed on the cross for you. Holy communion should remind the congregation of this body.

In October 1524 Luther reported with surprise that this interpretation was already "running rampant far and wide."[16]

Carlstadt's view did not convince Zwingli, and it disappeared from the discussion soon after the Zurich reformer proposed his own variant in the summer of 1525: all previous theories had misconstrued the function of the word "is." The words of institution are an interpretation, not an equation. Jesus says "is" (*est*) and means "signifies" (*significat*): the bread signifies my body. The congregation that assembles around the bread and wine is thus referred to Christ in Heaven, who has been sitting at God's right hand since His ascension.

Luther was concerned with preserving the corporeality of Christ's presence, and thus stressed the last part of the controversial sentence, "my body." As God was truly incarnated and came into the world bodily, so real is His corporeal presence in the eucharistic elements of bread and wine.

IT HAS been said that Luther held a more comprehensive position, one which integrated "faith in salvation," while Zwingli thought in more rational, realistic, and thus practical categories.

Regarding Zwingli as the more practical, rationally oriented reformer is based on an accurate observation. It is the same social critique that erupted among the iconoclasts and accompanied the anticlericalism of the cities. A citizen, say, of Zurich, like Zwingli, saw the difference between the Middle Ages and the Reformation above all in the contrariety of the sacramental, sacerdotal Church and a spiritually unified, true community of faith. It was in the urban Reformation that long-harbored social resentment against privileged clerics made real inroads;[17] here is the anticlerical tendency one searches for vainly in Luther.

This is not to challenge the earnestness of Zwingli's search for the correct eucharistic doctrine.[18] But the congruence of theological solution and socio-political concerns makes two things clear: first of all, it explains why the eucharistic controversy raised such waves. For what historians today allow a

The Zurich reformer, Ulrich Zwingli. By Hans Asper, 1531.

paragraph of Reformation history was in the sixteenth century a pivotal issue and touchstone for pending decisions. The presentation of one's position on the Eucharist showed where one stood: on the side of the privileged clerics and ruling elite, or in the ranks of the citizens unified in true faith.

It also becomes clear that Zwingli started from the conviction that, properly understood, the Word of God described the "common good" and promoted its realization. Hence it was perfectly legitimate to take sociopolitical considerations into account in the course of scriptural exegesis. Zwingli's eucharistic theology was thus oriented toward city and society. For Luther the common weal belonged to the realm of human freedom and was to be shaped according to reason and experience. The Eucharist, on the other hand, was a way not of shaping the world but of keeping faith, rendering comfort where there was doubt and lending strength in the battle against the Devil. But in the city the Devil had been shackled and appeared only as a lawbreaker. We sense optimism in the view: it was not an expectation of the Last Days but a hope for modern times.

The contrast between the community-oriented urban reformers and Luther, minister to a godless world, is sharp. Luther focuses on the individual Christian, not because the "individual soul" is more important "before God" than a responsible forging of political life, but because service to the world demands a stout heart. For it is not a question of honor and dignity, but—whether in city or country, townhouse or farmhouse—of resistance to the destructive power of the Devil. Political affairs make enormous demands on Christians, and that is why they must be fortified in their faith.

Here lies the element of truth in the claim that Luther's position always links faith with salvation. Yet this applies to most of the reformers. In his tract *On the Babylonian Captivity of the Church,* written in the summer of 1520, Luther formulates this faith in a way that Zwingli could easily have accepted: "The mass as we know it is a promise of the forgiveness of sins made to us by God and confirmed by the death of His Son. . . . Where the promise is given to us by God, there the faith of the man who is eager for its fulfilment is necessary, so that it is clear that faith is at the very basis of our salvation, the faith that is dependent on His promise."[19] Not the emphasis on faith but the "dependence on the Word" separates Luther from Zwingli. This dependence became the essential feature of Luther's thoughts about the Lord's Supper, both in his debate with the pontifical Church and in his dispute with Zwingli and the other opponents Luther vilified as "fanatics."

Luther never really did justice to Zwingli. Nonetheless, it must be noted that in his dispute with the Zurich reformer, his conception of the Eucharist attained a profundity of thought for which the groundwork had been laid,[20] but which was now formulated in detail and made viable as a powerful tradition. A high price had to be paid for this profundity, and we must point out both the theological gain and the political loss.

First the loss: shortly after he made his decision for the Reformation in 1524, Landgrave Philip of Hesse recognized that the Evangelical movement would have to fight for survival on two fronts, not only theologically against the pope but politically against the Hapsburgs. It would be wrong to attribute a pan-European approach to Philip. But he had a feeling for the regional constellations of political power. Although he himself was a unique mixture of late medieval sovereign and enlightened ruler, he never considered the isolated territorial interests of Hesse, always seeking to secure them in the larger framework of the empire and the Hapsburg world imperium. He perceived the limits to his own rule more distinctly than any of the princes who dreamt of their own sovereignty and ultimately achieved it—but, apart from the Hohenzollerns in Prussia, only as rulers of politically and economically insignificant states.

Philip does not seem to have chosen the side of the Reformation for selfish or political motives. But shortly after his inner conversion, he began drawing political consequences from his profession of faith. First he strove to make a defensive pact with Electoral Saxony. His wish was realized in 1526 with the Gotha-Torgau treaty, but he could consider this treaty no more than the beginning of a larger pact system that would place the Evangelical estates in a position to hold their ground against pope and emperor. He wanted all the Evangelical territories and cities to unite. His ambitious plans were, however, foiled by the eucharistic controversy between Luther and Zwingli, which took on increasingly violent forms in the years 1525 to 1528. The Hessian landgrave was anxious to draft a treaty that allied northern and southern Germany and also included Evangelical Switzerland. Electoral Saxony, however, insisted that a unified profession of faith must precede the conclusion of any treaty to serve as the basis of the political alliance.

For two years Philip had been trying in vain to win Luther for his plans, when the imperial diet in Speyer (1529) made a move that could not be ignored: the imperial estates, overruling the minority of Evangelical estates, decided it was finally time to wipe out the Reformation, in keeping with the instructions of the Edict of Worms. The Evangelical estates lodged protests against the decision on April 19 and 20, thus gaining themselves the name "Protestants." The Protestants objected to the diet's transgression of authority "as in matters of God's honor and the salvation of our souls, each [estate] must stand for itself before God . . ."[21]

But Philip wanted more than just a protest against domination by the majority followers of the Church of Rome; he wanted tangible protection for the minority. Unlike his in-laws and cousins in Electoral Saxony, he was a prince who knew how to act promptly. He was still in Speyer when he invited Huldrych Zwingli to a religious colloquy. After a great deal of back-and-forth negotiating, it really did take place, in Marburg from October 1 to 4, 1529, and was attended by leaders of the Reformation from all over Germany, including the two opposing "heads," Zwingli and Luther. The discussion was substantive, the tone only rarely acerbic, but the agreement Philip had hoped for was not achieved.

Various transcripts show that the personal rancor between the two reformers had subsided, but both Zwingli and Luther stood their ground on doctrine. The Wittenberger cites the "clear words" of Scripture; they are unequivocal and overwhelming—so "submit"! The confession of Worms echoes in a different form: I am a captive of the Word, even if one cannot explain how the presence of Christ in bread and wine is to be imagined. The virgin birth and the forgiveness of sins are beyond our understanding in the very same way. Thus Christ instituted the Eucharist; "the Devil cannot get around that." Occasionally voices become shrill. Zwingli bases his view on Jesus' statement, "The flesh profiteth nothing" (John 6.63)—which must also apply to the Eucharist: "This passage breaks your neck." "Don't be too proud;" Luther retorts, "German necks don't break that easily. This is Hesse, not Switzerland."[22]

When the Marburg conference was over Luther wrote to his wife, we are "of one opinion in almost everything." But he added, "at the Lord's Supper, however, they will allow bread to be only physically and Christ to be only spiritually present. . . . I suppose that God has blinded them."[23]

The eucharistic controversy had for the time being thwarted Philip's attempt to construct a unified, anti-Hapsburg coalition. At the Diet of Augsburg the following year, the sad consequences became evident to everyone, for the Evangelicals were not in a position to work out a confession of faith acceptable to all. Apart from the Confession of Augsburg, the confession of the Lutheran estates, two further confessional documents were presented: Zwingli sent an account of his religious doctrines to Augsburg, and four southern German cities under the leadership of Strasbourg handed in their Tetrapolitan Confession to the diet. Only when the leader of Strasbourg's Reformation, Martin Bucer, years later accepted the Wittenberg view could the alliance Philip strove for finally be concluded—though without the Swiss.

Zwingli died soon thereafter. His death at the Battle of Kappel against the Catholic "Five Cantons" in October 1531 fully confirmed Luther's negative attitude toward the Zurich reformer. The prophecy of Marburg that he, Luther, would break his neck, had turned full force on the prophet himself. Zurich's defeat also convinced Philip to fall in line with the Saxons. His hoped-for alliance "for hasty rescue and defense" remained restricted to the empire.

In the sixteen years of its existence the Schmalkaldic League, the alliance formed by the Protestants in 1531, proved a successful defensive force: in July 1532 the Peace of Nuremberg, an important pledge of temporary toleration, was signed. For the first time the Protestant estates could negotiate as an independent, united party. The emperor was promised the help he needed to resist the Turks, and in return he and the Catholic estates had to accept the "Peace." The Nuremberg treaty was in reality little more than an uneasy cease-fire, but it foreshadowed the legal solution of the religious struggle in the empire as it was to be negotiated in Augsburg in 1555 and in Münster and Osnabrück in 1648.

Luther had welcomed the imperial pledge of tolerance as a divine gift; his assessment of the Hesse-Württemberg campaign against the house of Hapsburg in the summer of 1534 was altogether different. In a surprise attack Philip of Hesse succeeded in reconquering the hereditary land of Duke Ulrich of Württemberg, who had been expelled as a tyrant in 1519. Only since about 1530 had Luther reluctantly accepted the idea of a defensive military alliance and sanctioned the princes' right to resist the emperor should he violate the commitments made upon his election.[24] The Württemberg campaign could not purport to be defensive; it could appear only as an attempt to impose the Reformation by force of arms.

The Hessian expedition in Swabia proved that the defense pact also had offensive potential. The golden age of the Schmalkaldic League ensued: Pomerania and the cities of Augsburg, Kempten, Frankfurt, Hannover, and Hamburg joined. King Francis I of France and King Henry VIII of England established diplomatic contact with the league to exploit the division within the empire and the weakened position of the emperor. All Scandinavia became Lutheran in 1537 when Denmark (Sweden had already defected from Rome in 1523) elected a Protestant king, Christian III. This meant that the

Luther and Hus administering Holy Communion in both kinds, bread and wine, to the elector and his family.

Reformation could also be carried out in Christian's other states, Norway and Schleswig-Holstein.

Prominent circles in France evinced pronounced sympathies for the Reformation. In 1534 a Church of England independent from Rome was created by the king's sovereign decree. The Reformation was plainly on the advance. Once King Christian of Denmark joined the Schmalkaldic League in 1538, Landgrave Philip seemed to be very close to his objective of an anti-Hapsburg coalition, though not in the form originally intended. Philip's plan to unite *all* the parties to the Reformation in an alliance was not to be realized.

Supported by an insistent Luther, Electoral Saxony implemented the Confession of Augsburg, and especially the article on the Eucharist, as the charter of the league. This measure virtually forced Wittenberg's opponents to rethink their theological position. In 1536 a settlement on the issue of the

Eucharist was finally reached between Wittenberg and southern Germany. Even the four south German cities—Strasbourg, Constance, Lindau, and Memmingen—that had presented a separate confession in Augsburg in 1530 signed the eucharistic settlement. Nonetheless, Luther could not overcome his suspicion that political expediency had outweighed religious convictions and theological clarity. The Gospel can only be spread by the Word and not by politics, and even weapons cannot protect the Word.

The failure of the Schmalkaldic League one year after his death would not have surprised Luther. It was his firm conviction that there could be no blessings on offensive war and that wars waged for the sake of the Gospel were the work of the Devil. Because of this basic attitude Luther has been called apolitical, unrealistic, and even fanatic. But his concern was to distinguish faith and politics in such a way that pursuance of a policy of peace became all the more realistic the more consistently the cause of the Reformation was left to God. The Marburg colloquy of 1529 attests to the fact that the reformers, Luther and Zwingli alike, were steadfast in their refusal to subordinate their convictions to the demands of political calculation. That an alliance of all Protestants could not be achieved was the political price of the eucharistic controversy.

In determining the theological gains, we must first realize that agreement was reached in Marburg on decisive principles of Evangelical faith. But why could the eucharistic controversy not be marginalized enough to enable Luther to extend his hand to Zwingli in Christian fraternity? The gesture would have been so small and the political profit so great! To answer this question, the decisive underlying motives must be disentangled.

In a sermon he gave on Maundy Thursday 1518 about the proper preparation for holy communion, Luther uttered a much noted principle: "You will receive as much as you believe you receive. . . . Belief alone is the best and only condition, because it builds not on our works or powers but on the absolutely pure, enduring Word of Christ: 'Come to me, all who are weary and heavily laden.'"[25]

There is no way of telling whether Zwingli knew this sermon, though it immediately appeared in several Latin and German editions and was also printed in Basel a year later. He could certainly have accepted it completely and, as with other of Luther's writings, have seen to its dissemination. The passage from St. Matthew which Luther quotes in the sermon became Zwingli's motto as: "Come to me those who work(!) and are heavily laden, and I will give you rest" (Matt. 11.28).[26] Luther had formulated the fundamental religious questions not only for a Zwingli in Zurich but for the whole

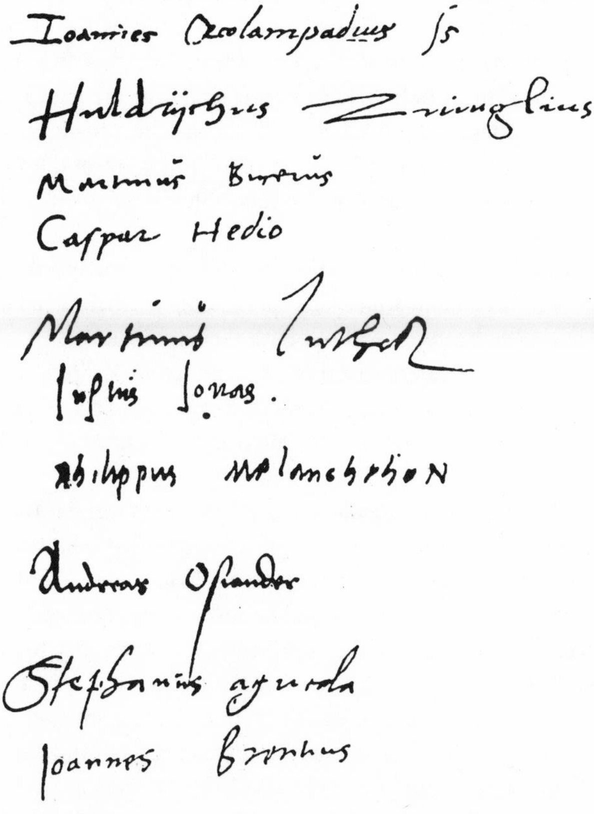

In Marburg the leaders of the Reformation in Germany signed the "Fifteen Articles," representing the fundamental principles of Evangelical doctrine. One problem remained unsolved: they did not agree at this time on "whether the true body and the true blood of Christ were really present in bread and wine." Marburg, October 1–4, 1529: Johannes Oecolampadius, Hyldrychus Zwinglius, Martinus Bucerus, Caspar Hedio, Martinus Lutherus, Justus Jonas, Philippus Melanchthon, Andreas Osiander, Stephanus Agricola, Johannes Brentius.

era, and he had answered them as well: belief liberates us from the insupportable burden of inner and outer compulsions.

To his sermon Luther appends a statement with a medieval touch to it, an important and revealing "appendix"; that it has received little attention can best be ascribed to the significance of what goes before. Luther: If you lack faith, then clutch the last anchor. Have yourself carried to church like a child and then speak without fear to Christ the Lord: "I am undeserving, but I rely on the faith of the Church—or of another believer. Whatever my situation, O Lord, I must be obedient to Your Church, which bids me to go to Communion. If I bring you nothing else, at least I bring you this obedience." And then, Luther continues, only believe firmly that you are not going to the Lord's Supper undeservingly. Christ will credit the obedience you have shown to the Church as the obedience of faith. The faith of the Church will as little abandon you, the adult, "as the infant that is baptized and saved by virtue of alien faith."[27]

This "alien faith" is the bridge between infant baptism and the real presence of Christ in bread and wine. The sacraments are beneficial and useful only if one has faith, but even without faith they are true.

This "alien faith" separates Luther not only from Zwingli and his followers but also from his own heirs. Modern Protestantism sees faith as individual fulfillment, and the idea of an "alien faith" outside the individual is foreign to it.

To comprehend Luther's distance from modern Protestantism, it must first be remembered that his treatment of the sacraments did not deviate in the least from the principle of "by faith alone." But he had to do battle on two fronts at the same time. On the one hand he wanted to teach Christians that they were not allowed to run to the Sacrament "like pigs to the trough, without fear and humility."[28] Because of this Luther had, since 1523, demanded an annual auricular confession (within the precincts of the church but not necessarily in the confessional) to prepare the faithful for holy communion.[29] There was no doubt that the words of the apostle Paul were true: "He that does not discern the body of the Lord eats and drinks himself to damnation" (1 Cor. 11.29). But Luther gave the passage a new interpretation: the apostle was not demanding "worthiness," for no one, not even a saint, is worthy before God. St. Paul was asking not for worthiness but for faith and confidence in Christ's promise of salvation: "Given for you." In dealing with careless "pigs," insistence must be on faith.

The case is somewhat different for repentant sinners and those suffering temptation, for whom the Sacrament had been "especially" instituted. This was the second front Luther faced, and it only really became clear in the course of the eucharistic controversy with the Swiss. The Swiss insisted on the rational question: what is the profit of the real presence of Christ in the Sacrament, what is the use of "flesh-eating"? The flesh is, according to Jesus himself, of no profit! How can insufficient faith ever be replaced by obedience? The Reformer from Wittenberg was unmasked as a "neo-Papist" and captive to the Middle Ages.

Luther's answer must be given careful attention: the profit of the eucharistic body lies in the fact that through faith in the bodily presence of Christ the tempted communicant need not rely on himself and his soul, for he is led out of himself and directed toward Christ. The unequivocal, "clear" words of the institution of the sacrament breach the narrow bounds of the psyche, pointing outward to the God who promises: "Here you shall find me."[30]

God is present everywhere, but there is a world of difference between "God being here" and "God being here *for you.*" The Devil knows the former, but he will never experience the latter. The whole Gospel is concentrated in that little word "here," without which one would have to search the whole of creation, looking here and asking there. But then no one could be sure he had found the eternal God in His multifarious creation "for himself." When you eat your bread at home, Luther says, God is near too. But if you accept it "here," then you eat His body—God becomes yours. God thus defines a "here" where he can be found with certainty so that he need not be "fanatically" sought "everywhere." But what does one find "here" in the Lord's Supper? The bodily Christ, the one everyone needs because we are more than mind and soul: "The mouth, the throat, the body which eats Christ's body should also profit from it so it will live eternally and be resurrected on the Last Day. . . . That is the heavenly power and the profit of Christ's body going into our body during the Lord's Supper."[31]

The benefit of the eucharistic controversy cannot be overlooked. Faith in the Word of God is essential for overcoming the spiritual-psychological focus on the inwardness of pious communion. What makes this so significant is that the Enemy, an expert on the single soul, loves individualism. He can penetrate the psyche and control it. He can twist and cripple even the believing Christian so that, lost in introspection, he despairs of God and the world. But there is one thing the Devil cannot do: he cannot become really present flesh. The call of the words of institution liberates the Christian from the clutches of self-analysis.

THE TRAGEDY of the eucharistic controversy was multi-faceted. In 1529 the dispute prevented the formation of a unified Evangelical front. The Schmalkaldic League could prepare only a "small German" religious peace, one that gradually enabled the confessions in the empire to coexist but left hundreds of thousands of Protestants outside the empire defenseless against persecution. In the era of the Thirty Years' War, even the "small German" religious settlement threatened to be dashed by the great powers. Scandinavian Lutheranism and militant Calvinism just managed to prevent the worst.

But the tragedy was even farther-reaching. Not only did the controversy thwart unity, it actually made it impossible for the various parties to listen to one another. The general vilification of opponents made it inconceivable for them to take each other's positions seriously. Luther was roundly attacked and ridiculed as a "flesheater." He was termed a "neo-Papist"—could anything have been more offensive to him? For Luther, on the other hand, the "perversion of the clear words of institution" proved that the Devil himself was at work. He was the master of a thousand arts and expert at twisting Scripture: "No matter how one looks at it, he is the prince of the world. Whoever does not know it should open his eyes and look around! . . . It is this very Devil who now subjects us to temptation through the fanatics."[32]

The personal confrontation in Marburg helped to objectify the dispute, enabling Luther to reduce the disagreement to the formula: "We are not of one mind. . . . We commend you to the judgment of God."[33] The Devil seemed to have been put at arms' length, but at a price: God's judgment had been invoked. The eucharistic controversy gave rise to fundamental questions that were insoluble at the time. Thus Marburg marked a profound, painful turning point in Reformation history, as the joy of having discovered the Bible to be the conclusive foundation of Evangelical faith could not remain undiminished when the reformers came to disagree over the "clear" text of the Scriptures.

The report which Andreas Osiander wrote to the council of the imperial city of Nuremberg is the most vivid account of the dramatic events at Marburg. It shows that Zwingli assessed the consequences the controversy would have on the progress of the Reformation "realistically" and was thus—from Osiander's Lutheran point of view—better at interpreting politics than Christ's words of institution: "Tears sprang to Zwingli's eyes so that many noticed it."[34] When Philip's chancellor urged the parties to come to an agreement, he received the reply: "I [Luther] know no other means than that they honor the Word of God and believe with us. To which the others answered: They could neither understand nor believe that the body of Christ was present."[35]

The disputants remained implacable; the division within the Reformation was complete.[36] Zwingli was not prepared to diverge from the reasoning behind his interpretation, and Luther absolutely refused to furnish cogent, rational arguments for God's instructions concerning the Eucharist. It is the corporal food we are obediently to take in, not its meaning: "I would eat dung if God demanded it."[37] The will of the Lord is not to be questioned; either one trusts in it or not. One "should close one's eyes," Luther says.[38] The miracle of the Eucharist can be expressed and pondered but not fathomed. This is a stance not very much in demand in our day, as it is suspected of being "blind obedience." Nor is Luther's way the way of European intellectual history, including Evangelical theology.

But where the perspective broadens and the myth of progress gives way to a recognition of the superhuman and supratemporal power of evil, Luther's adherence to the "incarnate" Word, the reality of God outside the human person, becomes an effective and powerful aid for bewildered Christians. The infant in its nonage at the baptismal font and the dying man receiving his last communion are not marginal figures in the Church of Christ. They stand for man at his weakest—whether at the beginning, the height of his powers, or the end of his strength. The idea that God is genuinely "there," outside the person, and can be found beyond the individual powers of thought and strength of faith is what the controversy of that time bestowed on posterity.

It is not only modern man who can make little sense of infant baptism and the real presence of Christ. But they are meaningful to man in conflict, to man between God and the Devil, who does not ignore Luther's words: We are beggars, that is true.

CHAPTER IX

Christianity between God and the Devil

False Alternatives

We may not deviate from the cause of truth, even if many, yes all are against it. For it is not only the case today that the great mass, with all the great lords, err and defend injustice. And though it is hard and difficult to bear such loneliness . . . we know God, who will be our judge, lives.[1]

This appeal, penned by Luther in the autumn of 1519, was not intended solely for the ears of his students or spoken cautiously within the protective confines of the lecture hall during one of his lectures on the Psalms. He had already made a similar statement in the summer of 1519, during his debate with Johannes Eck, his first German opponent. In the course of the Leipzig disputation, which received a great deal of attention (as the proceedings were recorded by four different people, the documentation is abundant), he had dared to challenge the divinely ordained supremacy of the pope as well as to reject the infallibility of councils. Certainly the pope was to be respected—as bishop of Rome; and the papacy was to be held in high regard—as an institution rooted in history and created in accordance with human law, "de iure humano." But the only standard of obedience was the Gospel, not an institution, be it called papacy or council. Luther's colleague and debate partner Andreas Carlstadt had urgently warned him that it would be courting disaster to provoke a dispute over the authority of the pope. It is not surprising that Johannes Eck did not let the opportunity escape to inform Luther's sovereign personally of the outrage in Leipzig: "Your Electoral Highness will certainly know how to judge whether spreading such views is permitted in Christendom."

Luther was not long in rendering account, as had been demanded of him: St. Peter undoubtedly had honorary primacy among the apostles, but this gave him no legal authority or supremacy, for "he does not have the power to make, send, govern, or ordain the apostles."[2]

This recognition of honorary primacy was forfeited when Rome balked at a thoroughgoing reformation, and preferred ruling by force to serving in love.[3]

Councils were something else again. Luther's assessment of their authority remained differentiated to the very last: it was not fundamentally the case that *all* councils had erred; it was the medieval Church assemblies that had proven themselves to be fallible. Had not the Fifth Lateran Council (1512–17) in 1516 openly overturned the Council of Constance and even declared the Council of Basel invalid? "And so the councils contradict each other so that we, who build on them, ultimately no longer know where pope, council, Church, Christ, or we must stand. . . . Thus we are forced to say, whether we like it or not: the council has erred."[4]

Only the four "main councils" of the early Church, from Nicea (325) to Chalcedon (451), had adhered to Scripture, explicated the Gospel adequately, and unswervingly defended it against heresy. These councils, which continued to speak for the whole of Christendom east and west, had still been free to make decisions—free of the pope. But since the Church of Rome had acquired power over Christendom, it was no longer possible or permissible to build on a council.

The loneliness of the truth seemed to be the consequence, but that would also mean the end of Church and congregation, the teachings of the Church and the bonds of the congregation. Was this the beginning of the "heroic" but anguished loneliness of Protestantism and the starting point for the multiplicity of sects, the confusion of opinions and counteropinions? The problem deserves careful analysis if we are to get to the bottom of the suspicion that the beginning of the Reformation of the Church already initiated its end.

The interpretation of Luther's actions as a breaking away from the Church is firmly anchored in confessional historiography. On the Protestant side the individualism of the nineteenth century and the personalism of the twentieth celebrated the Reformer as a fearless outsider and presented him as a prototype of modern man. Relying only on himself, he could assume and dared assume the responsibility to act before God and for the world in accordance with his own conscience and the dictates of the hour. That Luther's "basic theological views" did not include a doctrine of the Church is a nineteenth-century conviction that has persisted into our own time. Theodosius Harnack, the great nineteenth-century authority on Luther, implied this point of view in the title of his comprehensive introduction to Luther's theology: "with special reference to his doctrine of reconciliation and redemption."[5] Whereas the real Luther never lost sight of the Church, the Protestant Luther had.

The motto Harnack chose was a statement that seemed to document plainly Luther's special relationship to the two concepts mentioned in the title. It was, in fact, a central statement, and Luther had impressed it upon his students shortly before leaving for the disputation in Leipzig: only through the cross of Christ is God's Word revealed; the cross constitutes the only genuine theology—"Crux Christi unica est eruditio verborum dei, theologia sincerissima."[6] If this motto means that the way an individual conscience experiences the cross in tribulation and trust becomes the key to the Holy Scriptures, not only has the pope lost his position, but the Church has lost its place.

Catholic scholarship in its own way has long held this "separatist" view. One hears of a solitary monk who, in his quest for his own gracious God, was able to forge ahead to profound experiences and lofty discoveries. But unfortunately—thus Hubert Jedin's qualification—Luther showed no interest in the Church. Only later, when he encountered resistance, did he develop a doctrine of the people of God, as an emergency measure to justify his discoveries. Joseph Lortz, the "old master of modern Catholic Luther scholarship," ventured a far-reaching historical explanation of this sort in his much-quoted book, *The Reformation in Germany:* in the wake—or, should one say more pointedly, in the prison?—of the late medieval decline to subjectivism, the Church as a redemptive institution was outside Luther's field of vision. He came upon it only when it could no longer do anything but condemn him, and he was no longer ready to bow in obedience in order to preserve its unity.[7]

This would allow Luther's theology of the cross to be acknowledged as biblical and genuinely Catholic, provided it was integrated into a "true" appreciation of the Church, which can remain Church only under the leadership of the vicar of Christ and successor to St. Peter.

Luther himself would not have hesitated to reply: "emergency measure"—indeed, for what greater emergency is there than disclosing the captivity of the Church under the domination of the pope?

Luther's insistence on the unwavering theology of the cross supports neither the Protestant-individualist nor the Catholic-subjectivist interpretation. True theology does not attend to the superior achievements of its own wisdom, nor does it build on the moral strivings directed toward credibility and one's own righteousness. That, Luther concludes, is why it rejects the urge for power and thus avoids the competition among patriarchs, bishops, and monks. The theology of the cross consistently furthers the unity of the Church in the preaching of the Gospel and the heeding of God's commandments. But the Church of his day—it was an accumulation of schisms . . . Oh, dark, pitch-black blindness: "Quid est ecclesia hodie nisi quaedam schismatum confusio? . . . Caecitas, caecitas, caecitas."[8]

When Luther wrote these lines in 1519 his ties to Rome were still intact. Negotiations for a settlement were underway, and a nonpartisan judge seemed to have been found in Germany: Archbishop Richard Greiffenklau, elector of Trier. It was not until Rome broke with Luther that he felt forced to confirm this break himself. The heresy trial in Rome had by then ended in a bull threatening excommunication, *Exsurge Domine;* and when Luther's last letter to the pope did not bring about any rapprochement, he burned the pope's bull and his canon law outside the walls of Wittenberg near the Elster Gate.

Was this merely the final act of the heretical revolt against the Church Luther had started on October 31, 1517? Johannes Eck thought so from the outset. Ever since the posting of the ninety-five theses, Eck had been seeking to mobilize resistance in Germany. His weapons were effective: Luther was endangering the Church; he was a Bohemian schismatic, a heretic and an agitator, in short a Hussite. The Hussites' savagery in the wars against the Catholic empire had not yet been forgotten. Eck did everything to construct the image of Luther as a dangerous heretic and father of heretics. This agitation against him might be thought sufficient to explain Luther's violent reaction. But there was more at stake than his personal honor. What was the sense of reproaching him with Hussite arson when the burning concern was the plight of the Church?

Luther's "doctrine of the Church"—an inadequate, overly abstract concept for his view of the communion of saints—was not appended to his so-called subjectivism as an afterthought. Modern Luther interpretations, including enlightened Catholic ones, must be clearly contradicted on this point. Luther would have countered vigorously the ostensibly straightforward description found there of the sixteenth century as an "age of religious schism." Schism is not the result of the Reformation, it is its genesis and point of departure.

There is a Protestant Luther tradition that must be repudiated just as categorically, for it is chiefly responsible for the historical misrepresentation of Luther and has also created the heroic myth of the enlightened, educated Protestant. Luther does not stand for the alternatives of "truth not unity," "conscience not institution," "individual not community." His declaration of loyalty to the Church as the communion of saints in the *Grosser Katechismus* of 1529 should have ruled out such false alternatives. For the Church is "unified in love, beyond factions and divisions."[9] As long as the Protestant tendency to play off the invisible Church of the faithful against the visible institutional Church has not been overcome, this declaration will make no impression. These words are wrongly read as if Luther was thinking of the ideal Church, which can never and may never become real. Luther himself, however, had struggled from the very beginning to bring the Church of faith back into history, into the reality of his—even without him—unsettled time, back into the reality of his day. The visible, institutional Church must be measured according to the task set by the Lord.

Book of Psalms—Book of the Church

Between 1513 and 1515 Luther held what was probably his first course of theological lectures in Wittenberg, on the book of the Psalms. This is where we shall be able to discover whether the young Luther had really been intent on the communion of the Church from the beginning.

If he was already following what was later to be his usual timetable, he could be heard from nine until ten on Mondays, Tuesdays, and Wednesdays. Following lectures of this kind presupposes more than a knowledge of Latin. Apart from those of Luther's concepts that are taken for granted today, we also find ideas which, dating back to the Middle Ages, have become alien to us and may occasionally even seem daring. But once we have familiarized ourselves with his exegetical method, grasped the way he approaches a text, and developed a sense for the experiences the young professor wove into his biblical exegesis, we encounter that awareness of the Church which is incompatible with the prevalent view of the lonely Reformer without a Church.

The first lecture of the summer semester of 1513 was probably on August 15, after the dog-day holidays. Luther began it with a basic introduction about the proper "key" to understanding Scripture: it is the art of distinguishing between spirit and letter. That is what makes a true theologian. It is a gift bestowed on the Church by the Holy Spirit and does not spring from human cleverness. The Psalms are no more than the hollow letter if they are regarded as a liturgical task and droned out daily as part of the Divine Office, without inner understanding; that merely renders one insensitive and locks the heart. Only by pressing forward to the spirit, the spirit of Christ, will the person at prayer be released and revived, for the Book of Psalms is the book which prophesies Christ.

Erudite scholastic commentaries on the "labyrinth of the Psalms" are often in greater need of explanation than the actual text, to which Christ himself provided the key when he said: "Search the scriptures; for . . . they are that which testify of me" (John 5.39). This is the prophetic sense of the Psalms, testifying to the coming and the works of Christ. But this is by no means to exhaust the scope of the text; nor is it rendered obsolete by the coming of Christ. Its enduring spiritual value for today, after the arrival of Christ, is that its prophecy allegorically encompasses "all of Christ," the Lord and His Church. And the text goes still further, down to the life of the individual Christian, not as a creature in isolation but as a member of the Church Militant on earth: the tropological or moral meaning of the Psalms arms and strengthens man in his religious battle against sin and the Devil.

To demonstrate how this insight of the fourfold sense of Scripture is handled as an exegetical method, Luther falls back on traditional examples. Again and again he uses the alternatives of Jerusalem and Babylon or the several messages contained in the term "Mount Zion":

	Historical Interpretation	Allegorical (figurative) Interpretation	Tropological (moral) Interpretation	Anagogic Interpretation (in the light of the Last Judgment)
Jerusalem	the city of Judea	good people	virtues	rewards
Babylon	the city in Mesopotamia	evil people	vices	punishment
Mount Zion	the land of Canaan	synagogue	Pharisaic justice	earthly well-being
Mount Zion	the people of Zion	Church	Christian justice	eternal life

Luther employs this fourfold exegesis to expose the situation of the Church's struggle against the Jews and pagans, to arouse Christians from their lethargy, warn and fortify them, and to overcome their resistance to the "nuisance" and "folly" of the Christian faith.

Did students in August 1513 already realize the consequences of this design? Luther's text shows how goal-directed—directed at the Church—his exegesis of the prophecy of the Psalms is. Twice he plainly declares his intentions, and a third time he marks his position by conspicuous silence.

The introduction to his lectures on the Psalms, "the Preface of Jesus Christ," begins with a series of four scriptural passages, the last one indicating which Christ the Psalmist David—who was considered the author of the Psalms—foretold: "I know nothing except Jesus Christ, and him crucified" (I Cor. 2.2). This verse also furnishes the true interpretation of the Church: there is no Church save the Church Persecuted, which in its history participates in the sufferings of Christ. And: no one belongs to this Church save those who do not seek to escape tribulation and distress.

Luther became even more explicit in the second part of the introduction, in which he used carefully selected examples to demonstrate the Psalms' three levels of meaning—concerning Christ, His Church, and its members: "As Christ was hounded by the Jews, so too the Church is plagued by tyrants, heretics, and godless Christians."[10] The plague for the early Church is the era of martyrs. The recognition of Christianity by the emperor Constantine was followed by a period during which the Church needed councils and doctors of the Church to defend itself against dangerous heresies; finally, "in our time," the internal struggle has broken out against the godless *in* the Church, who have already advanced so far as to attain leading positions. "Contra tyrannos, hereticos, et impios principes ecclesiae":[11] today we are battling against tyrants, heretics, *and* impious prelates.

What Luther so conspicuously neglected in his opening lectures is the fourth level of the traditional fourfold system of interpreting Scripture: the anagogic interpretation, in the light of the Last Judgment. In the next two years he would occasionally assess this dimension separately, but it was no accident that he omitted it from his introduction. The prophecy of Christ in the Psalms reveals that the Second Coming is fast approaching. The future has already commenced, the end has begun. A "last meaning" in the light of a distant Return is superfluous: this future is now!

Luther's exegesis of the Holy Scriptures was inseparably linked with a "doctrine of the Church" from the very beginning. A year after receiving his doctorate, the twenty-eight-year-old professor prepared his comprehensive

In the jaws of hell the pope is crowned amidst the servants of the devil, an allusion to 2 Thess. 2. 4a: "[The Devil] opposeth and exalteth himself above all that is called God, or that is worshipped"

lectures on the Psalms in such a way as to enable him to assimilate the medieval tradition of scriptural exegesis while going on to develop it independently. The mark of Martin Luther is palpable from the very first sentence. But the personal quality is not created by his orientation toward Christ and certainly not by his use of the fourfold method of exegesis. The striking feature is his emphasis on the reciprocal relationship between Christ, Church, and Christian, and on Christ crucified constituting His Church and determining the life of every Christian. That is why the Church is imperiled again and again, and why Christians are tested by the Devil's might "also today."

Luther wants to show that the time of Christ has not become distant past but that it is continuing in history. The Church is hotly contested by God and the Devil. The adversary may change his disguises, but he always remains recognizably faithful to himself, whether as a Pharisee, Roman emperor, heretic, or ecclesiastical leader. The original idea of the Church, and thus its guidepost and touchstone as the budding Reformer saw it, is that of the Church of Christ crucified, the Church of martyrs who spread the Gospel through belief and profession of faith and not by means of earthly power and armed force.

The martyrs' *obedience* by faith is still so central to the young Luther that he cannot yet fit *justification* by faith as found in St. Paul's Epistle to the Romans into the fabric woven of Christ, Church, and the individual Christian. This will be achieved only as a result of his Reformation approach to the central passage of the Epistle—"The just shall live by faith" (Rom. 1.17). In his search for clarity Luther makes his way from discovery to discovery, his path beginning with the Church and staying with it to the very end. Looking back on his Psalm lectures a quarter of a century later, he could say in retrospect, "Ah, I was often glad when I had found the true meaning of a word; it illuminated a whole sentence for me."[12]

As the introduction proves, Luther's first lectures on the Psalms had been preceded by a number of discoveries. Fit together, they form the picture of a Church that already bears Reformation characteristics. Decisions made here prepared the way for the controversy over indulgences.

Church of Confessors—Church of Martyrs

The Church of Christ is not invisible. Though its power and treasures are concealed in God's hands and can only be viewed through faith, its testimony lays claim to space and a place in life and death, has a history, and also needs offices and office-holders. But when a reversal occurs in the Church, when its testimony is concealed and its possessions and wealth displayed, there is no alternative but to reform its very institutions.

In the autumn of 1515 Luther was still prepared to acknowledge the supremacy of the Church of Rome in the West as a later doctrinal and historical development,[13] but his ideal of ecclesiastical government was a college of bishops. The Church of confessors has no room for wrangling over preeminence and privilege. It knows offices and requires the cooperation above all of bishops and doctors, but all of them are there to serve and not to rule. They protect the preaching of the Gospel and supervise the administration of the sacraments. By virtue of his responsibility for preaching and teaching, the village priest is entrusted with the duties of both bishop and doctor in his parish. God's children are born through preaching; through the sacraments of baptism and communion Christ tears them out of the Devil's hands and fortifies them in distress and persecution.

The visible Church is never pure and immaculate; it will always be a "mixed body" (*corpus mixtum*) of saints and hypocrites. In periods of acute danger there will not be many who hold their ground and remain unflagging in their faith. Only a "handful" will stand fast to the end.

These are all basic ideas that can be found in Luther's first Psalm lectures. They will survive to become the principle underlying both the indulgence theses of 1517 and the article on the Church in the Confession of Augsburg formulated by Melanchthon in 1530. In 1537 Luther again called the Church back to its true foundations in the *Schmalkaldic Articles*: "Thank God, a child of seven knows what the Church is, namely the saintly believers and the sheep who hear the voice of their Shepherd."[14]

Luther offers a final account in his major treatise *On the Councils and Churches* (1539). There he names sermon, baptism, holy communion, absolution, ordination, and divine worship as six characteristics of the Church, and adds a crucial seventh one: God's people suffer persecution and are subject to hate, plagued by the Devil, world, and flesh. "As the seventh, one recognizes the holy Christian people outwardly by the relic of the Holy Cross, that it must undergo all the misfortune and persecution, all sorts of tribulations and evil (as the 'Our Father' prays) from the Devil, world, and flesh; inwardly mourn, be stupid, be frightened; outwardly poor, scorned, ill, weak, suffer; so that it can be like Christ, its head. And the reason for this must alone be that it holds fast to Christ and the Word of God, and suffers for Christ's sake, Matt. 5: 'Blessed are they who suffer persecution for my sake' . . . Where you see or hear such, know that this is the holy Christian Church."[15] The revolutionary character of this view of the Church is obvious. The Church of martyrs need only be compared with the outward magnificence and outward symbols of sovereignty of the medieval Church. And that is exactly what many of Luther's contemporaries did.

Yet even as bold a program as Luther's has a darker aspect, which should not be suppressed. Exhorting the persecuted to defenseless acceptance of the cross and passive suffering can reinforce the status quo and have so conservative an effect as to obstruct change and reform. Christians "must be pious, silent, obedient, prepared to serve the authorities and everyone with body and all one possesses, and to do injury to no man."[16]

"Pious, silent, and obedient"—is this not proof enough that Luther educated the Germans to subservience, to acquiesce to their superiors? That is no doubt how it looks when the "handful" becomes the established Church and the throne concludes a holy alliance with the altar. Pious silence becomes revolutionary, new and renewing again, only in times of war, when it becomes daring "to do injury to no man," when it demands courage to counter violence with peace. This is the courageous Church Persecuted that Luther is talking about, a Church that continues to worship and to serve the common good though it be "hanged, drowned, murdered, martyred, chased, tormented." Once again: "Where you see or hear such, know that this is the holy Christian Church."[17]

By demanding that even in times of persecution a Christian must not isolate himself from society but must serve it, Luther indicates that he does not want to divide divine worship from the common good, Christian from citizen.

Oppressed and yet obliged to uphold the state—this is the historical basis of the distinction between Church and State, and the place to start if we are to find our way in the maze of debate over Luther's oft-misunderstood distinction between Christian and citizen, God's earthly realm and God's realm of faith. Instead of a modern concept like "upholding the state," Luther would have preferred "carrying a sword," thinking not only of Christian soldiers but also of judges, magistrates, and all office-holders committed to serving the people. Luther's own behavior contradicts the caricature of servility to princes. His own princes of Electoral Saxony, though they had all afforded the Reformation their protection, are not spared, and they are all criticized sharply, where necessary to the point of disobedience. Conversely, however, one should not refuse to serve a persecuting government—a view antithetical to that of the medieval papacy, which claimed the right to release the subjects of a refractory emperor from their oath of allegiance and exhorted the people to rise up in active battle against the authorities for the sake of the Church. The true, persecuted Church, on the other hand, has no political ambitions that it would risk peace in the world to achieve, for it is the same adversary who is persecuting the Church and trying to impose chaos on the world: the Devil. He does not have a third realm; he brings confusion into the two realms, enticing the Christian to retreat from the world and boast before God.

The persecuted handful is Luther's theme. Does that mean he has nothing to say about Christians and Church in a tolerant world, where they are safeguarded by constitutions and concordats? The origins of the great indulgence controversy lie precisely in this kind of ostensible freedom. In the autumn of 1514, when no one could possibly have anticipated the consequences, Luther took up this very topic of tolerant endurance: absolute tolerance is total persecution—"Nulla persecutio tota persecutio." "Today the Devil is endangering the Church with the greatest conceivable persecutions, namely without persecution, with tolerance and security. Woe to us, who are so dazzled by satiety and well-being that we fall into the Devil's trap."[18]

Gospel for Sale

Luther's right to administer a warning cannot be denied, because a satiated, self-complacent Church will give offense to all but the satiated and self-satisfied. Yet does this criticism justify the rift in and struggle over the Church that sowed despair and hatred and spilled blood in the sixteenth century and for a long time thereafter? Are we not dealing with a radical who attempted to force through his heady dreams for the true Church with no regard for losses? Had a passionate dream turned his normally cool head? How can Luther have believed that the contemporary, historically rooted Church, which had no alternative but to assert itself in the hard business of politics, could survive in the defensiveless stance of a powerless communion of Christ? It would have been enough to remedy obvious flaws and bridle the abuse of power. But why attack the structure of the Church if, as experience had shown, it could prevail against kings and emperors, heretics and revolutionaries, only with the aid of a staunch, powerful papacy? What impelled this man to take a stand against authority *and* reality?

These questions do not arise from our modern viewpoint; they were already posed in Luther's time and were a source of anguish to him. That he pursued his convictions with utter self-confidence and steadfastness is a myth that has emerged with the passage of time. But his horror at the enormity of events did not render him speechless, for with the Scriptures at hand he was in possession of a "book that spoke" and helped him to find a twofold answer: for one thing, the Church of Christ crucified was neither a figment of the mind nor an idealist's dream. It was historical reality, the documented story of Christ and his witnesses. Moreover, no one would ever be capable of converting the triumphal, power-oriented Church. That was a task to be left for God on the Day of Judgment.

Let us begin with the historical reality of true Christendom: the apostles tell of the beginnings of the Church of confessors—how it was continually being pursued and oppressed. St. Paul presents the central message of the Gospel, explaining at the same time why the communion of believers is persecuted: "We preach Christ crucified, unto the Jews a stumbling block, and unto the Greeks foolishness" (1 Cor. 1.23). This passage was fundamental

The diabolical pope (Clement IV) preparing to behead the pious emperor (Conradin)

to Luther. Already a shaping factor in the exegetical work of his first Psalm lectures, it was frequently referred to later on, and, in the form of theses, presented with all its implications before his own order at the disputation in Heidelberg in 1518. Stumbling block, foolishness—these are the realities, because God conceals His majesty and, against all expectations, hopes, and convictions, transforms it into its opposite: weakness on the cross. The idea is intolerable to the world; it must be eliminated as blasphemy, even godlessness. It was consistent for the Church in imitation of Christ to have to attest to its faith with the blood of martyrs.

WHEN LUTHER spent four weeks in Rome for his order in 1511, it was not so much the classical monuments from the time of Rome's greatness that fascinated him as the sites recalling the shedding of Christian blood, the catacombs of St. Calixtus on the Via Appia, where so many thousands of martyrs lie buried. The Church of martyrs was already a guiding light to him during his monastic years.[19]

Other than this, the monk's knowledge of Church history was as incomplete as that of any other contemporary. When Luther was preparing himself for his doctoral degree in 1512, normal theological training did not include submerging oneself in the past and developing a historical approach. Nonetheless, the new spirit of the time did not pass him by. A sense of the past was stirred in him, and soon he grasped the necessity of subjecting legendary historical traditions to critical examination.

While he was studying at the philosophical faculty in Erfurt (1501–05), he moved in a circle close to the humanist Mutianus Rufus, although they were only to meet much later, in 1515. And it was from the Mutianus circle that his first student came, Johannes Lang, friar and friend. Lang introduced Luther to Georg Spalatin, who had been the circumspect middleman between the reformers in Wittenberg and Elector Frederick since late 1516.[20] Luther owed his love for the classical writers, especially for Virgil and Cicero, to the Erfurt humanists; through his contact with them he acquired a feeling for rhetoric and rhetorical figures, which he later considered crucial prerequisites for a proper scriptural exegesis. It was also his years of familiarity with the Erfurt circle that generated his respect for the achievements of a Johannes Reuchlin or an Erasmus of Rotterdam in rendering Hebrew and Greek more accessible and later made it so natural to him to consult biblical texts in their original language. He quickly came to treat as second nature what "scholastic obscurantists" mistrusted and even branded heretical in their battle against Reuchlin and Erasmus.

At the monastery Luther buried himself in the new editions of the Church Fathers that had broken in on the scholarly world, enabling Augustine or Hieronymus to be read completely and in their original form. This was by no means the norm, for the theology of the Middle Ages, still a time of manuscripts, was restricted to a small canon of patristic works, selections in so-called florilegia. During his Erfurt and early Wittenberg years Luther's interest in the Church Fathers was not, however, historical; he read them only in connection with scriptural exegesis. Moreover, crucial source material on the history of the papacy became available so late that Luther could only use it afterward. "At the beginning," he admits in 1536, "I was totally innocent of historical knowledge. I attacked the papacy a priori, as one says, meaning on the basis of the Holy Scriptures. Others now confirm my results a posteriori, on the basis of historical documents."[21]

"Christo Salvatori Deo optimo maximo. Georgius Spalatinus. Peccator." (Georg Spalatin. Sinner against Christ the Savior, the Lord God of the universe.) Luther's friend and disciple Georg Spalatin praying before the Crucifix. Woodcut by Lucas Cranach the Elder, 1515.

Not until early 1520 did he receive a copy of the newly published Hutten edition of Laurentius Valla's proof—demonstrated sixty years earlier—that the pope's claim to temporal dominion over the Western world rested on a forgery. The Donation of Constantine a fraud! This was more than the exposure of a brazen lie. It not only exacerbated the resentment the German nation already bore against Rome; it destroyed trust as well. By excluding emperors and kings, whole empires and countries from its communion through excommunication and interdict, the Church, hiding behind the cloak of law, had been leading man away from salvation in the name of God.

"Dear God, the vile cunning of the Romans," Luther wrote to Spalatin almost as soon as he had come into possession of Valla's disclosure. "You will

Was Gott selbst vom Bapstum hellt
Zeigt dis schrecklich bild hie gestellt:

The lascivious monster the Whore of Babylon has taken possession of Rome

be amazed at God's counsel for letting this lie survive for so long, even allowing it to make its way into canon law." Did this revaluation of all values, this perversion of Christendom, not provide incontrovertible evidence that the pope in Rome, acting under the guise of legality, against Christ in the name of Christ, was the expected Antichrist?[22]

THE QUESTION of historical truth was becoming ever more important to Luther. By early 1519 his historical documentation and interpretation of councils and Church decisions had taught him how unreliable canon law was. Preparing for the disputation in Leipzig, he studied Rufin's Latin translation of Eusebius' Greek history of the Church in the 1514 Strasbourg edition. In the course of his reading he discovered that the first genuinely ecumenical council, the Council of Nicea (325), had expressly granted Jerusalem, as mother of all churches, honorary primacy over Christendom. It was thanks to Eusebius that he became aware of the more remote churches in Greece, Asia Minor, Egypt, and North Africa, which were independent of Rome. The thirteenth thesis that he wanted to debate in Leipzig in the summer of 1519 resulted from this discovery of a universal Church: "I deny that the pope is the supreme head of *all* churches."[23] In the West—the Donation of Constantine was not yet known to be a forgery in Germany—the Pope could be tolerated, though not with uncurbed power. Eusebius also furnished Luther with the historical evidence that proved the papal thesis of the fundamental priority of spiritual power over temporal power to be untenable. The Council of Nicea had been convoked by Emperor Constantine, not by a Roman bishop. The historical Constantine thus became a weapon against the legendary power of the pope and served as the model for the Christian sovereign in Luther's *Address to the Christian Nobility* (1520) by demanding the convocation of reform council, even, if need be, against Rome's will. Where all Christians are priests, bishops, and popes by virtue of having been baptized, no individual can arrogate the right to discipline the whole Church.

Thus Luther could not speak of a Constantinian "fall" of the Church. The roots of decline were not to be found in a political act of imperial tolerance and patronage, as the left wing of the Reformation has assumed to the present day. On the contrary, the historical change that had occurred at that time demonstrated the power of the testimony of the persecuted Church to Luther. Nonetheless, the Constantinian era remained ambiguous in his eyes—not because the emperor had interfered in "spiritual matters" but because even a time of tolerance had not crushed the Devil, nor would it ever.

Hardly had the Roman soldiers stopped raging than heretics came in to take over Satan's work through different means. In later years Luther gratefully remembered the master of novices who had given him a treatise by Athanasius to read during his first year at the monastery. Thus had Luther learned about Arius and how he had attacked that persecuted confessor of Christ, Bishop Athanasius. Like the early martyrs, Athanasius had had to flee, but, despite all he was subjected to, he had never lost faith.

How was it then in one's own time, when the Church was not only tolerated but powerful, respected, even feared? Had the present power of the Church checked the power of the Devil? Certainly not, declared Luther in the autumn of 1514, when he was discussing the first verse of Psalm 69: "Save me, O God; For the waters are come in unto my soul." St. Paul's Epistle to the Corinthians was once again the guiding principle of his exegesis: ". . . God chose what is foolish in the world . . ." (1 Cor. 1.27).

It was not as if the time of trouble had passed into history and the Church were now striding ahead unchallenged along the road to Paradise. The waters were up to their necks as much as they had been when Christ was crucified and His Church of apostles and martyrs was a frightened, despised handful. Now the situation was reversed, there was peace and security. The pressure of diabolical persecutions came not from outside but from inside.

All of us, Luther felt, even the leaders of the Church, are being lulled into a false sense of security and imperiled. Secular priests and monks alike are offering indulgences and peddling salvation from the treasure of Christ and the martyrs. As if we ourselves are not charged by God to contribute to the treasure of the Church and could afford to rest on the merits of the saints! Like the prodigal son, we have run away from our parental home and are squandering our inheritance. This is the ultimate, but also the cruelest persecution. It will thin the ranks as never before. St. Paul had already predicted: "For when they shall say: 'There is peace, there is no danger,' then sudden destruction cometh upon them, as travail upon a woman with child; and they shall not escape" (1 Thess. 5.3).[24]

The warning of 1514 does not yet contain the sweeping attack on the sale of indulgences of three years later, when the treasure of the Church had been transformed into the treasure of the "most sacred Gospel of grace." Nonetheless, some decisive ideas in the ninety-five theses of 1517 were taken over from the Psalm lectures. The ninety-second thesis, which none of Luther's opponents reacted to, takes up the warning of 1514:

92. Away then with all those prophets who say to the people of Christ, "Peace, peace," and there is no peace.[25]

This is an appeal directed against a Church which teaches and lives as if Christendom had found the road to progress and was no longer being persecuted. The last three theses can thus be understood as a call to be vigilant and to fortify the persecuted Church under the sign of the cross:

93. Blessed be all those prophets who say to the people of Christ, "Cross, cross," and there is no cross.
94. Christians should be exhorted to strive to follow Christ, their head, through punishment, death, and hell,
95. and thus be confident of entering heaven through many tribulations rather than through the false security of peace.[26]

The Future of the Church: Reformation between Failure and Success

After the Reformation breakthrough Luther would no longer make the hope for peace with God dependent on the individual's experience of the cross in the inner domain of repentance. The Christian's confidence must rest on God's forgiveness of his sins.[27] But what remained, and would remain to the very end, was the new Reformation view of the Church. The fundamental decisions of the Reformation were not based solely on new theses concerning the doctrine of justification and the freedom of the Christian.

The various phases of exploration and discovery were preceded by Luther's general view that by means of His Word in the Old and New Testaments, God led His people in imitation of the suffering Christ. Though in their disobedience they develop into an exultant conquering power, they would have to be bidden back to the Church of martyrs in service of the world.

To recall to its Lord a Church clinging tenaciously to disobedience must evoke severe opposition and prove perilous to the point of martyrdom. In the spring of 1520, presumably before the bull threatening excommunication had reached him and a year before the imperial ban went into force, Luther could still muster a mixture of pointed irony and bitter earnest when he described the snares of the Inquisition to his students. They shielded the Church so thoroughly that "Christ, who went to his apostles through closed doors, would no longer be able to gain entry. He would not pass the test of faith, but be found guilty as a multiple heretic and disobedient son of the Holy See."[28]

Three years later, on July 1, 1523, Luther's predictions came true. The first martyrs of the Reformation were burned before the town hall of Brussels. Johann von Essen and Heinrich Vos, Augustinian monks from the monastery at Eisleben, Luther's birthplace, had gone from there to Antwerp, where they had disseminated "heretical" doctrines. As they were not prepared to recant, only the stake could be their destiny—Margaretha, Emperor Charles V's aunt and regent, would tolerate no religious conflict in the already troubled Netherlands.

As we know that Luther was disappointed not to have been allowed to bear witness to the Gospel with his life in Worms, we are not surprised to read the account of a Swiss student in Wittenberg named Johannes Kessler: "When he received the news of the two above-mentioned martyrs in written form, he began to weep inwardly and said: I thought that I should be the first to be martyred for the Holy Gospel; but I was not worthy of it."[29]

Were we not aware of Luther's discovery of the Church of confessors, which is in the very greatest danger in times without persecution, this lament would have to be regarded as a pathological mania for martyrdom. Joyfully he wrote to his friend Spalatin in 1523: "Thanks be to Christ, who has finally begun to let my, or rather His, prophecy bear fruit."[30]

"Finally bear fruit"—and that at the end of the years which all accounts of the history of the Reformation present as years of triumph and advance. Martyrdom as success is certainly an unmistakable warning that Luther did not measure the Reformation's "progress" or "failure" by approval and growth in popularity. Profoundly affected by the two Augustinian monks in Brussels who had given their lives for their faith, Luther almost immediately (August 1523) wrote the words to his first hymn, which was printed on placards and soon became widely known. The last lines of the final verse seem to forecast the victory of the Reformation:

Der Sommer ist hart vor der Tür
 der Winter ist vergangen,
die zarten Blumen gehn herfür.
 Der das hat angefangen,
der wird es wohl vollenden.[31]

[Summer is fast approaching, / winter is gone, / the delicate flowers are blooming. / He who began it, / is certain to consummate it.]

But Luther had long realized that this consummation would not signify the beginning of a new epoch in the history of man, with "Christendom

The "sixth seal" has been opened, and persecution is at its climax. "And the stars of heaven fell unto the earth . . . and the kings of the earth, and the great men, and the rich men . . . and the mighty men . . . hid themselves in the dens and in the rocks of the mountains" (Rev. 6.13–15).

under the cross" becoming the triumphal, ruling Church. Consummation did not belong to history; it was the Last Day, the glorious Second Coming of Christ, which would bring the eternal realm of peace and with it the final revaluation of all values. The road there was not one of continuous progress and guaranteed détente. Until then there could be no other peace and no greater success than the preservation of the Gospel. Whatever the price, whether property or life, the Gospel would be preached. Nothing could stop it.

Holding fast to the Gospel was indeed much, but it did not constitute a "success." For Luther reformation was the beginning not of modern times but of the Last Days.

Historians may conclude that depriving a secularized Church of its power is de facto one of the essential conditions for the dawn of the modern era and that all striving for a restoration of the power of the triumphal Church must mean a step backward into the Middle Ages. Their reasoning would have left Luther unmoved.

Lucas Cranach the Younger, The True Church and the False Church

The only progress he expected from the reformation was the Devil's rage, provoked by the rediscovery of the Gospel. The adversary would hurl himself at the Church with increased force, attacking from all sides and by all possible means. Before there could be consummation there would be intensified persecution, for a general reformation, as Luther had known since 1520, could not be expected from the pope, a council, or any "reformer." God Himself would bring about reformation through consummation; it would be preceded by the Devil's counterreformation.[32]

This somber vision might be suspected to have arisen out of the deep-rooted pessimism of the early years, when there was no way of knowing what would become of the Evangelical movement. Should not the genuine, surprising successes of the Reformation have been occasion for a new, "optimistic" interpretation of the visible renewal of the Church?

A glance at the final stage of Luther's life will shed light on the subject. Once again it is the martyrdom of an Augustinian monk that gives Luther the opportunity to offer an interpretation of his time. Robert Barnes, a monk from the Cambridge monastery, was burned at Smithfield on July 30, 1540, by order of King Henry VIII. Five years earlier, the scholar and statesman

Hans Holbein, King Henry VIII of England *(1509–47)*

Thomas More, having refused to accept the king as head of the Church of England and to take the oath of royal supremacy demanded of him, had been executed for his belief in the supremacy of the Church of Rome. Though the English Augustinian may not be as well known (unlike More, Barnes was not canonized), he was nonetheless a witness for his beliefs. Barnes could accept neither king nor pope as head of the Church of Christ. He had been condemned as a heretic and imprisoned once before but had regained his freedom by recanting and had then fled to Wittenberg in 1530.

In the summer of 1531 the situation appeared to have undergone a fundamental change. Barnes was now in Wittenberg on a royal mission, to obtain Luther's expert opinion on Henry's desire to gain a divorce from Catherine of Aragon so he could marry Anne Boleyn.[33] In 1533 Barnes was officially matriculated at the University of Wittenberg as "Oxford Doctor of Theology." At that time King Henry was particularly interested in cultivating friendly relations with Protestant rulers so he could keep them from taking part in the council the pope was expected to convoke. But once the situation inside England had changed with the legalization of the king's marriage to Anne, and Barnes continued to insist that "What God hath joined together, let no man put asunder" (Matt. 19.6), he was condemned and put to death at the stake.

In the very same year Luther published a German translation of Barnes' last confession of faith. In his foreword to the *Confession of Faith which Robert Barnes . . . Made in England,* he took stock of the progress of the "last twenty years":

> And it is a particular joy to me to hear that our good and pious companion at home and table [Barnes] has so graciously been called upon by God to shed his blood for the sake of His beloved Son and to become a holy martyr. Thanks, praise, and glory be to the Father of our dear Lord Jesus Christ, who has once again, as at the beginning, let us see a time in which His Christians, who ate and drank (as the Apostles of Christ say) with us and were genuinely merry, are pushed to martyrdom (that means Heaven) and sainthood before our eyes and away from our eyes and our sides. Who would have thought twenty years ago that Christ the Lord was so close to us and was eating, drinking, talking, and living at our tables and in our homes through His dear martyrs?[34]

The last words of the foreword show with eminent clarity what progress and success consist of: ". . . It shall become even worse. Amen." The Church shares the fate of its Lord, Luther admonishes to the very last, in that the evil one will not be intimidated; he does not shrink from any attack nor does he fear violence, "for God sleeps and conceals Himself, yes, in His creatures He is weak." The Devil and his specters "are very bold, and pursue the suffering and dying God."[35]

To sum up, it can be said that from his first lectures on the Bible to the end of his life, Luther's view of the Church remained unchanged and central to his convictions. The Church is visible, but as a suffering communion of Christians. It is endowed with great riches, which are accessible only through faith. It is unique and unified, but scattered all over the world. Bishops and doctors are its servants, allowing the Gospel to be preached in sermon, sacrament, absolution of sins, praise of God—and martyrdom: as in the days of the early Church so will it be till Judgment Day. Persecution and pressure will increase, and yet the adversary will not be able to vanquish the Church.

The Gospel, which Luther discovered in the course of the indulgence controversy, affords certainty that the individual Christian shares in all the riches Christ promised His Church in Word and Sacrament. It is, however, participation not in triumph and victory but in the history of the true Church, which, though apparently triumphant in the world, is still being pursued by the Devil and beaten by his forces. The Psalms had prophesied the history of the Church, and the apostle Paul had experienced it: "We are troubled on every side, yet not distressed; we are perplexed, but not in despair; Persecuted, but not forsaken; cast down, but not destroyed" (2 Cor. 4.8–9).

If we examine the conceptual framework underlying Luther's Reformation vision, it is hard to believe that he could have aroused and activated a whole era to the extent he did. The allegorical method of scriptural exegesis was already outmoded in the sixteenth century; Luther's division of Church history into epochs—the time of the persecutors, the time of the heretics, the time of the destroyers—is Augustinian and must have sounded rather odd to humanist ears. But thus it was that Luther uncovered a view of the Church that countless contemporaries felt to be genuine and realistic. The discovery that the wealthy, powerful Church was in fact a Church in captivity ignited the Reformation, a movement Luther himself interpreted only as a terrible prelude to a grand finale.

The idea that the battle for the Church was only a prologue to God's Reformation was ultimately not accepted by the Evangelical movement. Other forms of Church renewal, particularly in the cities of southern Germany and Switzerland and among the followers of John Calvin's Reformation, believed that the "ecclesia militans," the Church Militant, could already become victorious here on earth. Consequently Calvinism developed greater momentum and seemed to be more successful, pointing the way and setting the goals for an incipient modern era. Where the Wittenberg Reformation had established itself, be it in Saxony, where it had begun, or in Scandinavia, the notion of a defenseless Church was able to prevail—under the protective mantle of the state.

Times have changed. The protection has become unreliable and the shield brittle. The expectation of imminent doom has freed itself from the embrace of the progress-oriented optimism of the Enlightenment and is as timely today as it was in the late Middle Ages and early sixteenth century.

Luther's vision of the Church of confessors once again captures the reality of our days. Viewed and assessed the right way, it can be of enormous benefit to the Church universal . . . and to all those who suffered so long under her raised fist.

CHAPTER X

Wedded Bliss and World Peace: In Defiance of the Devil

The Delights and Duties of Marriage

"For the person who believes in an eternal heavenly life, this life loses its value." Thus the former theologian Ludwig Feuerbach repudiated Christianity. Faith and earthly love are mutually exclusive. The monastic way of life is in keeping with the nature of Christianity, but Christian marriage is a shallow lie because the true Christian is convinced that by believing in God, man becomes totally self-sufficient and thus needs no counterpart of the opposite sex.[1]

Though Feuerbach liked to quote Luther, the two were divided not only by centuries but by epochs; they were as remote from one another as the Middle Ages and the Reformation. What Feuerbach the critical philosopher presented as "the nature of Christianity" was the medieval sexual ethic with which Luther so vehemently took issue. It was the Reformer who excoriated repression of the sexual drive in the service of a higher perfection, in complete contrast to the "critical philosopher," who presented—and thus caricatured—this modern "higher perfection" as true Christianity. But Luther wanted to liberate the Christian faith from this distortion: he could not accept the oppression of people down to their most intimate moments and warned of its devastating effects on society.

There are undoubtedly those who should stay unmarried for the sake of God. "But these are rare; not one in a thousand can do it: it is one of God's special miracles."[2] God-given celibacy does not elevate to a higher, holier state, it is the result of a specific divine calling to undivided service to the Word.

This, however, is the exception, not the rule. Matrimony befits everyone.[3] It is a "divinely noble business."

> Whoever is ashamed of marriage is also ashamed of being and being called human, tries to improve on what God has made. Adam's children

> are and will remain human; that is why they should and must beget more men. Dear God, we see daily the effort it costs to live in a marriage, and to keep the marital vows. And we try to promise chastity as if we were not human, had neither flesh nor blood.
>
> But it is the God of the world, the Devil, who so slanders the marital state and has made it shameful—and yet allows adulterers, whores, and dissolute knaves to survive in high esteem all the same—that it would be fair to marry in order to spite him and his world and to accept his ignominy and bear it for God's sake.[4]

The above eulogy on marriage has nothing to do with an unrealistic, quaint concept of wedded life. On the contrary, from 1520 to 1525 Luther principally addressed the numerous nuns and monks who had entered monasteries or convents at a very early age and had renounced all claims to the family fortune. They were totally penniless; for them marriage was an economic gamble of the first order. Luther vividly depicted the risks run by members of orders who married without having learned a craft. Marriage entailed obligations, but whoever was willing to take them on should make the leap in the name of God. For him there was truth in the familiar witticism that "marriage and tournaments demand considerable courage."

The Fall had debased the conjugal act as much as it had man's highest intellectual achievements. Yet through marriage the egocentric lust for possession could be turned toward a partner. The combination of sexuality and egotism was not novel; it could have been discovered in medieval morality texts. Astonishing, however, is the way Luther spurned everything the Middle Ages held sacred. How could one want to compare "high reason" to "low instincts"! Luther's association of "higher" and "lower" powers in man shows that something decisively new was underway. The surprising element—one still highly offensive in the sixteenth century—was the assertion that sexual drives were a divine force or even God's vital presence. Luther found the scriptural basis for his view in a verse from the Book of Genesis. The passage became so important to him that he made repeated attempts to translate it into good German, ultimately deciding for the version: "Es ist nicht gut, dass der Mensch allein sei. Ich will ihm ein Gehülfen, die um ihn sei, machen" (Gen. 2.18),[5] which corresponds precisely to the King James Version: ". . . It is not good that the man should be alone; I will make him an help meet for him." Luther's exegesis of the text, informed by his thoughts on sexuality and marriage, is truly epoch-making. "This is the Word of God, by virtue of which . . . the passionate, natural inclination toward woman is created and maintained. It may not be prevented by vow and law. For it is God's Word and work."[6]

God's power is not confined to marriage; it is already present in the sexual instinct. Marriage is simply the right way to use it, the genuinely spiritual, divinely ordained status to live one's sexuality. Because the Devil hates God's life-giving power, he hates marriage with the same intensity and seeks to hinder the peace of God and to decrease the fruits of the earth.[7] At weddings God was—and still is—referred to as the "third party" to the union. For Luther God is so vitally present in the power of attraction between man and woman that he inspires the conjugal union and Himself constitutes the sexual bond of marriage.

What made Luther's theology so vivid and intelligible was not the outer rhetoric, but the connection of the Word of God with corporeality. Unlike those who had gone before him and those who followed him, he understood God's Word as truly creative: "God spoke and it was so." Thus the Word of God generates sensuous existence. The major schools of the Middle Ages, modern philosophical idealism, and contemporary, person-oriented theology all link the "Word" of God with the human "spirit," with conscience and always with man's conscious mind. The Middle Ages are faulted with the "sacramentalization" of grace and the Reformation invoked as a witness to the "spiritualization" of man.

Modern Christian thought describes the truly human being as responsible, as "responding" to the Word of God. If considered at all, his bones and ligaments, let alone his sexual drives, are no more than the requisite framework for his response. "The Word was made flesh" (John 1.14) is how St. John the Evangelist announced the miracle of Christ's birth. But depending on the denomination, theology has transformed "flesh" into either "Church" or "preaching." Feuerbach considered this "transformation" the essence of Christianity.

For Luther this spiritualization, this striving for the transcendental, was a perversion of Christianity. A just man does not become spiritual through faith, he *lives* out of faith; and this our life is created and intended by God. The first line of the Creed can be fathomed only out of human experience: "What do you mean," he asks in his *Large Catechism*," by the words 'I believe in God, the Father, the Almighty, the Creator . . .'? Answer: What I mean and believe is that I am God's creature, that means that he has given me and continuously maintains body, soul and life, limbs small and large, all the senses, intellect and reason."[8]

Even this unequivocal declaration did not escape misconstruction, restriction to intellect and reason. Sensuousness, and with it all the senses, was cast aside as irrelevant. The nobility of man is far above God's lowly creation—eating, drinking, clothes, food, wife and children. Both the new layman of the sixteenth century and the cultured citizen of the Enlightenment reveal themselves as the monks of times past. Luther saw the Devil at work in this monk. "Whoever is ashamed of marriage is also ashamed of being human": thus did Luther reject the vitiation of body, senses, and sensuality. It is the "god" of this world, the Devil, who has maligned marriage and made it "shameful"; one should marry "to spite and resist" him and his morals.[9]

No one in our century has dealt so thoroughly with Luther's sexuality as the Dominican Heinrich Seuse Denifle. His disgust for Luther demonstrates that hatred, too, can engender perception and the courage to say a great deal that has been politely pushed aside in our era of ecumenism.[10] Denifle sees Luther's "lust" as one of the main causes of the Reformation. Luther's experiences with his sexuality led him to believe that man's "primeval sin" was insuperable. His carnal instinct drove him to reinterpret the Scriptures so as to legitimate marriage "completely overcome by lustfulness."[11]

From sensuality to the Reformation! This image of Luther makes Luther's wife, Catherine of Bora, a whore as well as the core of Reformation theology. Protestants immediately disclaimed the thesis as slander, and today it no longer finds sympathy among the Catholic Luther scholars. Nonetheless, there is an undeniable consensus between Luther's slanderer and his defenders. Despite the Reformer, sexual drives are confused with man's "primeval sin." What nature wants is "unholy," something only for the dark hours of the night. One need only read Luther's *Wider den falsch genannten geistlichen Stand* (*Against the so-called spiritual estate;* 1522) to establish that he did not hesitate to speak plainly about the healthy elemental force of desire.

> A young woman, if the high and rare grace of virginity has not been bestowed upon her, can do without a man as little as without food, drink, sleep, and other natural needs. And on the other hand: a man, too, cannot be without a woman. The reason is the following: begetting children is as deeply rooted in nature as eating and drinking. That is why God provided the body with limbs, arteries, ejaculation, and everything that goes along with them. Now if someone wants to stop this and

> not permit what nature wants and must do, what is he doing but preventing nature from being nature, fire from burning, water from being wet, and man from either drinking, eating, or sleeping?[12]

Not only Heinrich Denifle considered this self-incriminating: "If the Protestants had found a Catholic writer before Luther who had written this, they would surely have branded him as unclean to the highest extent and corrupted to the core. And justifiably so."[13]

True, but not "justifiable"; the word cannot be left unchallenged! The lustful Luther deserved to be read and understood without the monkish priggishness of so-called cultivated citizens.

The tendency to make him "respectable"—and not Denifle's appalled outcry—explains why one of Luther's most revealing and engaging letters has been all but suppressed. In December 1525 he wrote to his friend Spalatin to say that he would unfortunately not be able to attend his friend's wedding. But Spalatin should not let himself be misled by the hidebound priests of the old faith in Altenburg because marriage was a gift of God. This was followed by an erotic passage, the second part of which was stricken from editions of Luther's letters very early on: "When you sleep with your Catherine and embrace her, you should think: 'This child of man, this wonderful creature of God has been given to me by my Christ. May He be praised and glorified.' On the evening of the day on which, according to my calculations, you will receive this, I shall make love to my Catherine while you make love to yours, and thus we will be united in love."[14]

The Emancipation of Eve

Instead of glorifying virginity and celibacy Luther discovered marriage and the household to be a worthwhile, fulfilling profession. From our present-day perspective his respect for the woman as housewife and mother does not do justice to her other gifts. The woman of today has long since proven herself outside the family.

The complaint that women are restricted to "children, church and, kitchen" does not, however, apply to the distribution of roles in Luther's marriage. Catherine's perceptible independence may have tempted him to sigh: "If I ever have to find myself a wife again, I will hew myself an obedient wife out of stone."[15] But his patriarchal irony should not cause us to jump to conclusions. The oft-criticized traditional roles passed down to us date back

Lucas Cranach the Elder, Women driving away monks and bishops, ca. 1526

to the Middle Ages and have persisted in large parts of Europe—with or without Luther's assistance. Luther did not consider it unmanly for fathers to wash diapers and make beds. People may sneer, but "God rejoices with all angels and creatures."[16] Conversely, he had his reasons for leaving the family finances and the administration of their property to his wife. Even if men could bear children the world would go to rack and ruin without women, because they know all about "spending and saving"—and that is what politics and government are all about![17]

There were also limits to his reevaluation of woman: he thought her less "intelligent" than the man and felt she should not "rule the roost" in politics and ecclesiastical government.[18] Nonetheless, Luther disposed of two gross prejudices that had shaped the clerical image of women. The first, which the *Hammer against the Witches* (*Malleus Maleficarum;* circa 1487) had once again drummed into the Inquisitors, was that women were sexually insatiable hyenas and thus a constant danger to men and their society. The second prejudice reduced women to "bearing children," the procreation of the human race and the reproduction of the male. Luther was familiar with and disgusted by both of these contemptuous theses. And though he advocated a distribution of roles because he believed women could not cope with pressure as well as men, he thought they were under the same burdens and of equal value as creatures.

Holy Matrimony: Love and Lust

In the bloodiest phase of the Peasants' War, Luther, who had already recommended marriage to so many as the way of the Gospel, decided to risk it himself. The time was not a random choice. He was well aware of the injustice and oppression the "common man" in town and country had to suffer. But violent resistance against the authorities, particularly in the name of the Gospel, was the work of the Devil—and only possible in the chaos of the Last Days. So the end must be near: "Only a short time and the righteous judge will come." The enemy now devastating the country hated the joys of marriage as intensely as he did peace in the world. That is why, Luther wrote to a friend, I want to marry my Catherine "in defiance of him" before I die. After all, I will not "be robbed of my heart and my happiness."[19]

A monk marry a nun? To shatter this taboo was to openly court disaster. The Luthers awaited the birth of their first child with growing suspense, for they were acquainted with the superstition that a two-headed monster would issue from a "sacrilegious" union of this kind. On June 7, 1526, Catherine Luther bore a son. The very same day Pastor Bugenhagen, who had also blessed their marriage, christened the boy Johannes. Relieved and happy, Luther reported to his relatives in Eisleben, a friend in Zwickau, and of course Spalatin that the child was healthy and without birth defects: "Little Johannes is cheerful and strong." Then paternal pride broke through: he was a good eater and drinker, thank God—"homo vorax ac bibax"![20] What would have become of the Reformation if Luther's first child had actually been handicapped!

Five more children were born, two sons and three daughters: Elisabeth (1527), Magdalena (1529), Martin (1531), Paul (1533), and finally, on December 17, 1534, Margaret. Two of the girls died very young; Elisabeth at only eight months and Magdalena at thirteen years. The Luthers grieved deeply for "Lenchen," who had helped them to overcome the painful loss of Elisabeth.

Luther expressed his joy over the children in his typical, vivid way: "I have legitimate children, which no papal theologian has—the three children are the three kingdoms which I acquired more honestly than [Archduke] Ferdinand did Hungary, Bohemia, and the Roman crown."[21] What it must have meant for his sons and daughters to live up to the expectations of the surroundings in and outside Wittenberg can hardly be imagined.

Luther was not, however, trying to raise a generation of kings. If they were suited for it, he wanted one son to be a soldier, the second a scholar, and the third a peasant. Everything turned out differently, of course. Despite all his father's opposition, Hans became a lawyer and later royal chancellery councilor in Weimar. He achieved the career his father, Martin, had been intended for! Martin, the second son, studied theology but never took up a clerical post, living instead as a private citizen in Wittenberg until his early death in 1564. Paul achieved the greatest renown. He studied medicine and

Lucas Cranach the Elder (?), Portrait of Lenchen (Magdalena) Luther (1529–42)

later became a sought-after doctor, first in Gotha and later with the elector of Brandenburg. The Reformer's only surviving daughter, Margaret, married a Brandenburg nobleman named von Kunheim.

Running the household in the roomy former Augustinian monastery required a firm hand and good planning. What Luther had at first reproved as arrogance in his wife proved to be a talent to think, act, and make decisions independently. She ruled an extended family judiciously. In addition to the parents and children there was Catherine's aunt "Muhme Lene," to whom Luther allotted her own room. Then there were two of Catherine's nieces living in the house, plus an ever-changing circle of students who found lodgings there. Finally, there was a never-ending stream of visitors—friends, people curious to meet the great man, or people with theological queries or soliciting Luther's intercession with the elector in their behalf.

Luther's respect for the head women had for finances undoubtedly went back to his experiences with his wife. The family had very modest means, especially during the first ten years, and Catherine had to work hard to make ends meet. The elector had made them a wedding gift of one hundred gulden. But the necessary renovation of the Black Monastery, which continued to serve the couple as a home, immediately devoured the whole sum.

As preacher at the city church Luther had been receiving an annual salary of less than nine gulden since approximately 1514. In 1523 this sum was still the only cash at his disposal, since his Augustinian professorship gave him free lodgings and, together with brewing rights, a claim to payment in kind but not to a salary. It was only in 1524 that Elector Frederick granted him an annual salary of one hundred gulden. The new Elector John ultimately accorded him two hundred gulden so that Luther would earn as much as Philipp Melanchthon. This equality of salary was maintained from then on, even when Elector John Frederick raised the salary to three hundred and in 1540 to four hundred gulden.[22]

Luther never earned anything from his writings; he refused to accept a penny from them. Even at a very low percentage the royalties from his countless and oft-reprinted works could have freed him from his constant financial problems. The sum of three hundred and later of four hundred gulden was a top salary for a Wittenberg professor at the time, but the big house, all the runaway nuns and monks the Luthers took in, and the continual guests made the household expensive to run. Luther calculated his annual expenses at about five hundred gulden. Catherine had to bridge the gap with the earnings from a farm, from gardening, pig-breeding, and beer-brewing, and by taking in lodgers. "Mr. Cathy," Luther mocked, but underneath the irony there was respect and recognition, because, as he ended his detailed statement of accounts for the year 1535–36, "the economy is the mainstay of state and Church."[23]

"Defiance of the Devil" is probably the worst reason for marriage ever recorded in the long history of the institution. Luther's defiance did not originate in presumptuousness but in conviction: the excommunicated heretic understood his marriage to Catherine of Bora, the runaway nun, as a God-given answer to false diabolical holiness. The twenty-year marriage of convenience became a happy one: "I would not give my Katie for France and Venice together."[24] In the intimacy of its patriarchalism their marriage could have been considered exemplary far into the twentieth century: "Katie, you have married an honest man who loves you; you are an empress."[25]

The reason for their happiness lay as much in Catherine's character as in her husband's nature. But the decisive factor was that both of them regarded marriage as a profession and divine vocation without the romantic expectations of love that were later to increase so enormously the number of disappointments and marital breakups. It is true that the two had not been passionately in love when they started out, but what began as fondness and gratitude for a new form of companionship developed into a firm bond of

Lucas Cranach the Elder, Portraits of Martin Luther at the age of forty-three and Katharina Luther, née von Bora, at the age of twenty-seven, 1526

love. The surviving letters are positive evidence of that. In his invitations to the wedding feast he was still circumspect, writing: "I do not love my wife, but I appreciate her."[26] As the years passed his reticence disappeared and Catherine became "my beloved wife." His many imaginative forms of addressing her in his letters are a piece of "marital literature" of their own: "The rich woman of Zulsdorff" (Catherine owned a farm there), "Frauen Doctorin Katharina Ludherin, living in body in Wittenberg and wandering in spirit in Zulsdorff, my darling to her own hand"[27]—and sometimes at her "feet."

"At table" fourteen years after his wedding he recounted the prosaic beginnings. Actually he had wanted to marry Ave von Schönfeld—he did not like Catherine because he thought her haughty. But God wanted otherwise and blessed me with "the happiest marriage."[28]

The beginnings really were extraordinarily unromantic. Pastor Johannes Bugenhagen married Martin and Catherine at the Black Monastery on June 13, 1525. It was a quiet ceremony with only a few friends in attendance. Before the wedding was celebrated on a larger scale and in the presence of parents two weeks later, they were already the talk of the town: the doctor had made the runaway nun Catherine his wife. Melanchthon, in keeping with his cautious temperament, expressed deep reservations, fearing that the cause of the Reformation would be harmed by such festivities in dark times—in the midst of the Peasants' War. He was not invited to the nuptials on June 13.

Hieronymus Schurff, the Wittenberg lawyer who had been Luther's legal adviser at the Diet of Worms, shared Melanchthon's opinion: "If this monk takes a wife, the whole world and the Devil himself will laugh, and all the work he [Luther] has done up to now will have been for nought." Their misgivings were not unfounded. In the hands of Counter-Reformation opponents Luther's marriage became a convincing argument for the monk's depravity. "Luther was not content to simply play with his aristocratic Ketten Borra but rather . . . breaking his own and the nun's vow to God—had her consent to become his alleged wife. Then . . . as soon as Luther's wedding bells rang, the lecherous monks and nuns put up plenty of ladders against the monastery walls and ran off together in masses."[29]

At that time the consummation of a marriage was attested to by a witness at the bridal bed. Luther's was Justus Jonas, his closest friend, who would also be found at Luther's deathbed. Jonas did not enjoy his task: "Yesterday I was present and saw the bridegroom on the bridal bed—I could not suppress my tears at the sight. . . . Now that it has happened and God has desired it, I implore God to grant the excellent honest man . . . all the happiness. God is wonderful in his counsels and works."[30]

"God is wonderful" does not mean that He is great but that He can astonish beyond belief, that He is unpredictable and acts counter to all expectations. Luther's wedding marked a radical break, as Melanchthon, Schurff, Jonas, and many others rightly felt. The Reformation had to take leave of the centuries-old ideal of the charismatic leader who, as an ascetic man of God, forsakes all things "worldly." Even among Luther's intimates in his own Wittenberg, his "defiance of the Devil" meant that he had to go his own lonely way. Luther sharply criticized the breaking of images that constantly accompanied the Reformation in the cities. Theological objections to images were either untenable or uncertain; experience, on the other hand, demonstrated images to be "sermons for the eyes." Luther's marriage was the genuine and far more offensive form of iconoclasm. It directed itself against the fiction of false saintliness in the hearts of the living and not against the depiction of dead saints. For him "saintly" meant to be near his "dear housewife," as he wrote to her in none too veiled terms: "I would like to be your lover now."[31]

Ten days before his death, in one of the last letters he wrote to his wife, Luther related that the negotiations that had taken him to Eisleben were grueling: "I suspect that Hell and the whole world are rid of all devils at the moment for they have probably all assembled here in Eisleben for my sake."[32]

After a few harsh lines about Jews and lawyers—for him, both a threat to justice in the name of the law—there was an important piece of information that would no longer have amazed his opponents: "We are living excellently. . . . The local wine is good, and the Naumburg beer is very good; the pitch in the local beer does not cause me any breathing problems. The Devil has spoiled beer in the whole world for us with pitch, and for you the wine with sulfur. But here the wine is pure."[33]

That Luther's Reformation found God-given space for love and good living already met with embarrassed disapproval in the Reformer's own time. German intellectual history, continuing the monastic tradition Luther had worked so hard to escape, disdained the world once more, identifying it with the Devil—though too enlightened to use his name.

These taboos had such an enduring effect that Luther's statements about the senses and sensuality remain primly unmentioned. But the Reformation turning point can only be fully gauged as an event and a revolution when it is understood that Luther's discovery of the righteousness of God also revealed the Devil to be the enemy of woman, world, and well-being.

Conscience need no longer distinguish between Heaven and earth. In one of his final letters to Catherine, Luther reminds her of liberation in faith *and* life through Christ "in swaddling": "I have someone stronger to care for me than you and all the angels. . . . So be at peace, Amen."[34] Though excommunicated and banned, Luther is at peace—with beer mug in hand.

Divorce and Bigamy

Luther was fully aware of the offensive character of his marriage. "Getting married has brought me so much contempt that I may hope that the angels are laughing and all the devils weeping."[35] Whether Luther's marriage was truly detrimental to the drawing power of the Reformation is difficult to tell. The hard line he took in his writings against the Peasants' War shortly before his marriage and his break with Erasmus at the end of the year presented much more of a problem to the "common man" and the scholarly world.

The way people judged Luther's marriage depended primarily on how they imagined the future of the Reformation movement. For a long while Melanchthon had continued to hope for a settlement with the Roman Catholics that would rescue the unity of the Western Church. He had invested all his energies in this cause—especially at the Diet of Augsburg in the summer of 1530. As a family man Luther could only constitute an obstacle on the road to unification. The fiercest attacks on Luther's marriage came from the juridical elite of the learned councilors, for they were still loyal to canon law. Everyone concerned with achieving a settlement could accept the idea of married secular priests, but for a monk to marry was opprobrious. The vows being broken had after all been sworn voluntarily.

But assuming that a Reformation of the *whole* Church was no longer possible in 1525, in that year of crisis Luther's marriage could indeed lend support to the innumerable Evangelical preachers who were already married. What Luther taught he now lived as well.

LUTHER'S COUNSEL as father confessor to Landgrave Philip of Hesse on December 10, 1539, could not so easily be condoned. Philip was one of the most forceful princely supporters of the Reformation. And it was he, of all people, who—with Luther's approval—made himself guilty of the crime of bigamy! The scandal arising from the landgrave's bigamous marriage had far-reaching political consequences. The strongman of the protective alliance of the Protestant estates of the empire, the Schmalkaldic League, was at the emperor's mercy. According to imperial law as promulgated by Charles V in the rules of the criminal court in Regensburg in 1532, bigamy could result in the death sentence. To avoid punishment Philip thus had to come to an arrangement with Charles V and conclude a separate peace in 1541: he was to halt all attempts to strengthen the Schmalkaldic League and desist from all activities against the emperor.

But Philip was not the only one compromised. Luther's reputation suffered lasting damage as well. Even today the fact that he advised Philip to enter into a bigamous union is—in good ecumenical harmony—interpreted by Protestants as "the greatest blot on the history of the Reformation" and by Catholics as the act of a devious scoundrel.[36]

Before Philip was nineteen (1523), he had wed Christina, daughter of Duke George of Saxony (†1539). Relations between George, Luther's bitterest foe among the princes, and his cousins in Electoral Saxony had always been strained; through Philip's marriage to his daughter, he was allied with the militant Protestant prince. This was the political side of the marriage, but the decisive reasons for the couple's estrangement were personal. Soon, after "not more than three weeks," Christina no longer appealed to the young landgrave. Later he complained about her unfriendliness, her "smell," and her alcohol consumption. But she cannot have been quite as repulsive as Philip made her out to be since the couple did, after all, have ten children, the last three of them after March 4, 1540, the date Philip married his second wife, Margarethe von der Sale.

Hans Guldenmund, Landgrave Philip of Hesse

He had already considered taking a second wife besides Christina in 1526. Had not the patriarchs of the Old Testament had more than one wife? When he sought Luther's advice on the matter in the autumn of 1526 (perhaps he was already trying to gain support in Wittenberg), he received a disappointing reply: no one, and above all no Christian, should have more than one wife. The example of the patriarchs of the Old Testament proved nothing, for what God had permitted them as an emergency measure in a polygamous world did not automatically apply "to me." Not only would an additional marriage cause a scandal, it could not be vindicated by the Word of God either. Only "great need" could overrule the "no."[37]

Luther did not deviate from this line. When Henry VIII, who had since 1509 been married to Catherine of Aragon, the emperor's aunt, procured expert opinions in Germany and Switzerland in 1531 in support of his plans to marry Anne Boleyn, Luther once again indicated that marriage was sacred: "Before I should approve of such a repudiation, I would rather let him marry a second queen." And to make sure there could be no misunderstanding, he concluded with the words: "Even if there should be a divorce, Catherine will remain queen of England—and she will have been wronged before God and man."[38]

Luther recognized certain grounds for divorce. If faith had been broken and a partner deserted, the union for life had been destroyed. The "innocent partner" should not be kept from remarrying.[39] But the one who had disrupted the marriage was pulled up short: "No, my friend: if you are bound to a woman, you are no longer a free man; God forces and commands you to stay with wife and child, to feed and rear them."[40]

Luther's "confessional counsel" of December 10, 1539, which will forever link his name with Philip's bigamy, ended with a remarkable statement, one that seems incomprehensible today: the public will regard Margarethe as one of the prince's "not unusual" concubines, so the scandal and talk will remain within limits.[41] The remark, undoubtedly not bereft of irony, is elucidated by the frank advice Philip's sister Elisabeth, widow of Duke John the Younger of Saxony (†1537), gave him. When her brother revealed his predicament to her, she suggested that he "take *one* bedmate instead of the *many* whores."[42] Elisabeth knew what she was talking about. The unmarried Elector Frederick the Wise, her father-in-law George's cousin, had his "bedmate" Ann Weller and, though discreet, made no secret of their relationship. Shortly before his death he wrote his two sons by the union into his will, leaving them Castle Jessen and an annual pension of one thousand gulden.[43] The "great men" were discussed candidly at Luther's table: "The secret marriage of princes and great men is a genuine marriage for God, although it is conducted without pomp and splendor."[44]

Elisabeth was familiar with these circles when she tried to reason with her brother. But Philip did not follow her advice. Not surprisingly, the opinions as to his reasons diverge. He decided, it is said, "rather to marry for reasons of conscience."[45] Or: it was pure sensuality that drove him, his moral dilemma was only feigned, for "he was not religious. He had now been following the new teaching for fifteen years."[46]

The debate about Philip's morals diverts us from the decision Luther had to make. The Strasbourg reformer Martin Bucer had assured Luther that the landgrave had already been avoiding the Lord's Supper for years because of his moral dilemma, as Philip himself related, since "the peasants' feud,"[47] meaning for nearly fifteen years. It looked as if only an additional marriage could keep him from further excesses. The statement Luther had once made regarding the marriage of the English king now also became his counsel to Philip: divorce was out of the question; in case of emergency, the only alternative was a second marriage. Philip's first wife, Christina, agreed to the solution. She retained all her rights as a landgravine, and children from her husband's second marriage (seven sons were born) were to have no claims to power. Philip had to continue rendering her "friendliness," which he did: Christina bore him three further children.

Not a concubine but a second wife: that could have put an end to the whole affair. From a modern vantage point the solution was not a milestone, but it was no scandal either. Luther's stubborn insistence on the inseparable nature of the first marriage is particularly striking in light of our—from the perspective of other cultures, hypocritical—acceptance of successive marriages while indignantly condemning simultaneous "polygamy." Then should the pastoral counsel given to Philip be extended to others as well? Absolutely not, said Luther; that is precisely why he insisted that his ad hoc advice was to be confidential: that it not create a legal and moral precedent, "let it remain secret."[48] As history shows, Luther's insistence on silence was in vain.

A proper assessment of the matter cannot consist in a Protestant defense of Luther by putting the blame on the medieval tradition of dispensation for concubinage, or in a claim of deception by Bucer, or in a condemnation of the mendacity of the depraved, syphilitic Landgrave.

Wherever blame is placed, the fact remains that Luther came to a decision which, contrary to his own opinion, is genuinely exemplary. There is Christian counsel which bursts the seams of moral convention, whether unwritten or codified in law. Luther himself insists that the Gospel teaches of a higher law, the Law of Love—however dangerous in practice—which is to be directed to the unique needs of the "neighbor," who may well encounter dilemmas which no law can foresee. Luther gave his advice unwillingly and hesitantly, but he did not shirk his pastoral responsibility, for example, by referring Philip to experts in civil law.

In this case as well, Luther had distinguished between the inflexible law and the Gospel of grace. Though public law is a precious gift, it is subject to the blind legal code of generalized regulations, which cannot differentiate between precedence and exceptions, between normal cases and emergencies. But the Gospel sees the individual and seeks his welfare in the maze of moral obligations. The law was not thereby abrogated, and that is why Luther's ministerial advice was to remain secret. The Gospel risks unconditional love, and that is why such counsel could be given. Here Luther

So dire is the situation! By the standards of justice and law, the pope and cardinals deserve to swing from the gallows. From left: *Cardinal Albrecht of Mainz, Bishop Otto of Augsburg (?), Cochlaeus (?), the Pope.*

is so different from the Reformation in the cities, and from Calvin's Reformation: biblical counsel is not to be confused with bourgeois morality. Not making this distinction means unmaking Luther's Reformation.

Chaos and Peace

December 10, 1539, was the day Luther advised the landgrave to take a secret additional wife. This was the "black day" in the history of the German Reformation, or at least that is what can still be read in a widely used Protestant handbook of Church history that has otherwise undergone numerous revisions and corrections over the past seventy-five years.[49] "Dies ater" it says in its classical erudition, for middle-class sensibilities have been offended.

In comparison, Luther's writings against the Jews, which in turn cannot be isolated from his writings against the papists and peasants, evidently seemed far less offensive. But Luther assailed all three groups with deadly ferocity, urging the authorities to take decisive action. As early as the summer of 1520 his reply to the claims of the papacy as revealingly formulated by Silvester Prierias could hardly have been plainer: "If we punish thieves with the gallows, robbers with the sword, heretics with fire, why do we not defend ourselves all the more with all weapons against these perpetrators of destruction, these cardinals, these popes, this whole filth heap of the Roman Sodom, who are unceasingly destroying the Church of God, and wash our hands in their blood."[50]

The attacks he leveled against the rebelling peasants in May 1525 were equally virulent.[51] His *Ermahnung zum Frieden* (*Admonition to Peace*) was a two-pronged assault denouncing alike the injustices of the princes and landed nobility and the inadmissable mixing of Gospel and violence by the peasants. Filled with the impressions of a ten-day journey through convulsed Thuringia, Luther hastily added an appendix to the *Admonition: Against the Robbing and Murderous Hordes of Peasants.* Here we can find the sentence that was to style him "toady of princes": "Such strange times are these that a prince can be more deserving of Heaven by shedding blood than others by praying."[52] Luther's language veritably trembles with rage and indignation:

> So dear lords, free here, save here, help here. Have mercy on the poor, stab, slay, strangle here whoever can; if you die doing it, good for you: a more blessed . . . death you can never receive.[53]

When the old Luther called for measures against the Jews twenty years later, he included cruelly exact instructions. In his pamphlet *Of the Jews and Their Lies,* he suggested how these "children of the Devil" should be treated.[54]

> *Firstly,* that their synagogues or schools should be burned down and what will not burn should be razed and covered with earth, that no man will ever see a stone or cinder of it again. . . . *Next,* that their houses should be broken and destroyed in the same way. For they do the same things there as in their schools. For that they can be put under a roof or stable, like the gypsies. . . . *Thirdly,* that all their prayer books and Talmudists, in which such idolatrous lies, curses, and blasphemies are taught, should be taken from them. *Fourthly,* that their rabbis should be forbidden, at the risk of life and limb, to teach from now on. Because they have lost their office for good reason. . . . *Fifthly,* that escort and road should be completely prohibited to the Jews. For they have no reason to be in the country, being neither landlords, nor officials, nor peddlers or the like. . . . *Sixthly,* that they should be prohibited from usury and that all their cash and fortunes in silver and gold should be taken from them and put in safekeeping. . . . *Seventhly,* that young, strong Jewish men and women should be given flail, axe, hoe, spade, distaff, spindle, and be left to earn their bread by the sweat of their brows. . . . For, as all can see, God's wrath over them is so great that gentle mercy will only make them worse and worse, and harshness little better. So away with them at all costs.[55]

The very first sentence of this program, which can safely be termed a pogrom, is left out in modern translations:

> We must exercise harsh mercy with fear and trembling, in the hope that we could save some from the flames and embers. We must not avenge ourselves. They are under God's wrath—a thousand times worse than we could wish it upon them.[56]

What he actually does wish upon them is, however, bad enough.

It is not only Luther the *old* man, worn out by work, overtaxed by worries, at the end of his strength, who has spoken here. Nor is it all merely verbal acerbity characteristic of the times. The Reformer had made similar appeals for resistance to the "exploiting Romanists" in 1520 and the "plundering peasants" in 1525. Three times the limits of his view of the Devil, which brought liberation and progress in so many respects, were demonstrated. As a result of his constant awareness of the Devil's might, Luther had learned to apply the distinction between law and the Gospel and discovered the boundary between passive belief in God and active participation in shaping the world.[57] Against the background of a world pervaded by the Devil, Luther had discovered the joy of life. And ultimately the moral pressure of the Devil had led him to do battle against that fatal human disease, the oppressive "superego" of conscience. But where the battle against Satan's forces leads to collective judgments in the face of a rapidly approaching doomsday, the voice of the prophet becomes a shrilly fanatical battle cry. That, too, is Luther.

How can one and the same man insist on the Gospel of love as opposed to public morals and decency in the case of bigamy and at the same time arm the authorities with the sword, charging them, as guardians of the law, to employ even pogrom and massacre as a means of restoring order?

The natural condition of the world is chaos and upheaval. It is never left to itself, but is always the battleground between God and the Devil. Like a father sustaining and supporting his family, the temporal authorities protect the welfare of all men. It is a Christian duty to make a contribution in both family and society to the survival of the world in the struggle against chaos.[58]

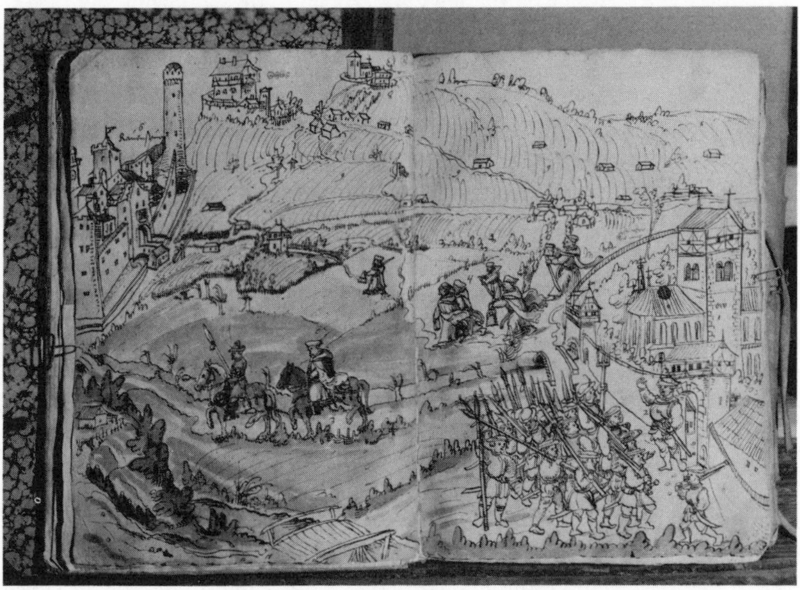

A peasant army at the gates of a monastery

There is a fatal connection between fighting the Devil in papists, peasants, and Jews and the subsequent use of the cry for reformation to rally "God's troops" against "God's enemies."

Darkness at Noon: Luther and the Jews

The Third Reich and in its wake the whole Western world capitalized upon Luther, the fierce Jew-baiter. Any attempt to deal with the Reformer runs up against this obstacle. No description of Luther's campaign against the Jews, however objective and erudite it may be, escapes the horror: we live in the post-Holocaust era. Under the spell of nightmarish terror, it is difficult to peer through the shadows of history, making clear judgments, passing a just sentence, as we grope our way along the path between aggressive accusation and apologetic explanation. Guilt-ridden voices abound, but our era requires far more than verbal repudiation: it calls for detailed information and an unvarnished view of the past. It needs collective anamnesis in the painful encounter with an epoch in which the modern world emerged. For this is not a matter of a German past which, once overcome, will free civilization from future fear of the Darkness at Noon.

Luther's late writings on the Jews are crucial to this agonizing but necessary task of remembering. The time to begin is August 1536, when Elector John Frederick of Saxony, Luther's magnanimous patron and staunch defender of the Reformation, decreed that the Jews were to be driven out of his electorate.[59] The elector was employing a means that had long been religiously sanctioned in Christendom and was thus no bolt from the blue to the Jews. Homelessness had become their fate in medieval Europe. But there was no getting used to it. Whenever they were expelled, they suffered renewed, severe hardship.

The elector had to be persuaded to rescind his measures or at least to mitigate them and grant Jewish merchants the right to pass through the electorate. The man most suited for the task was Josel von Rosheim, acknowledged far beyond his Alsatian home as the spokesman of the Jews, "governor of all Jewishness in the empire."[60] But who was to procure him access to the court of Electoral Saxony? There seemed to be a man at hand, a certain Martin Luther of Wittenberg, who in 1523, as a friend of the Jews, so it seemed, had bravely exposed himself to his opponents' suspicions. After all, who at that time could stand to hear that as Luther put it, "Jesus Christ was born a Jew" and that these despicable Jews, whom God had disowned, were of the same lineage as Christ; we, who think so highly of ourselves as Christians, are heathens, only "in-laws and aliens"—so far had the reformer dared to go.[61]

Contact with the supposed "friend of the Jews" in Wittenberg was established by Wolfgang Capito, a reformer from Strasbourg. Capito was a well-known Hebraist and, though perhaps no "friend of the Jews" himself, had great respect for Jewish erudition.[62] With Luther's help the elector was to be convinced to change his mind. When Luther refused, it was surely an unpleasant, inexplicable surprise for Josel von Rosheim and probably for Capito as well. Even today this refusal is often judged to be the decisive turning point in Luther's career from friendliness to hostility toward the Jews. Luther himself would have denied any such turning point, for he emphasized that he was and had always been of the opinion that the Jews should be treated in a "friendly way"—so as not to put any obstacles in the way to their conversion by God. He adhered firmly to this view to the end, though the "friendliness" turned into harsh "mercy," which was for him the only alternative to expulsion, the last means of keeping the Jews from being driven out.

Josel von Rosheim had mistakenly hoped he would receive help from Wittenberg and thus be able to pursue a policy protective of the Jews, but protecting the Jews was not part of Luther's task. He urged the temporal authorities to take steps to "rehabilitate" the Jews since the authorities were responsible for the welfare of the state and therefore for deciding on improvement and protection or expulsion. For the temporal authorities the relevant legal norm was one that, long before Luther, Swabian scholar Johannes Reuchlin had formulated in defense of Jewish wisdom. As the Jews' knowledge was to be employed in the service of Christians, he demanded that the Jews be protected as "guest citizens"—as long as they bowed to the laws of the land. But if they brought harm to the common weal and would not allow themselves to be improved, they were to be driven out.[63]

For Luther the Jews were doing anything but improving.

What was worse, encouraged by their misreading of his own words, they had become more daring, defaming and cursing Jesus of Nazareth and regarding Christians as their "worst enemies," so much so that "if you could, you would [now] rob [all Christians] of what they are and what they have." However, the decision not to speak for the Jews in Saxony hinged on the analysis that they were appealing to religious tolerance while irreligiously rejecting their own God . . . the Father of Jesus Christ. Nothing would prevent the misery of exile unless "you accept your cousin and Lord, the beloved crucified Jesus, along with us heathens." That Luther spoke of the Jews as "cousins of Jesus" was not intended to convey unconditional acceptance to "opponents" of Christ: "Would you kindly accept my advice, . . . Because for the sake of the crucified Jew, whom no one shall take from me, I would gladly do my best for all you Jews, unless you should use my favor for your stubbornness. This is what you should know."[64]

Three days before his death Luther added an "Admonition against the Jews" to his last sermon, held in Eisleben on February 15, 1546. It clearly illustrates the change Luther had undergone in old age. There had been no transformation of friendship into enmity; only the measures proposed for an effective policy of improvement and conversion had changed: The Jews are our public enemies; they do not cease to defame Christ our Lord, to call the Virgin Mary a whore and Christ a bastard, "and if they could kill us all, they would gladly do so. And they often do."[65] Nonetheless, "we want to practice Christian love toward them and pray that they convert."[66]

In his letter to Josel von Rosheim Luther had still taken the opportunity to address the Jews directly, exhorting them to convert. But now he spoke to the Christian temporal authorities: the Last Judgment is fast approaching, so woe to those temporal rulers who have neglected their duty to protect Christendom! Now is the time for defense against the storm troopers of the Antichrist, whether they descend upon Christendom from the outside in the form of the Turks, subvert the preaching of the Gospel and order in the empire from inside the Church like the pope and clerics beholden to him, or, like the Jews, undermine the public welfare from the inside. Luther had discovered this concatenation of Jews, pope, and Turks as the unholy coalition of the enemies of God long before he began leveling his massive assaults on the Jews. Now that the terrors of the Last Days had been unleashed, the Church and temporal authorities were forced into their own defensive battle, one without the promise of victory but with the prospects of survival. Christian rulers, you should "not participate in the sins of others, you must pray humbly to God that he should be merciful to you and allow your rule to survive."[67]

The measures had changed from "friendliness" to "harsh mercy"; what had not changed was Luther's view of the Jews. It was as it had been since a young professor of the Psalms had discovered the Jews to be obdurate foes of God. They had to convert, there was no way around it. They had to become once again what they had once been: true children of Abraham, the true sons of Israel! But for the Jews as Jews there was no hope. They had to turn away from their devilish, Christ-defaming schools and synagogues, "but where they do not, we should not tolerate or suffer them among us."[68]

This was not an appeal to the mob to rise up in a surge of riotous patriotism and attack the Jews in cruel revenge, for Luther had unequivocally prefaced his reeducation program with the statement: "We must not avenge ourselves."[69] His demands were directed at the temporal rulers, the princes and nobility.[70] They had, for the sake of money, tolerated accursed usury and thus watched the common man being robbed of all he had by the Jews; now they were to abandon their policies toward these enemies of God and Christ. The subject of exploitation was not new; it can be traced back to pre-Reformation social reform pamphlets. "Out with the Jews" was a common rallying cry in the streets and from the pulpits. Luther, on the other hand, did not advocate expulsion; he sought to preserve "tolerance," tolerance only, of course, for the purpose of conversion. That is the attitude that stayed with him to the end of his life. But the approach of the Last Days fixed temporal limits to the period in which tolerance could be exercised.

The authorities are warned not to become accessories to "the sins of others"; this undoubtedly referred to violations of the civic law alleged against the Jews. Not only were the Jews accused of blasphemy and denounced as usurers, they were also charged with infamous crimes constituting a public danger, with desecration of the Host and the Body of Christ and the ritual murder of children. Masses of them were condemned to the stake.[71] The theme of "Jewish crimes" was already popular in the late Middle Ages and was invoked again later, in 1541, by Johannes Eck.[72] In his most scathing tract against the Jews, *Of the Jews and Their Lies* (1543), Luther did not attempt to diminish this fear of the criminal offenses of the Jews. But the vehemence of the diatribe arises not from the warning against possible crimes of individuals but from his unrelenting attitude toward collective Judaism, which endangered Christians not only by deeds but also by words. That is why Luther advised the authorities to burn synagogues as schools of lies, to confiscate rabbinical books or—if no other means worked—to expel those Jews who would not be converted.[73] Because Jewish "blasphemy" was beginning to have effects, measures to protect Christianity had become necessary.

BUT THE "sins of others" had a further dimension, surely the central one to Luther, namely the rejection of Christ. By no means unique to the Jews, it was attributed above all to the pope and his curia: "But now I am not astonished at the Turks' or the Jews' blindness, obduracy, wickedness. For I must see the same in the holiest fathers of the Church, pope, cardinals, bishops. O thou terrible wrath and incomprehensible judgment of God's high majesty."[74] Luther had long known of this intimate connection without calling for expulsion. But with the approach of the Antichrist, the only way out was a final separation—not only from the Jews, however! As Luther neared the end of his days on earth, the issue was not a Turkish crusade, or hatred of Rome or the Jews, it was upholding the Gospel against all enemies in the confusion of the Last Days.

The terrible tragedy of the relationship between Jews and Christians in world history can be studied in concentrated form in the history of this one man. As a Reformer he was "a product of the Jews," more precisely of his reflections on Israel as the people of God and repudiator of Christ. He saw in the Jews' resistance to the Reformation, to the rediscovered Gospel, an obstinately persistent estrangement from God[75] and thus a newly formed alliance of all the forces inimical to God.[76] In his tract *Of the Jews and Their Lies,* and summarized again in his final *Admonition* (part of an untitled sermon given in Wittenberg, 1546), the concept of a tolerance that leaves room for conversion is certainly retained. But his imminent expectation of the Last Judgment lets him interpret and evaluate the "signs of the times" so as to keep this tolerance within very narrow bounds, as it is the very last chance to avert expulsion. Luther's Reformation unquestionably did nothing to improve the political and social lot of the Jews.

Though his attitude toward the Jews remained medieval, even in the last phase of his life he never took over that medieval hatred for the Jews as "murderers of Christ" which subjected them "in a Christian spirit" to the rage of the mob. His views led beyond the Middle Ages in two ways. For one thing, the reception of his impulses in his own circle must be noted. We should not identify the Reformation movement with Luther to such an extent as to neglect the nuances of various views among a series of Luther's distinguished students. Justus Jonas, his close collaborator and the translator of his Jewish tracts, and the Nuremberg reformer Andreas Osiander did not implicate the Jews in the final struggle with the Antichrist and his armies. In their Evangelical faith they hoped for a common, liberated future for Jews and Christians in the Last Days. Secondly, the later Reformation hymns of a Paul Gerhard (†1676) or a Jakob Revius (†1658) were not the first to instill the idea that "It is not the Jews, Lord Jesus, who crucified You."[77] The Wittenberg Hymnal of 1544 already contained a verse which, though not expressly attributed to Luther, was so similar to what he wrote and preached over the years that it must be regarded as written by Luther's hand.[78]

> Our great sin and sore misdeed
> Jesus, the true Son of God, to the Cross has nailed.
> Thus you poor Judas, as well as all the Jews
> we may not upbraid inimically,
> for the guilt is ours.[79]

In the anguish of the Last Days the ever-existing alliance of God's enemies challenged Luther into radical opposition. But precisely this view of history has a converse side, pointing to the future. In the mirror of Jewish history Luther discovered "us wretched Christians,"[80] who are also links in the threatening chain of evil. Through the Jews he found out who we actually are: by nature always heathens and enemies of God, hypocrites like the Jews when, before God, we rely on good pedigree, law, and works.[81] The revelations in the Jewish mirror were incredible: "Jews"—penetrating the Church, to make matters worse, having managed to get it firmly into their clutches. Such sharp criticism of the Church was suited to attacking at the roots the Passion-oriented piety[82] that instilled intense hatred and for centuries made Holy Week in Christian Europe a particular time of terror for the Jews.[83]

But solidarity in sin between "us wretched Christians" and the Jews loses its penitential and reformatory force if "Reformation" is understood as having already led true Christians out of the bondage of ecclesiastical despots, the final Babylonian captivity before the end. Such Protestant triumphalism permits heretics, papists, Jews, and "us wicked Christians" to be looked back upon as past history. Then the "Jewish probe," prophetic gauge in the service of the Reformation struggle for the Church at the beginning of the end, is no longer safe from exploitation as a racist final solution. Through the Jews Martin Luther unmasked the capability of Christians to ally themselves with the primeval enemy of Heaven and earth. Eliminating this shocking view of Christians results in a destructive view of the Jews. Once this fundamental theological structure has collapsed, the anti-Judaism found in Luther— as in the Christian faith as a whole—becomes a pawn of modern anti-Semitism.

CHAPTER XI

The Man and His Deeds

Conflict and Character

When Luther left Worms he was thirty-seven years old and at the height of his powers. But who this man was remained unclear. Unanticipated events had placed him in a political arena where often his voice was heard but his personality became blurred. Moreover, his behavior was molded so decisively by convictions that it is often difficult to differentiate accurately between personal traits and the duties of office. But anyone wishing to encounter Luther the man must risk the attempt. As a monk Luther was trained to read his own soul, and his critical self-analysis is an excellent guide for anyone trying to find access to him. His negative judgments were never exaggerated; the two unfavorable qualities he emphasized in himself were confirmed by his contemporaries: extreme irascibility and verbosity. He found an "official" excuse for his excess verbiage in his Saxon lack of breeding and thick-headedness.

His short temper has been partially excused by the fact that he was continually doing battle and simply "exploded" when the pressure became too great. With that we have indeed touched upon the unpleasant aspects of Luther's personality. The steadfastness and religious conviction that distinguished him in Augsburg and Worms also limited the number of his friends and followers. His personal charisma could be a burden to his surroundings. There is little sense in trying to look for excuses, however suggestive.

The facts speak plainly, but they must be understood historically, in the context of events. The Diet of Worms was an experience that left its mark on Luther; he could not shake it off. He was the only reformer whose freedom of movement was seriously inhibited. The only places he could move about freely were Electoral Saxony, later Hesse—and after Duke George's death, Ducal Saxony. But it was not only Luther the traveler who was restricted. Against his will he had become the symbol of the Reformation. He could not say a word that would not be heard and pondered everywhere. Worms had given a provincial theologian influence in the world. Thus a single sharp remark made in the privacy of his own home was spread far and wide—and often exaggerated.

Waging war on the Devil for the sake of God leaves little room for subtlety. "If God is for us, who can be against us!" (Rom 8.31). The words of St. Paul determined the Reformer's encounters with Erasmus, Carlstadt, and Zwingli. Many of Luther's diatribes resemble public exorcisms and are futile as attempts to persuade persons of different opinions of the rightness of his position. Thus it is probably no coincidence, and only seemingly a consequence of rhetoric, that Luther rarely used the commonly employed scholarly qualification "if I am not mistaken"—*ni fallor*—but made generous use of his favorite expression, "certainly"—*immo.* Luther's certainty left its mark on German academic linguistic usage. Where Anglo-American scholars qualify their statements with an "I am inclined to believe," the Germans say "it is patently obvious." This, too, is part of the Luther heritage—its negative aspect, and a watered-down version at that.

Luther's impatient, caustic treatment of opponents was probably connected with his short temper and volcanic temperament. But the linguistic usage we have observed points beyond the man to the culture-shaping power of the protracted interconfessional conflict. Not only did the professor from Wittenberg set off the conflict, he also experienced its effects from the very start. That makes it difficult to judge his disposition, because it is not easy to be even-tempered if few really will listen to one's arguments. Luther had already been on the defensive since 1518. Silvester Prierias, the Italian curial theologian, and Johannes Eck, the German professor, launched their attacks on him at approximately the same time. Their calculated insults, denunciations, and accusations of heresy were the antithesis of academic restraint. Luther's irony and great dialectic skill succeeded for a surprisingly long time in objectifying a debate whose fires had been stoked in Ingolstadt and Rome. He was extremely eloquent in expressing his concern about the Church, his integrity in questioning tradition, and his personal struggle for clarity.

The Leipzig disputation in the summer of 1519 revealed the enormous pressure Luther was under in the ostensibly equal contest with Eck. Never Eck's match as a debater, Luther was soon maneuvered into the position of the accused. For one-and-a-half days Eck took every opportunity to defame his opponent directly or indirectly, unequivocally or with innocent ambiguity, as a "Hussite" and "Bohemian heretic." Luther's repeated protests went unheeded. On the afternoon of July 5 Luther could no longer contain himself. Violating all the rules of disputation, he interrupted Eck twice. The next morning at seven, he could bear no more of Eck's barbs and spontaneously changed over to the German language to demonstrate to non-theologians that his rights had been infringed.[1] In subsequent years laymen would preside over Reformation disputations from the start: the search for truth was too important to leave to academic theologians.

In his exhortation of 1520 Luther sounded relieved; the burden seemed to have been lifted from his shoulders: "The time for silence is over, the time to speak has come."[2] The Reformer had never maintained silence, but now he abandoned the defensive and launched a counterattack—in a language everyone could understand: German, the national tongue. This was the perfect role for Luther. Only now did his keen, original mind and his fresh, vivid language develop their full scope.

At the Diet of Worms he was prepared to admit that he had occasionally been too hard on his adversaries.[3] If he was thinking of Prierias or Eck, psychohistorians will have to be cautious in drawing conclusions about his character. Even the meekest of his contemporaries would not have reacted differently to their attempts to denounce rather than debate.

But once he had discovered the Gospel and recognized the targets of the Devil's attacks, Luther became less and less capable of distinguishing between adversaries and people who simply did not agree with him, between diabolical temptations and divergent opinions. Certainly he did not seek an open clash with Erasmus and waited almost a year, until late 1525, to counter the humanist's attacks. But in letters to his friends Luther began speaking disparagingly of the "philologist" much earlier: like Moses in ancient times, Erasmus could lead the people of God a certain distance, but ultimately he had to stay behind in the desert because he could not reach theology. Such barbs did not remain secret, nor were they intended to; Luther's assessment had been addressed to a mutual acquaintance. Erasmus was stung: I am Moses? Well, who does Luther think he is, Jesus?[4]

Following generations can only be grateful that Luther entered into a dispute with the humanist because it enabled the cause of Erasmian humanism to be clearly differentiated from that of the Reformation. "The truth," Luther wrote in May 1522, "is mightier than eloquence, the Spirit greater than genius, faith more than education."[5]

How gifted was the man who could express this antithesis in a single sentence! Centuries later, equating humanism with linguistic elegance and education still seems accurate. This letter, too, did not come to Erasmus' attention by coincidence, although Luther emphatically repudiated any idea of a conflict: "I will not challenge Erasmus, even if he provokes me now and then."[6] But a clear provocation of his own followed hard upon his protestation of restraint: Erasmus can "conquer" others with his rhetoric, but if he decides to attack me, "he will see Christ, who fears neither Hell nor the powers of Heaven. . . . I know what this man is like since I am well practiced in discerning devilish thoughts."[7] It was inevitable for Erasmus to feel he was being confronted by an insufferably arrogant contemporary.

In the stormy history of interconfessional conflict, criticism of Luther the man has so often been used as a weapon against the Reformer's convictions that experts in the field of Reformation history have felt compelled to defend the Reformer's character for fairness' sake. Luther's visceral identification with Christ in his dispute with Erasmus shows, however, that where the Reformer suspected the Devil's involvement, he could no longer distinguish between a man and his opinions, or between error and lie. That is probably why he ultimately sought conflict with Erasmus, as his constant gibes prove. Even a last offer of truce, which Luther made Erasmus by letter, was formulated in such a way as to leave the humanist no choice but to begin a public dispute. Luther sensed the Devil in Erasmus and wanted him to come out and reveal himself.

Luther's conflict with his older colleague Andreas Bodenstein von Carlstadt was a similar case. As representatives of Wittenberg reform theology, both of them came out against scholasticism in 1517. In 1519 they debated with Eck in Leipzig, Carlstadt always preceding his younger colleague (he had already been an established professor when Luther received his doctoral degree). In less turbulent times Carlstadt would have gone down in the annals of history as an important scholar. He did not cling fearfully to school traditions and found his way from scholarstic scholarship to patristic writings. From Thomas Aquinas and Duns Scotus he turned—at Luther's instigation—to Augustine. Ten years earlier, when Luther was not yet in Wittenberg, he had been the first university professor to learn Hebrew and, using Reuchlin's grammar, study the Old Testament.

Carlstadt was a man engaged in a continual search. A negative evaluation would have it that he was fickle, a positive one that he was always open to new impulses. All his life the obedience that issues from faith and the implementation of divine justice were more important to him than Christian freedom and justification by faith before God. His ideal of establishing a truly Christian community, the "Christian city of Wittenberg," through ecclesiastical and social reforms met with particular enthusiasm in reformed Switzerland. And it was there that he was to end his days, as a professor at the University of Basel.[8]

As in the case of Erasmus, Luther's conflict with Carlstadt was precipitated by the basic differences between them, which do not vanish even if we can demonstrate how badly Luther behaved toward him. Either the Reformation establishes God's kingdom on earth or it leads to a relative "improvement," helping Christians to unite and gather strength. In the first case the Old and New Testaments are God's blueprints; from them we can glean the instructions we need to construct a true community in and for God, however symbolic or geographically limited it may be. Then the city becomes a monastery under the abbot Jesus Christ, and the vows that responsible Christians take at baptism demand obedience to the rule of life which God has provided in the Scriptures.

But if reformation is the preaching of the cross of Christ for the purpose of gathering the faithful, then it does not effect "progress." It offers defiance to the Devil in the turbulence of the Last Days through preaching and sacrament. "Improvement of the world" through political and social reforms is both necessary and possible. But it is carried out under the terms of Christian freedom, not according to the "prescriptions" of biblical law. Then moral preconceptions must be reviewed and those who are weak, hesitant, or think differently must be treated charitably; then it is time to take reasonable, if basically limited, survival measures. The steadfast believers will assemble and stand firm in their faith and trust in the coming of God's reformation. This reformation does not reconstruct the monastery walls; it protects and effects practical reason in the world against old and new legalism. Thus there are worlds between the two colleagues from Wittenberg; their conflict is suprapersonal and cannot be reduced to differences in character.

Certainly these differences indeed existed. Carlstadt was probably embarrassed to find Johannes Eck so obviously much more interested in triumphing over Luther, although he himself had been the first to challenge the professor from Ingolstadt. But Luther, too, was always touchy when he was not regarded as having been the first "to start the matter." Still, rifts in the Wittenberg leadership only became visible when decisions about practical reform measures had to be made after the Edict of Worms (May 26, 1521). The conflict was sparked off by the question of how the reform of religious life and society was to look in detail once canon law had lost its relevance. Had it been up to Carlstadt, the divine law of the Scriptures would have determined the lives of secular community and church congregation.[9]

Luther was suspicious of a new rule of law guiding religious worship and public life. At first he shrank from a break-up of the Wittenberg coalition. But once Carlstadt had given up his professorship and moved to Orlamünde, the hostility came to the surface. When Carlstadt removed the images from churches there and refused to baptize children, Luther smelled danger. He sensed that the new pastor in Orlamünde was an instrument of the Devil, desirous of burdening and confusing the consciences of the faithful. In the future Luther would condemn anything resembling Carlstadt's ideals as fanaticism or diabolical strategy.

It is, in fact, true that neither Erasmus nor Carlstadt would have enabled all Christians to achieve freedom. The "enlightened" reforms of the one would have remained a privilege of the educated elite, and the reformation of the other would have been forced on all. If both of them had been successful in shunting Luther aside, Christendom would soon have been confronted with the alternative of "education or Bible." Luther's realization of these consequences could only reinforce his inclination to identify Christ so closely with his own interpretation of the Gospel that contradictions could hardly help being associated with untruth, denial, or the machinations of the Devil.

Historians will admit that only an "Evangelist" who firmly knew himself to be on Christ's side could have given the Reformation its thrust. But where resistance to the Papal State, fanaticism, and Judaism turns into the collective vilification of papists, Anabaptists, and Jews, the fatal point has been reached where the discovery of the Devil's power becomes a liability and a danger.

Luther saw himself as called to proclaim the Gospel, pushed and driven by God, against his skill and will. This concept of his "office" permits of no easy conclusions about his character. He performed his "duties" with a confidence of judgment and action that seemed to overcome all questioning, searching, hesitation, and doubt. If we judge Luther only by his "official" face, we shall never get to know the sensitive, sorely tried, frightened Luther, or the acrimonious one.

IT WAS not only Luther's opponents who found him obstinate and difficult. He was often a burden to one of the most gifted of his contemporaries, his fellow-professor and Greek teacher Philipp Melanchthon. Several times the younger man wanted to leave Wittenberg. Because of his respect for Luther's personality and judgment, he feared Luther's ire and suffered under his occasional withdrawal of affection. Melanchthon was living proof of the charismatic aura Luther must have radiated. He never doubted that it was Luther's vocation to be "the charioteer of Israel," and thus a common basis always remained on which they could agree despite their differences.

How dependent the "Erasmus of Wittenberg" was on Luther's theological judgments could be seen whenever Melanchthon had to make decisions on his own. Whether Luther was in exile at Wartburg Castle (1521–22) or nine years later, when he was keeping the sparrows and ravens company at Coburg Castle, far from the events of the Diet of Augsburg (1530), and finally after Luther's death, Melanchthon sorely missed the older man's reassuring presence. Luther's total awareness of the threatening power of the Devil always remained totally alien to Melanchton, however. The Devil was for him one among many dangerous forces and could be beaten, providing that sufficiently judicious measures were taken.

Melanchthon's ability to systematize was far superior to the impulsive Luther's; and Luther openly admitted that without Melanchthon's methodological talents, his own work would have choked on its verbosity and been lost. Melanchthon did more than simply represent the cause of the Reformation; he gave it a viable form and a lasting structure. That is why he has come down to us as "Praeceptor Germaniae," teacher of Germany. The contentious Reformer could bow in respect before Melanchthon's scholarly power; that is the difference between Luther and later admirers of Luther.

Luther and the Art of Language

Luther and his friends could often be found at the table in Luther's home, the former Augustinian monastery, discussing the events of the day and exchanging reminiscences. Many of these conversations "at table" were recorded and later published. The Luther of these conversations likes to speak as an experienced elder statesman in the service of God, but always in such a way as to disclose his weaknesses and errors of judgment as well. His table talk is living proof that it was never his intention to make his public persona as an Evangelist into a monument for posterity.

On the contrary, the Evangelist was sure of himself when it came to the Word of God, but Professor Luther knew his limits—and thus his strengths as well, as we see from his ridicule of certain colleagues' clumsy attempts at biblical exegesis. During his sojourn at Wartburg Castle he devoted himself to a task that began by demonstrating his shortcomings to him but that was to guarantee his fame in centuries to come: the translation of the New Testament into German. When Luther returned to Wittenberg in March 1522, after almost ten months of solitude at Wartburg, he brought with him a draft of the translation.[10] Before it was printed he went through the manuscript with Melanchthon, who was a fine scholar of Greek, and they consulted specialists to clarify problematic points. The New Testament appeared in German in September 1522—hence the common designation "September Testament." Though the translation was Luther's, he realized it could not have been completed without his colleagues' help. In January he had written to Wittenberg from Wartburg Castle: "In the meantime I have begun the Bible translation although the task by far exceeds my powers. Only now am I discovering what translating really means and why no one has thus far dared to associate his name with an undertaking of this kind. I would not be able to cope with the Old Testament at all without your proximity and help. . . . The task is so large and important that we should all work on it, as it is a public work and serves the common good."[11]

It took another twelve years for this goal to be reached and the last book of the Old Testament to be translated. In September 1534 the first complete Wittenberg Bible appeared. The translation played a major role in shaping the modern German language, yet it became a genuine folk Bible, carrying the cause of the Reformation into every house, because Luther made use of living, colloquial German in his translation. He had truly listened to the common people—the language of the common man was not too lowly to be the language of God.

Luther's language in the mirror of tradition, Psalm 51.3,6–8:

O Got erbarm dich mein: nach deiner micheln erbermbd . . .
Dir allein hab ich gesündet und tet das ubel vor dir:
das du werdest gerechthaftigt in deinen worten
und uberwindest so du urteylst.
Wann sich ich bin entphangen in den ungangkeyten:
und in den sünden entphieng mich mein mutter.
Wann sich du hast liebgehabt die wahrheit:
du hast mir eroffent die ungewissen
und die verborgen ding deiner weisheit.
(*Mentelin-Bibel,* 1466; after the Vulgate)

Erbarm dich iber mich, o got, nach deiner grossen
barmhertzikayt . . .
Dir hab ich allein gesündet / und vor deinem angesicht
übel gethon /
das du gerecht seyest in deinen worten /
und überwindest, so man dich urtaylet.
Dann ich bin wie du sichst in sünde empfangen worden /
und meyn mutter ward meyn in übelthaten schwanger.
Jedoch hast du die warhayt liebgehebt / und ungewisse
verborgne

ding deiner weyßhayt mir geoffenbaret.
(*Ottmar Nachtgal* [Luscinius], 1524; after the Vulgate)

Erbarm dich mein, o got, nach deiner barmhertzigkait . . .
Dir / allein dir hab ich gesündet / und das böß in deinen augen hab ich gethan /
darumb wirst du gerecht sein so du röden wirst /
und wirst rain scheinen so du richtten wirst.
Nym war in der sünd bin ich zu der geburt berait /
und in der sünd hat mich empfangen mein muter.
Nym war die warhait hast du begert in der mauren /
und in verborgenhait hast du mir zuwissen thon die weißhait.
(Caspar Amman, 1523; after the Hebrew original)

Gott sey myr gnedig nach deyner guete / . . .
An dyr alleyne hab ich gesundigt / und ubel fur dyr gethan.
Darumb wirstu recht bleyben ynn deynen worten /
und reyn erfunden wenn du gerichtet wirst.
Sihe ich byn ynn untugent gemacht /
und meyne mutter hat mich ynn sunden empfangen.
Sihe du hast lust zur warheyt /
Du lessest mich wissen die weysheyt heymlich verborgen.
(Martin Luther, 1524; after the Hebrew original)

The King James version of the same passage reads:

Have mercy upon me, O God, according to thy loving kindness . . .
Against thee, thee only, have I sinned, and done this evil in thy sight: that thou mightest be justified when thou speakest, and be clear when thou judgest.
Behold, I was shapen in iniquity; and in sin did my mother conceive me.
Behold, thou desirest truth in the inward parts: and in the hidden part thou shalt make me to know wisdom.

Luther's translation of the Bible is justly celebrated as a major achievement. Its acclaim is merited because the German Bible did not remain a linguistic work of art; it became a book of the people.[12]

His work on the Bible translation makes plain that Luther was more than an unshakably certain Reformer. His claim to being the first called to the

Title page of the Complete Bible, *from the Wittenberg 1541 edition*

office of preacher of the Gospel was something he never allowed to be challenged; he saw his experience as *the* Christian experience, and his long search led him to a truth that inspired his contemporaries with new goals. Luther lived at a time when truth was still indivisible, and the "Evangelist" was firmly convinced that he alone represented that truth. The claim brought him the reputation of being a loner. He had championed the cause of the weak and the laymen, but among theologians he tolerated only listeners and disciples.

The history of the Luther Bible shows us a completely different Luther, one who knew his limits and was well aware that the translation could only be accomplished cooperatively. He never considered the task to have been mastered. Before dinner every Wednesday and Thursday from the summer of 1539 to the beginning of 1541, he assembled his council of experts, his "Sanhedrin" as he called them, at his home so that a further, thorough revision of the translation could be made among competent colleagues. "We are beggars." The sentence Luther wrote on a scrap of paper shortly before his death mirrors worldly wisdom, not dying resignation, and stems from experience with his work on the Bible, its translation into common speech. His earliest biographer allows us a glimpse into the laboratory:

> When the whole German Bible had gone out for the first time and one day of tribulation taught the next, the Doctor began work on the Bible from the beginning again with great seriousness, industry, and prayer; and because the Son of God himself had promised He would be present where people gathered in His name and prayed for His spirit, Doctor Luther immediately organized a Sanhedrin of his own, made up of the best people available at the time. Each week they came to the Doctor's monastery for several hours before dinner. . . . After the Doctor had first looked through the earlier published Bibles and in addition consulted Jews and experts in foreign languages and asked old Germans for proper terms (once he had several sheep cut up so a German butcher could tell him what every [organ] of the sheep was called). He used to come to the consistory with his old Latin and new German Bible, always bringing the Hebrew text as well. Master Philippus [Melanchthon] always brought the Greek text along. . . . Everyone had already prepared himself for the text that was to be discussed and had looked through Greek and Latin, as well as Jewish exegetes. Then, as president, he proposed a version and let everyone speak and listened to what everyone had to say with reference to the quality of the language or the exegesis of the old doctors.[13]

The open-ended and thus necessarily common search for the right translation does not preclude certainty of faith, nor does trust in the Word of God make critical study of the text superfluous. The Scriptures do not reveal themselves to everyone in the same way, and many a man gets lost in them, as Luther explains in the vivid words of Pope Gregory: "An elephant drowns in this sea [of Scripture]; a lamb that is looking for Christ and perseveres, stands on firm ground and reaches the other side."[14] It is not he who knows everything but he who allows himself to be guided that finds solid footing in the Bible.

St. Augustine's distinction between knowledge and wisdom, cognition and faith, is central here. The fact that apart from schooling his intellect, man needs training as a human being between God and the world has been repressed again and again in Western tradition. The magic word *scholarship* has led to a reverent acceptance of scholarly systems or marginalized "great masters" from the Middle Ages to our day, in an often curious oscillation between over-confidence and tired skepticism.

The "elephant" Luther sees "drowning" in the Scriptures finds credulous successors until, swept away by the spirit of the age, it must yield to a new giant, which unmasks its predecessor as unsuited for swimming and exposes it to ridicule. The ever-new "masters" of philosophical innovation ride high for a time with their Plato or Aristotle, Hegel or Heidegger, each one promising to be a reliable guide to the safe shore. Luther does not deny the importance of his philosophical training. But, in contrast to scholastic tradition, he does not construct a scholarly system. Nor does he offer "dogmatics" that purport to provide security but for their credibility actually depend on the reliability of the philosophical underpinnings.

The confession "We are beggars" does not merely define a position before God, it is an admission of Luther's fallibility before his fellow man. Luther's earliest biographer concludes the history of the Reformer's life with the statement: "God guard all theologians to keep them from becoming masters in or over Scripture."[15]

Wine, Women, and Song

Luther was neither a self-contained loner nor a self-sufficient individualist. At Wartburg Castle he experienced how detrimental isolation was to scholarship and how fatal the effect of sustained solitude was to one's spiritual life. The Devil likes to have the Christian alone, for then he can heap him with worries and depression; I know Satan well, "know the tricks he likes to play on me; he is a sad, sour spirit, who does not like the heart to be glad."[16]

But God is the God of joy. Dark thoughts cannot be avoided, yet Luther comforts a depressed friend; it is the same as in nature: you cannot stop birds from flying over your head, but you can stop them from nesting in your hair. So seek company, play cards, or do something else you enjoy—and do it with a good conscience, for depressions come not from God but the Devil. Luther is speaking from experience.[17]

Apart from theology, music is God's greatest gift. It has much in common with theology because it heals the soul and raises the spirits. Luther had already enjoyed singing and making music as a youth. Without music man is a stone, but with music he can drive away the Devil: "It has often revived me and relieved me from heavy burdens."[18] Cards, music, and company—they are divine gifts.

We cannot find the apt saying "Who loves not women, wine, and song will stay a fool his whole life long"[19] in Luther's writings. The Reformer's admirers protested indignantly against such nonsense being imputed to their hero. And they were right! Luther would have been much more offensive by insisting with St. Paul that believers are fools for Christ: Who loves not women, wine, and song, will never be a "fool" his whole life long.[20]

The discovery of the world and earthly joys against the background of the adversary's threat to morality separates Luther from both monastic and puritan morality. German Lutheranism, with its cultural ideal of making music at home, has preserved a precious part of the Luther heritage. But when a cheerful round of cards is disdained as unrespectable or even disreputable, Luther has lost the game.

PEOPLE IN the world need company, believers need their congregation. Even where the individual stands before God in his unmistakable individuality, he needs intercession, the communal presence of others. Church communion means "that no believer ever lives alone or dies alone, but is protected and borne by the communion of saints."[21]

Because of his genuine piety, Luther increasingly gains general recognition beyond confessional boundaries today. But it is recognition coupled with the suspicion that the Reformer indulged in misdirected individualism and thus had no sense of communion within the Church. It is true that prayer involves a highly personal, individual approach to God; the knowledge that Christ died and was raised from the dead "for me," not for institutions, nations, or denominations is one of the non-negotiable features of Reformation theology.

Luther was at Coburg Castle on May 29, 1530, when he learned of his father's death. This was clearly the time for solitary prayer, as Veit Dietrich, who was with him, reported to Catherine Luther in Wittenberg: after reading the news of his father's death, "he immediately takes his Psalter, goes into the chamber and cries so much that he could not think clearly the next day."[22] Luther wrote to Melanchthon: "My dear Philipp, I have just [on this Pentecost] heard that my father has died." The son's bereavement for his father was right and proper—"through him God gave me life, through his sweat he fed and raised me—I am too beaten to write any more."[23] He was so close to his father that two nights earlier he had dreamt that he had lost a large tooth, so large that his amazement would not cease. On the Sunday after that his father was dead.[24] At the time a dream of this kind was popularly believed to be an omen of the imminent death of a relative.[25]

The grieving Luther retired with his Psalter, a book that reflects the entire range of human feelings, from exultant joy to the deepest sorrow. Since his monastic years the Psalms had been his prayerbook for all situations. At the monastery he had learned to identify with the psalmist of times past, to let the words become his own and thus to fit himself into the totality of Christian experience. Here, in the solitary chamber, stood a mourning son; though alone before God, he was not a lonely individualist far-removed from the communal experience of the Church. The Psalter, brimming with life and Luther's daily companion, preserved him from becoming dejected.

Praying to God and trusting that his prayers of intercession for the Church in its battle against the Devil would be heard and answered were sources of strength in Luther's life. Many a letter of his ends with the words: "Remember to pray for me." This might at first be regarded as a pious convention, as if Luther were keeping up old monastic habits, which he actually did. He could write: "Vale, ora pro me"—farewell and pray for me.[26] But as a rule his appeal for intercession sounded more urgent. He fell ill and knew exactly: you there in Nuremberg or Naumberg or wherever, you did not think earnestly of me, you were slack in your intercession. Since the Reformation was not the work of man but the task of God, the only thing left to the Evangelical movement was intercession, imploring help and inciting God on to intervention.

TALKING ABOUT Luther the son brings us to the question of Luther the father. As a parent he could display childlike imagination; for example, he penned a precious tale in Coburg and sent it to his eldest son, Hans, for his fourth birthday:

> I know a beautiful lovely garden. There are many children in it with golden garments, picking up beautiful apples under the trees, and pears,

cherries, prunes, and plums; they sing, hop about, and are happy; they also have pretty little horses with golden bridles and silver saddles. I asked a man whose garden it was whose children they were. He answered: they are the children that like to pray and learn and are pious. Then I spoke: Dear man, I, too, have a son. His name is Hansichen Luther. Wouldn't he like to come into the garden, too, so he can eat such lovely apples and pears, and ride such lovely little horses and play with these children? Then the man replied: "If he, too, likes to pray and learn and is pious, he should come into the garden too.[27]

When his daughter Magdalena died on September 20, 1542, at the age of thirteen, the grieving father composed the epitaph for his beloved child, to console his wife:

Ich, Lena, Luthers liebes kindt,
Schlaff hie mit allen heiligen glindt
Und lieg in meiner rueh und rast.
Nu bin ich unsers Gottes gast.
Ein kindt des todts war ich zwar,
Aus sterblichem samen mich mein mutter gebar,
Itz leb ich und bin reich in Gott.
Des danck ich Christi blutt und todt.[28]

[I, Lena, Luther's beloved child / Sleep gently here with all the saints / And lie at peace and rest / Now I am our God's own guest. / I was a child of death, it is true, / My mother bore me out of mortal seed, / Now I live and am rich in God. / For this I thank Christ's death and blood.]

All in all, Luther the family man is not much different from Luther the public persona. Be it at home or on the pulpit, at the lectern or the desk, as an authority on politics or a pamphleteer, his personal experience is always present.

But that makes it difficult to judge him fairly. The personality of an Erasmus or a John Calvin retreats into the background even in personal correspondence. The humanist writes as if afraid disclosures about himself might get into the wrong hands, or as if, in the back of his mind he were already thinking about the future publication of his correspondence and adapting the contents to prospective readers. The Geneva Reformer Calvin is not worried about the future. He makes a more stoic impression, distinguishing clearly between himself and his office, rarely yielding to deep emotions. With Luther feelings force their way everywhere. He does not merely teach a theology that encompasses the whole human being, spirit and soul, body and emotions; he himself is passionately present, not only teaching life by faith but living faith himself.

Luther Today: A Test

Where would a man like Martin Luther fit in today? What kind of job would he be suited for?

Were there still a university in Wittenberg (it was merged with the University of Halle in 1815), he would not likely be offered a professorship there; nor would it be any different in Heidelberg or Marburg. It is the Erasmian type of ivory-tower academic that has gained international acceptance. If there were a chair somewhere, whether in Harvard or Holten, it would be futile to look for his name on the list of applicants—one must follow a call, be driven against one's will.[29] Should he nonetheless be shortlisted by a department of religion, the problem would arise of what subject Luther should teach today. The professor of biblical theology would probably be best suited for the present-day field of practical theology.

But for that he would be too conservative and far too pious, as well as being too Catholic in approach and too strongly committed to the Middle Ages—in short, he would not be up-to-date. He would be an indisputably successful teacher, but as a colleague he would be irksome and unwilling to bow to majorities. The modern trend toward ecumenism would cause him particular problems because he would not be prepared to suppress those questions that divide Christians. He was driven by singular notions about the Devil and the Last Judgment. With respect to the Devil he had not yet experienced the Enlightenment and would seriously have to let himself be asked this question: "What would he have done without the Devil, without the possibility of attributing the grotesque and embarrassing contradictions in his personal history to Evil personified?"[30] How strange his answer would sound, that he would be even worse off without the Devil, for God, too, would then have become remote! Whether the discoveries of modern psychology would have changed his mind cannot be determined; he distrusted solutions that were "self-evident" and learned to see contradictions as proof of the proximity of truth.

He would certainly be an unpredictable ally in faculty politics. He might take an interest in curricular reforms, as he had in the autumn of 1517, and even present comprehensive plans that would be popular among the students who filled his lecture halls to the point of overflowing. But if, as in the summer of 1520, a great many of these students started fighting, as they had with journeymen painters, and caused a riot, he would preach publicly against them and even leave the meeting angrily when the rector and senate of the university tried to defend the students.[31]

He would be biting and sometimes overly rough toward colleagues with whom he disagreed. Where generalized judgments were concerned, he would outdo anyone, working himself up to furious tirades. He would rant against papists, Jews, lawyers, and high officials because he felt all of them strangled human life with suffocating laws that undermine the common good. He would hardly have bowed to anything like a minister of education—he was not "politically reliable."

A psychiatric analysis would rob Luther of whatever chances he had left of teaching at a present-day university. The diagnosis would be persuasive—*Paranoia reformatorica*—but the grounds for it must remain irritatingly uncertain, ranging from neurosis to psychosis, from Oedipus complex to mother fixation. Fear of the Lord and abhorrence of the Devil are indicators of disturbed childhood development. And disturbing is what they really are.

Of course there is an objection to this conceptual experiment of attempting to hire the sixteenth-century Luther at a modern university: a "child of his time" cannot simply be transplanted to an era centuries later. The distance between the dawn of the modern age and the twentieth century is vast. Historically we are separated by the Enlightenment, politically by the American (1776), French (1789), and Russian (1918) revolutions, and sociopolitically by the Industrial Revolution. Nevertheless, there is something to be learned from trying to imagine Luther as our contemporary because it is his personality and character that are at issue. Our anachronistic test is so illuminating because questions regarding his commitment cannot simply be shunted aside in an analysis of his person. The man and his cause are so intimately linked that any separation of the two will be at the expense of both. Even this speaks against offering Luther a professorship in our time, which prefers objective scholarship to a personal commitment and vision.

Sickness unto Death

The Reformation movement cannot be separated from Luther the man, but it would also be incorrect to see it as the consequence of his exposure to psychic pressures: Luther might be able to accept a diagnosis of *Paranoia reformatorica,* since "Reformation madness" includes the foolishness that is an intrinsic part of faith. And it can scarcely have been anything but this foolishness that enabled him to bear the burdens and pressures attendant on his role as a reformer—a role he did not want to play but which friend and foe alike forced upon the "Evangelist." One aspect of these burdens is particularly noteworthy. Luther's fear of God proved an overwhelming force before which human fears receded and lost their thrust. We can outline the range of this fear of God in five points:

Fear of the Lord is awe of the majesty of the Lord and fear of God's holy wrath: "If I could believe that God was not angry at me, I would stand on my head for joy."[32]

Faith and fear of the Lord are not mutually exclusive, but faith lives on trust in God's mercy and not the knowledge of His majesty. The faithful creep under the cross of Christ like chicks under the wings of the mother hen.

God's wrath is not directed against man but against his lack of faith: faith is the obedience demanded by God.

The Reformation discovery did not leave the "wrath of God" and the "fear of God" behind as outdated medieval concepts.

Faith is not individual self-protection. The Evangelical movement should build a wall of faith to protect the people.[33]

Despite the imperial ban and against the clear instructions of his prince, Luther left his exile at Wartburg Castle and returned to Wittenberg on March 1, 1522. Informing the elector of the grounds for his action, he cited this wall of faith providing protection from a wrathful God: "God has demanded that one should set oneself against Him as a wall before the people"—to change or stay His judgment. Luther cited the prophet Ezekiel: "And I sought for a man among them, who would build up the wall and stand in the breach before me for the land, that I should not destroy it" (Ezekiel 22.30).[34]

Luther returned to Wittenberg to erect the wall of faith that would protect the land from God's wrath over the oppression perpetrated by the mob and the papists. That is why he neither feared the emperor's ban nor needed the elector's protection: "I am coming to Wittenberg under far higher protection than that of the Elector. . . . Yes, I believe that I can protect Your Electoral Grace better than You me. . . . In this matter the sword should not and cannot counsel or help—God must work alone here, without any human care and aid. Thus he who has the greatest faith will furnish the best protection."[35]

This trust is the other side of the "phobia"; courage and contempt for the Devil issue from faith. When the plague was ravaging the city—above all between 1527 and 1529 and then again in the summer of 1542—Luther refused to leave Wittenberg with his colleagues. Some may flee the plague and find a healthier place to stay, but "public servants," preachers, mayors, judges, doctors, policemen, and neighbors of the sick who have no one to take care of them are "on duty" and must remain.[36] The letters from his last official trip are particularly impressive documents of his belief in public duty. With seeming heartlessness, he wrote to his wife: "Spare me your worrying, there is someone better to worry about me than you and all the angels; he lies in the manger and hangs from the Virgin's teats."[37] Zest for life is healthy and God-given, but worrying stems from the Devil and is a sign of weakness of faith and thus of disobedience. The others may leave—"for to flee dying and death and to save one's life is a natural instinct implanted by God and is not forbidden"[38]—but Luther cannot.

The knowledge that God's care sustains him in "office" is probably one of the roots of Luther's discovery of vocation. The farmer plowing his field, the craftsman producing his goods, and the sovereign capably judging and governing are as much doing God's work as the clergyman on the pulpit or in the confessional. They have all had a divine call to render service to the world, and thus they will also be judged by God.[39]

There is a clear professional hierarchy, with ruling princes at the very top. As Luther's concept of society leaves little room for control "from below," this phenomenon of obedience to authority is striking and offends modern democratic sensibilities. It is then easy to forget that the clouds of God's wrath and justice hang low: control "from below" is exercised "from above," by God Himself, with lightning speed and, where necessary, in a terrible way.

It is more than conceivable that Luther's intense, ever-present fear of the Lord was aroused at home, drummed into him at school, experienced during divine worship, and provided with a rational basis in the academic lecture hall. Whether it is an individual or a collective-social "phobia," Luther repressed nothing in this regard; he brought it to the surface and called it by its name.

Luther's age saw its own cause at stake in the battle against the false and for the true fear of God. By preaching, Luther had succeeded in convincing others that when one takes up the cross of Christ, which is God's ultimate Word, fear loses its destructive force. The underlying cause of the spiritual strain under which Luther had to live was the constant, radical questioning to which he subjected himself: are you alone wise, as opposed to so many throughout the centuries?—Look at what you have unleashed!

Since the summer of 1521 the number of problems arising from the break with an awesome tradition had been growing. Ideals that had been held sacred for centuries and to which Luther had been committed with every fiber of his being lost their strength of conviction and their validity. Priests were renouncing celibacy and openly getting married; their right to do so needed biblical substantiation and guarantees. Monks and nuns were running away from their monasteries and convents, eager to live a life pleasing to God in the world. How was this unprecedented breach of vows to be justified, and how was the new freedom of conscience to be protected against the licentiousness of the flesh? Priests were marrying and monasteries everywhere emptying, and the next question was already waiting to be answered: what did the biblical Lord's Supper have in common with hundreds of thousands of masses for the dead that were instituted out of piety in the interest of the deceased, with the purpose of effecting God's grace by means of the sacrifice of the mass?

Since approximately 1522 Luther had also been confronted by Catholics of a new sort, who were no longer seeking to defend the claims and privileges of Rome primarily by means of canon law; they argued on the basis of Scripture and were honest and earnest when they advocated traditional forms of piety. It was from their ranks that the reproach stemmed: considering the testimony of so many generations, how can Luther purport to know better? Then there were the princes, knights, peasants, and officials who were abusing the Gospel for their own purposes. What had once been the monopoly of pope and curia was now being done by people everywhere under the guise of "Evangelical freedom." Finally there was the attack from his own ranks: the followers of the Reformation fell out over the question of baptism and the Eucharist. It was all too much: "As if it were not enough that the pope, emperor, princes, bishops, and whole world hated me: now my own brothers are turning against me."[40]

Though these tribulations for the sake of the Gospel never reached the depth and intensity of personal anguish, they, too, continued to the end of his life. They are partly the expression, partly the result of the way Luther saw his own place in the reformation movement: he was an instrument in the hands of God, whose overpowering wisdom is hidden in history. Having worked out no historical plan and prepared no program of his own, he was in a weaker position than many of his prominent contemporaries like Thomas Münzer, the peasant leader; Ignatius of Loyola, founder of the Jesuit order; or John Calvin, the Geneva reformer. The only thing left for Luther was to wait for God's great reformation.

Overwhelmed by God, at the mercy of His power. The German poet

Rainer Maria Rilke expresses the experience in so unique, so timeless a way that it can help us to understand what Luther felt better than many a prosaic explanation could:

> Was wir besiegen, ist das Kleine,
> und der Erfolg selbst macht uns klein.
> Das Ewige und Ungemeine
> will nicht von uns gebogen sein.
> Das ist der Engel, der den Ringern
> des Alten Testaments erschien:
> wenn seiner Widersacher Sehnen
> im Kampfe sich metallen dehnen,
> fühlt er sie unter seinen Fingern
> wie Saiten tiefer Melodien.
>
> Wen dieser Engel überwand,
> welcher so oft auf Kampf verzichtet,
> der geht gerecht und aufgerichtet
> und gross aus jener harten Hand,
> die sich, wie formend, an ihn schmiegte.
> Die Siege laden ihn nicht ein.
> Sein Wachstum ist: der Tiefbesiegte
> von immer Grösserem zu sein.[41]

> [What we conquer are the small things, / and victory itself makes us small. / The Eternal and Un-common / does not want to be shaped by us. / This is the Angel who to the wrestlers / of the Old Testament appeared: / when the sinews of his adversaries / in the battle stretch metallically / he feels them under his fingers / like the strings of profound melodies. // Who was overcome by this Angel / who has oft from battle abstained, / he walks justified, upright / and proud out of that hard hand, / which as if molding, gently encloses him. / Victories are not inviting to him. / His gain is to be profoundly vanquished / by ever greater things.]

THE TENSION between the old and the new conscience was a further, and as we shall see, decisive aspect of the Reformation burden. Two verses of Luther's song "Nun freut euch lieben Christen gmein" ("Rejoice Together, Beloved Christians") provide an eloquent but unmistakably autobiographical statement of this tension:

Dem Teufel ich gefangen lag
im Tod war ich verloren,
mein Sünd mich quälte Nacht und Tag,
darin ich war geboren.
Ich fiel auch immer tiefer drein,
es war kein Guts am Leben mein,
die Sünd hatt' mich besessen.

Mein guten Werk' die galten nicht,
es war mit ihn' verdorben;
der frei Will hasste Gotts Gericht,
er war zum Gut'n erstorben;
die Angst micht zu verzweifeln trieb,
dass nichts denn Sterben bei mir blieb,
zur Höllen musst ich sinken.[42]

[I lay captured by the Devil / I was lost in death, / my sinfulness tormented me night and day, / in which I was born. / I also fell ever deeper into it, / there was nothing good about my life, / sin had taken possession of me. // My good works were good for nothing, / they were all worthless; / the free will hated God's Judgment, / it was dead to what was good; / fear drove me to despair, / so nothing was left to me but dying, / I had to sink to Hell.]

How impressive it is to watch Luther imbuing involved theological thoughts with experience, making them come alive and broadly understandable. The existential framework is, however, easily misunderstood, since it seems to imply that everything Luther experienced body and soul and described as sickness unto death was now past and overcome.

The conscience of man, of "old Adam," is geared to the standard of achievements before God and the world, and it is given to judging itself and others according to achievements. But the conscience of the man who has been justified by God builds on the achievements of Christ and is free of accursed self-analysis—"accursed" because the Devil abuses the conscience, establishes himself as the superego, and suffocates man with feelings of guilt.

In the Middle Ages captivity by the Devil, that fatal disease, was understood and branded as concupiscence, carnal lust. Luther liberated himself from this notion. For him "lust" was the diabolical drive to hold one's own before God and oneself through one's own achievements. Luther's hymns invite the congregation to allow God, through His Word and sacrament, to release them from the prison of the Devil's drives.

Luther's key statement, that the Christian is "sinner and just" at the same time, is the most pointed formulation of the moral revolution being carried out here. Against the background of the Middle Ages—which were by no means past in any respect—Luther can even be said to have been carrying out an immoral revolution. This became manifest when he wrote to Philipp Melanchthon from Wartburg Castle, appealing to the younger man's Christian conscience with the provocative words: sin bravely, but believe even more and rejoice in Christ—"pecca fortiter, sed fortius fide et gaude in Christo."[43]

"Sin bravely" is a challenge to fight the "old" conscience and cast it off as a suffocating yoke. "Believe even more and rejoice in Christ" is the call to the freedom of a Christian. Luther had accurately forecasted the obstacles that stood in the way of Evangelical freedom in the summer of 1519, during his second course of lectures on the Psalms. There would be "storms sweeping over the conscience" when faith clung to its hope in God without seeking refuge in good works. At that moment the idol of good conscience would demonstrate its power.[44]

The Christian walks a "straight and narrow way."[45] This is not a reference to the "straight gate" and the "narrow way" of those monks and puritans who forgo the joys of life on the "broad way" so as to maintain clear consciences. No, it is a difficult, a painful path because it leads to the nearly mystical experience of being torn out of one's conscience, the conscience that seeks peace in its own holiness.[46] Centuries of Western formation of conscience must be overcome if saying yes to God means saying no to one's own conscience.[47]

Psychology at the Deathbed

From 1527 on Luther's health began deteriorating so quickly as to constitute a crisis.[48] A year earlier he had already had a stone, of which he reportedly rid himself by eating a heavy meal—fried herrings and cold peas with mustard. At the beginning of the following year he was suddenly stricken with tightness of the chest caused by "a rush of blood to the heart," a feeling of oppression in the heart area, accompanied by painful buzzing in his ears. He was to complain frequently of these symptoms till he died. This time a herbal drink still brought relief.

Seven months later, on the morning of Saturday, July 6, 1527, Luther was seized by a serious depression followed by such violent circulatory disturbances that death seemed imminent. His father confessor, pastor Johannes

Bugenhagen; and his close friend Justus Jonas recorded the events of these days and Luther's "last words."

A Danish psychiatrist has assessed the two friends' eyewitness report as material evidence of Luther's psychosis.[49] In reality the document is a description of a moving deathbed scene and an impressive testament without pathological traits. Luther's real torments, which manifested themselves as melancholy, partly preceded and partly followed his illness, and they were intensified by a weakening of the body from which he was never completely to recover.

What had actually happened? At eight in the morning on July 6, 1527, Luther had pastor Bugenhagen summoned. He complained to him that he was suffering the most agonizing spiritual distress that he had ever experienced. Bugenhagen could not, however, find out what it was that was affecting Doctor Martinus so, and Luther himself could not furnish a more detailed explanation. Luther then confessed and asked for absolution. He also uttered the wish to receive the Lord's Supper the following day. After his confession Luther indicated what was troubling him: "Judged from the outside, on the basis of the life I have led, it may look as if I have been walking on a bed of roses. But God knows my life. . . . I have often tried to serve the world with outward dignity and holy seriousness. But God has not allowed it. The world cannot truly charge me with public crimes; that angers it all the more. . . . I shall pray to God to allow me not to offend anyone through my sins."[50] What Bugenhagen heard and reported still does not make clear just what lay so heavily on Luther's mind that morning. Nor do the following events produce greater clarity. The only thing that is evident is that Luther sensed death to be near.

On the evening of that Saturday Justus Jonas and his wife were invited to dinner, which was to be at five o'clock as usual. But when the two arrived Luther had already gone to bed. He tried to get up but fainted, pale and ice-cold. "O, Doctor Jona, I feel sick, get me water or what you have, or I will die."[51] Jonas managed to revive Luther by pouring water over him, but now the end seemed to be approaching; sapped of his strength, Luther prepared himself. When Bugenhagen returned around six o'clock, he found "the Doctor in bed" and heard "how, with clear words alternately in Latin and German, he called upon God the Father and Christ the Lord, and he commended all that he had done in the service of the Holy Gospel into the Lord's hands."[52] His term of office was over.

That is why Bugenhagen and Justus Jonas wrote their account. They wanted the world to know that to his very last breath Doctor Martin, the Evangelist, had held fast to his faith, that "Evangelical faith" had stood the test of the hour of death. That is why Jonas recorded Luther's last words: "My dearest God, You led me into the cause, You know that Yours is the truth and the Word."[53] Because Luther's death was treated as an official, public event, posterity gained this illuminating insight into the Reformation distinction between the correctness of teachings and the unworthiness of man. Both are expressed in his last confession: "I am fully conscious and certain that I have taught correctly from the Word of God, according to the service to which God pressed me against my will; I have taught correctly about faith, love, the cross, and the sacraments. Many accused me of proceeding too severely. Severely, that is true, and often too severely; but it was a question of the salvation of all, even my opponents. I was still intending to give all I had to write about Holy Baptism against Zwingli and the contemnors of the sacraments. But God has evidently decided differently."[54]

There was no trace of despair despite the factors that made it difficult for him to take leave: he regretted that he had not been found deserving enough to shed his blood for Christ, "as so many brothers have testified to their beliefs with their lives. But that honor was also withheld from Jesus' favorite apostle, John the Evangelist, although he wrote far more harshly against the pope than I was ever capable of doing."[55]

Once again the crucial point was his conviction that the Church of Christ was the Church of the persecuted and the martyrs, who truly bore witness to their crucified Lord.

Luther's second concern, too, was connected with his concern for the Church: who will deal with the mobs and fanatics that are now spreading more and more at the expense of the faithful and the Gospel? "O, Thou dearest God and Father, Thou hast given me many thousands of precious and noble gifts for others; were it Thy will, I would be happy to let myself still be used to glorify Thy name and be of use to Thy people. . . . O how the fanatics will cause havoc after my death!"[56] Who will now cope with the sectarians who will settle in far and wide if Christ does not prove mightier than Satan?"[57]

His last concern was for his pregnant wife—Elisabeth would be born five months later, on December 10, 1527—and his one-year-old son Johannes: "Lord God, I thank Thee for having allowed me to be a poor beggar on earth. I leave no house, property, or money. But you gave me a wife and children, I commend them unto Thee. Feed, instruct, and preserve them as Thou hast preserved me, O Thou Father of children and widows."[58]

It is thanks to Justus Jonas that one of Catherine Luther's prayers has survived: "My dearest Doctor, if it is God's will, I would rather know you to be with our Lord than with me. It is not a question of me and my dear child alone but of the many pious Christian people that still need you. Do not worry about me, I commend you to His divine will. God will take care of you."[59]

Finally the doctor arrived; it was Augustine Schurff, a professor of medicine. He wrapped the ice-cold patient in hot towels, especially his head and feet. The measures were effective. Downstairs friends waited in fear and trembling until Schurff returned with the news that Doctor Martinus had perspired a great deal and was now out of danger. The patient was still very weak and had to stay in bed; he could not give his planned sermon the next day, Sunday. But in the evening he was already able to get up. "God has brought him back to us, Christo gratia"—Christ be thanked.

He was not terrified by his encounter with death. As Luther himself reported, his physical recovery was speedy. What he had experienced at the outbreak of his illness as an assault by the Devil would, however, only really gain momentum as his health improved. He continued to be troubled by doubts about the Evangelical truth. What frightened him was that he did not know whether he could live up to it: "For more than a week I have been thrown back and forth in death and Hell; my whole body feels beaten, my limbs are still trembling. I almost lost Christ completely, driven about on the waves and storms of despair and blasphemy against God. But because of the intercession of the faithful, God began to take mercy on me and tore my soul from the depths of Hell."[60] Thus Luther wrote to Philipp Melanchthon on August 2, 1527, in words that provide immediate insight into his experiences. Luther was wrestling to find the merciful God!

This comes as a complete surprise and does not fit into the traditional picture of the Reformational discovery. It had, after all, looked as if, after much grumbling and cursing and desperate struggling, Luther had achieved the breakthrough in 1518 (possibly earlier, but not later) that had opened the gates of paradise to him—once and for all. Certainly Luther was no longer questioning the Reformation discovery that God bestows justification by faith without anterior or posterior conditions. He had only just attested to the fact that "I have taught correctly about faith, love, and cross." But certainty of faith does not exist once and for all, it is not a virtue one can possess, on which one can rely. Certainty of faith is a gift that "exceeds my powers."[61]

The plague that now swept through Wittenberg devastated the town, but Luther remained there with Bugenhagen and two other pastors—fear of the Black Death pales in comparison with the fear of the Devil's attack on one's soul.[62] "Satan himself is raging against me with all his might. . . . He affects me with indescribable spiritual weakness. . . . My hope is that the fight will benefit many, although there is nothing in this misery that my sins have not deserved. . . . But I know that I have taught the Word of Christ purely and truly for the salvation of many. That is what the Devil is angry at, that is why he wants to crush me together with the Word."[63] Shortly afterward he wrote to the same correspondent, Johannes Agricola, again: "World and reason have no idea how difficult it is to grasp that Christ is our justification, so deeply embedded in us—like a second nature—is the trust in works."[64] The Gospel is not merely too complex to grasp; the Gospel is repugnant to everyone whose conscience seeks justification in works!

In October he was still haunted by anguish and urgently requested Melanchthon to remember him in his prayers of intercession since he himself was a "miserable worm," plagued by the spirit of sadness: "I hope that the God who began His work in me will ultimately have mercy on me, for I seek and thirst after nothing but the merciful God."[65]

This was a further unequivocal statement: Luther was looking for the gracious God whom he had already been preaching and teaching for so long. The Devil had thrown him back to the monastery: "I have known these tribulations since my youth; but I never expected that they would so increase." On New Year's Day of 1528 the echo of his fears could still be heard: how "difficult" it is that our justification is hidden in God![66] The tension did not ease until the spring of 1528.

We can search for a psychological explanation for these dark days and months. At times he must have been overworked. The almost unimaginable rate at which he worked, the masses of letters and treatises, the lectures and negotiations make it very likely. He himself considered this explanation only to dismiss it. Overwork was not a decisive reason. It would certainly not be wrong for the emotional state he was in to be described as an illness, provided, however, that cognizance of the symptom is not taken for a diagnosis. Here was a highly sensitive human being afflicted by living in two eras at once, a disorder that physicians or psychiatrists might be able to ameliorate but cannot cure. Luther suffered through the conflict—unavoidable for medieval and modern alike—between the conscience and Evangelical reliance on God. Here is where the man and his deeds converge.

This is the sickness unto death which Luther uncovered: we cling to our achievements and cannot shake the need to prove ourselves before God and man, in life and in death. Luther's "neurosis" proves to be part and parcel of the Reformation discovery: we are beggars—that is true!

EPILOGUE

Luther as He Was

If Martin Luther walked down the street today, would anyone recognize him? Would at least Luther scholars slow down? There are certainly enough pictures of him. Lucas Cranach (†1553), who knew Luther well and thought very highly of him, executed at least five portraits of him; three oil paintings and two copperplates have survived. This impressive series, though shaped by the vision and conception of one and the same artist, seems to depict completely different figures. The ascetic face of the serious monk has nothing in common with the vigorous, bearded Luther as Junker Jörg except the broad forehead and the luminous eyes. There seem to be worlds between the monk and the squire, and yet there was only a year between the portraits, which date from 1520 and 1521. The eyes also give the face of 1532, immortalized by apprentices from the Cranach workshop, its individual stamp.

The last portrait, painted by Lucas Cranach the Younger (†1586) at the beginning of 1546, seems to focus on the eyes as well. Though the painting of the deceased Luther and his death mask show the man in all his dignity, they reveal death in all its indifference. The sparkling eyes are missing—and thus Luther himself is, too. Eyewitnesses—in the literal sense of the word—recounted that whoever spoke to Luther was riveted by the intensity of his eyes. After his interview with Luther in August 1518 Cardinal Cajetan spoke of the monk with the strange eyes. A Swiss student in Wittenberg provided a glowing description, calling them "deep, black, blinking, and glittering like a star"![1] They were all in agreement over the vivid play of his features clearly reflecting his volatile emotions. He was no stoic, nor did he look like one.

The oldest description of Luther's outward appearance dates back from the Leipzig disputation of 1519, which attracted many listeners who did not want to miss the theological contest between Carlstadt, Luther, and Johannes Eck. The surviving description is not specific enough to allow us to see his face, but it is an excellent sketch from a distance. It was written by the Leipzig humanist Petrus Mosellanus, of whom Luther thought very well, who had been offered the chair of Greek at the University of Wittenberg a year earlier, even before Melanchthon was offered the post.

Mosellanus describes Luther as a man of medium height, "haggard from worrying and studying, so that one can almost count his bones through the skin." Nonetheless, he makes the healthy impression of a man in the prime of life. He speaks in a clear, articulate voice and is courteous, even cheerful—but he criticizes "a bit too caustically and aggressively."[2]

How worn out and emaciated Luther was at the time of his Reformation discovery can be gathered from a remark he himself made about his physical condition. Though still thin at the disputation in 1519, he had already begun gradually putting on weight the year before. When he returned to Wittenberg from his successful disputation in Heidelberg in May 1518, his friends teased him, saying the Neckar region must have agreed with him because he had "filled out considerably"![3]

Being too thin was never mentioned again; he developed in the opposite direction, toward corpulence. Once he had been condemned to immobility at Wartburg Castle and was receiving regular meals, there were soon no traces left of his original gauntness. Visitors at Coburg Castle at the time of the 1530 Diet of Augsburg described him as stout, and shortly before his death he described himself as the "fat doctor." This was no exaggeration.

MOSELLAN'S REFERENCE to Luther as courteous is surprising—that is a virtue no one attributed to the later Reformer; and the records of the Leipzig disputation provide only partial confirmation. In direct comparison with Eck it was easy to be courteous. The aggressiveness for which the humanist faults him is more convincing. In his prolix introductory speech, Mosellan admittedly demanded a style of debate so dignified, so restrained that it would have been more suited to a Platonic symposium than to a bitter fight that was to separate doctrinal truth from error. But Mosellan's view was correct: Luther never denied having an overly sharp tongue; his tendency to use such heavy ammunition genuinely damaged his reputation in cultured circles.

The good humor Mosellan mentions is particularly noteworthy. It prevails despite all the cares that mark Luther's face. Luther was an emotional man; his temperament was like a volcano, liable to erupt in any situation, especially when he felt exuberant. His opponents sensed this and rejected it as being unfitting for a monk. They relate disapprovingly that throughout the Leipzig disputation the professor from Wittenberg was wearing a silver ring—with an amulet against evil—and that he was holding a flower, occasionally even smelling it![4]

Mosellan also mentions the flower, though not as criticism. Yet it seems an unusual way of appearing at a disputation. The fact is that Luther loved nature and observed and admired it with keen eyes. He liked to relax in his garden, and, in defiance of the Devil, delighted in flowers, especially roses, as God's gift.[5]

Joy of life is not something that simply exists, it must be worked at. Even in our century, with holidays and relaxation legally established as a human right, the joy of life is an art that cannot be bought. Space and time can be provided, but joy needs practice.

The oft-invoked piety flourishing on the eve of the Reformation had two different faces: one a tendency to laicize the Church, the other a tendency to clericalize the world. People feasted, celebrated, and drank at church consecration festivals and carnival. But everywhere, particularly north of the Alps, there was a growing inclination to criticize luxury and merriment as if even laymen had taken monastic vows.

In the foreword to the new edition of his best-known book, *Enchiridion Militis Christiani,* Erasmus of Rotterdam coined a slogan welcomed far and wide: the ideal city is a monastery writ large. With this he had put into words a long-existing tendency that would later lend credibility and thrust to the Reformation in the German cities. The time was crying out for a new breed of educated, responsible laymen. But the new layman was the old monk. Thus a second Reformation was engendered. Luther had made room for the joy of life, but it was crushed by puritanism before it could properly come into its own. Luther's often shocking battle for inner freedom included defending pleasure and merriment: the old monk was really a new layman.

NOT ONLY trials and tribulations, quarrels and cares left their mark; so did serious illness. Virtually the only health problem we know of up to the year 1520 is the accident that nearly cost him his life, when his sword pierced an artery. On the way to Worms Luther was seized by a bad fever, but only after he was at Wartburg Castle does he truly seem to have been plagued by physical complaints for the first time.

The legend has stubbornly persisted that Luther experienced his Reformation breakthrough as the end of an agonizing bout of constipation. The unsavory story goes back to one of Luther's own statements: this cloaca is where I made my discovery. All the rest was freely but colorfully invented. The fact is that he did not begin suffering from hemorrhoids and possibly anal fissures[6] that made bowel movements into a virtual torment until he was at Wartburg Castle, well after he had already been pronounced a heretic and put under imperial ban. He had had his first problems in Worms, but now he was plagued as never before: "My ass has become nasty," he complained in German in a Latin letter.[7] Once he described to his friend Spalatin, who belonged to the small circle of friends who knew where he was hiding, that after five days of constipation his bowel movement had caused him such pain "that I nearly gave up the ghost—and now, bathed in blood, can find no peace. What took four days to heal immediately tears open again."[8] Illnesses were never so private to him that he would have wanted to suppress the details. The more extreme the situation, the more quickly he resorted to the German language, for Latin was too far removed from a scream of pain. The portrait of Luther showing us the Reformer only from the neck upward does not let us see the rest of his body racked with pain.

The passage that follows the frank description in his letter to Spalatin is typical of his attitude toward illness: "I am writing you this not to evoke your pity, but so that you can congratulate me. . . . By this misery I am incited to prayer, which is what we need most: to do battle with Satan by praying with all our might!"[9]

Only at the beginning of October 1521 did a remedy Spalatin obtained from the court physician of Electoral Saxony bring relief. Luther had been suffering from constipation for six months,[10] and it continued to be a problem, one which would be joined by others—headaches with buzzing in his ears, tightness of the chest, stones, and gout.

In 1530 the forty-seven-year-old Luther was a middle-aged man—we would assume. He himself felt old: "The years are piling up."[11] He needed glasses now, and at Coburg Castle complained that he could not see a thing with the badly made ones sent to him from Wittenberg. He attributed both his headaches and the ear infection from which he was never again to be completely free to the bad Coburg wine. He was exasperated by a shin infection kept open artificially for some time by a tube to drain the pus. Even on his last trip the tube was still in his leg.

In February 1537 the Protestants were faced with a decision that tested their consciences and their savvy alike. The pope had called for a council in Mantua, and the question under consideration was whether the Protestant imperial estates should participate, whether they were even allowed to participate in an "unfree," meaning papal, council. In Schmalkalden, which already belonged to Hesse, representatives of the princes and cities concerned assembled for extensive consultations. Wittenberg, too, took part. Luther fell so seriously ill during the negotiations that friends thought his death imminent, as they had ten years earlier and would again ten years later. He was probably suffering from several kidney stones so unfortunately placed that,

Probably the last portrait of Luther, drawn by his valet, Reifenstein, in a book belonging to Melanchthon. Melanchthon added the following words:

Doctor Martin Luther
Alive I was your plague, o pope,
Dead I shall destroy you.
He died in the year 1546
He lived for 63 years
The 64th year was the year of his death
It was the 18th of February when he encountered death,
at night between two and three o'clock.
On the 22nd of the month he was buried in the Castle Church of Wittenberg.

He is dead, yet he lives.

as Matthäus Ratzberger, the physician treating him, reported, he "could pass no water." His whole body became so bloated "that one could do nothing for him but expect the end."[12]

A year later Luther still vividly recollected all the remedies that had been tried on him: "Had I died of my stones in Schmalkalden, I would already have been in Heaven for a year now, free of all ills. At that time I was so terribly tormented by the doctors: they gave me as much to drink as if I were a huge ox and treated all my limbs, even sucking at my private parts."[13]

Nothing helped, so Luther asked to be allowed to die in his "fatherland," Electoral Saxony. The departure to Gotha was planned but put off for a day: "Philipp Melanchthon detained me for a day with his incurable belief in astrology, for it was new moon."[14] On the way back, the bumpy road may have given the fatally ill Luther the decisive push back to life. In the early hours of February 27 the stone was dislodged and "he almost drowned in his own water."[15] Luther had escaped with his life once again;[16] the "stargazer" had been right!

His physician Ratzeberg closes this part of Luther's biography with the remark that Luther never recovered from his kidney stones. Judging from the work he did, Luther was not an "old man" even in his final years. But occasionally he yearned for the end or dreamt of retiring from "office": "Then I could dedicate myself completely to my garden." But these were passing thoughts. Illnesses were so plainly a plague of the Devil that he put up desperate resistance to them. Patient acceptance of suffering as divinely ordained destiny was anything but pious unless there was nothing left to be done. But diet and medical cures were there to be made use of in the fight for health against the Devil.

Luther must have had a very strong constitution, or he would never have been able to bear strain, overwork, and constant physical ailments for so long. But there is a deeper source for his exceptional vitality. Health is God's domain; death the Devil's intent. Luther learned to draw life from the struggle against the Devil. For the just shall *live* by faith, and "life" does not begin in Heaven. According to the medieval *memento mori,* in the midst of life we are surrounded by death. Luther's faith enabled him to vigorously turn this on its head: "In the midst of death we are surrounded by life."

NOTES

Following is a list of abbreviations used in these notes:

EA lat.var.arg.	*D. Martini Lutheri Opera latina varii argumenti,* vols. 1–7 (Frankfurt, Erlangen, 1865–73).
WA	*D. Martin Luthers Werke: Kritische Gesamtausgabe, Abteilung Werke,* vols. 1– (Weimar, 1883–).
WABr	*D. Martin Luthers Werke: Kritische Gesamtausgabe, Briefwechsel* [Correspondence], vols. 1–18 (Weimar, 1930–85).
WAT	*D. Martin Luthers Werke: Kritische Gesamtausgabe, Tischreden* [Table Talk], vols. 1–6 (Weimar, 1912–21).
WADB	*D. Martin Luthers Werke: Kritische Gesamtausgabe, Die Deutsche Bibel* [The German Bible], vols. 1–12 (Weimar, 1906–61).
AWA	*Archiv zur Weimarer Lutherausgabe,* vol. 2: *D. Martin Luther Operationes in psalmos 1519–1521,* part II: Psalm 1–10 (Cologne, Vienna, 1981).
H. Bornkamm, *Martin Luther*	Heinrich Bornkamm, *Martin Luther in der Mitte seines Lebens: Das Jahrzehnt zwischen dem Wormser und dem Augsburger Reichstag,* ed. K. Bornkamm (Göttingen, 1979).
M. Brecht, *Martin Luther*	Martin Brecht, *Martin Luther. Sein Weg zur Reformation 1483–1521,* 2d ed. (Stuttgart, 1983).
Th. Kolde, *Augustiner-Congregation*	Theodor Kolde, *Die deutsche Augustiner-Congregation und Johann von Staupitz: Ein Beitrag zur Ordens- und Reformationsgeschichte nach meistens ungedruckten Quellen* (Gotha, 1879).
Köstlin-Kawerau, *Martin Luther*	Julius Köstlin, *Martin Luther: Sein Leben und seine Schriften,* 5th ed., ed. G. Kawerau, 2 vols. (Berlin, 1903).
Reichstagsakten [Proceedings of the Imperial Diet]	*Deutsche Reichstagsakten, Jüngere Reihe. Deutsche Reichstagsakten unter Kaiser Karl V.,* vols. 1–, ed. Historische Kommission bei der Bayerischen Akademie der Wissenschaften (Gotha, 1893–; 2d ed. [reprint] Göttingen, 1962–).

Werden und Wertung der Reformation — Heiko A. Oberman, *Werden und Wertung der Reformation: Vom Wegestreit zum Glaubenskampf,* 3d ed. (Tübingen, 1989).
English edition: *Masters of the Reformation: The Emergence of a New Intellectual Climate,* trans. D. Martin (Cambridge, New York, Melbourne, 1981).

1. A GERMAN EVENT

1. *WABr* 1.235, 88; ca. 25 Oct. 1518.
2. *Akten und Briefe zur Kirchenpolitik Herzog Georgs von Sachsen,* ed. F. Gess, vol 1 (Leipzig, 1905), introduction, lxvii.
3. *Neues Urkundenbuch zur Geschichte der evangelischen Kirchen-Reformation Reformation,* ed. C. E. Förstemann, vol. 1 (Hamburg, 1842), 259.
4. *WABr* 1.82f. This document should be dated 31 Dec. 1517 instead of 1518.
5. *WA* 12.220, 4–14.
6. *WABr* 1.261, note 1; cf. *WAT* 5, no. 5375c; summer 1540.
7. *EA lat. var. arg.* 2.426–28.
8. *WABr* 1.234, 70–73; 25 Oct. 1518.
9. "Ea autem sunt partim contra doctrinam Apostolicae Sedis, partim vero damnabilia." *WABr* 1.234, 73f.; Nov. 1518. Cajetan explicitly noted that he had judged Luther's conformity with the true faith on the basis of the Holy Scriptures alone—and of canon law. Ibid. 233, 14f.
10. *WABr* 1.250, 22. The cautious Frederick explained his standpoint on the Luther question only once, in this very letter to Cajetan, dated 7 Dec. 1518.
11. *WABr* 1.281, 31–34; 20 Dec. 1518.
12. *Reichstagsakten* 4.604, 18–22.
13. *Reichstagsakten* 1.867, 7; 870, 19–871, 1; 876, 16f.
14. *Reichstagsakten* 2.581, 28–582, 2.
15. *Reichstagsakten* 2.595, 23–25, 34f.
16. Cf. W. A. Reynolds, "Martin Luther and Hernán Cortés: Their Confrontation in Spanish Literature," *Hispania* 42 (1959): 66–70; 45 (1962): 402–04. See above all Hernán Cortés' three highly interesting reports to Emperor Charles V from 1520 to 1524: *Die Eroberung Mexikos,* ed. C. Litterscheid (Frankfurt, 1980).
17. Karl Brandi, *Kaiser Karl V: Werden und Schicksal einer Persönlichkeit,* vol. 1, 7th ed. (Munich, 1964), 93.
18. *Reichstagsakten* 1.853, 5–10.
19. *Reichstagsakten* 1.671f.; 676f.; 690–93; 703f.; 860.
20. Georg Mentz, *Johann Friedrich der Grossmütige 1503–1554,* part 1 (Jena, 1903), 18f.
21. *Reichstagsakten* 2.526, 24–32.
22. *Reichstagsakten* 1.873, 9–14.

23. *Reichstagsakten* 2.496, 3–8.
24. *WABr* 2.305, 11f.; 28 Apr. 1521.
25. *Reichstagsakten* 2.579, 3–5.
26. *Reichstagsakten* 2.581, 23–582, 2.
27. *WABr* 2.305, 13–15; 28 Apr. 1521.
28. *Reichstagsakten* 2.555, 37, note 1.
29. "Warnung an seine lieben Deutschen," probably written in October 1530, shortly after the Diet of Augsburg, and published in April 1531. *WA* 30 III. 290, 28–291, 9. For National Socialist exploitation, cf. H. Werdermann, "Martin Luther und Adolf Hitler: Ein geschichtlicher Vergleich," lecture held on Reformation Day (October 31, the date the posting of the 95 theses), 1935 (= *Der Ruf! Eine volksmissionarische Schriftenreihe* 4), 2d ed. (Gnadenfrei i. Schlesien, 1937), 4.
30. *WA* 30 III. 285, 15f.
31. Dedicated to his loyal, stalwart Wittenberg student, Nikolaus von Amsdorff, on 23 June 1520. *WA* 6.404, 11f.
32. *WABr* 2.120, 13–15; to Spalatin, 7 June 1520.
33. *WABr* 2.167, 6, note 1.
34. *WABr* 2.48, 22–27; to Spalatin, 24 Feb. 1520.
35. *WA* 6.325–48.
36. *WA* 6.336, 9–10; Decretum Gratiani I, Dist. XL, cap. 6; *Corpus iuris canonici,* ed E. Friedberg, vol. 1 (Graz, 1959), col. 146.
37. *WABr* 2.120, 6–8; to Spalatin, ca. 7 June.
38. *WA* 6.329, 17f.
39. The text of the Donation of Constantine can be found in *Das Constitutum Constantini* (The Donation of Constantine), ed. H. Fuhrmann, *Fontes Iuris Germanici Antiqui* 10 (Hannover, 1968).
40. *WA* 6.463, 35f.; 464, 26–30.
41. *WA* 6.434, 11–13.
42 *WA* 6.405, 27–406, 18.
43. *Ulrichs von Hutten Schriften,* ed. E. Böcking, vol. 5 (Leipzig, 1861), 302.
44. *WA* 6.406, 21–407, 8.
45. *WA* 6.407, 7f.
46. *WA* 6.446, 14f.
47. *WA* 6.469, 8–11, 16f.; cf. beginning of the *Address to the Christian Nobility* (*WA* 6.405).
48. *WABr* 2.232, 72f.; Ebernburg, 9 Dec. 1520.

II. A MEDIEVAL EVENT

1. *WA* 30 III. 387, 6–10; letter from Jan Hus to the congregation in Prague.
2. *WA* 50.34, 16f.; 1536.
3. *WAT* 1. no. 624; 294, 19–23; autumn 1533.

4. *WAT* 3. no. 3403b; 306; 9f.
5. *Die Schriften des Heiligen Franziskus von Assisi,* ed. K. Esser and L. Hardick (Werl, 1972), 96.
6. See Brian Tierney, *Origins of Papal Infallibility, 1150–1350: A Study on the Concepts of Infallibility, Sovereignty and Tradition in the Middle Ages* (Leiden, 1972).
7. Only a "semi-official" text was available to me: "Our Father-in-Heaven, Rock and Redeemer of Israel, bless the State of Israel, the beginning of the sprouting of our redemption . . ." Cf. E. L. Fackenheim, *The Jewish Return into History: Reflections in the Age of Auschwitz and a New Jerusalem* (New York, 1982).
8. *WA* 50.323, 36–324, 8; 1538.
9. *WA* 50.362, 7; cf. *Deutsches Sprichwörter-Lexikon,* ed. K. F. W. Wander, vol. 1 (Darmstadt, 1964), col. 415, no. 27.
10. Bernard of Clairvaux, *Sermones super Cantica Canticorum, 1–35,* Sermon 33. *S. Bernardi Opera,* vol. 1 (Rome, 1957), 245.
11. *WA* 3.417, 1–425, 11; Ps. 69, 1–5.
12. *WA* 3.425, 7f.
13. *AWA* 2.606, 2–4; 1519–21.
14. *AWA* 2. 615, 1–3; Ps. 10.16.
15. *WA* 3.422, 5.
16. *WA* 38.105, 8–20.
17. *WA* 6.459, 31; 1520.
18. *WA* 7.21, 1f.
19. *WA* 7.26, 4–7.
20. *WA* 7.21, 3f.
21. *WA* 6.258, 25.
22. *WA* 6.465, 25–467, 26.
23. *WA* 6.227, 29–32; Sermon von den guten Werken, March 1520.

III. AN ELEMENTAL EVENT

1. Heinrich Heine, *Zur Geschichte der Religion und Philosophie in Deutschland* in: *Sämtliche Schriften,* ed. K. Briegleb, vol. 3 (Munich, 1971), 539.
2. For the debate since E. H. Erikson, *Der junge Mann Luther* (Hamburg, 1970); see also *Psychohistory and Religion: The Case of Young Man Luther,* ed. R. A. Johnson (Philadelphia, 1977); U. Becke, "Eine hinterlassene psychiatrische Studie Paul Johann Reiters über Luther," *Zeitschrift für Kirchengeschichte* 90(1979): 85–95.
3. *WA* 18.299, 25–29; "Ermahnung zum Frieden auf die zwölf Artikel der Bauerschaft in Schwaben," 1525. Cf. Johannes Wallmann, "Ein Friedensappell: Luthers letztes Wort im Bauernkrieg," in *Der Wirklichkeitsanspruch von Theologie und Religion: Ernst Steinbach zum 70. Geburtstag* (Tübingen, 1976), 57–75.

4. *WAT* 3. no. 3566 B; 416, 24; 1537.
5. *WA* 38.338, 6; in *WAT* 4, no. 4640; 414, 6f., with special emphasis on the contrast between world and God.
6. *WA* 53.511, 28–34; 1543.
7. *Nuntiaturberichte aus Deutschland 1533–1559 nebst ergänzenden Actenstücken,* ed. W. Friedensburg, vol. 1 (Gotha, 1892), 541, 14–18.
8. Indicated by O. Clemen in 1934; *WABr* 5.287f., note 14. Presented in its full scope by Ian D. K. Siggins, "Luther's Mother Margarethe," *Harvard Theological Review* 71(1978): 125–50; with comprehensive bibliography. Heinrich Bornkamm already noted that Luther's grandmother, a Ziegler, had been confused with his mother. Cf. H. Bornkamm, "Heinrich Boehmer's 'Junger Luther' und die neuere Lutherforschung," in H. Boehmer, *Der junge Luther,* ed. H. Bornkamm, 5th ed. (Stuttgart, 1962) [Leipzig, 1939], 358f.
9. *WABr* 1.610, 20–22; to Spalatin, 14 Jan. 1520.
10. *WAT* 2. no. 1559; 134, 5–12; May 1532.
11. *WAT* 3. no. 3566b; 416, 24–26; 1537.
12. *WAT* 4. no. 4707; 330, 9f.; 1539. *WAT* 5. no. 5373; 99, 10f.; 1540.
13. *WA* 17 II. 475, 11–15; 1527.
14. *WA* 15.45, 1–47, 14; 1524.
15. *WABr* 2.563, 7; 15 June 1522. Cf., however, O. Scheel, *Martin Luther: Vom Katholizismus zur Reformation,* vol. 1, 3rd ed. (Tübingen, 1921), 70–97.
16. We owe this demythologization to R. R. Post, *The Modern Devotion: Confrontation with Reformation and Humanism* (Leiden, 1968).
17. *WA* 56.313, 14.; cf. *WA* 3.648, 26.
18. *WAT* 5. no. 5362; 95, 1–7; *WA* 30 III. 491, 37.
19. *WABr* 1.11, 39; Erfurt, 22 April 1507.
20. Cf. O. Clemen, *WABr* 1.13f.
21. *WABr* 1.15, 2; 28 April 1507.
22. *WABr* 1.16, 1–21; 17 March 1509. Johannes Braun is mentioned once more in the letters when Luther requests the Erfurt Augustinian prior Johannes Lang to pass on Luther's Gotha chapter sermon to Braun. *WABr* 1.52, 8; 30 Aug. 1516.
23. *WABr* 1.257, 2; 25 Nov. 1518.
24. *WABr* 1.515, 75–78; 3 Oct. 1519.
25. *WA* 1.48, 21; 1515; similarly in one of his last table talks, Eisleben 1546. *WAT* 6. no. 6809; 206, 21. Cf. *Deutsches Sprichwörter-Lexikon,* ed. K. F. W. Wander, vol. 4 (Darmstadt, 1964), col. 1113, no. 1251.
26. *WAT* 3. no. 2982b; 131, 20–26; 1533.
27. *WAT* 6. no. 6830; 217, 26f.
28. *WAT* 6. no. 6832; 219, 30–40. Cf. M. Osborn, *Die Teufelsliteratur des XVI. Jahrhunderts* (Berlin, 1893) [Hildesheim, 1965]; H. Preuss, *Die Vorstellungen vom Antichrist im späten Mittelalter, bei Luther und in der konfessionellen Polemik* (Leipzig, 1906); H. Obendiek, *Der Teufel bei Martin Luther: Eine theologische Untersuchung* (Berlin, 1931); H. R. Gerstenkorn, *Weltlich Regiment zwischen*

Gottesreich und Teufelsmacht: Die staatstheoretischen Auffassungen Martin Luthers und ihre politische Bedeutung (Bonn, 1956); K. L. Roos, *The Devil in 16th Century German Literature: The Teufelsbücher* (Bern, Frankfurt a.M., 1972).

29. *WAT* 6. no. 6827; 215, 40–216, 9.
30. *WAT* 5. no. 5284; 44, 8f.; 1540.
31. *WAT* 6. no. 6827; 216, 9–11.
32. *WAT* 4. no. 4035; 92, 39; 1538.
33. *WAT* 5. no. 6250; 558, 13f.
34. *WA* 1. 44–52; 50, 12–20.
35. *WA* 1.50, 24f.; *WA* 4.681, 29f.
36. *WABr* 2.421, 11–13; Dec. 1521.
37. *WABr* 1.52, 2; 30 Aug. 1516.
38. Cf. caricature of the pope, no. 10 in *WA* 54, appendix. Cf. *WAT* 6. no. 6817; 210f.
39. Cf. especially R. W. Scribner, *For the Sake of Simple Folk: Popular Propaganda for the German Reformation* (Cambridge, 1981), 81f.; with bibliography.
40. *WA* 30 II. 646, 1; 1530.
41. *WA* 1.50, 25; 4.681, 20–30; cf. 4.612, 8–17.
42. Catalogue, *Stefan Zweig Exposition*, Jewish National and University Library (Jerusalem, 1981), no. 52.

IV. THE ROAD TO WITTENBERG

1. *WAT* 2. no. 2788; 660, 24–26, 28f.; 1532.
2. *WAT* 6. no. 7029.
3. *WAT* 1.143, 10f.; 1532.
4. Cf. E. Kleineidam, *Universitas Studii Erffordensis: Überblick über die Geschichte der Universität Erfurt im Mittelalter 1392–1521*, part 2 (Leipzig, 1969), 146.
5. W. Urban, "Die 'via moderna' an der Universität Erfurt am Vorabend der Reformation," in *Gregor von Rimini: Werk und Wirkung bis zur Reformation*, ed. H. A. Oberman (Berlin, 1981), 311–30; 315–29; including further bibliography.
6. Kleineidam, *Universitas*, part 2, 147.
7. Bartholomaeus Arnoldi de Usingen, *Parvulus philosophiae naturalis* (Leipzig, 1499), fol. 138[r]; cited by E. Kleineidam, "Die Bedeutung der Augustinereremiten für die Universität Erfurt," in *Scientia Augustiniana: Festschrift Adolar Zumkeller*, ed. C. P. Mayer and W. Eckermann (Würzburg, 1975), 395–422, 405; cf. W. Urban, *Die 'via moderna' an der Universität Erfurt*, 320.
8. "Sum Occanicae factionis . . ." *WA* 6.600, 11; Oct. 1520.
9. *WAT* 2. no. 2544a; 516, 6f.; March 1532.
10. *WA* 6.195, 4f.

11. *WABr* 1.171, 71–76; May 1518.
12. *WABr* 1.88, 22–89, 29; 8 Feb. 1517.
13. Cf. *Werden und Wertung der Reformation,* 131f.; M. Schulze, "'Via Gregorii' in Forschung und Quellen," in *Gregor von Rimini* (Berlin, 1981), 1–126; 97f.
14. Kleineidam, *Universitas,* part 2, 227.
15. Cf. H. Junghans, "Der Einfluss des Humanismus auf Luthers Entwicklung bis 1518," *Luther-Jahrbuch* 37(1970): 37–101.
16. *WAT* 1. no. 116; 44, 21–23; 1531.
17. *WAT* 1. no. 116; 44, 21f.
18. *WAT* 1. no. 119; 46, 24f.; 1531.
19. *WAT* 4. no. 4707; 440, 9f.; 1539.
20. *WAT* 4.440, 14–18.
21. *Constitutiones OESA ad apostolicorum privilegiorum formam pro reformatione Alemanie* (Nuremberg, 1504), chap. 15.
22. *Constitutiones,* chap. 15.
23. "Misericordiam Dei et vestram." *Constitutiones,* chap. 15.
24. *WA* 47.590, 6–10.
25. *Constitutiones,* chap. 18.
26. *WAT* 1. no. 1222.
27. *WAT* 4.303, 13f.; 1539.
28. *WABr* 6.439, 9–21; 28 March 1533.
29. A. Kunzelmann, *Geschichte der deutschen Augustiner-Eremiten,* part 5 (Würzburg, 1974), 10.
30. Cf. B. Hamm, *Frömmigkeitstheologie am Anfang des 16. Jahrhunderts: Studien zu Johannes von Paltz und seinem Umkreis* (Tübingen, 1982), 271f.
31. A. Kunzelmann, *Geschichte der deutschen Augustiner-Eremiten,* part 5, 420f.
32. 30 Dec. 1475; Th. Kolde, *Augustiner-Congregation,* 421; document 5.
33. Th. Kolde, *Augustiner-Congregation,* 119f.
34. *Dokumente zu Luthers Entwicklung* ⟨*bis 1519*⟩, ed. O. Scheel, 2d ed. (Tübingen, 1929), no. 536.
35. *WA* 43.378, 37f.; 381, 40–382, 8.
36. *WABr* 1.11, 28; 22 April 1507.
37. *WA* 1.44, 15; 45, 34.
38. R. Weijenborg, "Luther et les cinquante et un Augustins d'Erfurt: D'après une lettre d'indulgences inédite du 18 avril 1508," *Revue d'histoire ecclésiastique* 55 (1960): 819–75; 822.
39. B. Hamm, *Frömmigkeitstheologie,* 58–84; 291–99; 328f.
40. Cf. R. Weijenborg, "Neuentdeckte Dokumente in Zusammenhang mit Luthers Romreise," *Antonianum* 32(1957): 147–202; cf. W. Eckermann, "Neue Dokumente zur Auseinandersetzung zwischen Johann von Staupitz und der sächsischen Reformkongregation," *Analecta Augustiniana* 40(1977): 279–96.
41. G. Kawerau, "Aus den Actis generalatus Aegidii Viterbiensis," *Zeitschrift für Kirchengeschichte* 32(1911): 603–06; 604.

42. Johann von Staupitz, *Sämtliche Schriften, Abhandlungen, Predigten und Zeugnisse,* vol. 2 (*Lateinische Schriften 2),* ed. L. Graf zu Dohna and R. Wetzel (Berlin, 1979).
43. Cochlaeus alleged he had learned from Augustinians that Luther "ad Staupitium suum defecisse." *Ad semper victricem Germaniam paraclesis* (Cologne, 1524), fol. C2; cited by H. Böhmer, *Luthers Romfahrt* (Leipzig, 1914), 8f.
44. Cf. B. Lohse, *Mönchtum und Reformation: Luthers Auseinandersetzung mit dem Mönchsideal des Mittelalters* (Göttingen, 1963), 267–72.
45. Letter to Braun on 17 March 1509; *WABr* 1.17, 43f.
46. Köstlin-Kawerau I. 101f. Concerning the city of Wittenberg cf. H. Junghans, *Wittenberg als Lutherstadt* (Berlin, 1979).
47. *WAT* 2. no. 2255a; 379, 15–17, 1531.
48. *WA* 47.392, 10f.
49. *WA* 31 I.226, 11–17; 1530.
50. *WA* 51.89, 20–23; 1545.
51. *WAT* 4. no. 5010; 612, 11; 1540; *WAT* 6. no. 6777; 183, 3f.
52. *WA* 54.220, 1; 1545.
53. *WA* 38.212, 3f.; *WAT* 3. no. 3428; 313, 5f.
54. *WA* 38.212, 4f.; *WAT* 3. no. 3428; 313, 6f.
55. Cited by H. Böhmer, *Luthers Romfahrt,* 111.
56. *Reichstagsakten* 3.397f.
57. *WAT* 3. no. 3403b; 306, 9f.
58. O. Scheel, *Dokumente,* no. 539.

V. THE REFORMATION BREAKTHROUGH

1. *WABr* 11.67, 7f.; to Elector John Frederick, 25 March 1545.
2. *WAT* 6. no. 6647; 95, 14–18.
3. *WAT* 2. no. 1351; 66, 1–7; 1532.
4. *WAT* 4. no. 4007; 73, 15–24; 12 Sept. 1538.
5. *WA* 54.186, 14–21; 1545.
6. *WA* 54.187, 3–5.
7. *WAT* 2. no. 1681; 177, 8f.; 1532; cf. *WAT* 4. no. 4192; 191, 31f.; Dec. 1538. Cf. U. Becke's remarks in "Die Welt voll Teufel: Martin Luther als Gegenstand psychohistorischer Betrachtung," diss., Marburg, 1981, 180–88.
8. Luther mentions later (ca. Christmas 1531) the rhyme about the devil who catches a monk reading the first breviary prayer of the day while sitting on the toilet:

   Diabolus: Monachus super latrinam
   non debes legere primam!
   Monachus: Purgo meum ventrem
   Et colo Deum omnipotentem;

Tibi quae infra,
Deo omnipotenti, quod supra!
[Devil: You monk on the latrine,
you may not read the matins here!
Monk: I am cleansing my bowels
and worshipping God Almighty;
You deserve what descends
and God what ascends.]

(*WAT* 2. no. 2307; 413, 14–19; 1531.)

9. *WAT* 1. no. 83; 31, 22; autumn 1531.
10. *WAT* 1. no. 724, 726; first half of the 1530s.
11. *WA* 54.186, 25–29; cf. 179, 27f.
12. D. C. Steinmetz justifiably criticizes the tendency to present Luther as a "logical product" of medieval influences. See *Luther and Staupitz: An Essay in the Intellectual Origins of the Protestant Reformation* (Durham, N.C., 1980), 142.
13. *WA* 2.489, 17–20; 1519; on Gal. 2.16.
14. *WA* 9.3, 19–21.
15. *WA* 9.7, 32; 14, 37.
16. *WA* 9.13, 21f.
17. *WA* 9.27, 22–24.
18. This remained a basic theme in Luther's thinking and was worked out programmatically in the disputation on man, *De homine,* from the year 1536. Cf. G. Ebeling, *Lutherstudien,* vol. 2: *Disputatio de Homine,* 2 parts (Tübingen, 1977, 1982).
19. *WA* 9.46, 16–20.
20. *WA* 9.62, 23f.
21. *WA* 9.65, 14–17.
22. *WA* 1.226, 26; Thesis 50; Sept. 1517.
23. *WA* 9.62, 19–24; cf. 84, 6–8.
24. *WA* 9.83, 9.
25. *WAT* 4. no. 5009; 611, 7f.; 1540.
26. *WABr* 1.70, 19–21; to Spalatin, 19 Oct. 1516.
27. *WAT* 1. no. 347; 140, 5; 1532.
28. Cf. G. Ebeling, *Lutherstudien* vol. 1 (Tübingen, 1971), esp. 148–95.
29. *WA* 1.233, 10–13.
30. *WA* 56.36, 11–23.
31. *WA* 56.255, 19.
32. *WA* 56.256, 1–4.
33. "Non enim dabitur gratia sine ista agricultura sui ipsius." *WA* 56.257, 30f.
34. As in May 1518; *WA* 1.540, 41–541, 15; Resolutiones. In Martin Brecht's view, the new concept first appeared in the sermon of 28 March 1518 (*WA* 2. 145–52; 145f.): "That was the Reformational discovery" (*Martin Luther,* 223).
35. There are already preliminary formulations concerning Rom. 3.21 in the course

of lectures on the Epistle to the Romans (*WA* 56.256, 25–257, 33; cf. 172. 16–173. 18), but the main contrast here is still between righteousness of God and righteousness of man.

36. *WA* 2.504, 25–27; 490, 34–491, 5.
37. *WA* 2.520, 27f.
38. That is also the reason for the terse formulation "simultaneously sinner and just," *WA* 56.272, 17; cf. 269, 30.
39. *WA* 54.179–87; after the translation by K. Aland, *Luther Deutsch* (Göttingen, 1962), vol. 2, 19f. For the question of the dating of the Reformational discovery described in this text, cf. E. Bizer, *Fides ex auditu: Eine Untersuchung über die Entdeckung der Gerechtigkeit Gottes durch Martin Luther.* 3rd ed. (Neukirchen, 1966) [1958]; H. Bornkamm, "Zur Frage der Iustitia Dei beim jungen Luther," *Archiv für Reformationsgeschichte* 52(1961): 16–29; 53(1962): 1–60; K. Aland, *Der Weg zur Reformation: Zeitpunkt und Charakter des reformatorischen Erlebnisses Martin Luthers* (Munich, 1965).
40. *WA* 4.318, 35–39; Ps. 118.24.
41. *WAT* 5. no. 5677; 317, 11–318, 3; 1546.
42. *WAT* 1. no. 674, 320 9f.; first half of the 1530s.
43. *WA* 43.582, 13.
44. *WA* 43.582, 30–32.
45. Thus K. A. Meissinger, *Luthers Exegese in der Frühzeit* (Leipzig, 1911), 36f. The same reproach, formulated more cautiously, is repeated forty years later: Meissinger, *Der katholische Luther* (Munich, 1952), 83.
46. *WAT* 5. no. 5511; 204, 24f.; winter 1542.
47. *WAT* 5.204, 17.
48. E.g., *WA* 3.81, 24f.
49. *WA* 30 II. 637, 19–22; 1530.
50. *WAT* 5. no. 6419; 653, 1–18.
51. *WAT* 1. no. 116; 44, 16–20; Nov. 1531.
52. *WA* 50.198, 25–29; Schmalkaldic Articles, 1538.
53. *WA* 18.689, 24f.; 1525.
54. *WA* 30 II. 535, 37–536, 2; 1530.
55. *WA* 1.52, 15–18.
56. *WA* 5.537, 16–22; Ps. 17.45.

VI. THE REFORMER ATTACKED

1. *WA* 30 I. 209, 22–210, 8.
2. For the power of fear in the Middle Ages cf. S. E. Ozment, *The Reformation in the Cities* (New Haven, 1975), 22–46; T. N. Tentler, *Sin and Confession on the Eve of the Reformation* (Princeton, 1977). Interpreted as part of a larger

phenomenon by B. Hamm, *Frömmigkeitstheologie am Anfang des 16. Jahrhunderts* (Tübingen, 1982), 218f.

3. *WA* 30 I. 210, 33f.; 1529.
4. *WA* 1.525, 4–6; 1518. Cf. D. C. Steinmetz, *Luther and Staupitz* (Durham, N.C., 1980); with further bibliography.
5. Johannes Manlius, *Locorum communium collectanea* (Basel, 1563), vol. 3, 14; cited by O. Scheel, *Martin Luther: Vom Katholizismus zur Reformation*, vol. 2, 3rd and 4th ed. (Tübingen, 1930), 367, note 1.
6. Cf. the critical edition of Johann von Staupitz, *Lateinische Schriften II: Libellus de exsecutione aeternae praedestinationis*, ed. L. Graf zu Dohna and R. Wetzel (Berlin, 1979).
7. *WAT* 5. no. 5374; 1540.
8. Johann von Staupitz, *Tübinger Predigten*, ed. G. Buchwald, E. Wolf (Leipzig, 1927), Sermo 20.168, 40; cf. 3.14, 11f.; 5.27, 11; 9.66, 38–41; 11.86, 11f.; 18.148, 40ff. Cf. "Teufel, Welt, Fleisch," in Staupitz, *Lateinische Schriften II*, 109, note 20.
9. Staupitz, *Tübinger Predigten*, 26.205, 40f.
10. *WAT* 2. no. 1490; 112, 10–14. In the course of his Psalm lectures, Luther mentioned Bernard of Clairvaux around Christmas of 1514 as a witness to the accentuation of Christ's wounds as the only refuge from the Devil, world, and flesh (*WA* 3.640, 40f).
11. *WA* 43.457, 32–463, 17.
12. First published in Leipzig in 1490–91. See the series *Spätmittelalter und Reformation* (de Gruyter, Berlin), the critical edition of Joh. V. Paltz, *Werke*, vol. 3 (Berlin, 1989), 155–284. For a comprehensive survey of the theology of Johannes von Paltz, see B. Hamm, *Frömmigkeitstheologie.*
13. *WABr* 2.264, 42–48; 9 Feb. 1521.
14. *WA* 43.582; 15; 31f.
15. Staupitz, *Lateinische Schriften II*, § 71, p. 156; §77, p. 158.
16. Staupitz, *Lateinische Schriften II*, §106, p. 184; §113, p. 190.
17. Concerning the externality of grace, see above all K-H. zur Mühlen, *Nos extra nos: Luthers Theologie zwischen Mystik und Scholastik* (Tübingen, 1972), 93–147.
18. *WA* 56.272, 17.
19. Cf. my article: "Simul gemitus et raptus: Luther und die Mystik" in *Kirche, Mystik, Heiligung und das Natürliche bei Luther*, ed. I. Asheim (Göttingen, 1967).
20. *WAT* 1. no. 352; 147, 3–14; autumn 1532.
21. *WAT* 5. no. 5348; 77, 6; Aug. 1540.
22. *WA* 51.543, 13f.; 1541.
23. *WABr* 1.188, 23; 8 Aug. 1518 to Spalatin, who was present at the Diet of Augsburg.
24. *WA* 2.609, 12–14; 1519.
25. *WAT* 1. no. 884; 442, 1–5; first half of the 1530s.

26. *EA lat. var. arg.* 1.273f.
27. *Werden und Wertung der Reformation,* 190–92, with note 89.
28. Ibid. 192, note 90.
29. *WA* 1.236, 22–30.
30. *WA* 1.525, 10–12; 1518. In early 1518 Luther had developed these thoughts—probably in a Lenten sermon—in the language of mysticism: *WA* 1.319, 27–31.
31. *WA* 51.540, 27; 1541.
32. J. Benzing, *Lutherbibliographie: Verzeichnis der gedruckten Schriften Martin Luthers bis zu dessen Tod* (Baden-Baden, 1966), nos. 87–89.
33. *WA* 51.541, 4–6.
34. *WA* 3.416, 27f.; 424, 22f.; gloss Ps. 68; approx. autumn 1514. For a circumspect reconstruction of the chronology of this course of lectures, see *Luthers Werke in Auswahl,* ed. E. Vogelsang (Bonn edition, vol. 5), 3rd ed. (Berlin, 1963), 40.
35. *Akten und Briefe zur Kirchenpolitik Herzog Georgs von Sachsen,* ed. F. Gess, vol. 1 (Leipzig, 1905), 29.
36. J. Benzing, *Lutherbibliographie,* nos. 90–114.
37. *WA* 1.245, 21–23; 246, 27f.
38. *WA* 1.324, 15.
39. See the letter to his councilors in Magdeburg, cited by W. Borth, *Die Luthersache (causa Lutheri) 1517–1524: Die Anfänge der Reformation als Frage von Politik und Recht* (Lübeck, Hamburg, 1970), 29f.
40. Cf. B. Tierney, *Origins of Papal Infallibility, 1150–1350: A Study on the Concepts of Infallibility, Sovereignty and Tradition in the Middle Ages* (Leiden, 1972), 273–81.
41. R. P. fratris Silvestri Prieriatis . . . in presumptuosas Martini Lutheri conclusiones de potestate papae dialogus (Rome, 1518); *EA lat. var. arg.* 1.341–77; 346f.
42. *EA lat. var. arg.* 1.347.
43. *WA* 1.647, 19–21.
44. *WA* 1.647, 33f.
45. For the following, cf. G. Hennig, *Cajetan und Luther: Ein historischer Beitrag zur Begegnung von Thomismus und Reformation* (Stuttgart, 1966); G. Müller, "Die römische Kurie und die Anfänge der Reformation," *Zeitschrift für Religions- und Geistesgeschichte* 19(1967): 1–32; O. H. Pesch, "'Das heisst eine neue Kirche bauen': Luther und Cajetan in Augsburg," in *Begegnung: Beiträge zu einer Hermeneutik des theologischen Gesprächs. Festschrift H. Fries,* ed. M. Seckler, O. H. Pesch, et al. (Graz, Vienna, Cologne, 1972), 645–61; *Lutherprozess und Lutherbann: Vorgeschichte, Ergebnis, Nachwirkung,* ed. R. Bäumer (Münster i.W., 1972).

46. Th. Kolde, *Augustiner-Congregation,* Exkurs 3; pp. 411f.
47. Cf. G. Müller, *Die römische Kurie und die Reformation 1523–1534: Kirche und Politik während des Pontifikates Clemens' VII* (Gütersloh, 1969), 113–88; 212f.
48. Cf. H. Wiesflecker, *Kaiser Maximilian I: Das Reich, Österreich und Europa an der Wende zur Neuzeit,* vol. 4 (Munich, 1981), 389–403; 395.
49. *Acta Augustana, WA* 2.23, 36–25, 3.
50. *WABr* 1.208, 4f.; 3 or 4 Oct. 1518; cf. the original discovered in an attic in Boston: *WABr* 12. 14, 15f.; 4 Oct. 1518.
51. *WAT* 2. no. 2668a; 595, 30–32 and b; 596, 27–29; Sept. 1532.
52. *WABr* 1.214, 13; cf. 217, 60; both 14 Oct. 1518; 243, 307; and Nov. 1518.
53. Cf. Th. Kolde, *Augustiner-Congregation,* 321. Cf. Staupitz's letter to Elector Frederick on 15 Oct. 1518; supplement 16, pp. 443f.
54. *WABr* 2.298, 8–13; 14 April 1521.
55. *Der Andere und Letzte Theil zu Wilh. Ernst Tentzels . . . Historischen Bericht . . .* (Leipzig, 1718), 38; cited by I. Höss, *Georg Spalatin 1484–1545: Ein Leben in der Zeit des Humanismus und der Reformation* (Weimar, 1956), 195, note 33.
56. *Die Depeschen des Nuntius Aleander vom Wormser Reichstage 1521,* ed. P. Kalkoff, 2d ed. (Halle, 1897), letter 18, 166f. (1st ed. Halle, 1886, *Schriften des Vereins für Reformationsgeschichte* 17, 133).
57. *Die Depeschen des Nuntius Aleander,* 171 (1st ed., 138).
58. *Die Depeschen des Nuntius Aleander,* 176 (1st ed., 143); cf. *1521–1971: Luther in Worms: Ein Quellenbuch,* ed. J. Rogge (Witten, 1971), 101, note 17.
59. *WA* 51, 543, 3–10; 1541.
60. *Die Depeschen des Nuntius Aleander,* 204 (1st ed., 162).
61. *WA* 7.834–38; *Luther in Worms,* 97–101.
62. This is the concluding sentence in German as presented in the later Wittenberg printing. The short form "God help me. Amen" is better substantiated. Cf. *Reichstagsakten* 2.555. Concerning the interpretation, cf. K. V. Selge, "Capta conscientia in verbis Dei, Luthers Widerrufsverweigerung in Worms," in *Der Reichstag zu Worms von 1521: Reichspolitik und Luthersache,* ed. F. Reuter (Worms, 1971), 180–207; esp. pp. 200f., note 46; B. Lohse, "Luthers Antwort in Worms," *Luther* 29 (1958): 124–34; M. G. Baylor, *Action and Person: Conscience in Late Scholasticism and the Young Luther* (Leiden, 1977), 264–67.
63. *Reichstagsakten* 2.654, 16–20.
64. Leopold von Ranke, *Deutsche Geschichte im Zeitalter der Reformation,* vol. 1, book 2, chap 4, 6th ed. (Leipzig, 1881) [Berlin 1839], 332 (ed. Munich, Leipzig, 1924, 348f.).
65. Leopold von Ranke, *Deutsche Geschichte,* 333 (ed. 1924, 350).
66. For Luther's influence and view of himself as a political counselor, cf. E. Wolgast, *Die Wittenberger Theologie und die Politik der evangelischen Stände: Studien zu Luthers Gutachten in politischen Fragen* (Gütersloh, 1977), 285–99.

67. Cf. W. Borth, *Die Luthersache,* Exkurs I, 168–71; H.-Chr. Rublack, "Gravamina und Reformation," in *Städtische Gesellschaft und Reformation: Kleine Schriften 2,* ed. I. Bátori (Stuttgart, 1980), 292–313.
68. First rejection of Hutten as early as Jan. 1521; *WABr* 2.249, 12–15.
69. *WA* 10 III. 400, 16–24; sermon on All Saints' Day 1522.

VII. LIFE BETWEEN GOD AND THE DEVIL

1. For a balanced characterization, one can still consult J. Huizinga, *Erasmus* (Haarlem, 1924). For an excellent account with more recent literature, cf. D. Tracy, *Erasmus: The Growth of a Mind* (New York, 1978).
2. "Duae res sunt Deus et Scriptura Dei, non minus quam duae res sunt, Creator et creatura Dei" (*De servo arbitrio; WA* 18.606, 11f).
3. *WABr* 1.171, 71–74; 9 May 1518. For Augustine cf. letter 82, *Corpus Scriptorum Ecclesiasticorum Latinorum* 34, 2.1898, 354; furthermore, 1 John 4.1; Gal. 1.6; 1 Thess. 5.21, Cf. also the second course of lectures on the Psalms; *AWA* 2.500, 6–8.
4. *AWA* 2.449, 14–17.
5. *WA* 18.781, 8–10.

VIII. DISCORD IN THE REFORMATION

1. *WABr* 4.282, 6–9; 17 Nov. 1527; cf. 325, note 8.
2. *WABr* 4.319, 9f.; 1 Jan. 1528.
3. *WA* 6.450, 1–21.
4. *WA* 6.408, 11f.
5. *WA* 10 II. 243, 33; 1522; for Thomas Münzer, whom Luther considered the prototype of a diabolically dangerous fanatic, cf. W. Elliger, *Thomas Müntzer: Leben und Werk* (Göttingen, 1975); E. Wolgast, *Thomas Müntzer: Ein Verstörer der Ungläubigen* (Göttingen, 1981).
6. *WABr* 2.427, 117–20; Jan. 1522.
7. *Grosser Katechismus,* part 4; *WA* 30 I. 212, 26–30.
8. *WA* 30 I. 218, 32f.
9. *WA* 30 I. 217, 15–38.
10. *WA* 30 I. 219, 22–26.
11. Cf. the parallel unmasking of magic in the "Nominalistic hammer of excessive belief in witches" (*Werden und Wertung der Reformation,* 221f).
12. Cf. B. Lohse, *Mönchtum und Reformation* (Göttingen, 1963), 167–69; B. Hamm, *Frömmigkeitstheologie am Anfang des 16. Jahrhunderts* (Tübingen, 1982), 294f.

13. Cf. the arguments in the debate between Kurt Aland and Joachim Jeremias: J. Jeremias, *Die Kindertaufe in den ersten vier Jahrhunderten* (Göttingen, 1958); K. Aland, *Die Säuglingstaufe im Neuen Testament und in der alten Kirche* (Munich, 1961); J. Jeremias, *Nochmals: Die Anfänge der Kindertaufe* (Munich, 1962).
14. *WA* 26.462, 4f.; *Vom Abendmahl Christi, Bekenntnis;* 1528.
15. *WA* 6.511, 26–38; 1520.
16. *WABr* 3.361, 16f.; 27 Oct. 1524.
17. Thus B. Moeller, *Reichsstadt und Reformation* (Gütersloh, 1962; revised ed., Berlin, 1987); cf. T. A. Brady, Jr., *Ruling Class, Regime and Reformation at Strasbourg, 1520–1555* (Leiden, 1978).
18. Cf. G. W. Locher, *Streit unter Gästen: Die Lehre aus der Abendmahlsdebatte der Reformatoren für das Verständnis und die Feier des Abendmahles heute* (Zurich, 1972).
19. *WA* 6.513, 34–514, 16.
20. Cf. my criticism of the thesis of "Luther's relapse into the Middle Ages" in *Werden und Wertung der Reformation,* 368f.
21. *Reichstagsakten* 7/2. 1277, 29–31.
22. Hedio's report in *Das Marburger Religionsgespräch 1529,* ed. G. May (Gütersloh, 1970), 23; cf. the account by Zurich professor Collins, ibid. 36.
23. *WABr* 5.154, 16; 4 Oct. 1529.
24. Cf. E. Wolgast, *Die Wittenberger Theologie und die Politik der evangelischen Stände:. Studien zu Luthers Gutachten in politischen Fragen* (Gütersloh, 1977).
25. Matt. 11.28; *WA* 1.331, 6–14; cf. G. Ebeling, *Luther: Einführung in sein Denken,* 4th ed. (Tübingen, 1981), 178–97.
26. *Huldreich Zwinglis Sämtliche Werke,* vol. 1 (CR 88) (Berlin, 1905), 82, 4f.
27. *WA* 1.333, 13–26.
28. *WA* 31 I. 416, 36–417, 1; 1530.
29. *WA* 12.215, 18–30; Formulae Missae. For the development of Luther's Eucharistic doctrine in the years 1523–27, cf. H. Grass, *Die Abendmahlslehre bei Luther und Calvin,* 2d ed. (Gütersloh, 1954); A. Peters, *Realpräsenz: Luthers Zeugnis von Christi Gegenwart im Abendmahl* (Berlin, 1960).
30. *WA* 23.151, 15; 1527.
31. *WA* 23.259, 4–7.
32. *WA* 23.71, 24–27.
33. G. May, *Marburger Religionsgespräch,* 56f.
34. Ibid., 56.
35. Ibid.
36. Cf. the clear outline of the basic differences by G. W. Locher, *Die Zwinglische Reformation im Rahmen der europäischen Kirchengeschichte* (Göttingen, 1979), 283–343.
37. G. May, *Marburger Religionsgespräch,* 19.
38. Ibid.

IX. CHRISTIANITY BETWEEN GOD AND THE DEVIL

1. *AWA* 2.422, 8–13; exegesis of Ps. 7.7–10; after the translation by Stephan Roth: *Das Erste Teyl der Lateinischen auslegung des Psalters Doctor Martin Luthers: Verdeudschet durch Stephanum Rodt* (Wittenberg, 1527), 266.
2. *WABr* 1.475, 352f.; August 1519.
3. *AWA* 2.85f.
4. *WABr* 1.471, 213–19; Aug. 1519.
5. T. Harnack, *Luthers Theologie mit besonderer Beziehung auf seine Versöhnungs- und Erlösungslehre*, 2 vols. (Erlangen, 1862), 1886.
6. *AWA* 2.389, 15f.; exegesis of Ps. 6.11.
7. J. Lortz, *Die Reformation in Deutschland*, 6th ed. (Freiburg, 1982) [1939/40], vol. 1, 394–96.
8. *AWA* 2.408, 23–26.
9. *WA* 30 I. 190, 7f.
10. *WA* 3.13, 28.
11. *WA* 3.13,25f.; *WA* 55 I/1.10, 7f.
12. *WAT* 4. no. 4149; 170, 21–23; 1538.
13. *WA* 4.345, 19–28.
14. *WA* 50.250, 1–4; 1537.
15. *WA* 50.641, 35–642, 7. 16f.
16. *WA* 50.642, 7f.
17. *WA* 50.642, 12–17.
18. *WA* 3.424, 11–14.
19. *WAT* 3.349, 29f; no. 3479a; 1536.
20. Cf. I. Höss, *Georg Spalatin 1484–1545: Ein Leben in der Zeit des Humanismus und der Reformation* (Weimar, 1956), 80, 89.
21. *WA* 50. 5, 26–28; 1536.
22. *WABr* 2.48, 22–49, 28; 24 Feb. 1520.
23. *WABr* 1.353, 24f.; Feb. 1519.
24. *WA* 3.433, 18–20; autumn 1514, perhaps shortly before All Saints' Day.
25. *WA* 1.238, 14f. Not even given further attention by Luther in his 1518 commentary (*WA* 1.628, 18f).
26. *WA* 1.238, 16–21; 628, 21–28.
27. *WA* 1.631, 23–32; 1518.
28. *AWA* 2.597, 19–22.
29. *WABr* 3.239, note 3.
30. "by creating new martyrs, for that region probably the very first." *WABr* 3.115, 14–16; 22/23 July 1523. It would not have eluded Spalatin that Luther speaks of "creating" martyrs the way the pope "creates" bishops and saints according to canon law.
31. *WA* 35.411–15; modernized version in *Kaiser, Gott und Bauer: Die Zeit des*

Deutschen Bauernkrieges im Spiegel der Literatur, ed. G. Jäckel (Berlin, 1975), 288–91.

32. *AWA* 2.605, 6–14; ca. March 1520. Cf. as early as *WA* 1.627, 27–34; May 1518.
33. *WABr* 6.179, 23–29; 3 Sept. 1531 to the Augustinian prior in Cambridge and Oxford doctor of theology Robert Barnes, who became a Protestant martyr nine years later by order of the king. Cf. *WA* 51.445. Cf. A. G. Dickens, *The English Reformation,* 2d ed. (London, 1964), 58f., 102–04.
34. *WA* 51.449, 7–17.
35. *WA* 51.569, 13–16; *Wider Hans Worst,* 1541.

X. WEDDED BLISS AND WORLD PEACE

1. Ludwig Feuerbach, *Das Wesen des Christentums* (1841), ed. K. Quenzel (Leipzig, 1904), chap. 18, 253–62.
2. *WA* 10 II. 279, 19–21; 1522. A year later Luther increased the number: there is not one Christian in a hundred thousand (*WA* 12.115, 20f.; 1523).
3. *WA* 12.94, 28f.; 1523.
4. *WA* 18.277, 26–36; 27 March 1525.
5. In 1523 Luther had translated Gen. 2.18 differently: "Ich will yhm eyn gehulffen gegen[!] yhm machen." *WADB* 8.42f.
6. *WA* 18.275, 19–28; 1525. For the comparison with Augustine, Gregory the Great, and Thomas Aquinas, cf. C. T. Wood, "The Doctor's Dilemma: Sin, Salvation, and the Menstrual Cycle in Medieval Thought," *Speculum* 56(1981): 710–27; with further bibliography.
7. *WA* 37.446, 1–447, 4; sermon 5, June 1534.
8. *Die Bekenntnisschriften der evangelisch-lutherischen Kirche. Hrsg. im Gedenkjahr der Augsburgischen Konfession 1930,* 5th ed. (Göttingen, 1963), 648, 9–16 (*Grosser Katechismus*); cf. *Kleiner Katechismus,* 510, 33–36.
9. *WA* 18.277, 26–35; March 1525.
10. In a significant and frank tribute from his own ranks, Denifle's style of treating Luther is characterized as follows: "The reader is almost overwhelmed by the force of the one-sided, destructive and mordant criticism that is aimed at annihilating the opponent" (H. Grauert, *P. Heinrich Denifle O. P.: Ein Wort zum Gedächtnis und zum Frieden: Ein Beitrag auch zum Luther-Streit* (Freiburg i. Br., 1906), 7f. First published in *Historisches Jahrbuch* 26(1905): 959–1018; 966). For the totally different style and open-minded approach of modern Catholic Luther research, cf. B. Lohse, *Martin Luther: Eine Einführung in sein Leben sein und Werk* (Munich, 1981), 240–43.
11. H. Denifle, *Luther und Luthertum in der ersten Entwicklung,* vol. I/1 (Mainz, 1904), 115.

12. *WA* 10 II. 156, 13–22.
13. H. Denifle, *Luther und Luthertum*, I/1, 113.
14. *WABr* 3.635, 22–28; 6 Dec. 1525.
15. *WAT* 2. no. 2034; summer 1531.
16. *WA* 10 II. 296, 31; 1522.
17. *WAT* 1. no. 1006; 505, 22–25; first half of the 1530s.
18. *WA* 50.633, 20–24; 1539; WAT 1. no. 1229; 611, 19–27; cf. *WAT* 6. no. 6567; 46, 37–40.
19. *WABr* 3.482, 81–83; 4(5?) May 1525.
20. *WABr* 4.210, 14f.
21. *WAT* 2. no. 2590b; 534, 12–14; April 1532. Thus the three children are Hans, Magdalena, and Martin.
22. Cf. the receipts for Luther's salary in the years 1534–42. *WABr* 12.423–27.
23. *WABr* 9.583, 147; 1536.
24. *WAT* 1. no. 49; 17, 10–12; summer/autumn 1531.
25. *WAT* 1. no. 1110; 554, 25f.; first half of the 1530s.
26. *WABr* 3.541, 8; 21 June 1525.
27. *WABr* 9.205, 1–3; 26 July 1540.
28. *WAT* 4. no. 4786; 503, 22. Cf. *WABr* 3, 474, 13–475, 14; to Spalatin, 16 April 1525. Concerning Ave, or Eva, von Schönfeld, cf. E. Kroker, *Katharina von Bora: Martin Luthers Frau*, 2d ed. (Zwickau, 1925), 45. 63.
29. G. Weyer, *Ephemerides, oder Kurtze Jahr und Tag-Geschichten vom Auff- und Untergang dess Lutherischen ersten Evangelij und des Melanchthonis Augsburgischer Confession*, 1679, fol. 54–56.
30. *Der Briefwechsel des Justus Jonas*, ed. G. Kawerau, vol. 1 (Halle, 1884), no. 90; p. 94, 3–9.
31. *WABr* 11.287, 36; 7 Feb. 1546.
32. *WABr* 11.286, 13–15.
33. *WABr* 11.287, 39–44.
34. *WABr* 11.286, 9–12.
35. *WABr* 3.533, 8f.; to Spalatin, 16 June 1525.
36. Köstlin-Kawerau, *Martin Luther II*, 478; J. Lortz, *Die Reformation in Deutschland*, vol. 2, 6th ed. (Freiburg i. Br., 1982), 247.
37. *WABr* 4.140, 14–17; 28 Nov. 1526.
38. *WABr* 6.179, 27f., 182, 150–53; to Robert Barnes (†1540), 3 Sept. 1531.
39. Very vivid in *WA* 30 III. 242, 9–243, 30; *Von Ehesachen*, 1530.
40. *WA* 30 III. 243, 23–25. For a balanced view with a bibliography of more recent literature see M. E. Schild, "Ehe, Eherecht, Ehescheidung, VII: Reformationszeit," in *Theologische Realenzyklopädie*, vol. 9 (Berlin, 1982), 336–46.
41. *Philippi Melanchthonis Opera quae supersunt omnia*, vol. 3 (CR3) (Halle, 1836) [Reprint Frankfurt a. Main, New York, 1963], 862. Cf. W. W. Rockwell, *Die*

Doppelehe des Landgrafen Philipp von Hessen (Marburg, 1904), 29; draft in supplement I, 312–18.

42. *Briefwechsel Landgraf Philipp's des Grossmüthigen von Hessen mit Bucer,* ed. M. Lenz, vol. 1 (Leipzig, 1880), 160.
43. Rockwell, *Doppelehe,* 152, note 2.
44. *WAT* 4, no. 3976; 50, 33–35; Aug. 1538.
45. Rockwell, *Doppelehe,* 19.
46. Lortz, *Die Reformation in Deutschland* 2: 246.
47. Thus Philipp to Luther (*WABr* 9.83, 13f.; 5 Apr. 1540).
48. *WABr* 9.90, 9; 10 April 1540.
49. K. Heussi, *Kompendium der Kirchengeschichte,* 16th ed. (Tübingen, 1981; 1907–09), 308, note 1.
50. *WA* 6.347, 22–28. According to Brecht this passage should be attributed to Melanchthon. But cf. *WA* 6.347, 22–24.
51. Cf. the excellent survey of modern literature in F. Winterhager, *Bauernkriegsforschung* (Darmstadt, 1981).
52. *WA* 18.361, 4–6. Cf. H. Bornkamm, *Martin Luther,* 330–36.
53. *WA* 18.361, 24–26. Very balanced with futher literature: J. Wallmann, "Ein Friedensappell: Luthers letztes Wort im Bauernkrieg," in *Festschrift Ernst Steinbach* (Tübingen, 1976), 57–75.
54. *WA* 53.417–552; 420, 29; 1543. For the subject of Luther and the Jews plus further bibliography, see my account in *Wurzeln des Antisemitismus: Christenangst und Judenplage im Zeitalter von Humanismus und Reformation,* 2d ed. (Berlin, 1983).
55. *WA* 53.523, 1–526, 16.
56. *WA* 53.522, 34–37.
57. Cf. B. Lohse, *Martin Luther* (Munich, 1981), 190–97.
58. On this subject cf. G. Ebeling, "Die Notwendigkeit der Lehre von den zwei Reichen," in *Wort und Glaube,* vol. 1, 3rd ed. (Tübingen, 1967), 407–28.
59. C. A. H. Burkhardt, "Die Judenverfolgung im Kurfürstentum Sachsen," *Theologische Studien und Kritiken* 70 (1897): 593–98.
60. Cf. S. Stern, *Josel von Rosheim: Befehlshaber der Judenschaft im Heiligen Römischen Reich Deutscher Nation* (Stuttgart, 1959).
61. *WA* 11.315, 25–27.
62. *WABr* 8.77–78; Wolfgang Capito to Luther, 26 April 1537.
63. *Doctor Johannsen Reuchlins . . . Augenspiegel* (Tübingen, 1511). Reprint in *Quellen zur Geschichte des Humanismus und der Reformation in Faksimile-Ausgaben,* vol. 5 (Munich, 1961), fol. H2^v
64. *WABr* 8.90, 1; 46–50; 32f.; 91, 56–60; Luther to Josel von Rosheim, 11 June 1537.
65. *WA* 51.195, 29–32.
66. *WA* 51.195, 39f.

67. *WA* 51.196, 4–6.
68. *WA* 51.196, 16f.
69. *WA* 53.522, 36; *Von den Juden und ihren Lügen,* 1543.
70. *WA* 51.196, 5.
71. Cf. the detailed explanation in *WA* 53.527, 15–31.
72. Johannes Eck, *Ains Judenbüechlins Verlegung: Wider die Verteidigung der Juden* (Ingolstadt, 1541). Eck's diatribe is directed against the Nuremberg reformer Andreas Osiander, who had dared to defend the Jews against the accusation of child-murder.
73. *WA* 53.526, 7–16; 528, 31–34. Cf. 520, 33–521, 7. In the same year, 1543, two further tracts concerning the Jews appeared: *Vom Schem Hamphoras* (*WA* 53.579–648) and the comparatively moderate *Von den letzten Worten Davids* (*WA* 54.28–100), in *Luther seine Argumente gegen die rabbinische Schriftauslegung ausbaut, um die Messiaserwartung als Christusverkündigung auszuweisen.*
74. *WA* 53.449, 26–29.
75. It is the religion of achievement, that "reasonable" principle of give and take, that wishes to gain the merciful God for itself by means of its own rites, laws, and works while bypassing the person and works of Christ: "Das ist religio Papae, Iudaeorum, Turcarum . . . 'si sic fecero, erit mihi deus clemens.'" *WA* 40 I. 603, 6–10.
76. For the range of medieval concepts of the Antichrist cf. M. Reeves, *The Influence of Prophecy in the Later Middle Ages: A Study in Joachimism* (Oxford, 1969), esp. 358–74; "Some Popular Prophecies from the Fourteenth to the Seventeenth Centuries," in *Studies in Church History, 8: Popular Belief and Practice* (Cambridge, 1972), 107–34; esp. 122f; and B. McGinn, *Visions of the End: Apocalyptic Traditions in the Middle Ages* (New York, 1979).
77. Jacobus Revius, *Over-ijsselsche sangen en dichten,* ed. W. A. P. Smit (Amsterdam, 1930), 222; Cf. *Protestantse poëzie der 16de en 17de eeuw,* ed. K. Heeroma (Amsterdam, 1940), 179; L. Strengholt, *Bloemen in Gethsemané: Verzamelde studies over de dichter Revius* (Amsterdam, 1976), 116–20.
78. The first appearance I have found is in *Ein Sermon von der Betrachtung des heiligen Leidens Christi,* 1519: "Alßo vill engster soll dir werden, wan du Christus leyden bedenckst, Dan die ubeltether, die Juden, wie sie nu gott gerichtet und vortrieben hatt, seynd sie doch deyner sunde diener gewest, unnd du bist warhafftig, der durch seyn sunde gott seynen sun erwurget und gecreutziget hatt, wie gesagt ist" (*WA* 2.138, 29–32). Cf. *WA* 9.652, 16–24 (1521); *WA* 28.233, 1f. (1528).
79. *WA* 35.576. Cf. *WAT* 6.257; no. 6897.
80. Already in the first course of Psalm lectures, cf. *WA* 3.564, 31f.
81. In the eighteenth century Johann Georg Hamann (†1788) employed this view of the Jews, in accordance with Luther's ideas, autobiographically: "I recognized my own crimes in the history of the Jewish people, I read [in it] my own

autobiography, and thanked God for His forbearance toward this His people, because nothing could be better justification of my own hopes of similar treatment" (Johann Georg Hamann, *Sämtliche Werke,* ed. J. Nadler, 6 vols. 1949–57, vol. 2, 40, 25–29; cited by O. Bayer, "Wer bin ich? Gott als Autor meiner Lebensgeschichte," *Theologische Beiträge* 11(1980): 245–61; 254).

82. B. Blumenkranz has presented an interesting collection, making no claims to completeness, of quotations on the Jews' sole responsibility for Christ's death: *Les Auteurs chrétiens latins du moyen âge sur les juifs et le judaisme* (Paris, 1963). Cf. also the results of his examination of the exegesis of the "Pro Iudaeis" prayer in the Maundy Thursday office: "Perfidia," *Archivum Latinitatis Medii Aevi* 22 (1952): 157–70; reprinted in *Juifs et Chrétiens: Patristique et Moyen Age* (London, 1977), vii.
83. "Hic est locus, ex quo debemus facere canticum und frolich sein, ut non sic recordemur passionis Christi, quomodo zusingen 'der arm Judas,' und stechen den Iudaeis die augen aus. . . . Yhr habt wol uber euch [Christen] zu weinen, quod estis damnatae et peccatrices. Ideo ipse flet et patitur pro nobis." ("Here now we should sing and be joyful that we do not carry the suffering of Christ in our hearts as much as we mock poor Judas and put out the Jews' eyes. You Christians have reason to cry over yourselves, you are the accursed sinners. That is why the Lord cries and suffers for you.") *WA* 36.136, 29–32, 36–137, 2; sermon on 24 March 1532.

XI. THE MAN AND HIS DEEDS

1. *WA* 59.472 1237–39, 1248 f.; 494, 1903–, 495, 1909.
2. Preface to his *Address to the Christian Nobility;* Eccles. 3.7; *WA* 6.404, 11f.
3. Two years later, on 29 May 1523, Luther named Hieronymus Emser (†1527) and Johann Fabri (†1541). *WABr* 3.76, 72; 77, 84–94. For Fabri's work as a Counter-Reformer, cf. *Werden und Wertung der Reformation,* 281–93; for Emser, ibid., 325f.
4. *WABr* 3.96, 19–21; 20 June 1523 to Oecolampadius in Basel, where Erasmus lived until 1529. For Erasmus' reaction on 21 Nov., cf. ibid., 97, note 5.
5. *WABr* 2.544, 12f.; 28 May 1522.
6. *WABr* 2.544, 19f.
7. *WABr* 2.545, 23–28.
8. Cf. R. J. Sider, *Andreas Bodenstein von Karlstadt: The Development of His Thought, 1517–1525* (Leiden, 1974); U. Bubenheimer, "Scandalum et ius divinum: Theologische und rechtstheologische Probleme der ersten reformatorischen Innovationen in Wittenberg 1521/22," in *Zeitschrift der Savigny-Stiftung für Rechtsgeschichte* 90, Kan. Abt. 59 (1973): 263–342; U. Bubenheimer, *Consonantia Theologiae et Iurisprudentiae: Andreas Bodenstein*

von Karlstadt als Theologe und Jurist zwischen Scholastik und Reformation (Tübingen, 1977).

9. Cf. U. Bubenheimer, "Andreas Rudolff Bodenstein von Karlstadt: Sein Leben, seine Herkunft und seine innere Entwicklung," in *Andreas Bodenstein von Karlstadt 1480–1541: Festschrift der Stadt Karlstadt zum Jubiläumsjahr 1980,* 5–58; with further bibliography.
10. Cf. K.-H. zur Mühlen, "Luthers deutsche Bibelübersetzung als Gemeinschaftswerk," in *Eine Bibel—viele Übersetzungen: Not oder Notwendigkeit,* ed. S. Meurer (*Die Bibel in der Welt* 18) (Stuttgart, 1978), 90–97; with further bibliography.
11. *WABr* 2.423, 48–56; to Amsdorf, 13 Jan. 1522.
12. *Die Luther-Bibel: Entstehung und Weg eines Volksbuches,* ed. G. Hammer et al. (Stuttgart, 1980), 13.
13. *Mathesius' Predigten über Luthers Leben,* ed. G. Buchwald (Stuttgart, 1904), 186f.; and Johannes Mathesius, *Ausgewählte Werke,* vol. 3: *Luthers Leben in Predigten,* ed. G. Loesche, 2d ed. (Prague, 1906), 315f.; cf. *WADB* 4. xxixf.
14. *Mathesius' Predigten,* 189; *Ausgewählte Werke,* 319; *WAT* 5. no. 5468; 169, 6f.; 1542.
15. *Mathesius' Predigten,* 189; *Ausgewählte Werke,* 319.
16. *WABr* 5.327, 95–97; 20 May 1530.
17. *WABr* 5.374, 18–41; 19 June 1530.
18. *WABr* 5.639, 23f.; 1 Oct. 1530.
19. On this subject cf. Köstlin-Kawerau, *Martin Luther II,* 681f.
20. Cf. esp. H. O. Burger, "Luther im Spiegel der Tischreden," *Germanisch-romanische Monatsschrift* 54(1973): 385–403.
21. *WABr* 2.152, 23–153, 25; 20 July 1520.
22. *WABr* 5.379, 17–19; 19 June 1530.
23. *WABr* 5.351, 33–36; 5 June 1530.
24. *WABr* 5.379, 22–24; 19 June 1530.
25. Modern psychoanalysis interprets dreams of this sort differently, as a loss of strength, power, or potency. Freud himself mentions a popular belief that this dream is understood to indicate the death of a relative. See S. Freud, *Studienausgabe,* vol. 2: *Die Traumdeutung,* 3rd ed. (Frankfurt, a.M., 1972; 1900), 380; for the first time in the 1911 edition.
26. *WABr* 2.631, 46, Dec. 1522.
27. *WABr* 5.377f.; 19 June 1530; *Martin Luthers Briefe in Auswahl,* ed. R. Buchwald, vol. 2, 2d ed. (Leipzig, 1909), no. 191, pp. 86f.
28. *WAT* 5. no. 5490c; 186, 19–26; Sept. 1542.
29. *WABr* 2.368, 7f.; 1521.
30. E. H. Erikson, *Der junge Mann Luther: Eine psychoanalytische und historische Studie* (Frankfurt a.M., 1975; Munich, 1958), 256.
31. *WABr* 2.142, 8–143, 24; 147, 15–17; 151, 15; 163, 4–164, 10; 1520.

32. *WA* 37.176, 6f.
33. *WABr* 2.476, 20f.; 479, 36f.; 1522.
34. *WABr* 2.461, 66–70; to Elector Frederick, March 1522. This idea is recurrent with Luther; cf. the letter to Melanchthon of 27 Oct. 1527. *WABr* 4.272, 4–8.
35. *WABr* 2.455, 76–456, 85; March 1522.
36. *Ob man vor dem sterben fliehen möge; WA* 23.338–79; 1527.
37. *WABr* 11.286, 8–10; 7 Feb. 1546.
38. *WA* 23.347, 6f.; 1527; cited by H. Bornkamm, *Martin Luther,* 497.
39. Cf. G. Wingren, *Luthers Lehre vom Beruf* (Munich, 1952).
40. *WABr* 4.279, 8f.; ca. 10 Nov. 1527.
41. Rainer Maria Rilke, *Sämtliche Werke,* ed. E. Zinn, vol. 1 (Wiesbaden, 1955), 459f.
42. *WA* 35.423, 6–424, 3; *Evang. Kirchengesangbuch,* no. 239.
43. *WABr* 2.372, 84f.; 1 Aug. 1521.
44. *AWA* 2.303, 20; 319, 3.
45. *AWA* 2.318, 11; cf. Matt. 7.14.
46. *AWA* 2.318, 3f.
47. *AWA* 2.312, 12.
48. Cf. the detailed account of the events in Köstlin-Kawerau, *Martin Luther II,* 168–78; and the sensitive interpretation in H. Bornkamm, *Martin Luther,* 489–96. Luther's own account of the crisis can be followed from the letter to Spalatin of 10 July 1527 to the report to Linck on 25 February 1528; the tribulations had now become "more endurable" (*WABr* 4.221, 8f., 387, 8f).
49. P. J. Reiter, *Martin Luthers Umwelt, Charakter und Psychose sowie die Bedeutung dieser Faktoren für seine Entwicklung und Lehre,* vol. 2 (Copenhagen, 1941), 576–83.
50. *Dr. Johannes Bugenhagens Briefwechsel,* ed. O. Vogt (Stettin 1888–99; Gotha, 1910) [reprint Hildesheim, 1966], 69, 19–70, 4. This prayer in Jonas's version is in F. Schulz, *Die Gebete Luthers: Edition, Bibliographie und Wirkungsgeschichte* (Gütersloh, 1976), nos. 47 and 279.
51. *Der Briefwechsel des Justus Jonas,* ed. G. Kawerau, 1st half (Halle, 1884), 105, 4f.
52. *Bugenhagen Briefwechsel,* 66, 8–15.
53. *Briefwechsel Justus Jonas,* 1.105, 21f.
54. *Bugenhagen Briefwechsel,* 66, 27–67, 8; cf. *Briefwechsel Justus Jonas,* 1.106, 6f.
55. *Bugenhagen Briefwechsel,* 66, 13–19.
56. *Briefwechsel Justus Jonas,* 1.106, 10–15.
57. *Bugenhagen Briefwechsel,* 67, 13–15.
58. *Bugenhagen Briefwechsel,* 67, 16–21; *Briefwechsel Justus Jonas,* 1.106, 31.
59. *Briefwechsel Justus Jonas,* 1.106, 34–40.
60. *WABr* 4.226, 9–13; 2 Aug. 1527.
61. *WABr* 4.228, 4; 12 Aug. 1527.
62. *WABr* 4.232, 24–26; 19 Aug. 1527.

63. *WABr* 4.235, 9–16; 21 Aug. 1527.
64. *WABr* 4.241, 28–242, 30; 31 Aug. 1527. This statement, written to his student Johannes Agricola, had to take a position on the way inspections were to be carried out in Electoral Saxony. The issue was to cause the most serious Reformation dispute apart from the question of the Eucharist. Luther writes about the dangers in such a way here as to allow Agricola to assume that Luther is on his side in the struggle against the promulgation of the law. Cf. the account by J. Rogge, *Johann Agricolas Lutherverständnis: Unter besonderer Berücksichtigung des Antinomismus* (Berlin, n.d.) [1960], esp. 109–18. Luther can take Melanchthon's side by virtue of the same experience (*WABr* 4.272, 13–21).
65. *WABr* 4.272, 30–32; 27 Oct. 1527.
66. *WABr* 4.319, 6–16; 1 Jan. 1528.

EPILOGUE: LUTHER AS HE WAS

1. Johannes Kessler, *Sabbata,* book 2, ed. E. Egli and R. Schoch (St. Gall, 1902), 65, 4f.
2. *Dr. Martin Luthers Sämmtliche Schriften,* ed. J. G. Walch, vol. 15. 2d ed. (St. Louis, 1899), 1200.
3. *WABr* 1.173, 11f.; 18 May 1518.
4. *WABr* 1.530, 56, with note 15.
5. *WABr* 4.148, 15f.; 1 Jan. 1527.
6. *WABr* 2.357, 18; 13 July 1521.
7. *WABr* 2.334, 6; 12 May 1521.
8. *WABr* 2.388, 29–33; 9 Sept. 1521; cf. the first account of 12 May, *WABr* 2.333, 34–38.
9. *WABr* 2.388, 33–35.
10. Cf. *WABr* 4.324, 81; Justus Jonas to Luther, 3 Jan. 1528; and Luther's precise information in order to help the town clerk of Nordhausen: *WABr* 4.342, 18–31; 6 Jan. 1528.
11. *WABr* 5.316, 16f.; 12 May 1530.
12. *Die handschriftliche Geschichte Ratzeberger's über Luther und seine Zeit,* ed. Chr. G. Neudecker (Jena, 1850), 105f.
13. *WAT* 3. no. 3733; Feb. 1538.
14. *WAT* 5. no. 5368; summer 1540.
15. *WAT* 3. no. 3746; Feb. 1538.
16. Cf. further information in *WABr* 8.46–48.

CHRONOLOGICAL OUTLINE

English titles to Luther's works are given as they appear in Martin Luther, *Works*, 55 vols., ed. Jaroslav Pelikan and Helmut T. Lehman (St. Louis: Concordia Publishing House, and Philadelphia: Fortress Press [formerly Muhlenberg Press], 1955–86). The *Small Catechism, Large Catechism,* and *Schmalkaldic Articles* are not included in this edition but are available in any of the editions of the Book of Concord (the Lutheran confessional writings).

Events in the Age of the Reformation	*Events in the Life of Martin Luther*
1453–56 Johannes Gutenberg: printing of the Vulgate	
1466 or 1469 *Desiderius Erasmus of Rotterdam (†1536)	
ca. 1480 *Andreas Bodenstein von Carlstadt (†1541)	
	1483 November 10: Born in Eisleben November 11: Baptism
1484 *Huldreich Zwingli (†1531)	1484–96/97 Youth and early schooling in Mansfeld
1485 Division of Saxony into electorate and duchy	
1485 *Johannes Bugenhagen (†1558)	
1486 *Johannes Eck (†1543)	
1492 Discovery of America by Christopher Columbus	
1493 *Justus Jonas (†1555)	
1493–1519 Emperor Maximilian I	
1496 Marital alliance between the house of Hapsburg and the royal house of Spain	
1497 *Philipp Melanchthon (†1560)	1497 Attends school in Magdeburg

*Asterisk indicates a birth date.
†Dagger precedes a death date.

1500 *King and Emperor Charles (I)V (†1558)

1498–1501 Attends Latin School in Eisenach

1501 Matriculates at the University of Erfurt; studies at the arts faculty

1502 Foundation of the University of Wittenberg

1503 Johannes von Staupitz (†1524) becomes vicar general of the Augustinian Observant congregation

1505 Master of arts examination; begins studying law in Erfurt
July 2: Surprised by a thunderstorm near Stotternheim, Luther vows to become a monk.
July 17: Enters the monastery of the Augustinian Eremites in Erfurt

1507 Pope Julius II offers an indulgence for the rebuilding of St. Peter's in Rome

1507 April 3: Ordained at the Cathedral Church of St. Mary in Erfurt

1509 *John Calvin (†1564)

1509–47 *King Henry VIII of England

1510/11 Luther sent to Rome because of the Observant controversy

1511 late summer: final transferral to Wittenberg

1512–17 Fifth Lateran Council

1512 October 18/19: Receives the degree of doctor of theology; becomes professor of biblical theology

1513–21 Pope Leo X

1513–15 First course of lectures on the Psalms (*Dictata super Psalterium*)

1513–45 Albrecht of Brandenburg, archbishop of Magdeburg and (from 1514) of Mainz, administrator of Halberstadt; deeply in debt as a result of cumulation of offices

1515–47 King Francis I of France

1516 Erasmus of Rotterdam: *Novum instrumentum,* the first Greek edition of the New Testament

1515/16 Lectures on the Epistle to the Romans

1517 January: Johannes von Staupitz, *Büchlein über die Prädestination* (Little book concerning predestination)

1517 September: Luther's disputation against scholastic theology—fundamental repudiation of

Johann Tetzel promotes indulgences in Brandenburg and Magdeburg regions; half of the proceeds going toward the debts of Albrecht of Mainz

Aristotelianism
October 31: Posting of the ninety-five theses at the Castle Church of Wittenberg and demand that Archbishop Albrecht of Mainz put an end to the abuse of indulgences
Luther is denounced in Rome by Albrecht; the curia takes the theses as an attack on the authority of the pope.

1518 *Dialogue Concerning the Authority of the Pope,* treatise by the Dominican Silvester Prierias, court theologian of Roman curia
Imperial diet in Augsburg

1518 April: disputation in Heidelberg in the milieu of the chapter of the German Augustinian congregation

October 12–14: Questioning by Cardinal Cajetan after the Diet of Augsburg; Luther refuses to recant
December 8(?): Elector Frederick rejects Cajetan's petition to extradite Luther or banish him

1519 January 3: Death of Emperor Maximilian
June 28: Election of Charles V as king of Germany

1519–21 Hernán Cortés conquers and destroys the Aztec empire in Mexico. Ferdinand Magellan and his men make the first voyage around the world

1519–21 Second course of lectures on the Psalms (*Operationes in Psalmos*)
June 27–July 16: Disputation in Leipzig, with Luther and Carlstadt against Eck
Condemnation of Luther's theology by the Universities of Cologne and Louvain

1520 Johannes von Staupitz gives up his post as vicar general of the Augustinian congregation
October 23: Coronation of Charles V in Aachen as "elected Roman Emperor"

1520 Hutten and Sickingen offer Luther their help
June 15: Papal bull threatening excommunication, *Exsurge Domine*
August: *Address to the Christian Nobility of the German Nation*
October 6: *The Babylonian Captivity of the Church*
October 10: Luther receives the bull threatening excommunication
November: *The Freedom of a Christian*
December 10: Burning of the bull *Exsurge Domine* and canon law before the Elster Gate in Wittenberg

1521 January 27: Opening of the imperial diet in Worms
April 17/18: Wounding and conversion of Ignatius of Loyola (†1556)
December: Philipp Melanchthon's *Loci communes,* the first systematic survey of Reformational theology

1521 January 3: Excommunicated by Pope Leo X
March 6: Summons to the Diet of Worms
April 17/18: Questioning at the Diet of Worms before the emperor and empire; Luther refuses to recant
May 4: Taken into protective custody by his sovereign near Eisenach on his way home from the diet
May 4–March 1, 1522: at Wartburg Castle as Junker Jörg
May 8: Edict of Worms, signed by the emperor on May 26; imperial ban imposed on Luther and his followers

1521/22 "Wittenberg troubles"

December–end of February 1522: Translation of the New Testament in eleven weeks

1522–23 Pope Hadrian VI
Beginning of the Reformation in Zurich

1522 March: Luther's return from Wartburg; Eight sermons (*Invokavit sermons*) against the reform measures introduced in Wittenberg (*The Eight Wittenberg Sermons*)
September: The New Testament appears in print ("September Testament")

1523 March 6: Edict of the Diet of Nuremberg: enforcement of the Edict of Worms postponed; Hadrian VI presents to the Diet of Nuremberg a renewal program (papacy's admission of guilt)
July 1: The first martyrs of the Reformation, Augustinians Johann von Essen and Heinrich Voss from Antwerp, burned at the stake in Brussels

1523 Luther resumes his lectures
December: Working out of an Evangelical liturgy (*Formula missae*)
Major writings: *Dass Jesus ein geborner Jude sei* (*That Jesus Christ Was Born a Jew*); *Von weltlicher Obrigkeit* (*Temporal Authority: To What Extent It Should Be Obeyed*)

1523–34 Pope Clement VII

1524 Landgrave Philip of Hesse joins the Reformation
August: Beginning of the peasants' revolts in southwestern Germany

1524 October 9: Luther abandons his religious habit
Major writings: *Brief an die Fürsten zu Sachsen von dem aufrührerischen Geist*

Erasmus of Rotterdam: *De libero arbitrio* (*Concerning Free Will*)
Thomas Münzer's diatribe against Luther: *Hoch verursachte Schutzrede wider das geistlose sanft lebende Fleisch zu Wittenberg* (Speech against the Mindless Soft-living Flesh in Wittenberg)

(*Letter to the Princes of Saxony Concerning the Rebellious Spirit*), against Thomas Münzer; *An die Ratsherren aller Städte deutsches Landes, dass sie christliche Schulen aufrichten . . . sollen* (*To the Councilmen of All Cities in Germany That They Establish and Maintain Christian Schools*)

1525 Charles V defeated at Pavia
Francis I of France taken prisoner
Peasants' War in Thuringia
March: Twelve Articles of Memmingen
May 5: Death of Frederick the Wise
May 15: Annihilation of the Thuringian peasant army at Mühlausen
1525–32 Elector John the Steadfast

1525 April: *Ermahnung zum Frieden auf die zwölf Artikel der Bauernschaft* (*An Admonition to Peace: A Reply to the Twelve Articles of the Peasants in Swabia*); to which is added at the beginning of May: *Against the Robbing and Murdering Hordes of Peasants*
June 13: Marriage to Katharina von Bora
ca. July: *Ein Sendbrief von dem harten Büchlein wider die Bauern* (*An Open Letter against the Hard Book against the Peasants*)
November/December: *De servo arbitrio* (*Bondage of the Will*); against Erasmus
From 1525 on: Eucharistic controversy

1526 June 25–August 27: First Diet of Speyer: crushing of the Reformation put off
August 29: Battle of Mohacz: Ludwig II of Hungary defeated by the Turks
1526–30 Visitations of churches and schools in Electoral Saxony

1526 June 7: Birth of his first son
June: Signs of serious illness
Writings: *Ob Kriegsleute auch in seligem Stande sein können* (*Whether Soldiers, Too, Can Be Saved*)

1527 May 6: "Sacco di Roma": imperial army's sack of Rome

1527 March/April: Eucharistic treatise: *Das diese Worte Christi, "Das ist mein Leib," etc. . . . noch feststehen* (*That These Words of Christ, "This Is My Body," etc., Still Stand Firm against the Fanatics*)
Summer: Illness, severe depressions
November: *Ob man vor dem Sterben*

fliehen möge (*Whether One May Flee from a Deadly Plague*)
December 10: Birth of daughter Elisabeth

1528–42 Bugenhagen reforms conditions in churches and schools in the sphere of influence of the Saxon Reformation

1528 March: *Vom Abendmahl Christi, Bekenntnis* (*Confession Concerning Christ's Supper*)
August 3: Death of daughter Elisabeth

1529 February 26–April 12: Second Diet of Speyer
April 19: Protest of the Evangelical estates
September/October: Vienna besieged by Sultan Suleiman

1529 *Vom Kriege wider die Türken* (*On War against the Turk*)
March: *Kleiner Katechismus* (*Small Catechism*)
May 4: *Grosser Katechismus* (*Large Catechism*)
Birth of daughter Magdalena ("Lenchen")
October 1–4: Religious colloquy of Marburg: No agreement in the eucharistic controversy

1530 June 20–November 19: Diet of Augsburg
June 25: Presentation of the *Confessio Augustana;* Huldreich Zwingli and four cities (Strasbourg, Constance, Lindau, Memmingen) each have their own confessions delivered
August 3: *Refutatio* by Roman Catholic theologians; Charles V declares the Protestants to be defeated.

1530 April–October: Luther at Coburg Castle during the Diet of Augsburg.
May: Death of father, Hans Luther
Important tract: *Vermahnung an die Geistlichen versammelt auf dem Reichstag zu Augsburg* (*Exhortation to All Clergy Assembled at Augsburg*)

1531 Foundation of the Schmalkaldic League: protective alliance of the Protestant estates under the leadership of Electoral Saxony and Hesse
October 11: Zwingli killed at Kappel

1531 Death of mother Margaret
Warnung an seine lieben Deutschen (Warning addressed to his beloved Germans)

1532 Religious Peace of Nuremberg: Protestants granted free exercise of religion until a general council is convoked

1532–47 Elector John Frederick I, the Magnanimous, of Saxony (†1554)	
	1533 *Von der Winkelmesse und Pfaffenweihe* (About private Mass and ordination)
1534 February 24–June 25, 1535: the Anabaptists' "Kingdom of Christ" in Münster Introduction of the Reformation in Württemberg Separation of the English church from Rome: Act of Supremacy of the Church of England under King Henry VIII Foundation of the Jesuit order by Ignatius of Loyola	1534 ca. September: First complete edition of Luther's translation of the Bible (the *Complete Bible,* or *German Bible*)
1534–49 Pope Paul III	
1535 May 12: Protestant ordination established	1535 November 7: Negotiations with nuncio Pietro Paolo Vergerio at Wittenberg Castle about Protestant participation in the papal council 1535–45 *Lectures on Genesis* 1535–46 Dean of the theological faculty
1536 Wittenberg Concord: agreement between the Wittenberg Reformation and the southern German Reformation on the Eucharist Introduction of the Reformation in Denmark by King Christian III	1536 January 14: Disputation *Über den Menschen* (*The Disputation Concerning Man*) Disputation *Über die Rechtfertigung* (*The Disputation Concerning Justification*) December: the *Schmalkaldic Articles*
1537 February 9–20: Bundestag at Schmalkalden; negotiations about attendance at the papal council in Mantua; Schmalkaldic League extended for ten years; Melanchthon's treatise *Über die Gewalt des Papstes* accepted	1537 Serious illness during the Bundestag in Schmalkalden
	1537–40 Dispute over the meaning of biblical law

1538 Nuremberg League of the Catholic estates against the Protestants

1539 Religious Truce of Frankfurt; limited toleration of the Reformation
Introduction of the Reformation in Ducal Saxony and Brandenburg

1539 *Von den Conciliis und Kirchen* (*On the Councils and Churches*)

1539–41 A further revision of the Bible translation

1540/41 March 4: Bigamous marriage of Landgrave Phillip of Hesse
Religious colloquies in Hagenau, Worms, and Regensburg

1540 September 27: Jesuit order approved by Pope Paul III

1541 Nikolaus von Amsdorf: first Evangelical bishop (in Naumburg)
Introduction of the Ecclesiastical Ordinances of Geneva

1541 March: *Wider Hans Worst* (*Against Hans Worst*)

1541–53 Duke (from 1547: Elector) Moritz of Saxony

1542 War between the Schmalkaldic League and Duke Henry of Wolfenbüttel
Introduction of the Reformation in Braunschweig (Brunswick)

1542 January 6: Luther's will
September 20: Death of daughter Magdalena

1543–46 Archbishop Hermann von Wied's attempt to establish the Reformation in Cologne fails

1543 Nicolaus Copernicus (†1543), *De revolutionibus orbium caelestium*

1543 January: *Von den Juden und ihren Lügen* (*Of the Jews and Their Lies*)

1544 *Die Hauspostille* (a book of sermons)
September: *Kurzes Bekenntnis vom heiligen Sakrament* (Short confession of the Holy Sacrament)

1545–63 Council of Trent, opened on December 13, 1545

1545 March 5: Preface to the first volume of the complete Wittenberg edition of the Latin writings
Wider das Papsttum zu Rom, vom Teufel gestiftet (*Against the Roman Papacy, an Institution of the Devil*)

1546 Introduction of the Reformation in the Electoral Palatinate

1546 February 14: Last sermon in Eisleben—against the Jews
February 18: Death in Eisleben

February 22: Funeral at the Castle Church of Wittenberg; funeral sermon held by Melanchthon

1546/47 Schmalkaldic War
April 24, 1547: Protestants defeated by the imperial troops at Mühlberg
May 19: Capitulation of Wittenberg: Elector John Frederick forced to cede electoral dignity and electoral lands to Duke Moritz

1555 Diet of Augsburg: imperial estates agree on a religious compromise

SUBJECT INDEX

INDEX OF NAMES

Note: Page numbers in italics indicate illustrations.